ETERNAL VIGILANCE

ETERNAL VIGILANCE

GUARDING AGAINST THE PREDATORY STATE

RALPH L. BAYRER

Library of Congress Control Number: 2020904693
ISBN: Hardcover   978-1-7960-9325-4
                 Softcover   978-1-7960-9324-7
                 eBook   978-1-7960-9323-0

Rev. date: 06/17/2020

To order additional copies of this book, contact:
Xlibris
844-714-8691
www.Xlibris.com
Orders@Xlibris.com
809640

CONTENTS

Chapter 1 The Free Extended Order of Human Cooperation (FEO)...... 1

The small government/high liberty model gets it right. That model is the optimal form of governance for maintaining individual liberty and producing wealth for all segments of society. It is predicated on: (1) the civil and property rights of free individuals and (2) a circumscribed government limited to ensuring security, enforcing contracts, preventing fraud, and preserving the federal rights of the states. These values represent the leading edge of societal evolution, in which tribal values and medieval thinking gave way to more individual autonomy, less communal meddling, and arm's length (impersonal) financial and commercial transactions.

Chapter 2 Governmental Predation is Ubiquitous 28

The inclination to predation is in our genes; it is ineradicable. We have millennia of experience with predation between and within societies. Examples of predation under tyranny and modern kleptocracies are commonplace and intuitively obvious. Predatory instincts hidden inside democratic governments also abound. They hide in the form of good intentions and high sentiment so as to extract wealth from society in favor of special interests and unachievable utopian goals.

Chapter 3 Controlling Political Predation 46

Societal evolution has produced political mechanisms to control predation. Even prehistoric man found ways (usually intuitive methods) to prevent one man from becoming despotic. These methods, however, grew less and less effective as societies grew larger and rulers more distant from those ruled. Nonetheless, using philosophy and institutional trial and error, societies have found ways to control the worst forms of predation and their effects on the free extended order. It was the U.S. Constitution that established the most evolved form of social organization at the date of its ratification.

On the basis of good intentions and sentiment lacking scientific foundation, progressive forces found ways to undermine the bulwarks of liberty provided by the Constitution, leading to mis-governance and enormous costs.

Escaping constitutional limits, progressive forces pursued good intentions on an increasingly unaffordable scale. This involved making impossibly expensive promises that surely will not be honored in the long run and will impair growth so as to lead to likely future fiscal crises.

The forces of human nature that have led to our financial predicament are universal. There are some, like Greece, who have made a mess of things still un-remedied; others, like Brazil, have great potential but always cycle back to instability. More useful examples are those of New Zealand, Sweden, and Canada who, through utopian policies, hit financial barriers that left them no choice but to commit to deep reform, whose outcomes provide lessons for all.

Other democratic governments have escaped this dynamic through effective institutional control of predation; examples include Switzerland, Germany, the Netherlands, Singapore, and Hong Kong (New Zealand and Sweden after their deep reforms). Of course, their methods differ from those outlined in the U.S. Constitution, suggesting for consideration alternative institutional methods of controlling political predation.

Despite the superior performance of the FEO worldwide and a multitude of cautionary examples, progressive leftist forces are uncowed and remain in full attack mode. Lacking a historical perspective, they employ now-discredited medieval notions such as "fairness" that are as unworkable now as they were then. To do this, they have developed an impressive updated array of seductive arguments that are based on sentiment and good intentions but are oblivious to scientific evidence and historical precedent.

In the aid of reform and renewal, the first order of business is to point the way forward and meet the ideological threats head-on with an analytic framework and evidence.

With clear empirical principles in hand, we can reform our political system by restoring the spirit and efficacy of the original Constitution; perhaps amending it to limit our free-spending ways and to secure our liberty and property.

DEDICATION

I dedicate this work to my life partner Kenneth Vincent George for his many years of loving support for this project.

INTRODUCTION

**"Our civilization depends, not only for its origin but also
for its preservation, on what can be precisely described
only as the extended order of human cooperation."[1]
– Friedrich von Hayek**

**"Men are qualified for civil liberties, in exact proportion to
their disposition to put moral chains upon their appetites: in
proportion as their love of justice is above their rapacity."
– Edmund Burke[2]**

"The price of liberty is eternal vigilance."– Thomas Jefferson

This book is a renewed call for eternal vigilance in the defense of liberty, whether against simple tyranny or vis-à-vis the state as a predatory agent. Its central argument is that man's discovery of ways to successfully cooperate with his fellow man on community, national, and global scales in the face of ubiquitous predatory instincts is his greatest achievement and the foundation for all advanced civilizations.

We are well into the beginning of the twenty-first century. We enjoy immense human accomplishments in the areas of material well-being and self-governance, yet we confront a bewildering array of forces attacking the very foundations of that success. More alarming is the prospect that these attacks have already so weakened our social structures that we will leave an unaffordable and debilitating inheritance to future generations. These circumstances may well be the single most important political challenge confronting our society – and, indeed, almost all modern societies. One key to successfully addressing this challenge is a better

---

[1] W. W. Bartley III, ed., Hayek, F.A. *The Fatal Conceit: The Errors of Socialism* (Chicago: The University of Chicago Press, 1991), 6.

[2] Ibid, 29

understanding of human nature itself – its predatory side as well as its creative/productive side.

Nobel Prize winner Friedrich von Hayek identifies human cooperation as the basis for meeting humans' material needs when he characterizes civilization itself as an *extended order of human cooperation.*[3] The achievement of civilization was not so much learning to cooperate fruitfully since, as Hayek notes, this occurs spontaneously according to basic economic laws. Civilization's great achievement was protecting this system of cooperation that spontaneously unfolds from the predatory forces that are as deeply rooted in human nature as ambition.

Accordingly, this book's main theme shows how societies developed the essential values and institutions that optimize the functioning of that extended order. That order exists everywhere human communities exist; it can function well or clumsily. However, since its optimal form exists alongside liberty and freedom of all kinds, the book examines governance in terms of the predicates of what this author characterizes as a *Free* Extended Order of Human Cooperation (FEO).

In the face of predation, particularly within government, keeping the extended order free is no mean feat. If predation is not checked, vibrant wealth creation ebbs to a trickle. With effective control, however, wealth creation and all other human aspirations become more realizable – liberty, good health, a clean environment, and self-actualization by maximizing one's talents. While societies have made great advances in these areas, predatory instincts continue to operate in various forms, becoming more ingenious with each generation. They cannot be controlled by paper constitutions or political institutions but require eternal, vigilant oversight by the people.

More specifically, to further clarify these concepts, this book: (1) defines the elements of the FEO, (2) characterizes the forces of predation that must be countered to realize its benefits, (3) outlines the institutions that have arisen to combat such predation – notably the U.S. Constitution, (4) shows how those institutions have been undermined (at an enormous cost) over the last century, (5) identifies the lessons available from the experience of others as this predation is a human phenomenon that occurs everywhere, (6) defines the core nature of the current political/philosophical debate as science versus sentimentality, and (7) shows how we can restore the constitutional heritage most supportive of the FEO.

The Free Extended Order

According to Hayek, in order to understand economic activity, it is essential to view it culturally and sociologically in light of the ability of members of society to cooperate. The more freely people cooperate, the better. In all societies, individuals

---

[3]   Ibid, 6.

must engage in cooperative economic transactions to get their own needs met and survive. In primitive societies, expulsion from the group is equivalent to a death sentence; no individual can survive on his or her own. Cooperation allows division of labor and comparative advantages, which in turn unleash the possibilities of exchange, support individual creativity and initiative, increase productivity, produce consumer surpluses, and best utilize humankind's distributed intelligence.

The specific ways in which cultures produce extended orders were the result of evolutionary processes – i.e., as societies step-by-step discovered the most evolutionary-fit values, procedures, and institutions. Conceptually, society should be viewed as an organic whole that operates according to value systems. To take just one example of fundamental societal value shifts: as recently as a thousand years ago, Europe and indeed all civilization functioned in a decidedly pre-FEO mode. Medievalism was as preoccupied with the notions of social justice, just prices, and just wages as the members of today's far Left. Virtually all pre-modern societies held that all aspects of the economy and of an individual's status and employment had to be regulated to avoid any injustice.

As Adam Smith would later write, these views are totally incompatible with any modern economy. He saw clearly that the individual can judge better what product of his efforts is likely to have the highest value, the nature of competition, and risk-reward than any government entity. In that light, societies would have to move-on in terms of their values and institutions to achieve the benefits of the modern era. Fortunately, most of the advances occurred without the need of government direction.

Indeed, the extended order as explained by von Hayek arises *spontaneously* as innate human ambition is shaped by basic economic laws such as supply and demand, comparative advantage, and free-market prices. In this process societal wealth is automatically generated because all honest, freely-entered transactions result in a consumer surplus and all those participating in the FEO benefit (albeit to varying degrees). Governmental interference, however well-intended, is more likely than not to have unintended consequences that reduce overall well-being. The fact that advanced economic-countries are wealthy despite extensive government involvement doesn't mean they couldn't be far wealthier still.

A central element of the FEO that has become increasingly evident over the last millennium is the protection of private property. As explained by another Nobel Prize winner James Buchanan, the essence of private property is that, before trade can take place (that is, before goods, services, or titles can be exchanged), there must be a way to determine what belongs to each individual. This right to property is the basis for mutual exchange, which then allows the forces of comparative advantage to unfold, generating vastly more wealth. In principle, such trade arises through individuals' calculations of their own advantage, and no government action is required. However, when property rights are weak or non-existent, marketplace uncertainties multiply. Then each actor must take costly measures to protect his interest in transactions or, as is equally likely, may forgo such transactions altogether.

As powerful as this concept is for understanding the modern world, the predicates of the FEO are under continual attack by predatory political forces. They are also obscured by academia and the mainstream media to an astonishing extent. To be sure, many of these attacks are well-intended, but the reality remains that they rely heavily on sentiment rather than empirical learning and represent a regression to a medieval outlook on life.

Controlling Predation

While the elements of the FEO unfold naturally and spontaneously, protecting them from predation is far more sociologically complex. Attacks on the FEO take many forms and grow out of human nature itself. The most thuggish go back to time out of mind. Our very genetic makeup predisposes us to violence and predation against others when social circumstances permit it or even seem to require it for our own survival. Indeed, prehistoric tribal life shared characteristics with the societies of our primate relatives, the chimpanzees; one of these characteristics is a murderous distrust of outsiders. Anthropologists estimate that one quarter of early human populations routinely died from intertribal warfare.[4] As civilization expanded, such behavior simply expanded apace; witness the Mongol invasions of Central Asia and Europe and the Viking attacks on northern Europe.

Eons of social evolution were needed to keep predation within tolerable (but not optimal) boundaries. Actually, the more overt such predation is, the easier it is to implement corrective measures. We have armies to protect us from foreign adventurers, parliaments to counter would-be tyrants, police to deal with thugs, and prosecutors to take on fraud. But what about the more veiled forms that imbed and weaken virtually every form of government?

Amazing as it now may seem, Aristotle conducted a broad analysis of this question a full two and a half millennia ago; he concluded:

> All forms of government tried by man have perverse deviations from ideal forms because of man's ubiquitous predatory impulses: i.e., democracy as rule by the crowd, for the benefit of the dominant majority; oligarchy as rule by the few for the good of that few; tyranny as an unconstitutional assumption of power by one man for his own satisfaction.[5]

---

[4]   John J. Miller, review of *Constant Battles* by Steven LeBlanc, *The Wall Street Journal*, April 20, 2003.

[5]   Russell Kirk, *The Roots of American Order* (Washington, DC: Regnery Gateway, 1991), 90-91.

A central reason for all such dysfunctional social behaviors is that the potential for self aggrandizement through the aegis of government is unavoidable; as noted by Deepak Lal: "A universal feature of polities is the ubiquitous predatoriness of the State. This merely reflects the necessary monopoly of coercive power and the inevitable maximization of net revenue that self-interested governors will then extract from their subjects."[6] One could say that the more sophisticated the society is in this regard, the more subtle the forms of predation.

The last century has shown how the FEO can be smothered by misguided universal utopian programs or continuously undermined by regulations and taxes that pander to special interests. James Madison clearly foresaw these possibilities and believed (or hoped) in the efficacy of institutional checks and balances to keep such propensities manageable. In the event, even though these measures have fallen short, one of the modern world's greatest achievements is the extent to which we have succeeded. Moreover, the potential solutions are ever clearer: constitutionally protected liberty and property and enforced limitations on government.

James Buchanan analyzed the basis for this conclusion: An extended order is relatively infertile without a government to protect wealth; yet, at the same time, it can be threatened by a government that has too much power to intervene in the free workings of the economy. As will be discussed in Chapter One, he identifies principles describing how individuals agree to give up some of the freedom of action in exchange for others doing likewise in order to efficiently protect their property. However, without sufficient safeguards, once the government can intervene without clear demarcations in the economic sector, it can slip into areas not justified by cost-benefit considerations. Moreover, once that door is opened, the majority can transgress agreed terms for collective action so as to prey on the minority.

These ideas must have been considered when leaders such as the Founding Fathers identified forms of government that could put individual liberty at risk. Indeed, this is the view that underlies the U.S. Declaration of Independence and the U.S. Constitution. These very ideas are also expressed in Madison's *Federalist Papers*, which will be discussed below.

Moreover, a number of other societies have struggled to find appropriate measures to limit government. In the event, the solution was not the product of one great mind; it developed as various societies dealt with would-be tyrants here and there, exigency by exigency. The solutions evolved over centuries. Because the U.S. colonies benefited from this long evolution (whose historical traces are well documented), the U.S. Constitution illuminates how governmental systems can protect liberty by countering man's propensity for predation.

---

[6]   Deepak Lal, *Unintended Consequences*, 16.

The U.S. Constitution

In constructing a new government, the Founding Fathers had the benefits of English history and personal experience of the traditional rights enjoyed by free Englishmen. To be sure, the English had only an unwritten constitution, but it included key documents such as the Magna Carta and the British Bill of Rights, which clarified central concepts. This tradition extended further in the New World, where colonists living under the benign neglect of the crown had to establish their own rules of governance three thousand miles from England. At first these efforts were merely pragmatic and drew on their British inheritance. Then, at the beginning of the Revolution, to make their vision based on that experience clear, a number of the colonies wrote constitutions defining the roles of the governor and the legislature and their interactions. So the Founding Fathers brought a remarkable sense of history as well as extensive firsthand experience to their task of designing a national constitution.

The new U.S. Constitution, which was in no way intended to be revolutionary, would mirror the structures of state governments by including executive, legislative, and judicial systems. However, the Founding Fathers added checks and balances in line with the writings of Montesquieu. This choice was informed by a classically liberal, Lockean worldview that transcended the specific features of government. For example, the Declaration of Independence sets "life, liberty, and the pursuit of happiness" front and center. Jefferson's choice of the words "pursuit of happiness" emphasizes the government's protection of individuals so they can pursue opportunities; this certainly entails protection of individual property. According to the Declaration of Independence, the appropriate role of government is to secure those rights.

While the Convention began with a ready-made template for the broad structure of government, its specific features were the subject of extensive debate. They discussed how best to secure individual liberty, limit taxation, protect small states from the large, and other issues. In working through the details, they added something substantially new to the constitutional end-product: a strong distrust of central government. This grew out of their unique circumstances; they had been subjects of a King, had suffered under an overbearing Parliament, and had been part of a fractious confederacy. It is self-evident that the first two factors could easily lead to a distrust of large government per se as well as a desire to limit the power of the Chief Executive and check the functions of the legislature.

The third factor, their experience under the Continental Congress, made them wary of free ridership, of taxes, of trade barriers advantaging one state over another, and of the potential dominance of large states over smaller ones. The solution reconciling these factors was a federal republic that limited the power of the central government to levy taxes and further limited its powers of control to those enumerated.

This distrust of a strong central government that informed the drafters of the Constitution extended throughout the colonies; the issue arose in every one of the subsequent state ratifying conventions.[7] The people had to be reassured that the language of the Constitution was adequate in this regard. To that end, the state conventions were promised later amendments to the Constitution that would irrevocably limit federal power. Indeed, that was the purpose of Amendments Nine and Ten of the Bill of Rights, which reiterated that Congress had only the enumerated powers and that all the rest were reserved to the states and the people.

In hindsight, given what we now know about the predicates of the FEO, the Constitution was wise beyond its years. It was serendipitously structured along what would become known as classical-liberal lines and established an optimal system for rapid economic growth. To begin with, the drafters were aware of the importance of private property and of the value of a common market (the purpose of the Commerce Clause) and explicitly protected these predicates in the document. However, the general mistrust that led to strict limitations on a strong central government happened to also support the FEO. In effect, the economy was left free to grow efficiently, without governmental direction and guided by natural economic forces. We simply needed to keep the central government small, let the states compete with one another for the best results, protect property, discourage monopolies, and we were well set for the future.

It worked famously for over a century: The United States rapidly became the world's leading industrial and economic power, the beacon for millions of immigrants. However, then utopians in the shape of Progressives entered the political picture. While not necessarily predatory, they could only achieve their objectives by employing government power in predatory ways. And they could do so only by either amending the Constitution to remove limitations or by ignoring its provisions.

Undermining the Constitution

Unfortunately, at great cost to the country, the Progressives were able to use both of those approaches to circumvent constitutional constraints. At first this was accomplished through the appropriate, albeit highly difficult method of amending the Constitution, first to allow a federal income tax and then to change the method for selecting U.S. senators. However, to broadly realize their utopian goals, Progressives needed a faster and less politically onerous way of proceeding.

---

[7] Pauline Maier, *Ratification: The People Debate the Constitution 1787-1788*. New York: Simon & Schuster, 2011.

The solution was to undermine the Constitution's legitimacy in the public mind and then to simply ignore its limitations.

One leading argument, championed by Woodrow Wilson, was that the Constitution was outdated. He employed an irrelevant truism: The country had changed significantly since its founding. Certainly, the needs of a large, industrial economy are very different from those of a small, agrarian one, but why did that require changes to the Constitution when the system was manifestly working well for all?

Other progressive arguments relied on even more vague notions, such as, for example, that the Constitution must be a 'living' document to keep up with the dynamic changes of modern economies. However, nothing in the Constitution relies on the kind or size of the economy. It was crafted to deal with *human nature*, which had not changed over the years. In particular, in a large, wealthy country, why should the federal government need to insert itself into the private sector through income redistribution or by financing healthcare and pensions? If anything, as was already occurring on a substantial scale, individuals could get their needs met through work, savings, insurance, and cooperative efforts. Why would a bureaucratic one-size-fits-all solution be superior?

That implicit question led to another progressive argument: that the powers of science, which had only been proven in the physical realm, could be harnessed to rule citizen's affairs in the sociological and political arenas as well. In that light, the wisdom of science combined with the beneficence of government was to ameliorate the conditions of working people – whose lives, while materialistically far better than they had been, were still difficult. These ideas, however, were all sentiment and little science. If anything, distributed intelligence within the FEO will surely outperform a 'wise,' scientifically informed government.

The Progressives offered a Faustian bargain of the kind Madison feared: a mess of utopian porridge in exchange for our birthright of liberty. Rather than a constitutional right to pursue happiness by making the most of our innate talents and energy in life, we were to look to the larger community and the government for these things. The obvious negatives were dismissed: the cumbersome risk-averse nature of bureaucracy and the desire of many people for a free-ride, which together would surely lead to high opportunity costs and other unintended consequences.

The central error of progressive arguments was a failure to recognize that the Constitution was not designed to optimize operations in a given economic arena, but to deal with the unavoidable dark side of human nature.

The full onslaught of progressive thought came with the New Deal, during which Roosevelt decided to simply bypass the language of the Constitution by convincing the Supreme Court to ignore features like the Enumerated Powers

Clause. After he threatened to pack the Court, the justices ceased their efforts to enforce the Constitution in economic affairs.

And the United States has been paying the price ever since.

The Fiscal Predicament

The country's growing fiscal imbalances can be traced to the statist, actuarially unsound programs launched in the New Deal as well as their more recent mutations, all of which are a retreat from the principles of the FEO. Restraint was abandoned in virtually all areas of the economy: Good intentions ran fiscally amok, quasi-monopolistic programs were tolerated and nanny-state regulations created excessive waste.

To assess the present predicament, we must begin with the increasing inability of a Congress free of constitutional restraint to do its job of passing balanced budgets that limit spending within the nation's means. The United States has seen deficits of half a trillion to over a trillion dollars a year for the last decade, and the national debt has reached some $22.8 trillion (October 2019), not much less than the entire GDP. These annual deficits and accumulating debt leave us extremely vulnerable to a still more ominous problem: the future tsunami of unfunded entitlements contained in Social Security, Medicare, and Medicaid. These programs alone, measured in current dollars, account for many times the nation's entire GDP.

The burden of the federal regulatory state, while less evident to the eye, presents comparable fiscal problems. There is virtually no part of the economy out of the reach of the federal reach. The federal government has concluded that its wisdom is so superior to the workings of the FEO that it can impose its one-size-fits-all approaches on the banking, industrial, educational, and housing sectors, to name a few. Not only do these regulations stifle innovation and investment, but compliance costs due to internal oversight, auditing, and legal perils pervade our society, creating a substantial drag on fiscal growth.

While most of the examples in the book are drawn from the United States, the arguments are universal. After all, this book discusses the negative sides of human nature and how societies have learned to address them. The experiences of other countries – for good or ill – can inform our efforts to address these inescapable problems.

The Universality of the Challenge

An examination of several examples from other countries shows that progressive principles, by whatever name, are not *sui generis* to the United States. The seductive appeal of utopian promises by a central government resonates in virtually all democratically elected representative governments. This pattern strongly suggests that there is an almost universal weakness in any democracy (as Aristotle mentioned) that lacks the checks and balances needed to protect individuals from the predatory side of human nature.

There is insight to be gleaned from other countries' experiences, both those that have gotten it right, proceeding along a path similar to ours, and those that have gotten it painfully wrong. Two common themes are particularly noteworthy. The first is the clear superiority of the FEO as the model for modern societies across the globe, as demonstrated by numerous studies, notably *The Index of Economic Freedom.*[8] The second theme is the political temptation presented by private and corporate wealth to buy votes.

This book will review a variety of cases to glean the lessons from them. Specifically, it will show how countries such as Sweden and New Zealand, operating under progressive instincts similar to those in the United States, eventually hit a financial wall, leaving them no practical option but to reform in the direction of smaller government and freer markets. Others, like Hong Kong, Singapore, and Switzerland, got it right all along and continue to prosper. And others, such as Greece, which has been unable to implement adequate reforms, remain financially shaky, living on handouts from their neighbors. Still others become failed states, such as Venezuela and Zimbabwe.

Of all these examples, that of Singapore is the most telling. At the end of the Second World War, Singapore was still a part of Malaya; it was a poor, new entity without natural resources. Seven decades later, having followed the precepts of the FEO (without giving it that name), it has a standard of living higher than that of the United States.

Despite mountains of evidence, the political Left, along with their enablers in academia and the media, continue to argue against this reality.

The Ongoing Debate

The arguments deployed against the FEO have evolved considerably over the last century or so. Initially, they had to counter the monumental advances already enjoyed by all classes of society. The FEO is a system in which each individual

---

[8]   Terry Miller and Anthony B. Kim, *2016 Index of Economic Freedom: Promoting Economic Opportunity and Prosperity* (The Heritage Foundation and *The Wall Street Journal*, 2016).

strives to maximize his own success through foresight and hard work, purchases insurance to deal with life's bad luck, and allows a small, limited government (preferably primarily local) to help those truly unable to cope. Progressives took these circumstances for granted without truly understanding their significance and became preoccupied with those lagging behind. They argued that the coming of the modern industrial age and the rise of social science justified changes to the constitutional/economic model bequeathed to us to better meet the needs of the people and achieve greater social justice. They simply asserted (without evidence) that their economic model – one that required a large government – was better.

For a century, they got their way with extensive social programs, income-redistribution and smothering regulation. To be sure, poverty continues, but in contrast to Marx's time, few people still live in grinding poverty; almost none among the working class. However, by circumventing the Constitution and employing FEO-hostile ways, progressives left an impossibly expensive tab for the future. Moreover, as some foreign examples show, the big-ticket items of poverty, pensions, and healthcare could be have been addressed in ways far more empirically sensible and actuarially sound.

Without grinding poverty as a credible theme, the Left has moved on to other arguments to justify big government and income redistribution, such as medieval ideas of social justice and income equality. However, this will be a hard sell, since the electorate is not likely to conclude that high-school dropouts deserve the same income as a family with two professionals who spent years to develop skills that could serve society.

The FEO offers so much more than Progressivism to all classes of society. The hard truth is that wealth has to be created before it can be redistributed, and the production of wealth requires wariness of large government, an attitude inherent in the constitutional model bequeathed to the United States. Ultimately, the philosophic debate comes down to arguments based on intuition and sentiment, at which the Left excels, against those based on experience and empirical data, which the Left disregards when convenient.

What Next?

Given the deep problems currently facing the United States, this book's conclusions are not merely academic; they go to the heart of future politics. Indeed, the United States has lost its way and reached a political stalemate. It is encumbered by financial commitments that cannot be honored and which will likely result in a fiscal crisis of the first magnitude. In response, rather than politics as usual, a sea-change in public attitudes, even a 'Third American Revolution'[9] might be in order.

This book argues that the surest solutions will be found in a return to constitutional principles that are congruent with the FEO. A relatively simple solution would entail a sea change in the electorate: if they recognized the failure of a century of Progressivism, the country could use normal politics to address the most pressing failures: health care, Social Security, Medicare and Medicaid, the educational system, and economically destructive regulations. Based on our own history and the successful examples of others such as New Zealand and Sweden, this is quite feasible. Moreover, there is an enormous pot of gold to be found in freeing the economy from the policies, programs, and mindsets currently hemming it in.

Even if such a change occurred in American values, a further troubling question remains: Do representative governments have an inevitable tendency to overpromise, over-borrow, and ratchet up the economy to ever greater instability? Perhaps, even though we have come a long way, man has not yet found an adequate solution to the conundrum of democracy posed by Aristotle. Are there additional procedural, structural, and/or constitutional remedies yet to be discovered? To find out, a further political impulse is likely required, probably induced by a major fiscal crisis and a public perception that the system is not working.

Whether driven by a broad change in political values or the impetus of crisis, at a minimum, effective changes would likely require a return to the spirit and the language of the Constitution as it was ratified. These changes would tie the hands of representatives and reduce the Supreme Court's ability to act against those principles. Perhaps it would be impractical to attempt such measures across the board; for example, at this point, restoring the full force of the Enumerated Powers Clause would probably produce politically unacceptable wide-scale economic disruption. However, a host of modest changes in accord with the FEO can reasonably be achieved. Some would enforce the spirit of the Constitution, some would complete the unfinished business of the Constitutional Convention, and others would explicitly address weaknesses in our body politic, such as issues related to balanced budgets and taxation.

In addition, modifying the ways we select representatives in Congress might well shift the incentives motivating those representatives so they serve the people rather than their parties and their own ambitions. Updated notions of the political values of "life, liberty, and the pursuit of happiness" could serve as guideposts. Indeed, given the vast potential of computers and the internet to expand our lives, these ideals are timelier than ever. Von Hayek's free extended order of human

---

9   As will be discussed in Chapter 10, the election of 1800, which rejected the Federalists, restored constitutional barriers to a strong central government to the extent that some historians have termed it the Second American Revolution.

cooperation – the engine of economic progress – can be supercharged by an internet-induced enhancement of human distributed intelligence.

This is where vigilance comes in. How can the majority of the electorate be brought to see the benefits of a smaller, libertarian government and to distrust the illusory promises of the ever-growing regulatory state? They need to understand that the regulatory, high-tax approach of large government is fundamentally at odds with the promise of the FEO. The electorate needs to recognize that good intentions are not enough and that the promises of the bureaucratic/regulatory state are not likely to be met.

*　*　*

In short, this book describes the empirical foundations of free and flourishing societies as well as the threats they face from ubiquitous human predation, even under representative government. It outlines how protections of the FEO were serendipitously incorporated into the U.S. Constitution and how our body politic undermined those protections. It analyzes the political seduction that was used to accomplish this and suggests how things can be put right by a focus on the constitutional rule of law, by renewed protection of individual liberty and private property, by balanced budgets, and by honoring the principles of federalism.

CHAPTER 1

THE FREE EXTENDED ORDER OF HUMAN COOPERATION

"Little else is requisite to carry a state to the highest degree of opulence from the lowest barbarianism, but peace, easy taxes, and a tolerable administration of justice: all the rest being brought about by the natural course of things." – Adam Smith[10]

Around the world, state policies are the principle determinant of growth and prosperity – but in the sense that less is more. As we shall see, a light touch favors growth; a heavy hand encourages stagnation or poverty. To many this seems counterintuitive given the government's repeated, ongoing claims to fight poverty, make public investments, or create new centers of industry. The argument for limited government depends on Hayek's conclusions that innovation and growth occur naturally when government is limited to a protective role. Unfortunately, this is rarely the case because of inappropriate government intrusion into the economic realm; commonly traced to predatory special interests or misguided utopian thinkers.

To make this argument, this chapter demonstrates the simple truth of Adam Smith's observation that opulence is a *natural course* of things. However, simple is not necessarily easy. Much of Smith's insight of more than two centuries ago was (of necessity) more intuitive than empirical, drawing on specifics of the political

---

10   Lecture in 1755, quoted in Dugald Stewart, "Account of the Life and Writings of Adam Smith LL.D.," *Transactions of the Royal Society of Edinburgh*, Jan. 21 and Mar. 18, 1793, section 4, repr. In *Collected Works of Dugald Stewart*, ed. William Hamilton (Edinburgh: Thomas Constable, 1854), vol. 10, 1-98.

economy of his day. The modern world has come a long way in its understanding of these things and can now validate Smith's insights, showing that he was wise beyond his time. Accordingly, the first part of this chapter addresses Smith's assertion that opulence results naturally.

However, that is only the first half of the equation. Since growth and wealth creation occur spontaneously, only a light hand of government is essential to nurture the process. But why shouldn't government be able to tap this wealth to meet social needs? The answer is that at a certain point, government extraction of wealth begins to smother the economy, making everyone poorer than they need to be. So, the second part of the chapter describes deleterious types of government intervention in order to identify its proper limits. Ubiquitous human predatory instincts, which arise even under representative governments, makes identifying appropriate limits a tricky proposition and thus a subject for closer examination.

To begin, we examine how modern economic theory and growing empirical evidence from all kinds of national economies continue to underscore Smith's simple wisdom. Since his time, other economists, notably Friedrich von Hayek, have provided analytical frameworks that allow the average person to connect the dots so as to see what is important and why. Smith postulated the *invisible hand* to describe the macro-working of the economy; von Hayek introduced the idea of the *extended order of human cooperation*.[11]

Hayek's concept is useful because it captures the nature of economic transactions as they are carried out by separate individual actors who simply respond to basic economic laws while optimizing their immediate knowledge of markets. Envision a system in which key decisions are made by those who are most knowledgeable and who have the most at risk, rather than waiting for guidance from above. Does a bureaucrat a thousand miles away really know better than local actors how to build a widget, or make a timely investment, or price the widget, or incentivize a workforce? Hardly! It didn't work in the Soviet Union, nor in the 1930's New Deal America.

Using von Hayek's concept, this chapter will show how society spontaneously generates economic advancements and wealth creation when government resists the impulse to exploit or to forbid what comes naturally. The chapter is divided into three parts. The first shows how a *free* extended order spontaneously responds to economic laws and therefore requires government protection but not intervention. The second part outlines the type of government that can best maintain that free order, and the final part examines how governmental regulation and taxation (which can be forms of predation on behalf of societal factions) sap the vitality of this free order. Overall, a societal model based on personal freedom is better than one of governmental good intentions. With that idea firmly in mind, we will be better equipped to vigilantly protect our rights and liberties.

---

[11]   Bartley III, W.W., ed., Hayek, F.A., *The Fatal Conceit: The Errors of Socialism.*

THE EXTENDED ORDER

Hayek's extended order is, of course, an abstraction and no more a tangible entity than capitalism or democracy. But it can be understood in practical ways that explain how humans most effectively coordinate economic efforts. According to Hayek, to understand the nature of the modern economy, it is essential to view it culturally and sociologically in terms of the ability of members of society to cooperate freely in a great framework of institutions and traditions. He states:

> We have stumbled upon methods of ordering human economic cooperation that exceed the limits of [any one person's] knowledge and perception. …All this is possible because we stand in the framework of institutions and traditions – economic, legal, and moral into which we fit ourselves by obeying certain rules of conduct … [A]n extended order can come into being [because] … it itself constitutes an information-gathering process, able to call up, and put to use, widely dispersed information that no central planning agency, let alone any individual, could know as a whole, possess, or control. … [As is seen in biology, the extended order can benefit from] … evolutionary change … [that] tends towards a maximum economy in the use of resources…[12]

In short, humans follow certain rules of conduct that are based on tradition and culture, but not necessarily codified.[13] Societies develop through an evolutionary process in which, over time, the fittest values, codes of conduct, procedures, and institutions survive. As one example, no modern society still adheres to medieval values of just prices, trade hierarchies, and no-interest loans, all of which are totally incompatible with a modern economic system. Moreover, the evolutionary nature of society is evident in the degree to which the most successful cultures and societies have left dysfunctional atavistic instincts behind.

Essential to understanding the concept of the extended order is how individuals call upon widely dispersed information that no central planning agency could know as a whole. Man's knowledge is dispersed.[14] As Adam Smith wrote: "What is the species of domestic industry his capital can employ, and of which the produce is likely to be of the greatest value, every individual, it is evident, in his local situation, judges much better than any statesman or lawgiver can do for

---

[12]   Ibid, 14-15.

[13]   Ibid, 14.

[14]   Ibid.

him."[15] In short, economic actors with the best sources of timely information are most likely to balance risk and opportunity because they have 'skin in the game'; they are also the most likely to capitalize on emerging opportunities and thus produce superior results.

The extended order arises *spontaneously* as innate human ambition is shaped by basic economic laws such as supply and demand, comparative advantage, and free-market prices. Extended societal wealth is generated at the same time because all honest, freely entered transactions result in consumer surplus. When government forbids such transactions or decides it knows better how to transact them, its actions will too often mean that less total wealth is produced because of opportunity costs.

Natural Socio-Economic Forces

Due to material necessity and psychology, human beings are disposed to pursue wealth or – as Adam Smith noted, the propensity to truck, barter and exchange one thing for another. Indeed, they have little choice since no one man can satisfy all of his own needs; all depend on some form of cooperation with their fellow man. The nature of trade is shaped by economic realities such as the division of labor, comparative advantage, consumer surplus, and market prices. Most individuals may be unaware of these specific considerations, but they are quick to judge the combined effect of these forces on their own position in a given transaction.

Division of Labor

Division of labor occurs when a production process is divided into steps; each step undertaken by an individual skilled in performing that step. The overall process is vastly more productive than if one individual attempted to perform all the steps himself. Ludwig von Mises comments on the practical significance of the division of labor:

> If and as far as labor under the division of labor is more
> productive than isolated labor, and if and as far as man is able
> to realize this fact, human action itself tends toward cooperation
> and association; man becomes a social being ... [by] aiming at
> an improvement in his own welfare. Experience teaches that
> this condition – higher productivity achieved under the division
> of labor – is present because its cause, the inborn inequality of
> men and the inequality in the geographic distribution of the

---

[15]   Ibid.

natural factors of production, is real. Thus, we are in a position to comprehend the course of social evolution.[16]

Comparative Advantage

Another powerful motivation for exchange is comparative advantage. Economist David Ricardo defines this economic principle as the benefits that arise when one individual or group cooperates with a second individual or group that is less efficient in every regard than the first. Von Mises summarizes it as follows:

> The division of labor between two ... areas will ... increase the productivity of labor and is therefore advantageous to all concerned, even if the physical conditions of production for any commodity are more favorable in one of these two areas than in the other. It is advantageous for the better-endowed area to concentrate its efforts upon the production of those commodities for which its superiority is greater, and to leave to the less well-endowed area the production of other goods in which its superiority is less.[17]

David Boaz provides an example: If Friday can catch twice as many fish as Crusoe but can find three times as many ripe fruits in a day, then both of them will be better off if Crusoe specializes in fishing (even though he is less productive than Friday) and Friday specializes in foraging.[18] Under the same reasoning, societies should encourage individuals to focus on their greatest talents and to trade the produce of these talents for the greatest benefit to themselves and to society overall.

Consumer Surplus

Consumer surplus arises when both parties in a transaction freely exchange goods or services. As stated by Milton and Rose Friedman:

> The key insight of Adam Smith's *Wealth of Nations* is misleadingly simple: if an exchange between two parties is voluntary, it will not take place unless both believe they will

---

[16]   Ludwig von Mises, *Human Action: A Treatise on Economics* (Fourth Revised Edition), (San Francisco: Fox & Wilkes, 1996), 160-161.

[17]   Ibid, 159.

[18]   David Boaz, *Libertarianism – A Primer* (New York: The Free Press, 1997), 156.

benefit from it. Most economic fallacies derive from the neglect of this simple insight, from the tendency to assume that there is a fixed pie, that one party can gain only at the expense of another.[19]

In practice, a given resource or item will often have much more utility for one consumer than another. For example, the value of a personal computer, which enhances the consumer's productivity, is greater than the cost charged by the manufacturer under competitive conditions. Often the consumer might have been willing to pay more (as was the case in the infancy of PCs, when they were far more expensive than now). Economists define consumer surplus[20] as the aggregate amount that consumers to whom an article has the greatest utility would be willing to pay above the average market clearing price (determined by the intersection of supply and demand).[21]

Free Market Price Signals

In a free market, the forces of supply and demand generate prices that provide clear signals to producers and consumers: rising prices encourage new production and discourage consumption; falling prices have the reverse effect. More abstractly, Hayek argues that, through price signals, the free market draws on the distributed intelligence and knowledge of all participants in the economic system. David Boaz elaborates:

> Prices don't just tell us how much something costs at the store. The price system pulls together all the information available in the economy about what each person wants, how much he values it, and how it can be best produced. Prices make that information *useable* to both producer and consumer. Each price contains within it information about aggregate consumer demands and costs of production, ranging from the amount of labor needed to produce the item to the cost of labor to the bad weather on the other side of the world that is raising the price of the raw materials needed to produce the good. Instead of having to know all the details, one is presented with a simple number: the price.[22]

---

[19] Milton Friedman and Rose Friedman, *Free to Choose* (Harcourt Brace, 1990), 13.[From *Economics* by Gwartney et al., 27].

[20] The surplus is equal to the area above market price and below the demand curve created by the variables of price and quantity/time.

[21] James D. Gwartney, et al., *Economics, Private and Public Choice* (South-Western Cengage Learning, 2008), 55.

[22] David Boaz, *Libertarianism – A Prime*, 150.

This system is invariably superior to one that involves central planning because in it decision-makers who have the most at risk and are closest to consumers and markets generally have the earliest and most detailed knowledge of relevant circumstances, and thus are quickest to respond to circumstances.

Another gloss on the significance of free prices:

> [P]rofit is a reward earned by producers who increase the value of resources, whereas loss is a punishment imposed on producers who use resources in ways that reduce their value… The price of a product measures the value that consumers place on the product. The price of the resources, however, measures the value that consumers place on *other products* that could be produced with those same resources. … If the output the firm produces with that resource can be sold at a higher price than the price of the alternative outputs, then and only then will the firm earn a profit. Thus, profit is a reward to those entrepreneurs who are able to see and act on opportunities to put resources to higher valued uses.[23]

Spontaneous Order

Given these unseen basic economic forces – characterized by Adam Smith as an invisible hand – most economic activity requires little government action beyond maintaining a level playing field, preventing fraud, and providing security. In the modern era, it is difficult for most to understand, much less believe, that so much of modern life can take place without significant government involvement. Yet we shall see how advances in science, agriculture, banking, industry, and the computer/internet all came about spontaneously when economic actors tried to profit by meeting the needs of consumers. Hayek calls this ordering of the market according to unseen economic laws without government action "spontaneous order." Indeed, virtually all the principal underpinnings of the modern economy arose without government leadership as individuals and networks crafted solutions to systemic trading needs and sought to meet consumers' needs. This is how money, banking, law, commercial courts, and more were created. Chapter Four will summarize how civil society (without government interference) spurred the development of schools, healthcare, disability insurance, and pensions in Great Britain and the United States.

Von Hayek showed that liberty is crucial to the development of spontaneous order. This can be seen in two aspects of human action: the nature and distribution of actionable knowledge and the freedom of the individual to exploit new

---

[23]   James D. Gwartney et al., *Economics, Private and Public Choice*, 568.

opportunities, to respond to the unknown, and to cooperate or collaborate with others. To understand this, it is necessary to first step back from observable situations. For example, while it is intuitively easy to visualize the productive capacity of laborers on a factory floor who follow management's coordination and directives, it is far more difficult to recognize the coordination achieved by dispersed entities. This section will illustrate a process by which individuals and small groups across society, working under their own initiative, coordinate their activities to produce wealth through mutually agreed means despite physical and institutional separation.

Distributed Intelligence

Hayek introduces the idea of distributed intelligence with the observation that "civilization begins when the individual in the pursuit of his ends can make use of more knowledge than he has himself acquired and when he can transcend the boundaries of his ignorance by profiting from knowledge he does not himself possess."[24] This, however, is no mean feat. Hayek notes that the sum of knowledge exists nowhere as an integrated whole but only as separate, partial, and sometimes conflicting beliefs.[25] For example, it has been mentioned here that prices incorporate vast amounts of knowledge: scarcity and abundance, adverse events affecting commodities a world away, transportation costs, famine, strikes, and so forth. Moreover, the more complex an economic society becomes, the smaller the share of that knowledge that any one mind can command.

Distributed intelligence, of course, exists everywhere that man does because we could not survive without relying on one another, each with unique knowledge. The extent and specifics of that cooperation determine efficacy, the most instrumental element of which is the freedom individuals enjoy to harness their knowledge and intelligence with that of others. Examples can be found even in primitive circumstances, such as native crafts and the exchange of scarce items (such as salt or metals) between tribes. Each tribe benefits from the others' unique knowledge in their respective areas of expertise.

A more complex example from modern times shows the working of distributed intelligence in the production of something as simple as a wooden pencil. The author of the book *I, Pencil* points out that no one person knows enough to make a pencil alone.[26] One would have to know how to harvest the most appropriate lumber, find and shape graphite, find and process rubber for the eraser, and smelt and shape metal for the binder of the eraser, not to mention installing the graphite

---

[24]   Friedrich von Hayek, *The Constitution of Liberty* (Chicago: The University of Chicago Press, 1960), 22.

[25]   Ibid, 25.

[26]   Leonard E. Read, *I, Pencil* (Foundation for Economic Education, March 3, 2015).

inside the wood. The manufacturer/entrepreneur discovers sources for each key piece of knowledge and brings it all together for the market. But he himself has likely mastered none of these skills beyond the final stages of assembly. Similarly, he can't define the scarcity or abundance of the inputs into the process with any precision, but he can glean relevant information from price signals, which also let him judge the economics of his business model and assess his competition.

The power of distributed intelligence arises from the fact that "compared with the totality of knowledge which is continually utilized in the evolution of a dynamic civilization, the difference between the knowledge that the wisest and that which the most ignorant individual can deliberately employ is comparatively insignificant."[27]

To be sure, a bureaucrat has as much access to distributed intelligence as an entrepreneur. However, he is less likely to use it to his advantage. He has nothing at stake and is timid and boxed in by conventional wisdom. To avoid making mistakes or being second-guessed, he is virtually forced to make decisions based on what is already known and proven (and thus defensible) rather than on what might be possible. Not being wrong is more important to him than guessing right on an opportunity that will not benefit him personally. After all, the odds are against him; most new innovations don't succeed. But society vastly benefits from the few that do.

Moreover, imagine the future potential for enhancing distributed intelligence through the computer revolution, the worldwide web, and artificial intelligence, which surely represents a quantum leap in man's capabilities for extended free cooperation.

Hayek expands on the role of spontaneous order in this process. As the interactions of various actors became more efficient, actors agreed on 'rules' as part of the natural process as problems were solved by those most familiar with the matters at hand. Again, as discussed previously, solutions arise spontaneously to meet commercial needs, e.g., terms of trade, money, and commercial law. Hayek developed these ideas into a body of social theory, illustrating how human relationships can grow into complex, orderly, and clearly purposeful institutions that owe little to design. These institutions were not invented but arose from the separate actions of many men who did not even know what they were doing (in a larger sense).[28]

This process extends well beyond institution-building to mundane, everyday activities; individuals and small groups find better ways of doing things, increasing society's productivity bit by bit, and eventually their methods are emulated by others who do not wish to be left behind.

---

[27]   Ibid, 30

[28]   Ibid, 58-59.

In *The Constitution of Liberty*,[29] Hayek argues that liberty must play a critical role in this process if we want modern society to fulfill its potential. That is why this present book identifies the goal as the free extended order of human cooperation. According to Hayek, liberty enhances the functioning of the extended order because relative freedom from government interference enhances the utility of distributed, actionable knowledge. This freedom is also the best way to unleash creative individuals' abilities to exploit new opportunities, and it is the best way to prepare society for the unknown and unexpected, whether brilliant discoveries or widespread misfortune.

There are important reasons why the government is not the best actor to lead economic advance or even to deal with many emerging problems on a limited scale. Individuals in government are subject to the same limitations regarding knowledge as individual economic actors. Moreover, the nature of government necessarily favors rationalism in ways that attempt to subject everything to human reason shaped by past experience and values predictability, despite the unavoidability of the unknown and the unpredictability of unintended consequences. Per Hayek, "the rationalist who desires to subject everything to human reason is thus faced with a real dilemma. The use of reason aims at control and predictability. But the process of the advance of reason rests on freedom and the unpredictability of human action."[30] Finally, government, an agent of the majority, "is, of necessity, confined to the already tried and ascertained, to issues on which agreement has already been reached…"[31]

Placing the government in inappropriate roles defies Hayek's evolutionary theory, which demonstrates how complex, orderly, and purposeful institutions develop without a macro-design. This is partly because of the ways in which the individual actor can be wise beyond his immediate hard knowledge and beyond conventional wisdom:

> Not all knowledge … is part of our intellect, nor is our intellect the whole of our knowledge. Our habits and skills, our emotional attitudes, our tools, and our institutions – all are … adaptations to past experience which have grown up by selective elimination of less suitable conduct.[32]

This is the essence of evolutionary progress – i.e., the survival of the fittest, even though the specifics went unremarked for centuries. A practical consequence

---

[29] Friedrich A. Hayek, *The Constitution of Liberty* (The University of Chicago Press, 1960).

[30] Ibid, 38.

[31] Ibid, 31.

[32] Ibid, 26.

is that entrepreneurs can act more quickly on the basis of informed intuition than bureaucrats who must justify their actions using past experience and accepted conventional wisdom.

So, not only does the government know less than it thinks it does, but also, once it grasps the reins of the regulatory process, group think sets in and dissenters are inhibited. Hayek emphasizes that "above all, however, we should provide the maximum of opportunity for unknown individuals to learn of facts that we ourselves are yet unaware of and to make use of the knowledge in their actions."[33]

In short, society should create social capital through education and experience while giving that capital plenty of running room through personal liberation and freedom from oppressive regulation.

Examples of Spontaneous Order

History contains a multitude of examples illustrating how man has spontaneously developed solutions in response to immediate economic needs. These examples include prehistoric trade, medieval banking, agriculture, the Industrial Revolution, computers and the internet, and the vast undertaking of science itself.

Prehistory

Empirical evidence for spontaneous markets goes back to human prehistory, showing that trade is older than agriculture or any sort of regular production. Early trade involved the exchange of necessities not found in all locales, such as salt. Archeological evidence indicates that trade was conducted over long distances in the Paleolithic Age, at least 30,000 years ago. This trade resulted from efforts made by individuals who spotted opportunities for comparative advantage, however intuitively.

However, given the universal mutual hostility among these early societies, before trade could expand, new attitudes and institutions had to emerge. For example, in early Greece (among other places), the social construct of a 'guest friend' arose. This allowed outsiders to enter an otherwise suspicious, if not hostile, tribe to provide a mutually beneficial service.[34] With time, the increasingly obvious economic benefits of such individual efforts led to expanding trade networks. Athens' ensuing preeminence among Greek city-states arose from its prowess and success in trading.

---

[33]   Ibid, 30.

[34]   Ibid, 39

Medieval banking

In medieval times, the foundations of banking rose spontaneously in the context of simple serial trade fairs. These fairs had several unique advantages: The fairgrounds were protected by a special peace under the prince's rule; letters of obligation sealed with the fair's imprimatur were recognized as especially binding; the 'franchise' exempted merchants from reprisal or debts stemming from outside the fair for the duration of the fair; and the canonical prohibition of usury, which fixed a maximum rate of interest, was suspended.

Innovations that developed in the more advanced Italian city-states helped these fairs become the money markets of Europe. At every fair, a period of sales was followed by one of payment. These payments cleared debts contracted at the fair itself and also settled credits contracted at preceding fairs. This was an early form of bills of exchange; bills were written promises to pay a sum of money in a place other than where the debt was contracted. The Champagne fairs were so widely attended that most debts were made payable there, no matter where they had been contracted. Soon not only commercial debts but also loans contracted by individuals, princes, or religious organizations were settled at the fairs.

In addition, new free cities provided a protected niche for the new wealth generated from expanding trade. Since property rights were relatively secure, capital could be safely accumulated for investment. Over centuries, artisans became traders, traders became merchants, and merchants became bankers. Furthermore, many of the first bankers were descended from money exchangers – an essential job because of the plethora of currencies. These money exchangers grew rich in one of the few niches of the economy relatively free from control. But generally, medieval bankers were both merchants and moneylenders, naturally finding a use for their surplus capital.[35]

In all these matters, necessity was the mother of innovation.

Agriculture

Another less dramatic but equally instructive example of the power of innovation involves the growth of agricultural productivity. This was a process of incremental change carried out by many actors over a much longer period, making it an even better example of the extended order in which learning and experience are shared. One entrepreneurial farmer finds better farming methods and is imitated by others who spot new opportunities. Similarly, with the advent of science, one group learns how to apply new research to agriculture, and their methods are quickly emulated.

While they were assisted by institutions such as agricultural colleges,

---

[35]   Ibid.

individual actors brought about these changes. The last two centuries have seen spectacular advances. When the United States was founded, around 90% of the population lived on farms or plantations, producing food and raw materials.[36] Currently, a mere 1% of workers live on farms; they feed the entire country (and produce much more for export).[37] Farmers' incomes and standards of living have grown in proportion with the overall economy, but the greatest benefits have gone to consumers. For example, in the last sixty years, agricultural productivity in the United States has doubled and average consumer food expenditures have fallen from over 20% of disposable income to less than 10% today (per the U.S. Department of Agriculture).[38]

Nineteenth-century industry

In another example, the Industrial Revolution advanced rapidly because of individual innovators, especially in the areas of steel, petroleum, automobiles, and electricity. The example of the early petroleum industry is especially instructive. At the beginning of the nineteenth century, little was known about efficient extraction techniques, petroleum refining, or the distribution of petroleum-based products to consumers. Those who mastered these elements and (presciently) invested in key R&D reduced prices dramatically and created vastly expanded markets for the various fuels. During the first twenty years of the Standard Oil Company's operation, the price of gasoline declined from 58 cents to eight cents a gallon.[39] One advance assisted another; for example, inexpensive fuel made mass production of automobiles feasible. Even though these entrepreneurs became fabulously wealthy, it was consumers who reaped the lion's share of this new wealth.

Computers and the internet

The rise of personal computing and the internet is the most recent example of these truths. To be sure, the Defense Department's work on computer communication was an important ingredient. But it was the development of software and internet services in the private sector that spurred innovation throughout the economy.

---

36   Alan Greenspan and Adrian Wooldridge. *Capitalism in America* (New York: Penguin Press, 2018), 32.

37   International Labor Organization, ILOSTAT database. Data retrieved April 2019.

38   Edward Conard, *Unintended Consequences, Why Everything You've Been Told About the Economy Is Wrong* (New York: Portfolio/Penguin, 2012), 36.

39   Burton W. Folsom, Jr., *The Myth of the Robber Barons – A New Look at the Rise of Big Business in America, Third Edition* (Herndon, Virginia: Young America's Foundation, 1996), 83.

A few specifics make this abundantly clear, beginning with the astonishing performance of certain 'economic clusters' – notably New York City in finance and Silicon Valley in new technology. These clusters provide arenas where highly motivated, intelligent, and creative individuals in close proximity can cross-fertilize and rapidly implement ideas due to the availability of the necessary social and financial capital. This is spontaneous order in high gear.

Josef Joffe discusses the performance of Silicon Valley: In the 1940s, Professor Frederick Terman at Stanford University was determined to create "steeples of excellence" by building the capability of science and engineering at the university in conjunction with practical innovation in the private sector. The eventual outcome was what we now know as Silicon Valley. At the outset, he encouraged two of his students David Packard and William Hewlett to start a little electronics company, which eventually became the big Hewlett Packard.

He also was involved with Varian Associates which started with a few Stanford Affiliates to build the Stanford Industrial Park (renamed Stanford Research Park), one of the world's premier research groups, which spawned numerous entrepreneurial efforts. Notably, William Shockley, the inventor of the transistor launched a startup of Shockley Semiconductors. Subsequently, participants in that startup went on to found Fairchild Semiconductors. Then Gordon Moore and Robert Noyce left Fairchild to create Intel. Entrepreneurial efforts mushroomed: within twenty years, 65 new enterprises arose. Perhaps most notable, Sergey Brin and Larry Page founded Google, which licenses its Internet search technology from Stanford, where "the father of the Internet" Vinton Cerf had developed the TCP/IP protocol.[40]

Science

A similar phenomenon can be seen in scientific advancement, as summarized by Rosenberg and Birdzell: "The general acceptance of the experimental method made it possible for hundreds and even thousands of specialists to build the results of their individual research into a single store of information, usable across all sciences." This was made practical with the contemporaneous discovery of the printing press which empowered the efficacy of distributed knowledge. The system was dependent on the initiative of the individual scientist with very little hierarchical management. Like entrepreneurs, individuals could spot where their talents and insights might have the greatest payoff. Peer review provided quality control and the basis for further advance. "The resolution of conflicts on points of professional controversy was a process of achieving professional consensus.... On

---

[40] Josef Joffe, *The Myth of America's Decline: Politics, Economics, and a Half Century of False Prophecies* (Liveright Publishing Corporation, A Division of W.W. Norton & Company, 2014).

the whole, it is apparent that the Western Scientific community was more, rather than less, efficiently organized by reason of its lack of a hierarchy."[41]

Spontaneous Adjudication

Over centuries, the FEO spontaneously evolved approaches to problems. One example involved dispute resolution between ranchers and farmers in Shasta Country, California. Legal scholar Robert Ellickson found that neighbors solved disputes (e.g., cattle straying and doing damage) without appealing to formal legal institutions. They often did not know the letter of the law, so resolutions were driven by cooperation, mutual interest, trust, reputation, and the need to maintain a good working relationship.[42]

Kevin Williamson examined dispute resolution in the computer industry in Silicon Valley. He states that it is a truism that disputes over issues such as patents and complex contracts may be honest disagreements or malicious advantage seeking. The honest cases go to arbitration, and the malicious cases go to court.[43]

These examples illustrate the ideal functioning of the extended order. However, it should be obvious that, since the extended order describes how all human economic interactions respond to universal natural forces, it exists everywhere and at all times in some form. The subsequent sections will show that this order can best meet human needs when it is allowed to operate freely. The free extended order is our guiding beacon. And freedom means that the government must be limited to its proper place.

LIMITED GOVERNMENT PROVIDES
THE OPTIMAL SETTING

Since governments are made up of flawed men and respond to men's parochial ambitions, they can and generally do end up undermining the FEO. In addition to overt predation by favored interests, modern democracies have a tendency towards utopian thinking that is inimical to maintaining a light hand in government. Indeed, society's principle challenge over centuries has been identifying the proper role of government and establishing values and institutions to keep it within appropriate bounds. Man's inescapable quandary is this: While government plays an essential role in providing security and maintaining the rule of law, once a

---

[41]   Nathan Rosenberg &L.E. Birdzell Jr., *How the West Grew Rich: The Economic Transformation of the Industrial World* (United States of America: Basic Books, 1986), 254-255.

[42]   Kevin D. Williamson, *The End is Near and It's Going to be Awesome*,(New York: Broadside Books, an imprint of Harper Collins Publishers, 2013), 171-172.

[43]   Ibid, 176.

government has a monopoly on the use of force to protect society, it is too easy for it to use those powers to enrich individuals in the government through (for example) taxation, regulation, and utopian schemes to benefit special interests. The challenge has always been containing these predatory forces while enabling the essential government functions that benefit all.

Keeping government within proper boundaries requires, first, an understanding of what those boundaries should be – particularly vis-à-vis the predicates of the FEO. Fortunately, today we have ample theory and empirical experience to address that challenge. Two useful tools include a model developed by the economist James Buchanan and predicates for the FEO derived empirically by studies such as the *Index of Economic Freedom*[44] and *Economic Freedom of the World*.[45]

Buchanan's Model

The economist James Buchanan postulates a simple abstract model for identifying the powers and responsibilities that should be assigned to government. He presents a thought experiment: In the abstract, how would humans negotiate agreements for political cooperation – in other words, based on what principles would they agree to give up some of the freedom of action they enjoy under an anarchistic pre-government in exchange for their fellow men doing the same? While theoretical, this illustration offers insights for real-world considerations. In an anarchistic state, each individual can benefit from preying on the goods of others – if he can get away with it. As a result, collective human wealth production suffers because non-productive resources must be devoted to protecting material wealth.

Clearly, when individuals negotiate terms to respect one another's property, predation is reduced, and more effort can be devoted to production and less to protection. Even so, men, not being angels, invariably continue to look for safe ways to violate such agreements to benefit themselves. Thus, these agreements require some enforcement mechanisms (e.g., the protective state). Enforcement costs can never be zero, but they are far less when borne by government than if each individual had to protect his own wealth separately.

When such terms are negotiated, key elements of organized society fall naturally and logically into place. First, the terms (by definition) must identify what belongs to each individual – i.e., private property is defined. Clear property rights set the foundation for mutual trade, allowing the forces of comparative

---

[44]   Terry Miller and Anthony B. Kim, *2016 Index of Economic Freedom: Promoting Economic Opportunity and Prosperity* (The Heritage Foundation and *The Wall Street Journal*, 2016).

[45]   James Gwartney and Robert Lawson with William Easterly, *Economic Freedom of the World 2006 Annual Report*,(Canada: The Fraser Institute, 2006).

advantage to unfold and vastly improving society's ability to create wealth. In principle, such trade arises through each individual's calculation of his advantage, and no government action is required.

Thus far in this model, all rules would have been decided unanimously because when all participants agree to all terms, no participant's rights can be violated by the others' collective action. However, in the next area of human social interaction, the model becomes more complicated. The rule of unanimity must be relinquished when the government is allowed to provide services to society because it can do so more cost-effectively than individuals on their own or through cooperative groups. Individuals agree to this arrangement because everyone is better off overall, even though not every individual benefits from every governmental action. This feature may indeed be the Achilles' heel of the extended order under representative government. The danger is that, without sufficient safeguards, once the government is allowed to interfere in the economic sector, the majority can transgress the agreed terms and use their power to prey on the minority.

According to Buchanan, the logic of such a philosophical model leads to the conclusion:

> The protective state has as its essential and only role the enforcement of individual rights as defined in constitutional contract. The state is law embodied, and its role is enforcing rights to property, to exchanges of property, and of policing the simple and complex exchange processes among contracting free men. ... its task is conceptually limited to enforcing agreed-on rules. [46]

Indeed, this view underlies the U.S. Declaration of Independence and the U.S. Constitution as will be discussed in Chapter Three.

The implications of this model identify the aspects of the economy and society that should be shielded from government interference; first, anything individuals can do alone or in voluntary cooperation with others is outside the proper role of government, and second, the power of taxation must be kept on a tight leash. Thus, when the government is responsible for removing economic 'externalities' in ways that benefit all (national security and protecting health, infrastructure, etc.), those tasks should be subject to strict cost/benefit considerations and should not be undertaken in ways that establish quasi-governmental monopolies protected from the forces of competition. Without such limits, the government is simply too cumbersome, too prone to advance the interests of special factions, and too resistant to reform.

---

[46]   James M. Buchanan, *The Limits of Liberty, Between Anarchy and Leviathan* (Chicago: The University of Chicago Press, 1975), 163.

Predicates for a Free Extended Order in an Advanced Economy

The above discussion draws abstract boundaries around government to preclude undue interference in the economic private sector. However, there are many areas where government is essential, but it must act with an awareness of the needs of the FEO and a wariness of the unintended consequences that can follow the best of intentions. A growing body of empirical evidence illustrates the appropriate guidelines.

These boundaries are evident in the reports, the *Index of Economic Freedom* (*Index*) and *Economic Freedom of the World*, both published annually. Each of these reports ranks countries according to objective criteria that focus on the freedom of markets, the rule of law, the restraint of the central state, and sound macroeconomic policies. Both reports characterize these attributes as elements of 'freedom' – which in practice means freedom from the predatory state and freedom for personal initiative, for entrepreneurship, and for devolved decision-making.

The *Index*[47] identifies representative criteria, divided into ten areas[48]that define this freedom:

1) **Trade policy:** Government should encourage free trade to strengthen comparative advantage by reducing or eliminating barriers such as tariff rates, non-tariff barriers (e.g., import quotas and licensing requirements), and corruption in customs.

2) **Fiscal burden of government:** Top income tax rates, average tax rates, the top corporate tax rate, and government expenditures should be minimal.

3) **Government intervention in the productive economy:** Government consumption as a percentage of the economy, government ownership of businesses and industries, the share of government revenues from state-owned enterprises and government-owned property, and economic output produced by the government should all be minimal. Income redistribution and unnecessary regulation (which breeds legions of "proceduralists," monitors, auditors, and lawyers to second-guess private actors) can be sand in the gears of enterprise.

---

[47] Marc A Miles., Kim R. Holmes, and Mary Anastasia O'Grady. *2006 Index of Economic Freedom: The Link Between Economic Opportunity and Prosperity.* The Heritage Foundation and *The Wall Street Journal*, 2006.

[48] The annual publications of the Index over the years always measure ten indices, which year-to-year are substantively similar. However, the order and the specifics vary. This listing is from the *2006 Index*.

4) **Monetary policy:** Government should provide a stable currency and minimize inflation.

5) **Capital flows and foreign investment:** Government policies should facilitate foreign investment and local financing for foreign companies; treat foreign and domestic companies equally under the law; and impose minimal restrictions on foreign companies (including foreign ownership of businesses or land), or regulations impeding foreign investors and repatriation of earnings.

6) **Banking and finance:** There should be minimal government ownership of banks, restrictions on the ability of foreign banks to open branches and subsidiaries, and minimal government influence in the allocation of credit allowing these sectors to function freely. Banks should be free to offer all types of financial services, securities, and insurance policies.

7) **Wages and prices:** The private sector should not be burdened by minimum wage laws; companies should be free to set prices privately without government influence or price controls; and government subsidies that affect prices should be minimal.

8) **Property rights:** Property should be protected from extra-legal government influence over the judicial system, from government expropriation of property, from corruption within the judiciary, and from delays in judicial decisions that protect private property rights.

9) **Regulation:** The licensing requirements to operate a business should be economically justified, and business licenses should be easy to obtain. Labor regulations such as regulated work weeks, paid vacations, and parental leave impose burdens on businesses, as do select labor regulations and environmental, consumer safety, and work health regulations.

10) **Informal market:** Smuggling; piracy of intellectual property; and black markets for products, services, transportation, and labor should be minimal or non-existent.

In short, the FEO functions optimally when there is freedom for entrepreneurial efforts, when investment decisions are made by those who incur the financial risk, when unencumbered prices ensure clear market signals, when trade is free so comparative advantage comes into play, when property rights are protected, when contracts are enforced, and when the market is protected from governmental action that unduly siphons away wealth (and thus investment). These are measurable parameters that correlate closely and robustly with a country's economic performance. Countries that mostly adhere to these principles – which the *Index* calls "free" or "mostly free" –grow vigorously. Alas, most countries do not and are underdeveloped, stagnant, or chained by authoritarianism (see Chapter 9).

The power of these factors on the economy are dramatically evident in the areas of taxation and property rights.

Overall Taxation

Its power to tax has a particular ability to either nurture or undermine the FEO. Taxation and regulation beyond appropriate limits drains wealth from the system, slowing innovation, investment, and growth. This correlation takes effort to parse, but it is essential to understanding why large government should inherently be suspect. The implications of taxation go well beyond dividing the economic pie fairly. Wealth must be created before it can be divided, and tax policy is key to determining a country's economic potential. Politics is often viewed as a zero-sum game in which the outcomes of political battles merely determine which groups will benefit from the division of national wealth. But taxing the investor class to enable others to consume is largely self-defeating. The economy is not a zero-sum game. Indeed, by taxing the investor class, all income classes, including the supposed beneficiaries of income redistribution, do less well over time because of curtailed wealth creation.

Indeed, beyond modest levels, high tax rates on the investor class reduce growth rates, sometimes severely. For example, a study by the National Bureau of Economic Research found a strong correlation between individual income and savings rates – ranging from 5% savingsrates among the bottom quintile in income to more than 40% among the top 5% of the population. Not surprisingly, the higher-income groups are more willing to take and underwrite risk in their investments, whereas lower-income groups invest predominantly in their homes and not enterprise.[49] In the United States, the top 5% in income, who also have more savings and investments, already pay nearly 50% of all federal taxes.[50] Thus, attempts to tax this proportion of the population still more heavily to subsidize the consumption of lower-income groups would necessarily reduce investment – and ultimately jobs for those lower-income groups.

Richard Rahn's research on countries around the world demonstrates that high taxation reduces economic growth. More specifically, taxation rates beyond an aggregate of about 25% increase economic drag. He summarizes his findings with a simple curve comparing economic growth rates over time to aggregate tax rates.

---

[49]   Conard, *Unintended Consequences*, 90.

[50]   Ibid, 257.

The Rahn Curve

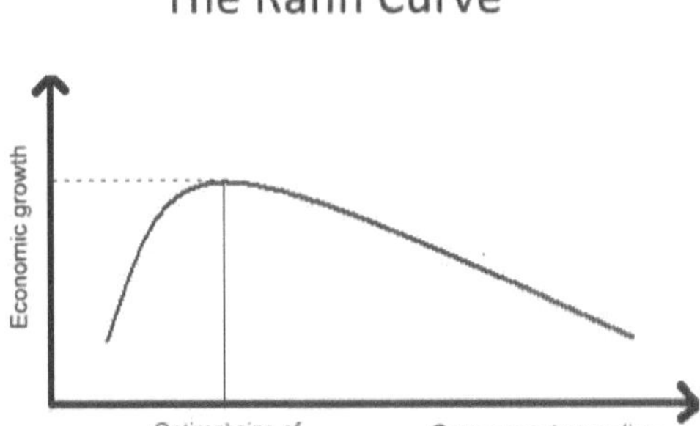

Source: Foundation for Economic Education, fee.org.

Key illustrative points on the curve include:

	Hong Kong/ Singapore	United States	Western Europe
Aggregate Tax Rate %	20	40	55
Average Growth Rate %	4	2 plus	2 minus

This data alone provides a key explanation for Singapore's spectacular growth in recent decades and Europe's relative stagnation.

Taxing Investment

While Rahn's work provides broad evidence for this concept, other studies provide more insight at the level of investment decision-making. Some examples regarding the interplay of innovation, intangible R&D, and taxation clarify this point.

Specifically, Edward Conard's *Unintended Consequences* portrays how wealth is produced naturally through innovation and then flows to all income classes.[51] This book examines the role of intangible investments in R&D in wealth generation and demonstrates how taxation can sap that productive force, eventually harming virtually all income segments of society.

As outlined in the earlier examples of spontaneous order, economic productivity increases with experience and human ingenuity. People learn to do more with less. That learning process is enhanced when entrepreneurship is relatively unfettered and investors are incentivized to bear intangible investment

---

[51]   Edward Conard, *Unintended Consequences,*(New York: Portfolio/Penguin, 2012).

costs commensurate with the risks involved. The innovation of the automobile assembly line is a case in point. Because the assembly line enabled the production of a greater number of cars with the same number of workers, it reduced labor costs per car and increased firm profitability (as well as wages paid). Enhanced profitability leads to higher income streams and increases a firm's capitalized value because the market anticipates enhanced future income in current net value. Modest capital investments directed by intangible R&D can produce a disproportionate increase in the value of an enterprise.

In virtually all areas of the economy, intangible investment in R&D is a key element of growth. Conard notes that since the Second World War, the U.S. economy has grown sevenfold in real terms, but physical inputs have grown only twofold. Most of the growth has come from intellectual capital, from workers such as product and process engineers, computer programmers, and strategic planners. In anticipation of the fairness argument, it should be noted that these individuals are disproportionately compensated in the United States because they produce a disproportionate share of the wealth.[52]

These results are not divorced from government policies, regulations, and taxes, so they vary considerably among countries. For example, the United States has proportionately higher rates of intangible investment than Europe. A 2006 Federal Reserve study, *Intangible Capital and Economic Growth*, estimates that intangible investments in the United States rose from about 7% of non-farm business output in the late 1970s to about 14% today. Comparable investments in Germany and France today are only about 60% to 70% of that; Italy's and Spain's are half.[53]

Some of the differences among countries can be traced to government policies; some might be a consequence of cultural attitudes towards entrepreneurship and risk-taking. Conard contrasts three wealthy societies – the United States, the European Union, and Japan – with similar access to education, science, and capital, which are essential inputs for growth. Yet productivity growth and GDP growth in the United States outperform those of the other two because of differences in intangible investment. He argues that financial incentives for risk takers and high performers in the United States are less burdened than in other countries, and this accounts for much of the difference. In the United States, upper income groups have more of the wealth, allowing them to make proportionately larger investments in innovation and, of course, reap proportional rewards: He estimates that one-third of the national income is derived from the efforts of the top 5% of the U.S. population.[54]

One element of his argument is that "successful, risky investments to discover and implement innovation will grow the economy faster than less risky investments

---

[52]   Ibid, 32.

[53]   Ibid, 46.

[54]   Ibid, 48.

that enlarge existing capacities in response to slowly growing demand."[55] The United States excels in the former, Europe (particularly Germany) and Japan in the latter. The United States is way ahead in internet business, having created companies like Google, Microsoft, Facebook, Intel, Apple, Amazon, and eBay. Europe has produced nothing comparable.

The highly publicized personal wealth of the entrepreneurs that created these enterprises is a small fraction of the consumer surplus they bring to society or of the wages captured by labor. Indeed, studies done by the Federal Reserve Bank of St. Louis have demonstrated that U.S. workers' share of national income has remained steady at about 70%. Moreover, the biggest ultimate beneficiary is the consumer, who garners over 90% of the wealth created through wages, lower prices, and consumer surplus.[56] Recall in the earlier example that enormous increases in farmer productivity benefitted the overall population more than the farmers themselves.

Seen in this light, policies that limit innovation and reduce productivity, such as unnecessary union work rules and dysfunctional government regulations, can have extensive impacts on economic growth rates. To be sure, such interference is always couched in the language of fairness and health protection, but rigorous cost-benefit testing is not always required of the regulators. Unverifiable social benefit claims enter the picture and as will be discussed, the Supreme Court defers to agency decisions even when ungrounded. A later chapter will provide examples of out-of-bounds government interference and the great cost it levies on wealth creation and the country as a whole. However, the government's power to tax economic activity can be just as pernicious, yet it is largely invisible to the average citizen.

On the topic of taxation, it is important to consider not just its reduction of corporate and personal income, but also its indirect effects on labor and consumer surplus. Conard demonstrates that taxing the investor class fails to achieve its larger purposes. Each dollar of investment that is lost to taxation reduces the net present value of future wealth by a greater amount.[57] Of course, some favored special interests are better off, but society as a whole is poorer.[58]

---

[55] Ibid, 31.

[56] Ibid, 36.

[57] Conard runs some numbers based on a continuation of historical patterns – i.e., high earners save about 40% of their income, successful investments earn on average about 7.5% per year, and labor together with consumers reap about 90% of all returns from such investments. He then estimates that $0.40 of investment produces a $3.65 net present value of future wealth; non-investors capture about $1.80 of this value. If, instead, the government taxes high-income dollars at a higher rate, thereby reducing investment, society loses that $1.80. Assume further that the government redistributes that taxed dollar across all income classes. Then the middle class (the middle 40% of income earners) would gain $0.40 directly but would have to forego $0.60 (40% of $1.80).

[58] Ibid, 259.

It is difficult to convince the electorate to accept this argument because society cannot see what does not happen, that is, the investment that never occurred and its results. However, the dismal economic results of the Obama era are highly illustrative. During his presidency, the federal government indulged in vast deficit spending (financed by borrowing from the investor class and abroad) and increased tax rates on the rich. Under the Obama administration, the United States slipped in the rankings of *The Index of Economic Freedom* from "free" to "mostly free" for the first time.[59] High levels of government spending and increased regulation in the finance, energy, and healthcare sectors took their tolls on economic performance. As a result, the United States experienced its most sluggish recovery from a recession in history, along with falling labor participation rates and a declining pace of business start-ups. The middle classes then saw continuous erosion of their real (post-inflation) incomes. Not surprisingly, in each year of that administration, average household income in real dollars fell.

Conard concludes:

> Because investment creates enormous value for consumers and wage earners, small reductions in profits and subsequent investment can have a big impact on wages, employment and the price of goods. The reduction in profitability can unwittingly destroy more value than well-intended regulations create.[60]

*　　*　　*

The above discussion cautions against government engaging in economic activities better left to the private sector by implementing inadvisable policies and overregulation, and by sapping markets' vitality through over-taxation. Later chapters will provide numerous examples of government programs that overstepped these bounds, failed to meet their objectives and cost the country dearly.

Private Property

The protection of private property rights is a key predicate for enabling the FEO: It frees individuals from dependence on the whims of the state and makes free exchange and trade possible. To repeat James Buchanan's conclusions, before trade can take place, (that is, before goods or titles can be exchanged), there must

---

[59] Terry Miller and Anthony B. Kim, *2016 Index of Economic Freedom: Promoting Economic Opportunity and Prosperity* (The Heritage Foundation and *The Wall Street Journal*, 2016), 3.

[60] Ibid, 39.

be a way to determine what belongs to each individual. Clear property rights are the basis for mutual trade, and as Tom Bethell notes:

> ... transferable (exchangeable) property rights are the key to economic efficiency, to amity between neighbors and peaceful relations in society more generally. ... When goods are owned in a well-defined way, and the rights to them are exchangeable, they will be purchased by those who value them most highly. Resources will be put to their highest-valued use.[61]

Paul Heyne of the University of Washington provides a telling example of this insight (cited by Bethell). As the Soviet Union disintegrated, news reports mentioned the apparent irony of food rotting in rural areas while grocery shelves were bare. The obvious question (at least to someone immersed in the free market system) arose: "Why didn't somebody transport the food to the cities?" However, under the rules of the Soviet Union, this transfer was not so easy to arrange: "Who owned the food that was going to waste? Who had authority to harvest it? Who owned the harvesting equipment? Who owned the trucks to transport the food to the cities? Who had fuel for the trucks? How was the food to be distributed once it arrived in the cities?"[62] Obviously, if there had been free agents along the way who had the necessary property rights, the cities' economic need would have quickly become a profit opportunity for actors spontaneously engaging their entrepreneurial instincts.

A collateral benefit is that when property rights and associated income are secure, individuals can contest government encroachment on their liberty in the courts as well as through the political process.

*   *   *

There may be no stone tablets enshrining the FEO, no general mathematical formulations to characterize it entirely, but one can look beneath the surface of things to perceive a framework for why it works the way it does. The above discussion has identified numerous markers for identifying an optimal FEO: (1) Natural, unalterable rules shaping economic action, together with mutable human activity, produce an extended order everywhere. (2) Those variable aspects of human governance can make this order *free*, and thus an optimal way to meet human needs. Taken together, they can be regarded as an FEO-*blueprint*, along the lines of the following chart.

---

[61]   Tom Bethell, *The Noblest Triumph: Property and Prosperity Through the Ages* (New York: St. Martin's Press,1998), 316-317.

[62]   Ibid, 323.

THE INVISIBLE HAND/SPONTANEOUS DEVELOPMENT PRODUCE A NATURAL ORDER

Basically Determined by:

Human Nature
- Human action/ predatory instincts
- Distributed intelligence
- Social capital

Economic Laws
- Supply and demand
- Price signals
- Comparative advantage
- Consumer surplus

But Mutable Policies Facilitate a *Free* Extended Order by:

- Enhancing social capital
  - Individual liberty
  - Private property
  - Values (Protestant ethic/classical liberalism)

- Enforcing unencumbered functioning of economic laws
  - Free markets
  - Sound currency/free flow of capital

- Controlling predation
  - Competition/avoiding monopolies
  - Rule of law
  - Small government

Seen in this light, the FEO is in effect the *natural* order of things in which human energy and ambition can best meet individuals' needs while creating the greatest prosperity for all if allowed to function freely. This frees economic motivation and enables distributed human intelligence to function to optimal effect. Human nature and economic laws define what is possible; various outcomes open to human ingenuity are determined by the social/political elements listed at the bottom of the diagram.

Adam Smith's light hand of government and von Hayek's FEO suggest some key takeaways:

- Individual liberty and protected property rights are paramount.
- Small government and modest taxation lead to growth, benefitting every income class.
- Government intervention in free markets should be viewed with suspicion.
- Governments should not favor one faction over another.
- Rule of law, particularly the tradition of common law, is essential to protecting the original constitutional vision of the United States and to protecting private property and individual liberties.
- Empowering individuals and building social capital are integral to exploiting the power of society's distributed intelligence, a key element of the FEO.

*　　*　　*

In short, this chapter shows how Adam Smith's dictums about the importance of a free economy and a light hand of government work everywhere humans implement them. Indeed, given the innate human ambition to thrive, growth is spontaneous and needs little direction. But keeping government in its proper role does require constant attention because of the predatory side of human nature and the human predilection to empirically unfounded utopianism. Having discovered a tolerable balance between establishing a basis for prosperous growth and checking governments prone to predation has been one of social man's greatest achievements. Nonetheless, because such achievements are not immutable (and are, as we shall see, under continual attack), the people must exercise vigilance to preserve them.

The next chapter elaborates on this ongoing challenge by more fully describing the predatory side of human nature in the context of government. Chapter Three discusses the evolution of human values and institutions that address this challenge and facilitate the FEO to function optimally. Subsequent chapters provide examples of both dysfunctional governments and effective FEOs in several countries so as to reinforce the conclusions of this chapter and to provide insights for protecting the FEO going forward.

CHAPTER 2

GOVERNMENTAL PREDATION IS UBIQUITOUS

"A universal feature of polities is the ubiquitous predatoriness of the State. This merely reflects the necessary monopoly of coercive power and the inevitable maximization of net revenue that self-interested governors will then extract from their subjects."[63] – Deepak Lal

Chapter One demonstrated that prosperity occurs naturally if it is allowed to unfold under the light touch of government. Unfortunately, it is not government's nature to touch lightly. Indeed, as Deepak Lal noted, government naturally becomes predatory regardless of initial good intentions – government cannot function without power, power corrupts, and all human institutions eventually aim to extend their sway. That, too, is a natural outcome of human nature. This chapter will examine many forms of predation threatening the FEO; the following one will outline mankind's evolutionary progress in finding ways to curb that predation.

However, to control predation, one first needs to understand the darker side of human nature – or, if that term is too strong, the non-Rousseauian side. We are all casually aware of ordinary lawbreaking such as muggings and theft, which wash around the fringes of most of our lives; as of 2017, the U.S. has about some 1.5 million in prisons and jails.[64] We are perhaps less aware of the wide-scale fraud that permeates our society, such as Ponzi schemes, fraudulent Medicare claims (which come to billions of dollars), and fraudulent attempts to collect tax refunds

---

[63]   Deepak Lal, *Unintended Consequences*, 16.

[64]   Department of Justice, Office of Justice Programs, Press Release, April 25, 2019.

due others. Yet, as we shall see, the real danger is when the wrong people obtain power, either as individuals or as part of factions.

For this chapter's analysis, predation can be defined as any behavior designed to extract unearned wealth from others through force, fraud, or rent-seeking (in other words, as rights granted by to government to transfer wealth or the ability to move wealth from one sector of society to a favored faction).

Governmental predation has existed since time immemorial, from the simplest tribal societies to highly complex forms of self-government. It is inevitable because it is irresistible for many; as Willie Sutton allegedly responded when asked why he robbed banks, "Because that is where the money is." Moreover, even individuals who are not self-seeking and who patently attempt to do good can convince themselves that such behavior is necessary for the greater good.

It is man's nature to do whatever it takes to survive, particularly vis-à-vis his competitors. He can easily calculate the relative advantages of work versus pillage. Richard Dawkins, author of *The Selfish Gene*, concludes: "We are survival machines – robot vehicles blindly programmed to preserve the selfish molecules known as genes."[65] At the end of the day, our first goal is survival, and passing on our genes to another generation is a close second. Unsocialized man instinctively considers using force to obtain another's hard-earned gains to achieve these ends. Of course, man evolves socially as well as biologically; indeed, social evolution is much faster. We improve our odds of survival by creating strong communities and cooperating productively. Nonetheless, even socialized man will consider fraud, manipulation, or freeloading if those seem to be his best options.

While most of us enjoy and take for granted the widespread peace and stability of socialized modern life, we generally do so complacently, unaware of or at least unconcerned about the brutality that still lingers below the surface of our political structures. Brutal behavior helped tribal societies survive throughout prehistory until some ten thousand years ago when new social forms arose – that is, when man moved from hunter-gatherer societies into settled agricultural communities. Ten thousand years is not long on the evolutionary time scale, so our genetic instincts have not changed. However, because of lack of attention, we are all shocked when our brutal instincts poke through. When we contemplate the horrors of the Holocaust, of the Gulags, of the Islamic State, our media and politicians figuratively wring their hands and seek to 'understand' how these things could happen. This is pure naïveté. Such phenomena are simply human behavior when the wrong people gain power. When governments make a mess of things, destroying wealth to the point of engendering violent change, it becomes more likely that such people will come to power.

When the center no longer holds, when local security is endangered, predatory groups naturally spring into existence. These can take form as inner-city gangs, the

---

65   Richard Dawkins. *The Selfish Gene* (Oxford: Oxford University Press, 1976).

Mafia, or the feudal lords that arise after an empire's decay, such as in Europe after the fall of the Rome and in Japan in the thirteenth century AD. Mark the words of Jose Ortega y Gasset[66]: "If you want to make use of the advantages of civilization, but are not prepared to concern yourself with the upholding of civilization—you are done ... Just a slip, and when you look around, everything has vanished into air." This is the most pressing argument for the electorate's vigilance.

All forms of predation cost society by sapping the vigor `of the FEO. Recognizing various forms of predation and the mechanisms they employ is the first step to controlling them. Examples begin with prehistoric tribes and extend to large-scale pillaging and conquests, religious wars, utopian movements such as communism, thuggish kleptocracies of the modern era, and even representative democratic governments.

HUMAN PREHISTORY

Our genetic tendencies predispose us to violence and predation when social circumstances permit it; this is evident as far into the past as we can see or infer. Early man's social behavior was not that different from that of chimpanzees, his near relative. He lived in groups and was intensely hostile to outsiders and prone to warfare with his neighbors. His life was not the idyllic existence imagined by Rousseau; it was extremely brutal. Steven LeBlanc outlines the specifics of this grim reality, writing that "prehistoric warfare was common and deadly, and no time span or geographic region seems to have been immune. ... in primitive societies, war was a much stronger demographic factor with on average about one-quarter of all men losing their lives in battle."[67] Even considering the dreadful killing fields of the twentieth century, modern man has not approached this mortality rate. But predation was not aimed so much at looting, for there was not much in the way of wealth. Rather, its purpose was to protect territory, the source of food, and to carry off females with whom to mate. However, it was often genocidal as well; other tribes were wiped out to ensure that the genes of the winning group survived. Identical behavior could be observed among aboriginal tribes in the Amazon and in New Guinea as recently as the last two centuries.[68/69]

---

[66]   Jose Ortega y Gasset, *The Revolt of the Masses* (New York: W.W. Norton & Company, 1932), chapter 10.

[67]   John J. Miller, review of *Constant Battles* by Steven LeBlanc, *The Wall Street Journal*, April 20, 2003.

[68]   Matt Ridley, *The Origins of Virtue: Human Instincts and the Evolution of Cooperation* (New York: Penguin Books, 1996), 186-187.

[69]   Jared Diamond, *The Third Chimpanzee: The Evolution and Future of the Human Animal* (New York: Harper Collins Publishers, 1992), 296-299.

PILLAGING ON A GRANDER SCALE

As civilization grew, such behavior often expanded apace. A few extreme examples include the Mongol invasions of Central Asia and Europe, the Hun invasions of central Europe, and the Viking attacks on northern Europe.

The Mongols

Will Durant describes how, in the thirteenth century, Genghis Khan conquered central Asia from the Volga to the Chinese wall. He and his followers came to kill, pillage, and carry their spoils to Mongolia. They employed ferocity as a weapon, striking their opponents with paralyzing terror and leaving no possibility of revolt. Just a few examples of their tactics illustrate the thoroughness of their policies. When they invaded Khurasan, they ravaged every town along the way. Merv was burned to the ground and over a million inhabitants were slaughtered; in Nishapur, every man, woman, and child was killed; Rayy, a city with 3,000 mosques, was laid in ruins and its entire population put to death. Later, the Mongols attacked Baghdad the seat of the Abbasid Empire: During forty days of pillage, much of the population was killed; libraries and treasures accumulated over centuries were plundered and destroyed within a week.[70] China was probably Khan's main target; he may have intended to steal everything, drive the peasants off the land, and convert all of northern China into winter pastures. In 1215, he destroyed more than ninety cities and left Beijing burning for a month.[71]

The Huns

In the fifth century, Attila had ambitions to become the most powerful man in Europe. In 441, he crossed the Danube, capturing Sirmium, Belgrade, Nish, and Sofia and leaving the economy of the Balkans in ruins for four centuries. In 447, he entered Thrace, Thessaly, and southern Russia and sacked seventy towns. In 451, Attila marched to the Rhine, sacking and burning Trier and Metz and massacring their inhabitants. On his way to Rome, he destroyed Aquileia so completely that it was never rebuilt.[72]

---

[70]   Will Durant, *The Age of Faith*, (New York: Simon and Schuster, 1950), 339-340.

[71]   Ian Morris, *Why the West Rules – For Now* (New York: Picador – Farrar, Straus and Giroux, 2010), 389.

[72]   Will Durant, *The Age of Faith*, (New York: Simon and Schuster, 1950), 39-40.

The Vikings

The Vikings ranged almost as far as the Huns. In the Middle Ages, they assaulted Scotland, Iceland, Ireland, England, Germany, France, Spain, Italy, Sicily, and Russia. Their primary objective was not instilling terror and destroying enemies but obtaining loot. Theirs was a society that "hungered for land, women, wealth and power and felt a divine right to share in the fruits of the earth."[73]

RELIGIOUS/ CULTURAL INVASIONS

The predators described above did not seem to need a rationale for their behavior. However, men's facile minds can certainly justify organized predation in the name of some supposed greater good, such as religion.

Islam

The Abbasid Empire's economic ascendency over other regions of Asia and Africa, and even over Western Europe, was overwhelming, and it lasted for a relatively long time – about two hundred years.[74] Its expansion was driven as much by predatory incentives as by religious zeal. The Arabs took advantage of a military vacuum after the military exhaustion of the Byzantine and Sassanid empires, which had dominated the Middle East. The founders of the first Islamic dynasty, the Umayyads, drew on a new religious creed to expand Arab power, and their empire grew remarkably over the subsequent century. They offered their victims three choices: Convert to Islam, pay tribute, or die. Durant describes how triumphant Arab armies swelled with hungry or ambitious recruits, requiring ever new lands to conquer if only to provide the soldiers with food and pay. Each victory required another,[75] and predation continued after conquest. Lal notes: "[C]onfiscations of private property, which became a striking feature of social life in the Muslim world, began in a very early period, and were due to the unique form of the Islamic predatory state."[76]

---

[73]   Ibid, 510.

[74]   Deepak Lal, *Unintended Consequences*, 54.

[75]   Will Durant, *The Age of Faith*, (New York: Simon and Schuster, 1950), 188.

[76]   Deepak Lal, *Unintended Consequences*, 56.

The Conquistadors

The Catholic colonization of the New World by Spain and Portugal was conducted under the banner of religious zeal, but in fact it was predatory in the extreme. The Spanish Queen wrote that the conquistadors' duty was to teach the Indians the Catholic faith. Pope Alexander VI donated all lands discovered or to be discovered in the Indies to Spain with the stated purpose that their settlers and inhabitants be converted to the Catholic faith. But the crown's real purpose was to finance a large government, maintain the largest armada in the world, and pay for numerous wars. The colonists became feudal lords over the Indians; silver and gold mines were the main sources of wealth.[77]

As one political commentator has observed, organized groups such as governments and corporations do things for two reasons. The first is the stated reason; the second the real one.

OVERT PREDATION WITHIN SOCIETIES

The above examples epitomize man's predilection for exploiting other groups that are seen as aliens. However, just as much predation has occurred within societies under other guises. This is not the wanton pillaging of the above examples, but rather controlled predation by the government or the elite on other members of society. However, the same human instinct is at work whenever individuals wrest wealth from others for themselves and their extended families. This may certainly be accomplished through the use or threat of force, but it is mostly done by manipulating political power. It will be instructive to examine this behavior in more detail in past traditional monarchies and modern kleptocracies.

Monarchies

European monarchs descended from feudal warrior chieftains. They developed a stable form of government that successfully protected their societies from the predatory attacks of others. In return, they received feudal dues and later taxes. Over the centuries, warfare continued to be common, so societies needed such feudal or aristocratic protection. As nation-states arose, the old feudal arrangements became obsolete, but it is human nature to cling to power, along with all its perquisites. The nobility exercised that power to extract as much wealth from their subjects as possible; that is, until negative effects led to revolt by other ambitious nobles or subversion by neighboring powers. One example is France during the height of its monarchy.

---

[77]   Guillermo M. Yeatts, *The Roots of Poverty in Latin America* (Jefferson, North Carolina: McFarland & Company, 2005), 37.

Louis XIV, the "Sun King," believed that the Bible upheld the divine right of kings. Further, to carry out their responsibilities, kings needed unlimited authority, which included the liberty to dispose of all property, whether it was in the hands of the clergy or the laity.[78] The splendor of his court at Versailles was legendary. His ministers battened on the country as well. For example, Voltaire reports that Cardinal Mazarin (who ran the country) amassed a fortune estimated at two hundred million francs by diverting military expenditures and selling crown jewels for his own benefit.[79] At a later time, Nicolas Fouquet, the Superintendent of Finance, lived in great splendor until he was convicted of corruption. He was said to have amassed the largest private fortune of his time.[80]

At that time, nearly all the French nobility equally exploited the people. As Durant notes, the nobility had become "a vestigial organ," taking wealth but only providing military service in return, which was of little value in post-feudal Europe. Though the peasants were no longer serfs at the time of Louis XVI, they were still subject to feudal dues and required to do unpaid labor: "In sum and on the average the surviving feudal dues took 10% of the peasant's produce or income. The ecclesiastical tithe took another 8% to 10%. Add the taxes paid to the state, the market and sales taxes, and the fees paid to the parish priest for baptism, marriage, and burial, and the peasant was left with about half the fruit of his toil."[81]

Kleptocracies

The modern world abounds with examples of governments that exploit their people and the extended order for the benefit of those who govern. These leaders, however, lack any pretension to the traditions that supported monarchs. This section deals with examples of charismatic leaders and their cliques who gained power to enrich themselves in an almost textbook fashion. A key characteristic of these states is leaders who depend on a specific source of wealth creation and are careful not to kill the golden goose (although they may come close through greed and misjudgment). It is dismaying how easy it is for such leaders to gain and maintain power.

The Dictator's Handbook[82] describes the basic steps by which a ruthless leader seizes and maintains power. These steps are not highly abstract or difficult to learn; indeed, they seem to be intuitive, even for men who are not especially

---

[78]   Will and Ariel Durant, *The Age of Louis XIV* (New York: Simon and Schuster, 1963), 15.

[79]   Ibid, 11.

[80]   Ibid, 19.

[81]   Will and Ariel Durant, *Rousseau and Revolution* (New York: Simon and Schuster, 1967), 928.

[82]   Bruce Bueno de Mesquita and Alastair Smith, *The Dictator's Handbook, Why Bad Behavior is Almost Always Good Politics* (New York: Public Affairs/The Perseus Books Group, 2011)

intelligent. The ease with which despotism is imposed and established has enticed opportunists over the ages; it is a fact of life. It survives because few men become heroes when facing the muzzle of a rifle. One need not be Machiavelli to decipher the rules.

Kleptocratic despots who wish to milk the system have little interest in gratuitous terror or slaughter for religious or ideological reasons, although they have no compunctions about using force. They require an ongoing source of wealth and a power base that includes subjects willing to do their bidding. What does it take to achieve and retain the essential elements of despotic power? They must:

- Seize power from the previous ruler or group – usually with armed force and confederates;
- Seize the chief source of national income;
- Eliminate rivals and other centers of power;
- Maintain power by keeping key supporters satisfied and instituting a police state through the judicious use of terror to keep the populace quiescent; and
- Establish an effective propaganda system to make it all appear legitimate.

A couple of examples taken from *The Handbook* illustrate the essentials of this process.

Liberia

Sergeant Doe was virtually illiterate and came out of nowhere. On April 12, 1980, he scaled the fence of the President's mansion with sixteen other noncommissioned officers to confront the president and ask why they hadn't been paid. He found himself in the President's bedroom and, seizing the opportunity, bayoneted the president and declared himself the new president. He immediately rounded up and publicly executed thirteen cabinet ministers. He suspended the constitution and banned all political activity. He replaced all important people in the government and the army with members of his own small Krahn tribe and increased the army's pay. Then, as is common in such revolutions, he executed many members of the revolutionary group to eliminate any competitors.

Moreover, he knew where the money was. Firestone Corporation leased land for rubber, and the Liberian Iron Mining Company was wealthy as well. He also obtained backing from the United States in exchange for basing rights. But he knew nothing about governance. The economy collapsed, foreign debt soared, and criminal enterprises became the entrepreneurial success model. Nonetheless, he survived because he controlled revenues and continued to pay the army well. He did not need majority support, merely enough confederates to control the army and suppress the populace.[83]

Zimbabwe

Robert Mugabe of Zimbabwe may have come to power via the ballot box, but he followed the above rules to enrich himself and stay in power despite a wretched record of economic mismanagement. He plundered the country's natural resources and exploited agriculture – notably expropriating white landowners and giving their farms to his family and supporters. They, naturally, knew little of agriculture so that starvation spread across what had been southern Africa's bread-basket. According to the *Handbook*, "Mugabe succeeds because he understands that it does not matter what happens to the people provided that he makes sure to pay the army. …he is a master of the rules to rule by …when it comes to paying off cronies, he has delivered. That is why no one has deposed him."[84] He subjected Zimbabwe to thirty years of misrule before, as an old man, he was finally deposed in 2018.

Other Examples

The Handbook lists many others who used national treasuries to enrich themselves: Uganda's Idi Amin, Haiti's Duvalier, Zaire's Mobutu, Sudan's Omar al-Bashir, and Iraq's Saddam Hussein. According to *The Handbook*, "[t]hey all typify the rule of successful autocrats – they know how to build, manage, and finance tight coalitions while enriching themselves."[85] *The Handbook* shows that until representative governments implement effective institutions to secure liberty, this approach is likely to be the default model for mankind; that is, upstart leaders will always be on the make to grab and maintain autocratic power.

UTOPIANS

The model of communism practiced in the Soviet Union is an extreme example of a modern utopian approach that drew on a predatory-state model. It is unique because here, predation was not conducted by and for a ruling class, although the new party elite did live materially better than the average Russian. This predation was done in the service of an unrealistic utopian ideal. The private

---

[83]   Ibid, 21-24.

[84]   Ibid, 38.

[85]   Ibid, 154.

sector was eliminated, its wealth confiscated to serve collectivist goals. This predation extended way beyond the financial and industrial elite to the entire middle class and private agricultural holdings (i.e., the Kulaks).

Terror and all the tools of the modern totalitarian state were used to uproot aspects of Russian culture, destroying values, institutions, social capital, and even the élan vital that are essential for a healthy society and leaving behind an ailing post-communist Russia. *The Black Book of Communism* summarizes the whole sorry history:

> Lenin and his comrades initially found themselves embroiled in a merciless "class war," in which political and ideological adversaries, as well as the more recalcitrant members of the general public, were branded as enemies and marked for destruction. The Bolsheviks had decided to eliminate, by legal and physical means, any challenge or resistance, even if passive, to their absolute power. This strategy applied not only to groups with opposing political views, but also to such social groups as the nobility, the middle class, the intelligentsia, and the clergy, as well as professional groups such as the military officers and the police.

> Sometimes the Bolsheviks subjected these people to genocide. The policy of "de-Cossackization" begun in 1920 corresponds largely to our definition of genocide: a population group firmly established in a particular territory, the Cossacks as such were exterminated, the men shot, the women, children, and the elderly deported, and the villages razed or handed over to new, non-Cossack occupants. ... The "dekulakization" of 1930-1932 repeated the policy of "de-Cossackization" but on a much grander scale. Its primary objective, in accordance with the official order issued for this operation (and the regime's propaganda), was "to exterminate the kulaks as a class."[86]

The number of casualties boggles the mind:

> - Tens of thousands of hostages and prisoners were executed without trial, and hundreds of thousands of rebellious workers and peasants were murdered between 1918 and 1922.

---

[86] Stéphane Courtois, Nicolas Werth, Jean-Louise Panné, Andrzej Paczkowski, Karel Bartosek, and Jean-Louis Margolin, *The Black Book of Communism: Crimes, Terror, Repression* (Cambridge: Harvard University Press, 1999), 8-9.

- The famine of 1922 caused the deaths of around five million people.
- Tens of thousands were liquidated in concentration camps between 1918 and 1930.
- Hundreds of thousands were liquidated in the Great Purge of 1937-1938.
- Two million "kulaks," or relatively prosperous farmers (and so-called kulaks), were deported between 1930 and 1932.
- Four million Ukrainians and two million others were starved to death by an artificial and systematically perpetuated famine in 1932 and 1933.

In addition to targeting specific economic and ethnic groups, the Soviet Union used terror to pursue its never-proven and unachievable goals. The arbitrary, random nature of these assaults cowed the general population. Take, for example, the Great Terror of 1937-1938. A purge calling for the arrest of all kulaks and criminals was launched on July 2, 1937. The victims of this operation included not only former Tsarist civil servants and White Guards, but the ambiguous categories of "socially dangerous elements" and "members of anti-Soviet parties." *The Black Book* states: "It appears that during 1937 and 1938, 1,575,000 people were arrested by the NKVD; of these, 1,345,000 (85.4%) received some sort of sentence and 681,692 (51% of those who were sentenced) were executed."[87]

Central offices sent out quotas in advance, and local NKVD (secret police) often simply picked up suspects by "reactivating" old lists. If the list of names on file was insufficient, any means necessary were used to round up suspects to "comply with the established norms."[88] Terror is an apt word for this process – one that pervaded all layers of society.

So, after all the five-year plans, regimentation, and forced labor, Russia remains a relatively poor country. In 2014, its per capita income was only $24,805; in the United States it is over $54,000.[89]

*   *   *

These examples should leave the reader with no illusions about human nature and the essential role of appropriate institutions in keeping it in check. However, these cases are much easier to conceptualize than, for example, predation under a representative government.

---

[87]   Ibid, 190.

[88]   Ibid, 191.

[89]   *2016 Index of Economic Freedom*, 361.

REPRESENTATIVE GOVERNMENT

The above examples may seem to be intuitive, even commonplace examples of governmental predation. They certainly set the stage for vigilance against despotism of all sorts, and the most obvious response is a strong parliament to limit monarchical ambition. But man is susceptible to other forms of governmental predation – namely, man against man within a society, or what James Madison termed *factions*. This is a far more sophisticated type of predation. It is virtually always veiled and often appears beneficent to the average eye. Yet, in the end, it enables many to grow wealthy at the cost of their fellow citizens.

To be clear, this kind of predation is not blatant corruption in the government or by special-interest groups (though that does occur). The predation discussed here occurs when individuals spot an opportunity to game a complex system to benefit themselves at the cost of others.

It occurs chiefly as an outgrowth of the third step of Buchanan's abstract model of governance, when individuals relinquish some personal freedom of action in exchange for allowing the government to undertake tasks because it can do so more economically than private collaborators. These individuals rely on the implicit proposition that the government will undertake such tasks only for *the general welfare*. In economic terms, the individual wishes to reduce the external costs of his labor, such as when the government builds infrastructure, maintains wealth and safety, improves social capital, and provides for the common defense. Conceptually, the presence of external costs and the possibility to reduce them through cooperative action is similar to the mutual gains obtained through trade that benefits all parties.[90]

Unfortunately, once this door is opened – that is, once a government has the authority to undertake a generalized class of actions, including the power to tax – the FEO is susceptible to predation. Who is to police the line between desirable, economically justified actions and those that are merely politically opportune? As later chapters will show, that line is difficult to guard, if for no other reason than that predatory forces are and always will be (as Deepak Lal observes) ubiquitous.

Indeed, it is inevitable that political forces will pursue predatory goals. This is because special-interest factions arise spontaneously; they tend to exploit the legislative system due to their nature, and a system that lacks sufficient checks motivates legislators to favor their own factions at the cost of the larger society.

Factions Arise Spontaneously

It could be said that humans are emotionally programmed to divide into factions. Given two sports teams, the populace will quickly and enthusiastically

---

[90]   Buchanan and Tullock, *The Calculus of Consent*, 189.

line up behind one or the other. More broadly, groups line up by religion, by world outlook, and by economic interest. Through political coalitions, these lineups morph into attempts to influence the legislative process. Madison understood this clearly over two hundred years ago when he wrote Federalist Paper No. 10, which will be discussed in the next chapter. But, in short, Madison recognized that factions arise from "the diversity in the faculties of men" and "the causes of faction cannot be removed, and the relief is only to be sought in the means of controlling its *effects*."

The electoral dynamic becomes defined by this phenomenon because factions must continuously pursue legislative actions that benefit their members to maintain the coalition.

Factions Exploit and Debilitate

Once formed, a representative body will invariably reflect such factions. In *The Rise and Decline of Nations*, Mancur Olson describes the dynamic whereby small, concentrated interest groups form and then use lobbying to influence the democratic process to attain their own ends. People who think they can benefit from such endeavors will seek out the most pliable representative. Those representatives will then make deals among themselves to form the necessary legislative majorities. He demonstrates how "the behavior of individuals and firms in stable societies leads to the formation of dense networks of collusive, cartelistic, and lobbying organizations that make economies less efficient and dynamic and politics less governable."[91]

Three obvious forms of factional predation are: (1) the majority of the population preys on a minority, (2) a small, special-interest faction pursues specific goals, and (3) predation is done in the name of a utopian ideal.

Predation by the majority

The most obvious example of predation by the majority is the use of electoral power to extract wealth from some minority under the guise of the "general welfare." In the United States, the top 1% of the population pays some 37% of all income taxes, while the bottom 49% pays only 3%.[92] In a past extreme, politicians thought nothing of taxing the income of the highest earners at a 90% marginal rate. In the current electoral cycle, candidates are offering free college, universal health care, preschool childcare and more, all to be financed by "the rich."

---

[91]   Mancur Olson, *The Rise and Decline of Nations: Economic Growth, Stagflation, and Social Rigidities* (New Haven: Yale University Press, 1982).

[92]   U.S. Tax Foundation, *Summary of the Latest Federal Income Tax Data, 2018 Update.*

Small-faction predation

Predation by a small faction, however, is equally endemic and potentially more insidious because it is far less visible. It occurs when the legislative process does what comes naturally – that is, when it empowers pork-barrel items, special regulatory provisions, crony capitalism, and tax favoritism in the normal give-and-take of the legislative process. Three typical methods involve overt or concealed income redistribution, subsidies supported by sentiment that appear so small that they are not worth fighting about, and regulations said to protect some favored class that effectively create quasi-monopolies. Each measure can be a potent source of votes for politicians because the beneficiaries desire them very much and the larger electorate hardly notices them – hence Bismarck's famous observation about the unsavory similarities between the legislative process and sausage-making.

In isolation, many predatory measures would not gain majority support. But because they are the product of a small group that desires them passionately while others are relatively indifferent, that group can combine with other groups to pass two or more measures, none of which could stand alone. This works politically because the costs are either small or hidden. The costs of any one piece of such special-interest legislation are probably very small when spread across the entire electorate and thus go unnoticed.

However, some such legislative behavior may be a necessary part of the system because of its role in assembling the votes to pass larger essential legislation. *The Calculus of Consent*[93] outlines this behavior in mathematical terms. While these deals may well lubricate the larger system, problems arise when over time, in large numbers, such special-interest groups contribute significantly to expanding deficits and sluggish economies.

Moreover, according to Deepak Lal, such redistribution invariably damages the FEO when payoffs to favored groups are a negative-sum game because of the losses they present to society, their economic distortions, and their transaction costs.[94] In aggregate, special pleading may benefit the average voter who seeks to get something from the rich, but it still results in overall losses (see earlier discussion of *Unintended Consequences*). Even more troubling, these tendencies lead to economically unsustainable behaviors in representative government, when they extract as much wealth as the market can bear.

---

[93] James M. Buchanan and Gordon Tullock, *The Calculus of Consent, Logical Foundations of Constitutional Democracy*(Ann Arbor: The University of Michigan Press, 1965).

[94] Deepak Lal and H. Myint, *The Political Economy of Poverty, Equity, and Growth* (Oxford: Clarendon Press, 1966), 12.

Utopianism

A third form of predation occurs when ideological good intentions undermine the FEO via self-defeating policies. This may involve putting one faction, such as unions or a particular minority, on a pedestal for special treatment, or pursuing some abstraction like 'social justice', or pursuing a goal of societal transformation in favor of extreme environmentalism. This is predation in the service of an idea because it invariably attempts to finance the implementation of the ideas from the wealthiest sectors of the economy.

The chief areas in which such impulses are pursued in the public arena are income transfer and regulatory action. The arguments advanced for income transfer are discussed more fully in Chapter Eight, but, in a nutshell, they fall under an abstract notions of fairness, of positive rights, and, of course, of alleviating the privation of our fellow beings. Despite these good intentions, the practical outcome is that the majority exploits a small minority. To be sure, many such efforts are well intended, and small groups may indeed benefit disproportionately. The problem is that, over time, weakening the FEO makes everyone worse off than they would otherwise have been.

The wider manifestation is nanny-statism, in which regulation is employed to pursue utopian goals that (it is argued) the people cannot be entrusted to pursue on their own. In recent decades, regulation has grown beyond legitimate health and safety concerns into extensive areas of economic activity. Supporters argue these regulations are necessary for the common well-being, but they are more often designed to protect special interests, from unions to tenants to dairy farmers. Not only is wealth redirected away from the productive sectors of society through the relatively inefficient hands of the government, but the commercial sector is increasingly bound up in regulation that stifles efficiency and innovation and requires layers of unproductive compliance officers. Moreover, once regulatory agencies are established, they, like all institutions, tend to grow, to expand their jurisdiction – that is, regulators want to regulate.

De Tocqueville foresaw the dangers of a tendency to over-regulate:

> I have no fear that … [members of democracies] … will meet with tyrants in their rulers, but rather guardians. … Thus … [the guardianship]… every day renders the exercise of the free agency of man less useful and less frequent; it circumscribes the will within a narrower range, and gradually robs a man of all uses of himself. …After having taken each member of the community in its powerful grasp, and fashioned them at will, the supreme power then extends its arm over the whole community. It covers

the surface of society with a network of small complicated rules, minute and uniform, through which the most original minds and the most energetic characters cannot penetrate, to rise above the crowd. The will of man is not shattered, but softened, bent, and guided: men are seldom forced to act, but they are constantly restrained from acting: such a power does not destroy, but it prevents existence; it does not tyrannize, but it compresses, enervates, extinguishes, and stupefies a people, 'til each nation is reduced to nothing better than a flock of timid and industrious animals, of which the government is the shepherd.[95]

An extreme version of this utopian impulse has been seen elsewhere: in the Soviet Union's attempts to create a "new Soviet man," who was to be more communal and less motivated by self-interest. This was executed via an extreme form of human tyranny, yet it failed utterly and created the opposite: an atomistic, demoralized, and distrustful population.

Of course, the regulatory effect is less dramatic in democratic regimes, but it is ongoing and problematically invasive. As discussed earlier, Mancur Olson describes the collusive, cartelistic, and lobbying organizations that make economies less efficient and dynamic and politics less governable.

Opportunistic Legislators

The key to understanding dysfunctional legislative behavior is that it is not so much a matter of venal individuals but of the incentives inadvertently built into the system itself. Let's examine legislators' tendency to serve special interests rather than the country as a whole –not always, but enough of the time. What incentives/ pressures do they experience; what behavior is induced?

Modern public-choice theory holds that politicians and bureaucrats are not exempt from self-interest and often pursue their own advancement rather than what is best for clients and taxpayers. When legislation affects individual incomes and wealth, votes necessarily have economic value, which opens the door to corruption of sorts – not necessarily bribery, though bribery occurs, but betraying one's principles and the good of the people in general.[96]

The driving force, whatever the form of representative government, is that legislators are possessed by the overriding ambition to be re-elected, regardless of the relationship of votes to political principles. James Buchanan's economic

---

95   *Democracy in America*, cited in *The Libertarian Reader*, edited by David Boaz (New York: The Free Press, 1997), 22-23.

96   James M. Buchanan and Gordon Tullock, *The Calculus of Consent, Logical Foundations of Constitutional Democracy*(Ann Arbor: The University of Michigan Press, 1965), 121.

analysis of the legislative process shows how legislators – just like any individuals involved in a decision-making process that has economic dimensions – seek gains from trade. This behavior is most evident when we examine votes cast over time: Individual legislators will exchange votes with other legislators for reciprocal support of one another's interests – the essence of *log rolling.*

In effect, power corrupts. Representatives are governed by self-interest, promises are easy to make with other people's money, and the electorate responds more to sentiment and self-interest than to principles. Moreover, successful politicians know how to dress up these ideas in the form of good intentions and sentiment that carry the day.

$$* \quad * \quad *$$

In short, factions are inevitable. Under a free representative government, factions simply respond to motivations created and allowed by the system; they pursue self-interest within legal bounds. As Aristotle foresaw, a society that unduly relies on the wisdom of individual men will be overrun by self-serving excuses and attempts at freeloading – a potentially fatal flaw of representative government.

Richard Epstein elaborates: "In the absence of any strong social or institutional constraints, a dominant faction could use its voting power or political clout to confiscate the wealth of political losers, or more subtly, to hobble their economic activities with legal restrictions."[97]

This political dynamic is not unique to the United States, even though it provides most of the book's examples; this issue lies at the heart of free representative government everywhere. Without adequate restraint, an electoral system that gives factions free rein undermines the FEO. As Hayek notes, "[I]t would seem that no advanced civilization has yet developed without a government which saw as its chief aim in the protection of private property, but that again and again the further evolution and growth to which this gave rise was halted by a 'strong' government. ... Sooner or later, however, they tend to abuse that power and to suppress the freedom they had earlier secured in order to enforce their own presumably superior wisdom ..."[98]

---

[97] Richard A Epstein, *The Classical Liberal Constitution – The Uncertain Quest for Limited Government* (Cambridge, Massachusetts: Harvard University Press, 2014), 21.

[98] W.W.Bartley III, ed., F.A. Hayek, *The Fatal Conceit: The Errors of Socialism* (Chicago: The University of Chicago Press, 1991), 32.

So, this is the heart of the central challenge mankind faces: how to live productively and cooperatively by keeping predation under control.

$$* \quad * \quad *$$

One goal of this chapter is to leave the reader with no illusions about human nature. Eternal vigilance is necessary to guard against that nature as well as against the predatory state. However, on the bright side, societal evolution, driven by an increasingly powerful FEO, has gradually developed values and institutions that can guard against predatory interests of all sorts. The next chapter examines millennia of mankind's efforts along these lines.

CHAPTER 3

CONTROLLING POLITICAL PREDATION

"But what is government itself but the greatest of all reflections on human nature?"[99] – James Madison

"Man's reason is the slave to his passions, and recognizing this about himself, man can organize his own association with his fellows in such a manner that mutual benefits from social interdependence can be effectively maximized."[100]

Mankind's long and endemic history of predation of man against man, between and within societies, is dispiriting. Say what you will, the instinct to take more than we've earned runs deep in human nature – as Madison noted, men are not angels. Nonetheless, societal evolution has produced political mechanisms to control predation. These mechanisms, however imperfect, are unequivocally impressive. Even prehistoric man found (usually intuitive) ways to protect society against despots. These methods, however, grew less effective as societies grew larger and rulers more distant from those ruled. Through philosophy and institutional trial and error, societies have found ways to support the FEO, which furthers the interests of all while it materially strengthens societies that adopt it. That is way of evolution: step-by-step innovation; survival of best practices. We must understand this evolutionary process if we are to protect the institutions we

---

[99] Federalist Paper no. 51.

[100] James M. Buchanan and Gordon Tullock, The Calculus of Consent, Logical Foundations of Constitutional Democracy (Ann Arbor: The University of Michigan Press, 1965).

have developed and address their shortfalls, which have become all too evident in recent years at home and abroad.

To that end, the following sections will examine the arc of the development of political values and institutions from man's prehistory through the modern age. Specifically, the chapter will argue that, in terms of maximizing human liberty and freeing the extended order of human cooperation, the U.S. Constitution as crafted in 1787 represents the epitome of political evolution to that time. In its conception, the Founding Fathers incorporated the best of human empirical wisdom concerning how man should organize his common affairs. Any shortcomings are not in its design but in its execution, as will be discussed in subsequent chapters.

What are the key elements of that design, how did the concepts behind them become evident over human history, and how did the designers of the U.S. Constitution access those concepts? The story begins with human nature itself, which can be observed in very small societies prior to conscious institutional design. But as societies grew, nature and instinct became insufficient to control over-ambitious men and clever factions. In short, the complexity of decision-making in larger groups, the growing distance between rulers and ruled, and the formidable challenge presented by the concentration of police and military power in the elite overwhelmed egalitarian instincts and traditional approaches.

As we shall see, sophisticated institutions suitable for larger societies include consultation with the people, restraints on the monarch (or equivalent), and checks and balances on legislative bodies. Such institutions evolved in Greece and Rome two and a half millennia ago. Unfortunately, in that form, they proved insufficiently robust to meet the political circumstances of their times. However, they represented important milestones on the road to liberty and representative government, even though another two millennia of trial and error would elapse before our effective modern institutions fully emerged.

For this evolution of institutions to continue over such a long period of time, key values had to be imbedded in the cultures of succeeding eras, passed down from earliest history in ways that continued to resonate with both the elite and the people. The most important of these values were: laws derive from tradition, political authority derives from the people, and even the rulers are subject to the law. While philosophy is often too abstract for the average person to wield pragmatically, when it is married to the empirical truth of human nature, philosophical principles come to life. Societies reach for such ideas in times of trouble and transition to identify the best way forward.

In this chapter, we shall see how the Founding Fathers consciously drew on such principles to design the country's new form of government. To be sure, initially, the Constitution only attempted to fix specific shortcomings of the Articles of Confederation. However, rather than merely amending those Articles, they chose to create a new structure from scratch based on first principles of human nature and historical experience. The essence of the challenge was to free individual ambition while curtailing the potential for societal predation.

This chapter's historical review starts with early human social existence; ends with the ratification of the U.S. Constitution. It is divided into five parts: (1) instinctive control of predation in tribal life, (2) the emergence of governing institutions compatible with the rule of law in the larger societies of Greece and Rome, (3) key values transmitted through the Dark Ages, (4) trial and error in Britain that produced robust institutions to protect liberty, and (5) the epitome of governance achieved by the U.S. Constitution.

CONTROL OF PREDATION IN TRIBAL LIFE

Human nature is egalitarian; we resist being subordinated. In keeping with that instinct, we don't like to be dominated, we like our freedom of action, we don't like being manipulated, and we wish to keep the fruits of our labors. Indeed, humans are well equipped emotionally to understand their own self-interests and to sense attempted manipulation. Moreover, they are instinctively attuned to their individual vulnerability vis-à-vis more powerful individuals or external predatory groups. Thus, in primitive tribal life, individuals quickly responded to domineering behavior by overly charismatic individuals in their community and to threatening alien tribes.

Therefore, early human societies evolved a range of mores and institutions for controlling oppression; these included shared values and peer pressure. David Sloan Wilson observes:

> Hunter-gatherers are egalitarian, not because they lack selfish impulses but because selfish impulses are effectively controlled by other members of the group; accomplished sociologically by a form of "reverse dominance." In human hunter-gatherer groups, an individual who attempts to dominate others is likely to encounter the combined resistance of the rest of the group employing reverse domination, ranging in intensity from gossip, to ridicule, to ostracism, to assassination. Self-serving acts are thereby effectively curtailed.[101]

At the same time, human nature is instinctively in tune with Hayek's "extended order of human cooperation." Only through solidarity can groups survive, and only through cooperation can they effectively reap the gains of specialization and

---

[101]   David Sloan Wilson, *Darwin's Cathedral – Evolution, Religion, and the Nature of Society* (Chicago: The University of Chicago Press, 2003), 21.

exchange. So, despite a competitive struggle by the individual for survival and the protection of one's progeny, successful groups incorporated powerful mores for cooperation. Wilson cites findings that small groups of humans are psychologically disposed to bind themselves into functional units. He particularly refers to *Order without Law*[102] which shows how people "spontaneously establish, enforce and largely abide by social norms in the absence of a formal legal system."[103]

This phenomenon can be observed in present-day African tribes, as described by George Ayittey:

> African societies that ruled themselves had all four units of government: a chief, an inner council, a council of elders, and a village assembly. ... The inner council served as the first test for legislation. ... [Then the chief] might take it to the council of elders. This was a much wider and more formal body comprising all the hereditary headmen of the wards or lineages; in essence, the council of elders represented the commoners.
>
> In matters of serious consequence, the chief had to summon all members of the council of elders. ... Routine matters were resolved by acclamation. Complex matters would be debated until the council reached unanimity. ... Generally, the chief would remain silent and watch the councilors debate. ... If the council could not reach unanimity on a contested issue, the chief would call a village assembly to put the issue before the people for debate. Thus, the people served as the ultimate judge of final authority on disputed issues. ...
>
> Freedom of expression was an important element of village assemblies. Anyone –even those who were not members of the tribe – could express his views freely. ...
>
> In theory, the African chief wielded vast powers ... [but] chiefs and kings were not above the law and had to obey customary laws and taboos. ... [There] were [injunctions] clearly designed to check despotic tendencies and misuse of power. ... Any violations could result in immediate destoolment (removal from office). ... [He] could be removed at any time ... if he was corrupt

---

[102]   R.C. Ellickson, *Order Without Law* (Cambridge, Mass. Harvard University Press, 1991).

[103]   Ibid, 27.

> or failed to govern according to the will of the people – and so
> he can be even in modern times."[104]

So, in smaller societies, mankind knows (intuitively and practically) to be wary of granting power to another, whether a charismatic hunter or the tribal leader. Key values of human governance appear in the most elemental human societies: Chiefs are bound by tradition and law and must consult the people on matters of mutual concern. However, as societies grew beyond the capability of groups to assemble easily, these modes of governance became impractical.

EMERGENCE OF INSTITUTIONS IN LARGER SOCIETIES

It would take millennia of societal evolution for human societies to regain in larger settings these original attributes of governance. Could mankind develop social institutions that could meet the same governing objectives and adequately protect individuals from a monopoly on force granted to an often impersonal and ambitious set of leaders? The basic elements were clear and emerged time and again: Leaders are bound by precedent, advised by a council of elders, and open to the voice of the people on critical matters of well-being. Unfortunately, in larger societies, much of this model could be perverted and did malfunction. Mankind through trial and error developed institutions that embodied these values and were sufficiently robust to survive the stresses of human ambition in times of societal turmoil.

Autocracy in the East

As societies grew larger (about three millennia ago), different cultures diverged in these matters. In Greece, original values were preserved in more sophisticated ways. In the East, however, under the aegis of religion, more and more societies fell under the sway of autocratic leaders. For example (per Will Durant) in Crete during the Homeric Era: "The power of the king ... is based upon force, religion, and law. To make obedience easier he suborns the gods to his use: his priests explain to the people that he is descended from Velchanos and has received from this deity the laws he decrees ..."[105] Such values were common in other despotisms of the East.

For example, in Babylonia, circa 2000 BC: "All the glamor of the supernatural hedged about the throne and made rebellion a colossal impiety which risked not

---

[104]   George Ayittey, *Africa in Chaos* (New York: St. Martin's Press, 1998), 87-89.

[105]   Will Durant, *The Life of Greece* (New York: Simon and Schuster, 1939), 10-11.

only the neck but the soul. Even the mighty Hammurabi received his laws from the god. … Babylonia remained in effect a theocratic state, always 'under the thumb of the priests.'"[106]

Autocratic religion also governed ancient Egypt. According to Durant:

> [T]he Pharaoh, with the help of the priests, assumed divine descent, powers and wisdom; this alliance with the gods was the secret of his prestige.[107] …The king was chief priest of the faith … It was through this assumption of divine lineage and powers that he was able to rule so long with so little force. Hence the priests of Egypt were the necessary props of the throne, and the secret police of the social order.[108]

Indeed, this was the case in much of the world: Egypt, Mesopotamia, India, China, and the Aztecs. Even in modern Islam, the religious principle of governance holds sway in ways foreign to the development of governing institutions in the West. The idea that power is derived from the people or from a social construct is foreign. Rather, according to Bernard Lewis "in the Muslim conception, God is the true sovereign of the community, the ultimate source of authority, the sole source of legislation."[109]

Religion was often conjoined with military force to control populations for the benefit of the elite. In effect, once societies grew larger than tribes and city-states, the people became more distant from their rulers, and rulers acquired a monopoly on military force. This made autocracy the default. As shown in the previous chapter, the corruption of power is so universally tempting and the mechanisms for exerting power so simple and intuitive that autocracy became ubiquitous – outside Europe. It is such a powerful institutional construct that there are virtually no examples of successful revolt against an armed, ruthless despot without external help.

Early Traditions Continue in the West

Societies outside Europe never restored the egalitarianism of early humankind and its respect for traditional laws and consultation with the people. The essential philosophical and institutional arrangements to control tyranny evolved in the

---

[106]   Will Durant, *Our Oriental Heritage* (New York: Simon and Schuster, 1954), 233.

[107]   Ibid, 163.

[108]   Ibid, 201.

[109]   Bernard Lewis, *What Went Wrong? The Clash Between Islam and Modernity in the Middle East* (New York: Perennial, an imprint of Harper Collins Publishers, 2003), 113.

West. Specifically, this evolution flowed from the Greeks through the Roman Republic to medieval Europe, Britain, and finally the United States.

Greece

While in the East, the ideas that power derives from the people and that rulers should consult all free men vanished early, they survived in the West, beginning with the Greek city-states. Governing values such as worth of each individual and the need for leaders to be bound by rule of law persisted in various forms. To be sure, there are many counterexamples over the last twenty-five hundred years; it was never clear sailing. Nonetheless, in the tapestry of Western culture, the thread of limited government and free individuals continues through that time, however tenuous it became along the way.

Signs of the continuation of early tribal values were evident as late as 1000 BC in Achaean Greece. According to Durant, the clan acknowledged a common ancestor and a common chieftain. The chieftain's citadel was the center of the city, and his power relied on usage and law. When the chieftain desired some united action, he summoned all free males to a public assembly and proposed his idea. They could accept or reject it, but only the most important members of the group could propose changes.[110]

A dramatic example of the explicit institutionalization of these values is the government formed by Solon in Athens in the early sixth century BC. It might appear that this construct leapt fully formed from Solon's mind, but the underlying values surely evolved from tribal governments. At the time, Athens, which had lost much of its strength, was threatened by neighbors such as Sparta, Corinth, and Megara; it was also disturbed by civil feuds. The city's situation was so desperate that virtually all citizens agreed to give Solon unprecedented authority to reform its political mechanisms and to administer the city. Accordingly, in 594BC, Solon was elected *eponymous archon*, the chief civil magistrate of Athens. Most of his peers would undoubtedly have seized the opportunity to make themselves a tyrant – as has often happened – but Solon did not, believing that a commonwealth could endure only through righteous order.

The reformed order was neither an aristocracy nor a democracy, but a system of checks and balances designed to stabilize the government. He increased the powers of the Assembly – the popular congregation of all free citizens – and, to make it more effective, he created a new Council of Four Hundred to prepare and guide city business. Executive authority was left in the hands of the old Council of the Areopagus, a kind of senate recruited from former religious, military, and civil magistrates. Solon argued that this combination of the old and the new councils would save the Assembly from rash action: "The ship of state, riding upon two

---

[110] Will Durant, *The Life of Greece*, 53.

anchors, will pitch less in the surf and make the people less turbulent." Again and again throughout history, republican forms of government would establish executive authority balanced by two assemblies (houses), one to represent the people and the other the elite.

To be sure, these reforms did not endure; tyrannies and other dysfunctional governments recurred. Nonetheless, according to Durant: "despite intervening dictatorships and superficial revolutions, Cicero could say, five centuries later, that the laws of Solon were still in force at Athens. Legally his work marks the end of government by incalculable and changeable decrees, and the beginning of government by written and permanent law."[111]

Continuing in Rome

At the same time that some Grecian city-states were establishing rule of law, Rome, which began as a city-state, was developing a more evolved republican government that incorporated checks and balances. Durant dates the first republic based on a Senate from 509 BC. This Senate, however, did not represent the plebeians, who used various forms of class warfare to press for a stronger voice in the government and for defined, secular, written laws. Eventually, in 454 BC, the Senate sent a commission to Greece to study Solon's form of government, as well as those of other lawmakers. On their return, they transformed the old customary Roman laws into the Twelve Tables, which were then publicly displayed in the Roman Forum. Durant states that this was "the first written form of that legal structure which was to be Rome's most signal achievement and her greatest contribution to civilization."[112]

While various specific forms evolved over centuries, the three chief elements of Roman government are the consular authority, the senate, and the *comita* (formal assemblies of the people). To check the senate, popular tribunes were chosen; they could veto senatorial actions. Once again, as in Solon's Athens, executive authority was hedged by two assemblies representing the people and the aristocracy. Polybius, a contemporary Greek who studied Rome closely, concluded that the Roman constitution was almost a literal realization of Aristotle's ideal constitution,[113] which will be discussed next.

---

[111]   Ibid, 118.

[112]   Will Durant, *Caesar and Christ* (New York: Simon and Schuster, 1944), 20-23.

[113]   Ibid, 25.

Aristotle's Analysis

Aristotle (384-322 BC) drew on the above histories as well as those of a multitude of Greek city-states to identify the ideal forms of government. He saw that, two and a half millennia ago, the Greeks and Romans identified and implemented formal governments designed to prevent tyranny and to establish checks and balances among a monarch, an oligarchy of interests, and the plebeians. However, he also recognized the problems in previous solutions. Despite Solon's structure, which remained a part of the system and of men's minds, Athens reverted to tyranny and dysfunction time and again.

While Aristotle believed that the Greek *polis* was superior to any other form of social organization, he did not conclude that any one form of government was necessarily best for all people; rather, he identified a mix of abstract possibilities.

Russell Kirk summarizes Aristotle's three forms of "right government" that could maintain general welfare: monarchy, aristocracy, and the commonwealth. By monarchy, Aristotle meant one virtuous man who would lead under a body of laws that limited his power. He defined aristocracy as the predominance of a class of men of high birth who were dutiful and filled with the spirit that would later be called *noblesse oblige*. And a commonwealth denoted the exercise of power by the majority – but a virtuous majority that respected the lawful rights of all classes.

Each of these ideal forms had perverse deviations: democracy could become rule by the crowd for the benefit of the dominant majority; oligarchy could mean rule by the few for the good of that few; and tyranny is the unconstitutional assumption of power by one man for his own satisfaction. These realities led Aristotle to advocate a mixed government (whose ingredients would vary depending on circumstances) that incorporated the virtues of each form.[114]

Whatever the mixture, Aristotle believed government should be dominated by the middle classes rather than aristocratic families or the *demos* (the more numerous artisans and sailors who held no property). It was the middle class of Athens and of many other states that supplied the infantry, bore the brunt of fighting, produced the most economically, and provided a model for stable family life. Aristotle's underlying view was that a polity is a community of friendship in which men have everything to gain by peaceful cooperation, as if they were so many parts of the human body; in effect, that man is a social animal.[115]

It is a testament to his unfinished work *Politics* that Aristotle was able to identify so many of the critical elements of good governance during a time of turmoil and rapid change in Greece; to most of his contemporaries, nothing was clear. He was, however, only too aware that good intentions and the knowledge of optimal forms of governance would only go so far. Indeed, he catalogued some

---

[114]   Russell Kirk, *The Roots of American Order* (Washington, DC: Regnery Gateway, 1991), 90-91.

[115]   Ibid, 90-91.

forces that undermined his precepts. First, he noted that, at that time, Athens' middle class was relatively small. And, as Russell Kirk points out,:

> In the second place, factitious disputes and struggles readily arise between the masses and the rich; and no matter which side may win the day, it refuses to establish a constitution based on the common interest and the principle of equality, but, preferring to exact as the prize of victory a greater share of constitutional rights, it institutes, according to its principles, a democracy or oligarchy ...[116]

Having considered the strengths and weaknesses of many governments, Aristotle was aware of the pitfalls that lay in the corruption of power, the greed of the rich, the envy by the poor, and the turmoil created by factions.

While he remained agnostic about the ideal form of government, he did establish a template for pursuing that goal. Specifically, he recommended implementing mechanisms that could restrain tyranny, drawing on the strengths of the most productive sectors of society (for a long time this was the landed, productive interests represented by an oligarchy) while ensuring that they work for all of society, and drawing on the wisdom of the people without opening the door to unstable, predatory majoritarianism.

* * *

It would take a long time for society to identify specific institutional methods to achieve Aristotle's ideals. Later societies established institutions to use oligarchs and the people to check potential tyrants, then to check oligarchs, and finally to filter out the most dysfunctional impulses of the people. Moreover, an evolution of values would have to accompany the development of institutions. These values needed the emotional resonance that could motivate people to resist, by force if necessary, ideas that tradition and experience indicate are not right or proper.

The next section will examine key milestones in this uneven evolution. It will consider (1) how the values essential for representative government survived the fall of the Roman Republic and the Dark Ages that followed the barbarian invasions and (2) the milestones in the development of more robust governing institutions to secure those values.

---

[116]   Ibid, 91-92.

SURVIVAL OF KEY VALUES

Over two millennia ago, the Roman Republic attained the highest advance in institutions that secured liberty for most citizens (except, of course, slaves), represented the people, incorporated checks and balances on power, precluded autocracy, and established the basis for a relatively free extended order. For centuries, Rome was the most powerful and prosperous political entity on the planet. It did not, of course, endure.

Tragically, the Roman Republic, which had endured for centuries, eventually deteriorated into an absolutist empire as the Senate gained more power during the Punic Wars and then failed to address the tensions between the patricians and the plebeians that overwhelmed republican politics with threats of civil war. Despite growing authoritarianism, Rome retained its values that preserved property and free trade. Consequently, under several emperors (beginning with Augustus), Rome reached its greatest size and level of prosperity.

Although the emperors paid lip service to the Senate and the Republic, their power came to be based on the legions. Then, over several centuries, Rome overextended its realm, was threatened by barbarian invasion, and resorted to desperate measures to survive. In the context of this book's narrative, it is noteworthy that, to finance its wars, Rome effectively smothered the FEO through heavy-handed regulation and taxation.

Little of the old Republic remained beyond its forms. Even those vanished when Rome fell to the barbarians. Nonetheless, the values themselves endured. This was made possible by a number of factors: The invading barbarians brought no effective alternative culture with them, the Catholic Church played a central role in preserving Roman learning, and power was fragmented among many political entities, making it impossible for any one of them to obtain despotic power.

The barbarian tribes that destroyed Rome did not engage in the savagery and destruction common to the Mongols or the Huns. Indeed, the Goths, Visigoths, Ostrogoths, Alemanni, and Franks were fleeing the savagery of the Huns and seeking a safe place to settle. In most instances, the Romans invited them into the Empire. They could be assimilated for the most part.

Furthermore, the barbarians' ancestors held political values not dissimilar to those of the Achaean tribes of Ancient Greece that had been transmitted to Solon's Athens. For example, the Germans had tribal assemblies composed of nobles, guards, and freemen who chose the chief and approved the proposals submitted to them.[117] More importantly, as Durant notes, their introduction to the Empire was by no means sudden. They interacted with Rome for centuries in trade and war; by the fourth century AD, they had had writing and a government of

---

[117]   Will Durant, *Caesar and Christ* (New York: Simon and Schuster, 1944), 479.

stable laws for a long time: "In general the invaders – above all, the Goths – were civilized enough to admire Roman civilization as higher than their own, and to aim rather at acquiring it than at destroying it; for two centuries they asked little more than admission to the Empire and its unused lands, and they shared actively in its defense."[118]

Of course, as Rome's centralizing power ebbed, the German settlers appropriated land and displaced the old aristocracy. However, they had little incentive to replace Latin civilization; they married into the old aristocracy and eventually respected the Church.

In addition, according to Durant:

> It was a happy accident that while the chaos of barbarian invasion was mutilating the legal heritage in the West, the Code, Digest, and Institutes of Justinian were collected and formulated in Constantinople, in the comparative security and continuity of the Empire in the East. Through these labors, and a hundred lesser channels, and the silent tenacity of useful ways, Roman law entered into the canon law of the medieval Church, inspired the thinkers of the Renaissance, and became the basic law of Italy, Spain, France, Germany, Hungary, Bohemia, Poland, even within the British Empire – of Scotland, Quebec, Ceylon, and South Africa. English law itself, the only legal edifice of comparable scope, took its rules of equity, admiralty, guardianship, and bequests from Roman canon law.[119]

This was all possible because the West was spared the despotism that ruled the rest of the world. Its fragmented power centers were incompatible with a concentration of military power in one man or one small group. Europe had feudal structures: a king dependent on and checked by landed barons, a multitude of kings jockeying for power, and an independent universal Church that also sought political power and countered the largest secular states. This political mix made it virtually impossible for a would-be despot to override the rich inheritance of values checking arbitrary government.

The following sections show how the essential concepts underlying modern representative government survived to inform later parliamentary governments in Great Britain and eventually the U.S. Constitution. The essential precepts established that political authority is derived from the people, rulers are subject to the law, and individual liberty and property are protected under the law.

---

[118]   Will Durant, *The Age of Faith* (New York: Simon and Schuster, 1950), 23.

[119]   Will Durant, *Caesar and Christ* (New York: Simon and Schuster, 1944), 406.

Political Authority is Derived from the People

Rome's philosophers (especially Cicero) and jurists (most notably Ulpian) codified the principles defining the source of political authority. Furthermore, the great jurists of Rome handed down to the Middle Ages and the modern world the essential view that "there could be only one immediate source of political authority, and that was the community itself, that there was no other source, neither the personal qualities of the prince, his greater wisdom and intelligence, nor force, nor, normally, the direct appointment of God, but only the community."[120] But the law was not merely a contemporaneous expression of the community or a product of the legislature; it also had to be grounded in principle." Proper principles were thought to be discoverable in the law of nature, which was viewed as divine and unchangeable and thus not to be abrogated by a legislature.

Jurists of the Middle Ages viewed law less as a product of legislation than as an expression of the community's customs – that is, its traditions. Any new positive law had to be confirmed by those who lived under it.

This notion endured through the Dark Ages and helped form the values we hold important today. More than a thousand years later, the U.S. Constitution would begin with the words "We the people." A key implication is that political institutions must access the voice of the people.

Rulers are Subject to the Law

Ulpian's *Digest* allowed the emperor unlimited legislative authority, but only because the people – in other words, the whole community – conferred it upon him. Emperors Theodosius II and Valentinian II agreed with this conclusion, stating that the ruler is bound by the laws as his authority is drawn from the law. Later, in the sixth century, Emperor Justinian noted that the Roman people were the original source of a ruler's authority.[121]

These views survived. In the ninth century, several centuries after the fall of Rome, Hincmar of Rheims, the most important ecclesiastical statesman of the time, set out these principles. He said that kings must govern their people according to the laws of their ancestors, which were promulgated with the general consent of the community. Gratian, the first great systematic canonist, articulated this principle again in the middle of the twelfth century in his *Decretum*. The principles were repeated in many countries in the thirteenth century: Bracton, an Englishman, held that England was governed by unwritten law and custom;

---

[120] A.J. Carlyle, *Political Liberty* (London: Frank Cass & Co. Ltd., 1963), 12.

[121] Ibid, 13.

in France, Beaumanoir wrote, "All pleas are determined by the Customs ... The king is bound to keep, and to cause to be kept, the Customs of his country."[122]

Carlyle also notes:

> This principle, that all merely human authority is limited, was derived from the Roman law, and was of the greatest importance in medieval thought and sentiment, for it meant that there neither was nor could be any such thing as an absolute political authority. This view was that of the theologians as well. It was St. Thomas Aquinas himself who said that while sedition was a mortal sin, it was not sedition to resist an unjust authority.[123]

Protecting the Individual

Rule of law is well and good – it prevents arbitrary rule and the corruption of power. Of course, the substance of the law is critical if it is to secure individual liberty and establish a basis for the FEO. Accordingly, this section reviews how values related to protecting individuals from arbitrary government action and to protecting their property evolved from the time of the Roman Empire through the Middle Ages.

Individual Worth

Two millennia ago, in Rome, Cicero argued that a government that failed to recognize the equality of all men in reason and in the possibility of virtue could not be good. He also said that, without a share in political authority, men cannot be properly said to possess liberty. The idea that power derives from the people is meaningless unless the value of each individual is recognized. Cicero defines this principle of equality:

> There is no resemblance in nature so great, ...no equality so complete, as that which exists among men, there is therefore only one possible definition of human nature; for that reason, by which men are superior to the mere animals, is common to all, men differ indeed in learning, but they are equal in the faculty of learning; there is no man or race of men who cannot attain

---

[122]   Ibid, 14.

[123]   Ibid, 12.

to that virtue. Nature has given to all men reason, and therefore law which is right reason commanding and forbidding.[124]

That belief was reinforced by Christian philosophy, which became widespread after the second century AD. In the Acts of the Apostles, St. Paul argues that all men are alike because they are all the children of the one divine nature, are all capable of the highest, and are all made for the same divine end: the communion of the soul with God.[125]

These values support the view that individuals should be protected from unjust laws and arbitrary government. These values were also institutionally fleshed out during the Middle Ages. For example, a king could not take action against the person or property of any of his subjects except by process of law. Carlyle states:

> This is expressed not only in the famous clause of Magna Carta (39) but in the equally important ... statement of principles of law in Spain. At the Cortes of Leon in 1188 Alfonso IX swore that he would not take action against any man except by judgment of the court, and in the Cortes of Valladolid in 1299 it was decreed that no one was to be killed or deprived of his property till his case had been heard by *fuero* [custom] and Law. This was also the constitutional law of France as testified by Gerson in the fifteenth century, and by DeSeyssel and Machiavelli in the sixteenth; cases between the king of France and a private person were subject to the jurisdiction of the Parlemens.[126]

Because a just government depended on the consent of the governed, institutions that could represent the community's authority and will were needed. That system had to be adaptable, not only to small communities, but also to nations, which were then slowly taking form. Utilitarian forms of representation existed in the larger cities of Italy, Germany, and the Low Countries as early as the twelfth century. Representative assemblies emerged in many locations across Europe. In Hungary, King Andrew was forced to sign the Golden Bull in 1222. This document required him to summon a diet each year, forbade the imprisonment of a noble without a trial, and forbade him to levy taxes on noble or

---

[124] Ibid, 3.

[125] Ibid, 5-6.

[126] Ibid, 19.

ecclesiastical estates.[127] In Spain, the Cortes of 1188 placed restraints on Alfonso IX.[128] According to Carlyle, the representatives of Spanish towns were first summoned to a kingdom-wide council a good hundred years before the Parliament of 1295 in England. Similar bodies arose in most parts of Europe.

Carlyle sums up with the observation: "Political freedom implies that all political authority is derived from the community, the community which is composed of men who are capable of directing and controlling their public as well as private lives to ends determined by themselves."[129]

Protecting Private Property

Not only is the protection of property essential to the FEO (as discussed in Chapter 1), it frees individuals from dependence on the government so they can play a crucial civic role. Prior to the Roman Empire, no legal system recognized private property without limitations. In Greece, Persia and Egypt, ownership depended on the superior or collateral rights of other authorities or parties. Tom Bethell opines: "The idea that principles of law were superior to authority and force, that justice was 'blindfolded' and (ideally) indifferent to persons, was something new to antiquity. Beyond the Roman perimeter, either a collectivist tyranny or a subsistence-level communalism generally prevailed."[130]

This Roman law regarding property was shaped in part by Greek philosophy, if not by the laws of its myriad city-states. For example, Aristotle asked whether the ideal property system would be "a system of communism, or one of private property?" He pointed out that communal arrangements tend to cause "a good deal of trouble.... If they do not share equally in work and recompense, those who work and get less recompense will be bound to raise complaints against those who get a larger recompense and do little work." He also notes that when many people could claim ownership of the same object, disharmony must ensue. However, when people have separate spheres of interest, they have fewer reasons to quarrel, and each man will apply himself to what is his own.[131]

Aristotle, like Solon before him, had hit upon key elements of sound governance, but his concepts were not institutionally tested and may well have been too advanced for the prevailing values of the Greek society. Yet, he had

---

[127]   Will Durant, *The Age of Faith* (New York: Simon and Schuster, 1950), 658.

[128]   A.J. Carlyle, *Political Liberty,* 19.

[129]   Ibid, 11.

[130]   Tom Bethell, *The Noblest Triumph: Property and Prosperity Through the Ages* (New York: St. Martin's Press, 1998), 61.

[131]   Ibid, 63.

planted the seeds of thought regarding property rights and sound governance that would be codified by the Romans.

The *Twelve Tables* (mentioned above) offer a clear glimpse of Roman property rights. Although only fragments of Roman law remain, Tom Bethell concludes from an array of examples that property was more respected than liberty and more secure than life.[132] Most property was presumed to be private. The legal scholars of the *Digest* specifically note public possessions, which included religious temples, flowing water, riverbanks and the seashore, stadiums and theaters, and city walls and gates. Valuable property such as land, houses, slaves, and farm animals were *res mancipi*, meaning that their transfer to another owner required a ritual or a court procedure. According to the historian John Crook, "Proof of title was therefore reasonably simple in Roman law."[133]

*   *   *

These crucial values– the people as the source of power, the rule of law, the equality of individuals, and the protection of private property – endured in the intuition and hearts of the people through the Dark Ages. This was largely due to the long transition of political change as well as serendipity of circumstance. Importantly, the Germans residing inside the Empire assimilated key values long before the actual fall of Rome. Custom and the Germans' acceptance of the Church, which preserved so much of the old order in philosophy and governance, played a role in this. Moreover, the fragmentation of political power throughout the Middle Ages effectively precluded despotism: Kings were balanced by their nobles; one ambitious state by the jealousies of multiple others. In addition, this milieu was particularly suitable for the growing independence of commercial states, which evolved a whole new set of societal values that were especially appropriate for a new FEO

Despite a favorable milieu, sound values, and embryonic institutions, most countries failed to take the next key steps towards representative government: establishing an effective institutional voice for the people and keeping kings in check. It was the centuries-long experience of Great Britain and then the United States that led to new essential institutions. The first challenge was countering the monarch by the aristocracy and both by commercial interests. For centuries, giving a political voice to the whole population was moot; most people were not represented due to limited electoral franchises. The egalitarian and more politically open American colonies led the way with the U.S. Constitution.

---

[132]   Ibid, 65.

[133]   Ibid, 68.

BEYOND VALUES – FINDING ROBUST INSTITUTIONS

Values instruct us as we shape the institutions that govern us and allow us to live our lives to the fullest. Nonetheless, time and again, as seen in Solon's Athens and republican Rome, institutions constructed in accord with the values discussed above succumbed to predatory political forces. Something more robust would be required. In Europe, the power of the king was often balanced against that of the nobility, but finding a voice for the commercial classes and eventually the broader population would be trickier and take centuries. Quasi-independent commercial cities led the way on a small scale. But it was Britain that, over a span of five centuries, established essential strong national institutions via a dominant Parliament and an unwritten Constitution supporting the liberty of the people.

The Commercial City-States

Recall Aristotle's belief that successfully mixing the monarchy, the oligarchy, and the demos would depend on the existence of a middle class, which needed to be much larger than it was in ancient Athens. Hindsight shows that this required a vast expansion of the extended order. When this happened, new commercial interests complemented landed interests in legislatures, and individual wealth transformed the values held by the demos. This process began in the later Middle Ages when the growth of commerce in the West nurtured new towns that attained a substantial degree of independence from their feudal overlords and required new forms of self-government.

Depending on the jurisdiction, autonomy was wrested from feudal overlords or from ecclesiastical authorities. For example, some cities began to resist paying baronial or Episcopal taxes or offered money for a charter, but in the end it often came down to force. Tours, for example, fought twelve times before winning its liberty.[134]

As in early tribal history, small towns readily established representative bodies to govern their affairs; these bodies administered taxes and provided governance compatible with emerging mercantile values. For example, the towns had to learn how to tax equitably and without ruining taxpayers. Money was raised predominantly from the burgesses. The quota each should pay was calculated based on his fortune, a form of principled taxation rather than arbitrary exaction.

According to Durant, "By the end of the twelfth century the communal revolution was won in Western Europe. The cities, though seldom completely free, had thrown off their feudal masters, ended or reduced feudal tolls, and

---

[134]   Will Durant, *The Age of Faith,* 638.

severely limited ecclesiastic rights."[135] These cities, which were far more evolved than the ancient city-states, played an important role in the evolution of the new nation-states of Western Europe. In politics, cities generally joined with the king against the nobility. When kings required revenues for their incessant wars, they looked to wealthy merchants in cities as well as the landed nobility. Almost from the beginning, the emerging consultative bodies included representatives from the towns and the commercial classes. In this way the emerging extended order protected its interests and helped shape new institutions.

British Milestones of Government

The strong institutions necessary for nation-states evolved in Britain. Key British milestones of government that resisted tyranny and protected liberty included the Magna Carta, the Model Parliament, the British Bill of Rights, and, inadvertently, the American Revolution. Each milestone was driven by national interests willing to threaten or even use force, to protect their rights against an overreaching monarch.

The Magna Carta

The first great documentary milestone was the Magna Carta, which established in writing the principles under which a monarch was bound to respect the rights of nobles. To be sure, restraints on monarchy, whether tradition or the threat of rebellion, had existed for centuries. England, along with most of medieval Europe, generally held that power flows from the community and the king is subject to the law. These values existed under feudalism, which entailed reciprocal obligations between monarch and the nobles and provided for the common defense while resisting the centralization of power. As Kirk puts it: "[t]he barons' jealousy of royal prerogatives, and the kings' perennial suspicion of unruly barons, generally maintained a tolerable balance of power."[136] Nonetheless, ambitious kings such as John invariably tested traditional limits.

In that instance, the nobility and prelates of Britain felt threatened by John's ambition and wanted more than tradition for protection. Given John's grasping history, when he became king of England in 1199, he was forced to seal a coronation oath affirming that "his throne was held by the election of the nation (i.e., the nobles and prelates) and the grace of God."[137] His acquiescence did not last. After years of expensive warfare, when he wanted to resume war with France, John

---

[135]   Ibid, 640.

[136]   Russell Kirk, *The Roots of American Order* (Washington, DC: Regnery Gateway, 1991), 193.

[137]   Will Durant, *The Age of Faith,* 674.

ignored his coronation oath and demanded *scutage* from a recalcitrant nobility. This was a payment of money given in lieu of military service. The nobles resisted by sending a deputation demanding a return to the laws of Henry I, which had protected the rights of the nobles and limited the king's powers. They threatened armed resistance and confronted the king at Runnymede on the Thames in 1215.

There John was compelled to sign the Magna Carta, which enumerated protections for the nobles. While many of its specific terms have lost relevance, it effectively established the "principle of the supremacy of law: the idea that an enduring law exists, which all men must obey. The king himself is one of those men under the law. Along with this principle ran a corollary principle – that if the king breaks the law, and invades the rights of his vassals, then barons and people may deprive him of his powers."[138] And, while it was expressly designed to secure the rights of the baronage, over time and under political pressure, those rights were extended to other classes of society.

Durant sums up the significance of this document as follows:

> The Great Charter deserves its fame as the foundation of liberties today enjoyed by the English-speaking world. ... [I]t defined and safeguarded basic rights; it established *habeas corpus* and trial by jury; it gave to an incipient Parliament a power of the purse that would later arm the nation against tyranny; it transformed absolute into limited and constitutional monarchy.[139]

And according to Winston Churchill, from that time on, government meant something more than the arbitrary rule of any man, and custom and law stood above even the king. It was this idea, perhaps only half understood, that gave unity and force to the barons' opposition and made the Charter which they now demanded imperishable.[140]

The Model Parliament

Subsequent ambitious kings would continue to test the system. Society, in turn, would have to entertain the use of force to preserve people's rights because institutions for mediating these conflicts had not yet been established. Such an institution arose at the time of Edward I, another ambitious king. To be sure, prior to his reign, the king and the ruling barons often met to deal with the

---

[138]   Russell Kirk, *The Roots of American Order,*195.

[139]   Will Durant, *The Age of Faith*, 677.

[140]   Winston S. Churchill, *The Birth of Britain* (New York: Dodd, Mead & Company, 1966), 253.

affairs of the realm; they sometimes invited representatives of the commons to take part in these deliberations. Over time, these representatives became a Great Council, which evolved to a more general parliament. In 1295, under financial pressure, Edward summoned a "Model Parliament," which represented all the estates – the barons, the commons, and clergy. At that time, contrary to tradition, he (like other kings before him) bucked tradition in an attempt to levy new taxes unilaterally. And, once again, the barons compelled a monarch to acknowledge restrictions on his ability to extract wealth from his subjects – in this case by issuing a Confirmation of Charters in which the king affirmed that, conforming to old custom, he would levy no extraordinary tax (beyond feudal dues) without the consent of his realm's estates.[141]

The British Bill of Rights

The seventeenth century saw a decisive train of events that led to parliamentary supremacy over the monarch, beginning with the beheading of Charles I and then the overthrow of James II. These events grew out of the rapid economic changes England experienced as it shifted from a feudal system to a mercantile one; estimates suggest that the Commons had come to represent much more of the national wealth than did the House of Lords[142]. When Charles I needed money to for religious and dynastic wars on the Continent, he resorted to taxation without Parliament's assent, to forced loans, to martial law, to the billeting of troops in private homes, and to imprisoning citizens without a warrant. In protest, Parliament drew up a Petition of Right demanding that the king agree not to resort to such measures again. Its resolutions included the right of *habeas corpus* for every man, the indisputable right of every freeman to have full and absolute property in his goods and estate, and the impropriety of the king or his ministers levying a tax, loan, or benevolence without common consent by an act of Parliament.[143]

Nonetheless, according to Russell Kirk, the Petition of Right did not assure the House of Commons that they had nothing to dread from Charles I; "Would it effectually restrain the king from asserting what he saw as his prerogatives in church and state if they ran counter to the wishes of Parliament?"[144] In the midst of this controversy, when Parliament confronted Charles about his continued collection of unauthorized taxes (as well as over issues involving the dismissal of his ministers), Charles dissolved parliament for a time, beginning a period

---

[141]   Russell Kirk, *The Roots of American Order*, 197.

[142]   Will and Ariel Durant, *The Age of Reason Begin.*(New York: Simon and Schuster, 1961), 201.

[143]   Winston S. Churchill, *The New World* (New York: Dodd, Mead & Company, 1965), 184-185.

[144]   Russell Kirk, *The Roots of American Order,* 261.

of "personal rule" (Parliament would not sit for eleven years). He proclaimed: "We shall account it a presumption for any to prescribe any time unto us for Parliaments, the calling, the continuing, and dissolving of which is always in our own power…"[145]

There was a prolonged struggle between Parliament and Charles as he sought the means to deal with, among other things, an invasion by Scotland. Many other heated issues involving religious conflict were in play as well. But throughout:

> [T]he majority of the House of Commons, and the Presbyterians and Independents, saw themselves as the champions of the people's rights and the Protestant truth. London, the mercantile class, and some of the great landlord proprietors stood by the claims of the House of Commons; whereas the backbone of the royalist party was made up of squires and of the bulk of rural interest.[146]

The conflict led to two civil wars; after years of fighting, Charles' Roundhead forces were defeated by parliamentary forces led by Oliver Cromwell. The result was Charles' beheading and the institution of the Commonwealth, which lasted for some years.

The monarchy was restored when Charles II came to the throne. Major constitutional issues remained dormant until he was succeeded by James II. He, like his Stuart predecessors, harbored views of rule by divine right. After one of the Protestant nobles rebelled, James seized the opportunity to act, unleashing a series of moves that suggested the possibility of re-establishing Catholicism. This threatened much of British nobility, the Church of England, and other powerful groups. Among other things, he asked Parliament to repeal the Test Act, which excluded Catholics from office and from Parliament. Moreover, as a sign of his absolutist views, he asked Parliament to modify the Habeas Corpus Act and to establish a standing army under royal command. Parliament refused. Nonetheless, James proceeded to appoint Catholics to office, flouting Parliament's authority.

In response, a large group of nobles invited William and Mary (James' daughter) to come from the Netherlands to replace James, who then fled to France. Parliament drew up a Bill of Rights that defined the grievances justifying James' ouster, explicitly asserted Parliament's legislative supremacy, and articulated the rights of citizens in the face of arbitrary governmental power. This revolution consolidated power in the hands of the landowning aristocracy, of the leaders of industry, commerce, and finance – broadly in opposition to the monarchy and the "squirearchy" of smaller landed proprietors, who, together with some of the

---

[145] Winston S. Churchill, *The New World*, 191.

[146] Russell Kirk, *The Roots of American Order*, 261.

noble families and commercial classes, considered themselves 'Tories'. This revolt protected property and commerce from a potential new despot.

So, over the span of a century, interest groups in England repeatedly demonstrated their willingness to raise armies and risk fortunes to defend their property and wealth against a monarch's unconstitutional acts and potential despotism. While these revolts resulted in ringing declarations in the Petition of Right and the Bill of Rights, it was the willingness to fight over principles that secured these rights for the English people.

Like the Magna Carta, the British Bill of Rights, in writing, explicitly asserted the legislative supremacy of Parliament and articulated the rights of citizens in the face of arbitrary governmental power. Moreover, it laid out principles that could justify the overthrow of a government. The English philosopher John Locke came to several conclusions based on these events and that document:[147] Political sovereignty belongs to the people and not to the king; the people delegate their power to a legislative body, Parliament, but might withdraw that power on occasion; and executive authority is derived from the legislature and depends on Parliament. Further, governments are formed through freely agreed contracts: Governors hold their authority only as a trust from the people, and when this trust is violated, the people may rightfully use their strength to undo tyranny – although this is only justified by heavy provocation.[148] The Bill of Rights established the principle of representative government firmly in England (although it was limited in practice since the great majority of the people were still not permitted to vote[149]).

It is clear that many Roman attitudes regarding private property survived the Middle Ages and were strongly held at the time of the Glorious Revolution. As mentioned previously, the House of Commons increasingly came to reflect the commercial rather than the landed classes. In his analysis of these political battles John Locke concludes: "The great and chief end of men uniting into commonwealths, and putting themselves under government, is the preservation of their property. … the supreme power cannot take from any man any part of his property without his own consent."[150] At that time, *property* entailed much more than physical assets; it encompassed the right to use and enjoy the benefits of one's own thought and efforts. Practically speaking, this consent could be given via a representative in a legislative assembly.

---

[147] John Locke, *Two Treatises of Civil Government*, as cited by Kirk, *The Roots of American Order*, 283-285.

[148] Ibid.

[149] It was not until a series of actions in the nineteenth and twentieth centuries that Parliament extended voting rights to the entire adult population.

[150] Bertrand Russell, *A History of Western Philosophy* (New York: Simon and Schuster, 1945), 632.

John Locke saw the implications of protecting private property as essential to preserving individual liberty. In *Civil Government*, he argues that the desire for life, liberty, and property are innate human qualities and that private and public interests are identical in the long run, although not necessarily over short periods. Equally importantly, given liberty, a community of citizens will act to promote the general good.[151] Locke was one of a group of philosophers who viewed government as one part of a social contract in which individuals give up certain rights for the common good in order to better secure more important rights. He was a forerunner of the modern writer James Buchanan, who (as discussed earlier) analyzes the economic implications of an individual's willingness to cede limited power to the government. More broadly, these views lead to the conclusion that the government's power can never exceed that which is required for the common good.

John Locke's writings were well known to the participants of the Constitutional Convention.

*　*　*

Even though other Western countries adopted elements of the same representative institutions, only Britain had established a workable whole for controlling potential despotism, protecting individual liberty, and thereby allowing the extended order to flourish. It was a stepwise evolution in which the body politic dealt with threats in a pragmatic advance towards secured liberty. But, because of limited voting rights, Britain had not yet guaranteed a voice to the demos; this would come a century after the Glorious Revolution. Britain's American colonists would successfully tackle that challenge after the Revolutionary War.

The United States' Advance

How did the American colonists on a sparsely populated continent far from European civilization end up creating arguably the most advanced form of government in human history to that time? Well, of course, they brought that civilization with them in the form of experience and culture. The rest was circumstance, necessity, opportunity, and genius leadership.

The Circumstances

At the time of the Constitutional Convention in 1787, the American confederacy of colonies had fought an agonizing eight-year war to protect their

---

[151]　Ibid, 615.

rights as Englishmen, but the institutions of that confederacy were manifestly insufficient for meeting the needs of the new country.

The backdrop was a revolution in which the colonists fought to preserve their rights as free Englishmen and also to protect their property against an overbearing Parliament and monarch. More specifically, the struggle began as a dispute over who had the power to tax the colonies, Parliament or the colonies' own legislative assemblies.

In hindsight, the dispute should have been resolvable through peaceful means as both sides had reasonable concerns. The British crown had protected the colonies (at great expense) during the French and Indian wars. It was only reasonable that the growing colonies begin to bear part of the financial burden of that defense; the question was how this should be accomplished. The king had two options: He could requisition the legislatures of each colony or tax the colonists directly. England unilaterally chose the latter course, bypassing the colonial assemblies via the Stamp Act and the Tea Act. But the colonists resisted, and England increasingly turned to force to uphold what it saw as parliamentary rights.

As summarized by Andrew Jackson O'Shaughnessy:

> [T]axation united colonial opposition more than any other grievance. The colonists regarded direct imperial taxes as a potential instrument of tyranny. They insisted on their right to be taxed exclusively by their own representatives, which they believed was essential to the influence and survival of their elected assemblies. The issue of taxation and representation raised a fundamental contest over sovereignty and the limits of British authority in America.[152]

As the colonists in Boston resisted and the British became more obdurate, as demonstrated by Parliament's Coercive Acts of 1774, which placed limits on the state legislature and even the local appointments to courts, the colonists felt that their worst fears were being realized. During the debate over the acts, Lord Germain, the Secretary of State for America, suggested "the Massachusetts council be appointed by the king, town meetings be abolished, the method of selecting juries be changed, and colonial charters be treated as revisable."[153]

In the colonists' minds, the conflict quickly moved beyond taxation to protecting their historical rights as Englishmen, as John Locke had articulated them: Government is agreed upon by free contract; governors hold their authority

---

[152]   Andrew Jackson O'Shaughnnessy, *The Men Who Lost America* (New Haven & London: Yale University Press, 2013), 52.

[153]   Ibid, 174.

only as a trust from the people; and when this trust is violated, a people may rightfully use its strength to undo tyranny, although only under heavy provocation.

The colonists did believe that governmental contract was being violated, and they did move to undo potential tyranny, prevailing after eight years of combat. Clearly, they had, through experience, imbibed the values of the British Constitution, which in turn reflected values that had emerged in the West since the time of Athens, as outlined above. More specifically, they were sensitized against predatory government in all forms, whether by a powerful monarch or a grasping Parliament. They wanted protection for their liberty and their property.

Another factor was that colonies had fought the war as a confederacy and still functioned as one. As Madison's historical research would illuminate, the fate of confederacies seem to follow universal laws once they have been freed from the common threat that united them. Indeed, as will be further discussed in Chapter Seven, other contemporaneous confederacies in Europe (the Helvetian and the Dutch) arose in similar defensive circumstances and addressed the problem of subsequent governance similar in many ways to the Americans. It took these other countries a couple of centuries to create modern unified governments, but the Americans accomplished this in four months' time.

The problem inherent in confederacies is the possibility of freeloading, if there is no enforcement mechanism or means of reconciling different interests. Most members will hang back in confrontations and battles if they believe that others will do the heavy lifting; as discussed in Chapter One, these actors will attempt to milk the political economy beyond their just deserts. Madison's comments on ancient and modern confederacies note the universality of this phenomenon. He examined Greek, Italian, Dutch, and Germanic confederations over thousands of years and states that virtually every case created "temporary stability, usually based on a political alliance against a common enemy that eventually dissolved into civil war, anarchy, and political oblivion."[154] He, of course, had first-hand evidence of these propensities; state governments had failed to meet their troop quotas and financial obligations throughout the Revolutionary War.[155]

These truths influenced the leaders of the Constitutional Convention when considering whether to amend the Articles of Confederation – thereby preserving a confederacy – or to create a more unified form of federal government.

Necessity

The shortfalls of the Articles quickly revealed themselves. In practice, the requirement of unanimity meant that the Continental Congress could take no

---

[154]   Joseph J. Ellis, *The Quartet – Orchestrating the Second American Revolution, 1783-1789* (New York: Vintage Books, A Division of Penguin, Random House LLC, 2015), 127.

[155]   Ibid, 129.

meaningful action at all. If fear of a strong central government is the paramount concern, this might not be a bad thing. After the war, however, the states shared too many problems that required collective action for that arrangement to be practical. Moreover, the failure to address these problems was creating mutual animosity, a potential for sub-alliances among the states, threats from abroad, and potential instability. What were some of the key areas in which Congress was unable to act but where action was essential?

Having been cut off from England, its greatest trading partner, in the immediate aftermath of the war, the states experienced a great economic slump: a 30 percent decline in national income. At the same time, collectively the states had a huge war debt: the Continental Congress had borrowed $51 million and the individual states another $25 million, with little prospect that the debt could be repaid given that the 'continental' currency had lost almost all of its value.[156]

Beyond dire economic circumstances, obvious problems created by lack of effective government included: states flouting their obligations under the collective peace treaty with England, an inability to negotiate trade agreements with other countries, growing protectionism among the states, and disagreements about how to treat the western territories beyond the original thirteen states. Moreover, many state legislatures, lacking checks and balances, sometimes suffered from the downsides of majoritarianism. For example, to alleviate fiscal struggles, they resorted to issuing unsupported paper money, undermining property rights, and undercutting the rights of creditors. Political instability manifested in Shay's rebellion in Massachusetts.

These problems were self-evident to the Founding Fathers. Indeed, in the first years after the war, a concerted effort was made to amend the Articles to give Congress a source of revenue, to empower it to negotiate trade with foreign countries, and to regularize the settling of the West. These efforts always failed, often because of the veto of a single state. So, it was patently obvious that the states' default position of collective action – that is, a confederacy – or even a confederacy with enhanced powers was not a workable solution.

These problems could not wait, and the Continental Congress had shown time and again that it lacked the governing authority to address them. What possibilities existed, and how could they be realistically entertained given the mutual jealousies of the individual states?

The Constitutional Convention

A number of the Founding Fathers, notably Madison, Hamilton, and Jay, were anxious to address these problems with an enhanced federal government of some kind. Such an opportunity, albeit limited, seemed to emerge when, in

---

[156]   Alan Greenspan and Adrian Wooldridge, *Capitalism in America*, 39.

1786, Virginia called for a convention separate from the Continental Congress to "consider how far a uniform system in their commercial regulations may be necessary to their common interest and their permanent harmony" and to propose appropriate amendments to the Articles.[157] That gathering failed to reach a quorum (though unbeknownst to them several state delegations were still underway). Rather than admit complete failure, five delegations recommended to their state legislatures that a general meeting be convened in the future for the same purpose, as well as to address *any other issues* that might need attention.[158] Over the following months, various legislatures considered the idea, and eventually, in February 1787, the Continental Congress endorsed a convention in Philadelphia as "the most probable mean[s] of establishing in these states a firm national government." However, the Congress also limited the convention's agenda to the "sole and express purpose of revising the Articles of Confederation."[159]

Washington, Madison, Hamilton, and Jay were ready to make the most of the new convention. While many states expected the convention to produce a limited answer to the shortfalls of the Articles, these men recognized the need to consider a new start based on first principles of government while preserving key elements of tradition. Once the door was opened to a congregation of well-read, experienced, and in several cases, brilliant men, the construction of the Constitution moved expeditiously –in light of the ground covered and the compromises that had to be reached.

Some historians characterize the outcome as a somewhat random accommodation of the individual interests of the delegates and their states. The deliberation on several issues, such as the representation of the smaller states, the new government's jurisdiction over trade, and the challenge of the slavery issue, might lead one to that conclusion. But these negotiations addressed details; the larger framework was in little doubt. Indeed, as the following section will demonstrate, the ancient traditions described in this chapter played a dispositive role.

In fact, given the traditions of the people, the vigilance of states in a confederacy, the choice of a republic versus a parliamentary construct, and the cautions of Montesquieu, one might say that the Constitution almost wrote itself. The following section will show how seven key considerations shaped the Constitution: (1) the incorporation of the political inheritance of previous millennia, (2) the choice of a republican form, (3) the need to address the shortfalls of the Articles, (4) the states' concerns about relinquishing the protections of a confederacy to a more unified form of government, (5) wariness of potential

---

[157] Michael J.Klarman, *The Framers' Coup: The Making of the United States Constitution* (New York: Oxford University Press, 2016), 103.

[158] Ibid, 109.

[159] Ibid, 119.

tyranny, (6) the need to give voice to the common man while minimizing the threat of majoritarianism, and (7) the need to preserve individual rights of liberty and property.

The rationale behind these considerations is outlined in notes from the Convention itself as well as in Madison's, Hamilton's, and Jay's analyses presented in *The Federalist Papers*.[160]

Political Inheritance

The framers of the Constitution were necessarily creatures of British tradition, which (as discussed previously) had been inherited from millennia of Western culture. Indeed, the preamble of the Constitution drew on the Greek, Roman, and medieval European belief that political power flows from the people as is evident in the preamble: "We the people of the United States, in order to form a more perfect Union ..." Moreover, the writers of the Constitution understood John Locke's idea that individuals are willing to give up certain rights for the common good in order to better secure other rights.[161]

In addition to sharing a political philosophy, the framers had concrete experience of institutions that could support these goals. Living under the terms of charters granted by the king but also under the benign neglect of their mother country (which was three thousand miles and often eight weeks' sail away), they had experience with creating their own governing institutions. These institutions presupposed the civil rights of free Englishmen; most local jurisdictions had a governor, an assembly, and a judicial system that incorporated trial by jury.

A Republican Form

The founders' extensive reading of history and their experience under both British law and under the constitutions of their state governments offered a variety of options, from parliamentary systems to republics. Of course, they could have amended the Articles of Confederation to form a new, quasi-parliamentary government. However, this was never seriously considered. From the outset, the "Virginia Plan" advanced by Madison assumed they would institute a republican form of government. For an example, they looked to, *inter alia*, the historical experience of the Roman Republic, which included a Senate, a popular Assembly, and a limited executive function.

One of the many perceived virtues of a republic was its ability to protect

---

[160] *The Federalist Papers*, ed. Roy P. Fairfield (New York: Anchor Books, Doubleday & Company, 1966).

[161] Bertrand Russell, *A History of Western Philosophy* (New York: Simon and Schuster, 1945), 632.

against unrestrained democracy by filtering the will of the people through representatives. In the words of Madison:

> Of the two great points of difference between a democracy and a republic are: first, the delegation of the government in the latter to a small number of citizens elected by the rest; secondly, the greater number of citizens and greater sphere of country over which the latter may be extended. ... The federal Constitution forms a happy combination in this respect [balancing local circumstances against national needs]; the great and aggregate interests being referred to the national, the local and particular to the State legislatures. ... Extend the sphere [of the republic], and you take in a greater variety of parties and interests; you make it less probable that the majority of the whole will have a common motive to invade the rights of other citizens. ... Hence, it clearly appears that the same advantage which a republic has over a democracy in controlling the effects of factions ...is enjoyed by a large over a small republic, – is enjoyed by the Union over the States composing it.[162]

This suggested a two-house structure, one to represent the people and another to balance the first. They understood that, for the houses to balance one another, they would need to be elected in different ways. The means to that end proved to be a major conceptual stumbling block in their deliberations, as will be seen below.

Addressing the Immediate Shortfalls of the Articles of Confederation

Once the construct of a republic had been chosen, the next tasks were twofold: the republic must be given sufficient enumerated powers to address the shortfalls of the Articles, and the residual rights of the people must be secured. This section discusses how these issues were addressed; the next shows how individual rights were secured by checks and balances among institutions, a Bill of Rights, and an independent judiciary.

The shortfalls of the Articles were addressed in straightforward ways:

1. The Constitution did not grant Congress plenary powers, but rather only the enumerated powers listed in Article I, Section 8. Moreover, the Tenth Amendment clearly states, "The powers not delegated to the United

---

[162] *Federalist Paper* no. 10.

<ol start="1">
<li>States by the Constitution, nor prohibited by it to the States, are reserved to the States respectively, or to the people."</li>
<li>The Constitution established a common market. To prevent states from erecting tariff barriers against one another or undermining foreign tariffs established by the new government, the Constitution included the Commerce Clause (Article I, Section 8), which states Congress shall have the power "to regulate Commerce with foreign Nations, and among the several States." Section 9 adds "that no Tax or Duty shall be laid on Articles exported from any State; No preference shall be given by any Regulation of Commerce or Revenue to the Ports of one State over those of another; nor shall Vessels bound to, or from, one State be obliged to enter, clear, or pay duties in another." Taken together, these powers established a common market essential to America's future prosperity.</li>
<li>It also provided for common defense. The same Section 8 states that Congress will provide for the common defense, while Article II, Section 2 makes the president the Commander in Chief of the U.S. Army and Navy and of state militias when they are called into the service of the United States.</li>
<li>Furthermore, the Constitution gave the states one voice in foreign affairs; Section 2 empowers the president (with the advice and consent of the Senate) to make treaties and appoint ambassadors.</li>
<li>Finally, the Constitution provides the federal government with a source of income. Article I, Section 8 empowers Congress "to levy and collect Taxes, Duties, Imposts and Excises to pay the Debts and provide for the common Defense and general Welfare of the United States; as well as to borrow Money on the credit of the United States; and to coin money." No longer would the federal government have to beg states for money or have its credit-worthiness mocked by foreign countries.</li>
</ol>

Of course, implementing these goals would depend on the appropriate functioning of the new governmental institutions. The framers gave particular attention to these, as will be discussed in later sections.

Reassuring the States

Imposing a "national government," even with only enumerated powers, was still a significant challenge. The states retained a confederacy mindset, which included distrust of or at least uneasiness about their compatriots: Large states aligned against small ones, mercantile against agricultural, and those with slaves against those without. Members of confederacies are always leery of relinquishing sovereignty to a larger governing entity without iron-clad protection of their core rights. The question, however, is how (given the experience of human history) power can be safely vested in the hands of a central government. The founders were acutely aware of Aristotle's concerns: Men are not angels, pure democracies and autocracies have fatal flaws, power tends to coalesce, power corrupts, and factions (who work for their own benefit regardless of the consequences for the rest of society) are inevitable in politics.

During the Revolutionary War and its aftermath, some states engaged in freeloading or in jockeying for advantage at the expense of the others. Moreover, the smaller states were wary of the potential power of the large states – Virginia, Pennsylvania, and Massachusetts.

Therefore, these fears needed to be addressed directly if significant political power was to be granted to a national government in a way that would be acceptable to the sovereign states. Moreover, given the attractions of power, the leaders of each state were not going to cede power to some new entity unless they could preserve some of their existing prerogatives and also gain something far better. Much of the Convention, therefore, was devoted to defining the specific relationships between the states and the new federal entity. The solution was fivefold: The Federal government would only have certain enumerated powers; the federal system would have a republican form; a Senate would directly represent the states in a bicameral legislature, and the states would have primary power in the Electoral College that would select the president.

Limited Powers to the Federal Government

The states were assured that they could safely cede power to the new government because the Constitution was contemplated to be the frame of a national government, of special and enumerated powers, and not of general and unlimited powers. Madison stated this clearly in *Federalist Paper* no. 45:

> The powers delegated by the proposed Constitution to the federal government are few and defined. Those which are to remain in the State governments are numerous and indefinite. The former will be exercised principally on external objects, as war, peace, negotiation, and foreign commerce; with which last the power of taxation will, for the most part, be connected. The powers reserved to the several States will extend to all the objects which, in the ordinary course of affairs, concern the lives, liberties, and properties of the people, and the internal order, improvement, and prosperity of the State.

Elsewhere, Madison added that "the proposed government cannot be deemed a *national* one; since its jurisdiction extends to certain enumerated objects only, and leaves to the several States a residuary and inviolable sovereignty over all other objects."[163]

These statements highlight the goals of the new Constitution: to create a common market and a strong executive to protect the country's interests abroad while protecting the people's safety and property at home.

A Federal System

The basic structure of the new government was to be federal; the power of the central government would be balanced by the residual sovereignty of the states. Notably, "the election of the president and the Senate will depend in all cases on the legislatures of the several States."[164] Practically speaking, no policy opposed by a majority of the states could be maintained.

The Senate, meanwhile, represented the states in the national government. According to Madison, "[The Senate] is recommended by the double advantage of favoring a select appointment, and of giving to the State governments such an agency in the formation of the federal government as must secure the authority of the former, and may form a convenient link between the two systems."[165]

Equal Representation of the States in the Senate

Probably the chief sticking point in the Convention was getting the support of the smaller states, which were leery of the large differences in population and size among states (more than half the population resided in Virginia, Pennsylvania, and Massachusetts). The successful compromise determined that the House of Representatives would be elected on the basis of population but that each state would have equal representation in the upper house, the Senate. Thus, in the Senate, the smaller states could band together to defend their interests against overweening ambitions of the larger states.

The Electoral College

Similarly, the Constitution gave the states a large say in the selection of the president. The president is selected by a state vote via an Electoral College whose votes have been certified by the state legislatures. According to Hamilton, "without the intervention of the State legislatures, the president of the United

---

[163]   *Federalist Paper* no. 39.

[164]   *Federalist Paper* no. 45.

[165]   *Federalist Paper* no. 62.

States cannot be elected at all. They must in all cases have a great share in his appointment ..."[166]

Vigilance Against Tyranny

The Convention was very much influenced by the writings of Montesquieu, who understood Aristotle's argument that neither monarchy, oligarchy, nor democracy alone could remain virtuous or stable over time and that a then-unidentified mixture of the three would be required. Montesquieu knew history, particularly the evolution of British government, which he believed represented the epitome of representative government to that date. As Durant says, "He thought he had found there, however, imperfect, his ideal of a monarchy checked by democracy in the House of Commons, in turn checked by aristocracy in the House of Lords; and he supposed that the courts of England were an independent check on Parliament and the king."[167] He points out how the three powers of government and two chambers of the legislature check and balance the others, thereby protecting the citizens' liberties.[168]

Montesquieu's ideas extensively influenced eighteenth-century political circles. Russell Kirk notes that his works were found in every British country house, as well as on the shelves of educated Americans; no other man was as quoted during the Constitutional Convention.[169] In short, he addressed an age-old political problem based on Britain's empirical experience. But his prescription also included a greater wisdom regarding the nature of man: A system can never rely on the virtue of a single man or even a small group of men to safeguard liberty. Individual ambition leads to the corruption of power.

The design laid out in the Constitution was reassuring, but only if the overall construct worked as intended. History held too many examples of rulers or legislative bodies who ignored tradition and law to create effective tyrannies. Checks on the president and the legislature would be essential to prevent them from misusing their power. Thus, according to Madison, "the great security against a gradual concentration of the several powers in the same department, consists in giving those who administer each department the necessary constitutional means and personal motives to resist encroachment of the others." He elaborated in the often-quoted words:

It may be a reflection on human nature, that such devices

---

[166] *Federalist Paper* no. 45.

[167] Will and Ariel Durant, *The Age of Voltaire* (New York: Simon and Schuster, 1965), 353.

[168] Ibid.

[169] Russell Kirk, *The Roots of American Order* (Washington, DC: Regnery Gateway, 1991), 350.

should be necessary to control the abuses of government. But what is government itself, but the greatest of all reflections on human nature? If men were angels, no government would be necessary. If angels were to govern men, neither external nor internal controls on government would be necessary. In framing a government which is to be administered by men over other men, the great difficulty lies in this: you must first enable the government to control the governed; and in the next place oblige it to control itself. A dependence on the people is, no doubt, the primary control on the government; but experience has taught mankind the necessity of auxiliary precautions.[170]

What auxiliary measures were taken to check the president and Congress?

Preventing Despotism

Since the founders feared despotism and had an aversion to monarchy, the new Constitution carefully hedged the selection of the chief executive. There was to be no "hero on horseback" sweeping all before him. The president was to be the creation of the states. According to Madison: "Without the intervention of the State Legislatures, the President cannot be elected at all. They must in all cases have a great share in his appointment, and will, perhaps, in most cases, of themselves determine it [via the Electoral College]."[171]

The Constitution included several provisions designed to restrain the president's power. He was to be an executive sworn to faithfully execute the laws passed by the legislature. He had no authority to unilaterally create laws on his own. While he could veto laws passed by Congress, both Houses of Congress together could override his vetoes. Moreover, his key appointments – the cabinet and the courts – would have to be confirmed by the Senate, as would treaties with other countries. Finally, in an extreme case, Congress could remove him from office via impeachment by the House and conviction by the Senate.

Preventing Legislative Tyranny

Since the legislature can be the strongest branch of government (and rightly so since it is the most direct representative of the people), care was necessary to prevent legislative tyranny that might abuse the rights of minorities. Madison wrote, "In republican government the legislative authority necessarily

---

[170]   *Federalist Paper* no. 51.

[171]   *Federalist Paper* no. 45.

predominates. The remedy for this inconveniency is to divide the legislature into different branches; and to render them, by different modes of election and different principles of action, as little connected with each other as the nature of their common functions and their common dependence on the society will admit."[172] In *The Calculus of Consent*,[173] Buchanan and Tullock demonstrate how such a construct protects minority rights by effectively requiring a super-majority of the electorate to infringe on the rights of the minority.

Even though the bicameral legislature itself and the division of power between the Houses provides substantial protection against a potentially tyrannical body, the Convention believed that further protections were required to guard life, liberty, and property. One such key measure was the president's power to veto congressional legislation. In the words of Hamilton:

> The first thing that offers itself to our observation is the qualified negative [veto] of the President upon the acts or resolutions of the two houses of the legislature; or, in other words, his power of returning all bills with objections, to have the effect of preventing their becoming laws, unless they should afterwards be ratified by two-thirds of each of the component members of the legislative body.

> The propensity of the legislative department to intrude upon the rights, and to absorb the powers, of the other departments, has already been suggested and repeated; the insufficiency of a mere parchment delineation of the boundaries of each, has also been remarked upon.[174]

> ...and the necessity of furnishing each with constitutional arms for its own defense, has been inferred and proved. ... Without [some kind of veto, the president]... would be absolutely unable to defend himself against the depredations of [the legislature].[175]

These provisions addressed the most overt forms of potential legislative tyranny. However, individual liberty required additional safeguards.

---

[172] *Federalist Paper* no. 51.

[173] James M. Buchanan and Gordon Tullock, *The Calculus of Consent, Logical Foundations of Constitutional Democracy* (Ann Arbor: The University of Michigan Press, 1965), 258.

[174] *Federalist Paper* no. 48.

[175] *Federalist Paper* no. 73.

Protecting the Individual

When ceding power to the state, the individual becomes vulnerable in two respects – his civil liberty and his property. The Constitution explicitly addresses both.

Individual Liberty

Almost without exception, the framers believed that, above all, the new Constitution had to preserve individual liberty and protect private property, reflecting Locke's writings and the principles expressed in the Declaration of Independence.

They conducted lengthy debates over how to best protect individuals from arbitrary government power. There was no question that the citizenry of the new United States would be afforded the rights and privileges that they had as Englishmen. The Constitution said nothing to the contrary, and that Constitution only assigned specific powers to Congress. Nonetheless, the antifederalists wanted this spelled out. To be sure, in *Federalist Paper* no. 84, Alexander Hamilton argued against the inclusion of a Bill of Rights in the Constitution, arguing that the inclusion of specific rights might be taken to mean that other traditional rights did not have the same protection. Nonetheless, the first Ten Amendments to the Constitution were quickly enacted to protect key rights of free men regarding speech, religion, and property (among others). This protected civil society and ensured that the voice of the people would always be heard.

Safeguarding Against Predatory Factions

In addition to safeguarding civil rights against *arbitrary* government, the Constitution needed to protect individuals from lawful majoritarianism in the legislature. This, as previously discussed, was an ancient question; even Aristotle expressed concerns about majoritarianism in democracy. Chapter Six will show how this concern influenced the establishment of representative democracy with universal suffrage in virtually all democracies. The United States, however, was the first to create the (then) missing piece in a governing edifice that provided checked universal suffrage and was congruent with the FEO. Madison approached this issue more directly than the other delegates, illustrating it with the need to prevent predation by popular and electoral factions. He wrote:

> It is of great importance in a republic ... to guard one part of the society against the injustice of the other part. Different interests necessarily exist in different classes of citizens. If a majority be

> united by a common interest, the rights of the minority will be
> insecure. … there are but two methods of providing against this
> evil …Whilst all authority in [a federal republic] will be derived
> from and dependent on the society, the society itself will be
> broken into so many parts, interests and classes of citizens [e.g.,
> agriculture, industry, finance, and commerce], that the rights of
> individuals or of the minority will be in little danger from the
> interested combinations of the majority.[176]

What factions did Madison anticipate? He warned against factions that might seek legislative support to take others' wealth. The quotes demonstrate his definition of factions: They arise almost inevitably from the unequal distribution of talent and wealth; they are inevitable and eradicable; their operations can be blocked by juxtaposing society's manifold interests; and the government's power of taxation is the focus of their ambitions and thus should always be subject to great scrutiny.

> By faction, I understand a number of citizens, whether
> amounting to a majority or minority of the whole, who are
> united and actuated by some common impulse of passion, or
> of interest, adverse to the rights of other citizens, or to the
> permanent and aggregate interests of the community.[177]

The diversity in the faculties of men, from which the rights of property originate, is not less an insuperable obstacle to the uniformity of interests. The protection of these faculties is the first object of government. From the protection of different and unequal faculties of acquiring property, the possession of different degrees and kinds of property immediately results; and from the influence of these on the sentiments and views of the respective proprietors, ensues a division of society into different interests and parties. … The latent causes of faction are thus sown in the nature of man… But the most common and durable source of factions has been the various and unequal distribution of property. Those who hold and those who are without property have ever formed distinct interests in society. … A landed interest, a manufacturing interest, a mercantile interest, a moneyed interest, with many lesser interests, grow up of necessity in civilized nations, and divide them into different classes, actuated by different sentiments and views. The regulation of these various and interfering interests forms the principal task of modern legislation …*The inference to which we are brought is,*

---

[176]   *Federalist Paper* no. 51.

[177]   *Federalist Paper* no. 10.

that the causes of faction cannot be removed, and the relief is only to be sought in the means of controlling its effects[emphasis mine].[178]

The influence of factious leaders may kindle a flame within their particular States, but will be unable to spread a general conflagration through the other States. A religious sect ... a rage for paper money, for the abolition of debts, for the equal division of property, or for any other improper or wicked project, will be less apt to pervade the whole body of the Union, than a particular member of it.[179]

There is no part of the administration of government that requires extensive information and a thorough knowledge of the principles of political economy so much as the business of taxation. The man who understands those principles best will be least likely to resort to oppressive expedients or to sacrifice any particular class of citizens to the procurement of revenue. It might be demonstrated that the most productive system of finance will always be the least burdensome.[180]

The principal counter to the inevitable operation of factions is the ability of a republican form of government to filter the passions of the electorate through their direct representatives and through the states themselves. It does this via a bicameral legislature and presidential veto power and by reserving some powers to the states and ensuring a balance of power among all branches of government.

In summary, the founders believed that the Constitution adequately protected the rights of the minority. In addition to the words of the new Constitution, an "unwritten constitution" had been inherited from Britain. This incorporated the traditional rights of Englishman, which (importantly) included property rights. The considerations in the unwritten constitution were imbedded in common law and so would shape the views of the new American judiciary. Finally, an unambiguous statement of inviolable individual rights, including protection of property, was included in the Bill of Rights (the first Ten Amendments).

Rule of Law/an Independent Judiciary

As discussed earlier, Montesquieu admired the British high judiciary, which provided a check on parliament. He saw this as part of a balanced government that combined elements of the monarchy with a parliament and a judicial branch. With this in mind, at the Convention, Hamilton emphasized the importance of an independent judiciary to maintain the Constitution's efficacy. Its duty is "to declare all acts contrary to the manifest tenor of the Constitution void. ... No legislative act, therefore, contrary to the Constitution, can be valid. ... A constitution is, in

---

[178]   *Federalist Paper* no. 10.

[179]   Ibid.

[180]   *Federalist Paper* no. 35.

fact, and must be regarded by the judges, as a fundamental law."[181] There and in an earlier paper, he emphasizes the importance of the courts' independence from the other branches, particularly from the legislature.

The validity of this concern can be seen in the progressive Left's efforts over the last century to pack the Supreme Court with members who believe in a "living Constitution" so they could ignore the clear requirements of the Constitution in favor of special factions. This opened the door to selecting justices based on their political predilections rather than on their knowledge of the law and commitment to deciding cases based on written law and precedent. Some examples are discussed in the next chapter, along with their costs to the country.

Competition Among the States

The central theme of this book is how man has discovered methods of self-government that respect the FEO. The new U.S. federal government would be a great advance in this direction, particularly because of its measures to limit (though of course not eradicate) the negative effect of predatory factions. State legislatures were unaffected by this innovation and had full latitude providing they did not encroach on the enumerated powers of the republic nor on the Bill of Rights.

Some of the delegates expressed concerns that state legislatures might fail to properly respect property rights, contracts, and sound money policies, so this hands-off federal approach did not come easily. Madison's Virginia Plan, which opened the deliberations, empowered the federal legislature to negate all state law that contravened the opinion of the national legislature regarding the articles of union. Charles Pinckney went further and proposed a veto allowing Congress to block all state laws that it judged improper.[182] However, such provisions were quickly determined to be non-starters on two grounds. First, the states would never agree to cede this much power; second, it would be impractical to monitor the activities of all the state Legislatures in so much detail. Yet the concern was real. The delegates decided that it was essential to guard the Constitution against adverse state action, so they included the Supremacy Clause and gave the judiciary the power to review state laws.

So, factions had a relatively free reign at the state level. That was simply a fact of life. As Madison noted, human nature made it impossible to eradicate factions; they could only find ways to limit their effect. Therefore, bad state policies would be countered not by law but by competition among the states. Bad policies have bad effects, such as slower economic growth and job loss. *The Wall Street*

---

[181]   *Federalist Paper* no. 78.

[182]   Michael J. Klarman, *The Framers' Coup: The Making of the United States Constitution* (New York: Oxford University Press, 2016), 155-156.

Journal noted how the states least hospitable to the FEO, California, New York, Connecticut, New Jersey, and Illinois, in recent years all had net out-migration of population as well as of total adjusted gross income.[183]People can vote with their feet as well as at the ballot box; governments eventually take notice and reform (several of the above states are slated to lose representatives after the next census). As Justice Louis Brandeis once noted, the states are the laboratories of democratic reform.[184]

Despite inevitable bad ideas, the system works because as Richard Epstein noted, competition is key in all aspects of public life to corral cronyism, special interests (particularly unions), and all forms of public quasi-monopolies. Not only can people move, but best practices will be noticed and adopted by other states. Two modern examples are the spread of right-to-work laws inhibiting the negative effects of union monopoly and charter schools/school vouchers that provide competition to the monopolies of public schools.

*   *   *

In summary, the Founding Fathers established a form of government that attained their chief goal of addressing the shortfalls of the Articles of Confederation. It provided the country with an energetic chief executive, a legislature that would provide for the common defense, and an open common market while protecting the liberties of a free citizenry.

Richard Epstein describes the philosophic mindset infusing the U.S. Constitution and its writers:

> Their entire debate rested on a sober and shared appreciation
> of the potentially corrosive effects of self-interest on human
> affairs, a modest confidence that our collective capacities with
> language and cooperation allow us to devise institutions capable
> of coping with these ever- present risks ... and a deep suspicion
> of government monopolies of all sorts and descriptions. At root,
> the classical view of American constitutionalism examined all
> legal interventions under a presumption of error.[185]

Their efforts also contained a deeper wisdom. The underlying values that helped shaped the specific features of the Constitution were also values in keeping

---

[183]   Editorial "Blue State Redistribution" (*The Wall Street Journal*, New York Edition, January 8, 2020) A16.

[184]   *New State Ice Co. v. Liebmann* (285 U.S. 262).

[185]   Richard A. Epstein, *The Classical Liberal Constitution – The Uncertain Quest for Limited Government*. (Cambridge, Massachusetts: Harvard University Press, 2014), 5.

with a free extended order, which supported enormous economic growth in the ensuing centuries.

Take a moment to appreciate this achievement. Sparsely settled in a remote corner of the civilized world, working from first philosophic principles and human experience, the Constitutional Convention crafted the most advanced form of government invented until then, the one best able to protect liberty in all forms (despite the limitations of human nature) in virtually all collective endeavors. To be sure, other countries, notably Switzerland, came up with comparable solutions that have worked well, as will be discussed in later chapters. Nevertheless, out of political expediency, it failed to address the horror of slavery. This would have to await a Civil War and amendments to the Constitution.

VIGILANCE GOING FORWARD

Virtually none of the supporters of the proposed Constitution believed it to be perfect. Nathanial Gorham of Massachusetts expressed serious doubt "that this vast country including the western territory will 150 years hence remain one nation."[186] Another apprehension was voiced by Benjamin Franklin, who, when asked what the Constitutional Convention had created, replied, "a republic, if you can keep it."[187] And, of course, the antifederalists were never fully persuaded of the virtues of the Constitution, despite the addition of the Bill of Rights.

Jefferson was not convinced that Madison and the other founders had found a way to control the inevitable human impulse for predation that could be unleashed by the power ceded to the government. He wrote: "Experience hath shewn that even under the best forms of governments those entrusted with power have, in time, and by slow operations, perverted it into tyranny."[188]

In the early nineteenth century, Senator John C. Calhoun also foresaw the inherent problem of relying on documents to corral raw political power:

> A written constitution certainly has many and considerable advantages, but it is a mistake to suppose that the mere insertion of provisions to restrict and limit the power of government without investing those for whose protection they are inserted with the means of enforcing their observance will be sufficient to prevent the major and dominant party from abusing its powers ...
> The end of the contest [between majority and minority parties]

---

[186]   Michael J. Klarman, *The Framers' Coup: The Making of the United States Constitution*, 628.

[187]   Bartleby,com, Great Books Online, *Respectfully Quoted: A Dictionary of Quotations*, 1989, No. 1593.

[188]   Internet: *BrainyQuoteDesktop*

> would be the subversion of the constitution ... the restrictions
> would ultimately be annulled and the government be converted
> into one of unlimited powers.[189]

Alas, those words were eerily prescient of the unfolding of politics in the United States in the twentieth century. But that is the subject of the next chapter, which will examine in detail how new, sophisticated forms of predation undermined key protections of the Constitution.

---

[189]   John C. Calhoun, *A Disquisition on Government* (New York: Liberal Arts Press, 1953), pp. 25-27.

CHAPTER 4

THE CONSTITUTION UNDERMINED

"It would seem that no advanced civilization has yet developed without a government that saw its chief aim in the protection of private property, but that again and again ... growth ... was halted by a 'strong' government ... Sooner or later ... they tend to abuse that power and suppress the freedom they had earlier secured in order to enforce their own presumably greater wisdom..."[190]
– Friedrich von Hayek

Let's review the bidding, as bridge players might say. Because of the ambitious, predatory side of human nature, no society developed an effective rule by the people that also protected individual liberty and reined in factions until the U.S. Constitution. The centerpiece of this creation was a central government that held limited powers and was balanced by the states in a federal republic. Serendipitously, this kind of limited central government not only protected liberty but also facilitated a robust FEO. Recall Adam Smith's proposition (presented in Chapter One) that prosperous growth is guided by an "invisible hand" and only needs the light touch of a government that performs essential societal tasks but wields powers of taxation, regulation, and income redistribution lightly.

However, as suggested by the Hayek quote above, history indicates that such a favorable state of affairs is unlikely to persist over a lengthy period under inevitable pressure of ambitious men and predatory factions. Chapter Two diagnosed the

---

[190] Friedrich von Hayek, edited by W.W. Bartley III, The Fatal Conceit (Chicago: The University of Chicago Press, 1988), 32.

subversive flaws in the abstract: legislators' ambition and opportunism, rent-seeking by special interests, and the inability of individual voters to foresee the negatives of sentiment and good intentions. These flaws appear in all forms of representative government. How did they play out in the new United States?

In its first century or so, the United States had a very good run of steady economic progress despite an exhausting Civil War. The flaws of representative government, such as corruption, cronyism, and factions that engage in special pleading, were evident in many of the states, whose legislatures were not as constrained as Congress. But on a national scale, the spirit of the Constitution regarding federal government was preserved.

Nonetheless, the United States had evolved into a very different country from the time of its founding. Profound economic and political changes presented unfamiliar challenges regarding the role of government. History and tradition offered no obvious solutions and did not indicate whether the scope of the federal government should be changed. Unfortunately, the country ultimately chose 'solutions' that ran counter to the temper of the Constitution at costs to all.

This chapter describes how key aspects of the Constitution were undermined by decades of progressive efforts, how the population's vigilance flagged, and how the Supreme Court abdicated its duty. In the twentieth century, constitutional protections were eroded by the kind of majoritarian forces anticipated by Aristotle, feared by Madison, and analyzed by Buchanan and Hayek. That reality underlies one of the most important stories of U.S. history in the twentieth century and is the focus of this chapter.

This story is not, for the most part, one of bad people pursuing self-interest, but of people who fail to understand the origins of the constitutional order by pursuing good intentions in harmful ways. They used sophisticated but faulty arguments that often carried the day. We now have a century of empirical evidence and painful experience with which to revisit these arguments.

To show how constitutional protections were weakened, the chapter will: (1) establish the economic and constitutional baseline of the first decades of the twentieth century, evidence of a superior U.S. political order, (2) describe the national transformation into an industrial, commercial country that raised the question of changing the form of government, (3) describe the *progressive* philosophy that promoted this change, (4) identify the key historical figures who implemented those changes and the milestones they reached, and (5) describe the failure of the Supreme Court to protect key features of the Constitution.

A TURN-OF-THE-CENTURY BASELINE

A century of experience had left the provisions of the Constitution essentially intact. To be sure, the federal government began to assume a much larger role by (for example) building railroads and in combating monopolies. But it could reasonably be argued that these functions were authorized by the Commerce Clause. When Congress attempted to go beyond its enumerated powers, such as by establishing an income tax, the Supreme Court pushed back. If the country truly wanted an income tax, they would have to establish it constitutionally through an amendment. This, of course, was eventually done and should have set the precedent for any further fundamental changes. If the country's new circumstances required deviations from the founding document, the reasons should be debated and, if necessary, the Constitution amended accordingly.

The prior century of experience demonstrated that a light hand of government and protection of individuals' natural rights had enormous payoffs. The United States had the most rapidly growing economy in the world, with a commensurate rising standard of living for everyone. It was a beacon for a flood of immigrants seeking to share those benefits. To be sure, life was not easy for many; there were slums and long work hours, and many suffered from the economic crises that arose from time to time. Unfortunately, it was these negatives, rather than the great advances, that attracted the attention of political philosophers, utopians, and muckrakers (among others), leading them to call for fundamental changes to our governing model. But they had a high hurdle to overcome: Our system was patently better than the alternatives, every aspect of the workingman's life was rapidly improving, and economic downturns were fleeting and self-correcting. Let's examine a few highlights.

From the beginning, the U.S. economy grew rapidly in manufacturing as well as agriculture. For example, in 1840, the United States ranked fifth in the world for manufacturing. By 1894, it reached first place, producing twice as much as Britain, the previous leader.[191] Importantly, per capita income rose apace: in 1914, the per capita incomes of the most developed countries were: U.S. $346, Britain $244, Germany $184, France $153, and Italy $108, respectively.[192] The country's economic model benefited every income class – perhaps some more than others, but still everyone. As standards of living increased, individuals could not only meet their immediate needs, but also provide for the vicissitudes of life such as illness and old age. Although some argued that the government should be responsible for these needs, as will be discussed below, it was increasingly clear

---

[191] Paul Johnson, *A History of the American People* (New York: Harper Collins Publishers, 1997), 531.

[192] Alan Greenspan and Adrian Wooldridge, *Capitalism in America* (New York: Penguin Press, 2018), 92.

that they could be addressed cooperatively through non-governmental means such as churches, work organizations, healthcare cooperatives, and fraternal organizations. As de Tocqueville marveled, the United States had an incredibly diverse civil society: "Americans of all ages, all conditions, and all dispositions, constantly form associations … to give entertainments, to found seminaries, to build inns, to construct churches, to diffuse books, to send missionaries; … they found in this manner hospitals, prisons, and schools."[193]

To be sure, economic progress didn't (and doesn't) follow a straight line; economic cycles led to booms and busts, largely due to banks' overexpansion of credit and eventual retrenchment. Nonetheless, despite temporary setbacks, the system worked; recessions were invariably self-correcting. The most dramatic example of this occurred just after the First World War. The country needed to retrench from massive war spending, which had been accompanied by a commensurate expansion of the monetary base by the Federal Reserve. The Reserve then shifted policies abruptly to reduce inflation, and the country went into a recession, which could well have turned into a depression.

The Harding Administration responded by quickly returning to the prior limited role of government and letting the system self-correct, reducing government spending and sharply reducing tax rates. For example, the top tax rate was reduced by half, to 25%, the excess profits tax was eliminated, gift taxes were repealed, estate taxes were slashed, and one-third of those who had paid taxes in the previous year were effectively removed from the tax rolls. Despite these cuts, the budget was balanced and the national debt was reduced from $24 billion to $16 billion. Furthermore, the Federal Reserve, whose rate increases had precipitated the recession, also played a role in the recovery by cutting the discount rate several times in 1921, leading to an increase in the money supply and easing credit conditions.[194]

To be sure, there was a sharp eighteen-month economic downturn (1920-1921). The economy, however, responded vigorously to what in later decades would be called 'supply side' economics, resulting in the period popularly known as the Roaring Twenties. Unemployment, which had been about 5% when Coolidge became president in 1923, fell to about 1% or 2%, and real dollar income for workers rose by 16% from 1923 to 1929.[195]

Given this record, how could the idea that economic development based on government bureaucracy would be more productive than that based on free markets and individual initiative gain traction? Therein lies a cautionary tale.

For several decades, one political party adopted a progressive political

---

[193] 4 Alexis De Toqueville, *Democracy in America* (New York: Mentor Books, 1956), 198.

[194] Burton G. Malkiel, "The Best Remedy" (New York: *The Wall Street Journal*, November 12, 2014), A13.

[195] Amity Shlaes, *The Forgotten Man* (New York: Harper Perennial, 2008), 37-39.

philosophy more and more. This party grasped the opportunity for fundamental change when the country grappled with the unprecedented hardships of the Great Depression. That political philosophy was rooted in uncertainties produced by a vast Industrial Revolution and was championed by numerous actors on the national stage.

A NEW SOCIETY EMERGED FROM THE INDUSTRIAL REVOLUTION

At the beginning of the twentieth century, U.S. society had to make sense of a host of developments: the new commercial order, continuing market imperfections, periodic economic crises, the promise of science, and the ongoing corruption and cronyism endemic to human nature at all levels of government.

A New Commercial, Economic, and Manufacturing Order

At the time of the American Revolution, the country was primarily agricultural. Thomas Jefferson believed that rural America's way of life was socially and morally superior to that of other societies.[196] He was suspicious of Hamilton's encouragement of commerce and manufacturing in the new country. While many of these values remained in the tapestry of men's beliefs, the country had moved decisively in the direction foreseen by Hamilton. How was the body politic to make sense of this?

Life was undoubtedly far simpler in the beginning: Farmers had to buy seed, sell to local markets, purchase at local stores, produce for themselves much of what they consumed, and perhaps take seasonal loans from a local bank. This economy could be easily grasped (if not fully understood).

However, life in the industrial age became very different and far less easily understood: Large industries were non-transparently linked to one another; laborers worked in a more impersonal environment and often felt disempowered; and distant, complex economic forces operated under the control of Wall Street, national banks, trusts, conglomerates, and the like. What is not understood can be fearsome, even if it occurs spontaneously and benefits everyone. These fundamental changes were compounded by the traumatic effects of economic cycles involving bank failures, bankruptcies, and a periodic lack of financial liquidity. The new economic order contained ample insecurity for politicians to exploit and for academics and intellectuals to ponder. And they did.

---

[196]   Stanley Elkins and Eric McKitrick, *The Age of Federalism* (New York: Oxford University Press, 1993), 199.

As expressed by Elihu Root in an address to the New York State Bar Association:

> The real difficulty appears to be that the new conditions incident to the extraordinary industrial development of the last half century are continuously and progressively demanding the readjustment of relations between great bodies of men and establishment of new legal rights and obligations not contemplated when existing laws were passed or existing limitations upon the powers of government were prescribed in our Constitution. In place of the old individual independence of life in which every intelligent and healthy citizen was competent to take care of himself and his family, we have come to a high degree of interdependence in which the greater part of our people have to rely for all the necessities of life on the systematized co-operation of a vast number of other men working through complicated industrial and commercial machinery. ... The relations between the employer and the employed, between the owners of aggregated capital and the units of organized labor ... present new questions for the solution of which the old reliance upon the free action of individual wills appears quite inadequate. ... [T]he intervention of that organized control which we call government seems necessary to produce the same result of justice and right conduct which obtained through the attrition of individuals before the new conditions arose.[197]

Nowhere here is it mentioned that the economic well-being of all classes had been increasing rapidly, that factory hours worked per week had been declining, and that targets of liberal sentiment such as child labor been shrinking just as rapidly. These proponents of change could point to the continuing difficulties of the common man without understanding how those difficulties fit into the FEO, advocating changes in government with an abundance of sentiment but without any real empirical insight.

Market Imperfections

Sweeping economic changes made people more aware of the workings of the economic order. They became more sensitive to their own lack of control, especially in regard to banks, trusts, and huge new corporate entities. New

---

[197] Samuel Eliot Morison, *The Oxford History of the American People* (New York: Oxford University Press, 1965), 811-812.

industries and their fabulously wealthy entrepreneurs – the railroad, steel, and petroleum industries – particularly captured the public imagination. The free market's "creative destruction" included much ruthlessness. Competitors were driven out of business and efforts were made to control prices and market share through pools, trusts, interlocking boards, and holding companies. Some companies' dominance of their fields, such as Standard Oil, aroused fears of monopolistic behavior that could harm the public.

Monopolistic behavior was manifestly incompatible with precepts of free markets, which relied on competition. Still, there was more than a little cognitive dissonance in this thinking since it ignored the benefits accruing to the entire population. Chapter 1 discussed how while individual entrepreneurs became extraordinarily wealthy, the vast bulk of economic benefits went to labor and to the consumer. For example, in just a few decades of the nineteenth century, prices of steel fell from $166 to $46 a ton, and petroleum from $16 a barrel to less than one.[198] These commodities obviously became more accessible to everyone as a result; hardly the phenomena associated with monopolies. Nonetheless, these large companies' public images were darkened by a number of writers who emphasized what they viewed as unscrupulous methods and downplayed the achievements, often calling these large firms "robber barons."[199] Particularly influential was Ida Tarbell's *History of the Standard Oil Company*. Was bigness alone an offense? What about tough competitive practices?

Certainly, monopolies were a concern. At that time, corporations were chartered in states and were not subject to federal regulation. However, only the federal government could control anti-competitive behavior nationwide. The Progressives found the power to do so in an expanded interpretation of the Commerce Clause. Accordingly, Congress passed the Sherman Antitrust Act in 1890, which stated "Every contract, combination in the form of trust or otherwise, or conspiracy, in restraint of trade or commerce among the several States, or with foreign nations is hereby declared to be illegal."[200] This was followed by the Clayton Antitrust Act of 1914, which prohibited a number of unfair trade practices.

In this area, rapid economic change seemed to require a more activist federal government. Were there other areas where this was also justified? Where was

---

[198]   Alan Greenspan and Adrian Wooldridge, *Capitalism in America, 132-133.*

[199]   From Wikipedia: The metaphor appeared as early as February 9, 1859, when *The New York Times* used it to characterize the business practices of Cornelius Vanderbilt. Historian T.J. Stiles says the metaphor "conjures up visions of titanic monopolists who crushed competitors, rigged markets, and corrupted government. In their greed and power, legend has it, they held sway over a helpless democracy."

[200]   Samuel Eliot Morison, Henry Steele Commager, and William E. Leuchtenburg. *A Concise History of the American Republic* (New York: Oxford University Press, 1977), 371.

the boundary between the Commerce Clause and the limitations imposed by the "enumerated powers" granted in the Constitution? These issues remained open.

Recurring Economic Crises

The entire population was periodically harmed by financial crises that were a feature of free markets for centuries. They resulted from speculation, overleveraging of credit, and bad governmental policies. In 1819, a panic was triggered by a credit crunch. Greenspan and Wooldridge note that "state banks across the South and West began to call in their loans on heavily mortgaged farms. The value of many farms fell by 50 percent or more. … The price of cotton dropped by 25 percent in a single day in 1819. … This panic set the pattern for a succession of panics in 1837, 1873, 1884, 1896, and 1907."[201]

Recessions could be viewed simply as a fact of life, a recurring cost that is far less than the overall benefits. However, two consequential financial crises occurred at the end of the nineteenth century and the beginning of the twentieth that spurred ideas for institutional change: the Panic of 1893, which produced a severe depression, followed by the Panic of 1907. While the latter mainly affected financial institutions, it led to a small decline in real wages and increased unemployment in the United States.

At that time, there was no Federal Reserve Bank and little understanding of macroeconomics, but there was a growing desire for tools to deal with financial panics. Even if recessions were unavoidable, for most people, knowing that a financial crisis might be around the corner leads to unease, increasing the potential of depositor runs on banks.

Political Corruption and Cronyism

Since predation is ubiquitous and factions are inevitable, no area of communal life is immune from corruption (e.g., bribery, vote trading), where money is involved. Corruption occurs in city halls, in state governments, throughout commerce, and even in churches. So, when journalists and reformers find evidence of corruption, it should not surprise. Instead, it should suggest the need for more political vigilance and proper enforcement; it should not be seen as an indictment of the system itself, which like all systems must cope with human nature.

In post-Civil War America, many new opportunities for corruption arose in ways that politics and the criminal justice system had not yet adjusted to. A vigorous press shed light on crony capitalism, monopolies, big-city political bosses, and patronage in the civil service – and many reports called for reform.

---

[201]   Alan Greenspan and Adrian Wooldridge, *Capitalism in America*, 42.

Examples, according to Samuel Eliot Morison, included: "Boss Tweed's stealing $100 million from New York City; ... Collis B. Huntington buying the California legislature and bribing congressmen to promote transcontinental railroad interests; Peter Widener obtaining street railway franchises by bribing aldermen..."[202]

At the beginning of the twentieth century, writers known as 'muckrakers' leveled their guns at political corruption and its link to corporations. One of the first was Lincoln Steffens, who wrote *Tweed Days in St. Louis* in 1902, followed later by a series called *Shame of the Cities*: "Philadelphia: Corrupt and Contented,""Pittsburgh, a City Ashamed," and "The Shamelessness of St. Louis."[203]

These problems captured the attention of the politically aware, who wanted to "return state governments to the people and end corruption." In Oregon, this led to the adoption of the initiative, referendum, direct primary, and popular recall of elected officials.[204] At the national level, the Seventeenth Amendment to the Constitution was passed. It required that U.S. senators be directly elected rather than appointed by state legislatures, which were often considered captive to special interests.

While most of the problems were found at the state and local levels, Progressives argued that some kind of systematic reform was required at the federal level as well.

*   *   *

So, in just a couple of generations, the United States had been economically transformed and had to confront social problems for which there was little precedent. But did the constitutional foundations need to be changed, and if so, how?

DID ECONOMIC CHALLENGES REQUIRE CONSTITUTIONAL CHANGE?

Several considerations seemed to suggest the possibility of a social reorganization. In particular, the rise of science married to utopian thinking and some examples from abroad indicated possibilities.

---

[202]   Samuel Eliot Morison, *The Oxford History of the American People* (New York: Oxford University Press, 1965), 732.

[203]   Samuel Eliot Morison, Henry Steele Commager, and William E. Leuchtenburg, *A Concise History of the American Republic* (New York: Oxford University Press, 1977), 503.

[204]   Samuel Eliot Morison, *The Oxford History of the American People,* 815.

The Promise of Science

The Industrial Revolution was, of course, made possible by the development of scientific knowledge, especially the ability to access the energy in fossil fuels, either directly or via electricity. That energy, combined with new systems for using human labor, such as the assembly line, vastly increased manufacturing productivity. Frederick Turner analyzed those new methods of labor in a framework of "scientific management." Corporate success led to the belief that rationality could be applied to a broad range of areas, including free markets, culture, and even the family. This implied that political discipline could overlay or even supplant spontaneous order. The wisdom of science combined with the beneficence of government would ameliorate the conditions of the working man, whose life, while materialistically far better than it had been, was still difficult.

These ideas, however, were all sentiment and little science. Their supporters believed that one-size-fits-all government programs and government extraction and then redistribution of wealth could produce superior results to one in which men bought insurance and joined volunteer-societies.

Nonetheless, the new beliefs led numerous writers to the seemingly obvious idea that government could and should lead the way. These ideas and experiences did not exist when the U.S. Constitution was created, so many concluded that existing constraints on the federal government should be revisited in the light of scientific advances. Yet advances had occurred spontaneously through the workings of the extended order with minimal government intervention, so why precisely should more government now be required?

Utopian Thinking

Utopian thinking was not a new development; the desire to reorder society to benefit everyone was seen as early as Plato's *Republic* two and a half millennia ago. Chinese Emperors attempted to control all economic transactions for an abstract good; St. Thomas Aquinas's *The Summa Theologica* described a perfectly ordered, fair, hierarchical society as did Sir Thomas More's *Utopia* and Karl Marx's *Communist Manifesto*. The egalitarian order of the original Jamestown settlement; and any number of idealistic communes in England and the United States also implemented such ideals. It is fair to say that these sentiments are so universal to the human psyche that they will invariably occur to well-intentioned thinkers who lack an empirical grasp of the past. This is what Hayek termed a "fatal conceit." Because very bright people can imagine ordering society differently to reach well-intentioned goals, they want to reorder individual decisions that optimize one's life in alignment with neutral economic laws in favor of their own preferences. The key question, of course, is how utopian goals should be pursued. The widespread attraction of such ideas is a recurring lure for ambitious politicians.

It was no different in turn-of-the-century America. Unprecedented affluence encouraged greater attention to those seemingly left behind. The muckrakers and the Progressives generally turned public attention to the most visible areas of seeming deprivation, such as difficult working conditions, slum housing, and child labor. And, as will be discussed, this thinking led to a desire for wholesale reordering of political and economic life.

Examples from Abroad

American writers and politicians were also influenced by foreign examples of governments that chose to pursue activist roles. While federal forms of governments such as those of the United States and Switzerland had constitutional safeguards limiting such behavior, other parliamentary systems were less fettered; parliaments have much greater freedom of action because the legislature and executive branches are combined. Without the equivalent of an "enumerated powers" guardrail, government expansion that favors majority special interests at the cost of minority rights is inherently easier. Later chapters will demonstrate how this dynamic played out in the twentieth century. But below we will see how it got an early start in Germany and Britain in the latter half of the nineteenth century. These two examples were especially beguiling to the Progressives.

Germany

Even though it was less free than the Anglo-Saxon countries, under the Kaiser Germany did have a representative government in the form of the Reichstag. To be sure, unlike other parliaments, the Kaiser held military powers that led to trouble down the line. However, the Reichstag was very important in domestic affairs. The Chancellor (Bismarck at that time) had to work to maintain majority support for his priorities.

After the 1848 uprisings against the established order in numerous parts of Europe, Bismarck was haunted by fears of revolution and was especially apprehensive of the socialist program. He tried, unsuccessfully, to get the Reichstag to restrict the freedom of the press and to make inciting class warfare a punishable offense. In particular, he tried (but failed) to limit socialist and communist meetings and publications.

So, he chose another avenue to address his apprehensions and to maintain working-class support for his conservative party: He became the pioneer of the social state. This helped him forge electoral alliances with other parties, especially those that adhered to paternalistic tradition, e.g., the ones associated with Catholicism.

Over a decade, he introduced Europe's first comprehensive welfare system. In 1883, he passed an act providing medical treatment for three million workers and their families; in 1884, another provided benefits and grants to incapacitated workers. In 1886, seven million workers were given accident and illness insurance, and in 1889, all workers were given a graduated pension at the age of seventy. All these actions were financed by workers, employers, and the state.

However, even in Wilhelmine Germany, there was pushback by those who understood the FEO, even if only intuitively. The classically liberal *Freisinnige* Party firmly opposed state socialism on principle because this approach violated personal freedom and could be seen as a step towards an omnipotent state.[205]

Britain

During this era, similar electoral impulses and calculations were at work in the British Parliament. The government swung between Conservative and Liberal majorities, but both parties were aware of the growing power of the unions and an upstart Labor Party. Under Disraeli, the Conservatives looked for ways to keep workers' allegiance. His government gave working men the vote in 1867 and then passed acts dealing with artisans' dwelling-houses, public health, factory regulation, and trade unions. Public education was also made compulsory.[206]

But the major impetus toward social democracy began after 1906 in initiatives supported by the Liberal and Labor Parties. These included money set aside for pensions on a non-contributory basis; a Trade Boards Act designed to stop "sweated labor" and to fix minimum wages; and the National Insurance Act, which insured all working classes against sickness. According to David Thomson, "taken in bulk the liberal legislation of the period meant that the State had at least accepted it a duty to promote the welfare of its citizens at the common expense."[207]

PROMOTORS OF FUNDAMENTAL CHANGE

All these changes in the United States and abroad worked their way into popular political writing and the thinking of American leaders. Moreover, the successes earlier Progressives enjoyed by attacking corruption and cronyism in government helped shape a template for broad political activism addressing more general problems. These successes naturally led to a broader movement to

---

[205] William Carr, *A History of Germany 1815–1945* (London: Edward Arnold Ltd, 1969), 150, 152, 157-158.

[206] David Thomson, *England in the Nineteenth Century 1815–1914* (Great Britain: Penguin Books, 1979), 181.

[207] Ibid, 200-201.

transform the United States, articulated by intellectuals, academics, jurists, and popular writers, eventually to be translated into action by political leaders.

Academicians and Jurists

The theoretical foundations for these ideas were developed by academicians such as Woodrow Wilson (when he was at Princeton) and jurists such as Louis Brandeis.

Woodrow Wilson

As an academician at Princeton University, Woodrow Wilson explored a theory of government that propounded a retreat from constitutional principles in favor of openness to more activist-government. Wilson came to believe that the president could and should take the lead in addressing what were perceived as national problems. He believed that constitutional restraints were outdated. Moreover, in his view, the president was positioned to take whatever grand steps he pleased as long as he could get Congress to go along with him.

Well before he became president, Wilson wrote several books challenging the theoretical basis for the enumerated powers that the Constitution granted to Congress. In *Congressional Government,* published in 1885, he argued for a parliamentary system. Later, in *The State*, he proposed that government should not be considered evil and advocated the use of government to allay social ills and advance society's welfare, verging on a defense of socialism. He argued that the British form of parliamentary government was still evolving in a more fruitful direction at the time of the American Constitutional Convention and that, had we decided how to structure the federal government a few decades later, we might have chosen somewhat differently.

Specifically, he admired the emergence of unitary parliamentary power to act without meaningful checks by the sovereign. He observed that, once a parliament can appoint the ministers who lead governmental departments, it effectively becomes both legislature and executive. Thus, as a body, it reflects the will of the people through representatives and has an immediate administrative mechanism to implement policy.

He argued that these evolutionary changes in the powers of parliament were in keeping with emerging Darwinian Theory, implying that government (a quasi-living entity) could evolve and become fitter and more useful to the people. In that light, he viewed the U.S. Constitution as outmoded, even an unfortunate straitjacket. Further, Wilson believed that America's intricate system of checks and balances caused the problems in American governance – that is, they were somehow unnatural and mechanical rather than organic. In one regard,

Wilson wanted to follow the German proponents of administrative power who believed that expert commissions would improve society faster and better than a government hampered by individual rights and the separation of powers.[208]

He presents a comprehensive exposition of his views in *Constitutional Government in the United States*, writing:

> It is difficult to describe any single part of a great governmental system without describing the whole of it. Governments are living things and operate as organic wholes. Moreover, governments have their natural evolution and are one thing in one age, another in another. The makers of the Constitution constructed the federal government upon a theory of checks and balances which was meant to limit the operation of each part and to allow to no single part or organ of it a dominating force; but no government can be successfully conducted upon so mechanical a theory.[209]

This was a curious misapplication of evolutionary theory – surely government should not be considered an organic being separate from the society it serves; particularly not representative government. A better reading of evolutionary theory would have been that societal evolution moves in the direction of fitter ways to organize; as was the case of the Constitution as written. The genius reflected in that document had balanced dangers of potential autocracy on the one hand and unchecked democracy on the other. With good reason, the Founding Fathers believed they had designed a government that protected individual liberty against excesses.

Wilson evidently was carried away by a desire to draw a clever, scientific-sounding analogy. But allocating powers within government is not "mechanical." Certainly, the American model, in which Congress formulates legislation that reflects the needs and will of the people and the president carries out that legislation has nothing particularly mechanical about it. The real issue that Wilson overlooked was: What should the government do; how and why was that limited by the Constitution's enumerated powers?

Moreover, Wilson, without a real argument or an empirical foundation, attempted to evade the wisdom of the Constitution by suggesting that it had somehow failed to keep up with the times, which to be sure are always changing. But the Constitution was designed to deal with the nature of man – that is, that "men are not angels." It did not define specifics regarding economic progress or

---

[208]   Adam J. White, "Betraying the Constitution," *The Wall Street Journal*, June 30, 2014, A9.

[209]   Woodrow Wilson, *Constitutional Government in the United States* (New Brunswick: Transaction Publishers, 2004), 54.

the growth of science and industry. The nature of man had not changed, and it still needed to be checked by the institutions of government.

Mark Levin found Wilson's conclusions revealing: "Clearly, Wilson dismissed not only the Declaration of Independence and the Founders' announced purpose for American independence, but the Lockean exposition on natural law, the nature of man, the social compact establishing civil society, and the essential ingredients of constitutional republicanism …"[210]

Wilson desired an activist federal government that operated outside the traditional confines of the Constitution, but he did not see the need to go through the arduous process of convincing the American people and amending the Constitution. His solution was to dismiss the importance of that legal doctrine and convince Congress and the courts to ignore it. He stated, "The president is at liberty, both in law and conscience, to be as big a man as he can. His capacity will set the limit; and if Congress be overborne by him … it will be from no lack of constitutional powers … but only because the president has the nation behind him, and Congress does not."[211]

On the topic of legal checks on unconstitutional behavior, he argued:

> It is remembered that the courts are the instruments of the nation's growth, and that the way in which they serve that use will have much to do with the integrity of every national process. If they determine what powers are to be exercised under the Constitution, they by the same token determined also the adequacy of the Constitution in respect to the needs and interests of the nation; our conscience in matters of law and our opportunities in matters of politics are in their hands.[212]

The obvious downside of this approach is that it relies on the sentiments *du jour* rather than principle, and it does not require public approval for amendments to common law. However, in fairness to Wilson's views, he did still strongly adhere to key elements of the United States' constitutional construct, supporting the Bill of Rights and the federal structure that divided power between the states and the federal government. For example, on the supposed powers assigned in the Commerce Clause, he inquires:

> May it regulate the conditions of labor in field and factory? …
> Clearly not … for that would destroy all lines of division between
> the field of state legislation and the field of federal legislation.

---

[210] Mark R. Levin, *Ameritopia* (New York: Threshold Editions, 2012), 189.

[211] Woodrow Wilson, *Constitutional Government in the United States*, 70.

[212] Ibid,167.

> Back of the conditions of labor in the field and in the factory lie all the intimate matters of morals and domestic and business relationship which have always been recognized as the undisputed field of state law.[213]

It seems clear that Wilson was of several minds regarding the Constitution. Unfortunately, the Progressives focused on his desire for an activist government that ignored constitutional limitations and disregarded his support of the division of power between the states and the federal government.

Louis Brandeis

Some eminent jurists, such as Louis Brandeis, had similar views about the courts – that they should ignore their role of protecting the Constitution in favor of facilitating a more activist and beneficent government. In 1917, he wrote that judges needed to recognize the new realities of the modern economic era:

> ... there actually came, with the introduction of the factory system and the development of the business corporation, new dangers to liberty. ... The individual contract of service lost its character, because of the inequality in position between employer and employee. ... Courts continued to ignore newly arisen social needs. They applied complacently eighteenth-century conceptions of liberty of the individual and of the sacredness of private property. Early nineteenth-century scientific half-truths like "The survival of the fittest," which translated into practice meant "The devil take the hindmost," were erected by judicial sanction into moral law.[214]

This breathtaking argument was presented without a shred of empirical evidence. Richard Epstein presents some basic data to contradict Brandeis's position. During the thirty-year period around Brandeis' remarks, average hours worked per week in manufacturing declined from fifty-nine to fifty, while average wages per hour tripled. Life expectancy increased from forty-seven to sixty years. One key issue for Progressives was child labor. During this period, without any government intervention, child labor declined (because of increasing prosperity) from 6% to 1.4% of workers.[215]

---

[213] Ibid, 171.

[214] Louis D. Brandeis, "The Living Law," *Illinois Law Review* 10 (1917), 461, 463-64.

[215] Richard A. Epstein, *How Progressives Rewrote the Constitution* (Washington, DC: Cato Institute, 2006), 5-6.

Epstein argues for a more empirically realistic view of the economy, demonstrating that a deeper appreciation of Lockean philosophy addresses Brandeis's concerns without direct government intervention. He argues:

> The main behavior to be protected [by the courts] is the freedom to engage in market competition – to make offers to do business with others. The private voluntary contracts that result are positive-sum games for the parties to them, and whatever harm ordinary contracts of sale and hire wreak upon competitors (and it is a real harm, no doubt) is more than offset by the gains to the parties and to consumers. We are all systematically better off, therefore, in a regime in which all can enter and exit markets at will than in a social situation in which one person, armed with the monopoly power of government, can license or proscribe the actions of others.[216]

Nonetheless, progressive jurists such as Brandeis and later Felix Frankfurter gained influence with progressive political leaders – clearly because their ideas helped open the door to the politicians' transformative ambitions.

Popular Writers

As discusses earlier, the desire to help others through the aegis of government is a recurring theme in human history. The warm sentiment is too compelling and the concept too facile for many with philosophic bents to resist. Two such writers and thinkers became influential in the Progressive Era – Edward Bellamy and Herbert Croly.

Bellamy's enormously popular work *Looking Backward, 2000-1887* envisioned a utopian, co-operative industrial society without profit or money. The book's popularity led to the formation of hundreds of clubs dedicated to the nationalization of industries and natural resources.[217]

Another influential writer of this era was Herbert David Croly (January 23, 1869–May 17, 1930), who was regarded as an intellectual leader of the progressive movement because of his books and his role in founding and editing the magazine *The New Republic*. His political philosophy influenced many leading progressives, including Theodore Roosevelt and his close friends Judge Learned Hand and Supreme Court Justice Felix Frankfurter (who strongly influenced the New Deal a quarter of a century later).

---

[216]   Ibid, 15.

[217]   Samuel Eliot Morison, Henry Steele Commager, and William E. Leuchtenburg, *A Concise History of the American Republic*, 503.

Croly's book *The Promise of American Life* (1909) laid out a program of progressive change which (in his view) would remedy the problem of the U.S.'s relatively weak national institutions with a strong federal government. He described democracy not as a government devoted to equal rights but as one with the aim of "bestowing a share of the responsibility and the benefits, derived from political economic association, upon the whole community." In a subsequent book, *Progressive Democracy* (1914), Croly rejected the thesis that the liberal tradition in the United States was inhospitable to anti-capitalistic alternatives and argued that working for wages was a lesser form of liberty.

Croly argued that America's liberal promise could only be redeemed by syndicalist reforms increasing workplace democracy, which would, in turn, require significantly stronger unions. Furthermore, the government would have to nationalize large corporations and implement a strong central government. Importantly, he argued that protecting only "negative rights," an idea that underlay the U.S. Constitution, was no longer adequate.[218]

Here, in a highly popular form, at least among a growing intellectual class, was a full-bore assault on the classical liberalism embodied in the Constitution as well as on what this book terms the FEO. Subsequent decades (apart from the Roaring Twenties) would see a steady progression towards realizing many of Croly's ideas.

Political Leaders

Many of these beliefs influenced U.S. political leaders during the first half of the twentieth century, most notably Theodore Roosevelt, Woodrow Wilson, and Franklin Roosevelt.

Theodore Roosevelt

Initially, as a Republican, Theodore Roosevelt believed the federal government should be truly national. He believed that the Constitution's General Welfare Clause gave the government the authority to do anything for the good of the country that the states could not do individually.[219] A better reading of the clause is the simple requirement that anything Congress does should promote the *general* welfare and never that of a specially favored group; this clause should not be understood to justify any action that could be said to produce a positive outcome. Roosevelt's broader interpretation, which gained wide support, was part of a philosophically slippery slope leading to bigger government and evasion of the Constitution's limitation on government by the enumerated powers.

---

[218]   *Wikipedia*, March 2017, *Herbert Croly.*

[219]   Samuel Eliot Morison, *The Oxford History of the American People*, 817.

Be that as it may, Roosevelt's early vision did not encompass all progressive ambitions; it aimed at restricting monopolies and increasing competition rather than instituting large government programs. He intended, not to make the rich richer, but to give a "square deal" to farmers, laborers, and small businessmen.[220] Still, he considered these issues the business of the federal government. He said: "I believe in corporations, but I believe they should be so supervised and regulated that they shall act for the interest of the community as a whole."[221]

Later, as the candidate of the Bull Moose Party in 1912, Roosevelt envisioned a larger role for the federal government. He insisted that "the rich man holds his wealth subject to the general right of the community to regulate its business use as the public welfare requires, and urged that the police power of the state be broadened."[222] The Progressive Party's platform indicates his philosophic shift. As socialist Eugene Debs put it, "the red flag of socialism had been replaced by the red bandannas of the Progressives."[223]

President Woodrow Wilson

The discussion above showed how Woodrow Wilson the academician developed the analytical foundations for transforming the United States. As president, however, he pushed relatively few reforms through Congress, but three of these were significant. The first two were laid *constitutionally* with the passage of amendments enabling federal income tax and the direct election of senators. The third, which created the Federal Reserve Bank, was based on an early Supreme Court ruling (during the Federalist Era) that concluded that a central bank was compatible with the enumerated powers clause of the Constitution.

Income Tax

All philosophy aside, the reality was that most of the changes the Progressives envisioned required money – and therefore required greater power to tax. An income tax made everything possible. Earlier nineteenth-century legislative attempts to impose an income tax (not proportionate to the census)were rejected by the Supreme Court on constitutional grounds. So, Progressives rose to the occasion and passed the Sixteenth Amendment, which was ratified in 1913.

The political dynamic shifted as a matter of course. Not surprisingly, the

---

[220] Ibid.

[221] Alan Greenspan and Adrian Wooldridge. *Capitalism in America,* 183.

[222] Samuel Eliot Morison, Henry Steele Commager, and William E. Leuchtenburg, *A Concise History of the American Republic*, 527.

[223] Ibid, 529.

character of Congress changed as well. Before the twentieth century, on average, most congressmen served only a couple of terms. According to the Congressional Research Service, during the nineteenth century, the average service time of representatives and senators remained roughly constant, although the average years of service was slightly higher for the first half of the century than the second. However, during the Progressive Era from the late nineteenth through the twentieth century, senators' average years of service steadily increased, from an average of just under five years in the early 1880s to a recent average of just over thirteen years. Similarly, representatives' average years of service increased from just over four years in the first two Congresses of the twentieth century to an average of approximately ten years in the three most recent Congresses.

In the twentieth century, Congress became more of a career path, with most congressmen attempting to stay in office for multiple terms. As more money became available and more of the economy open for meddling, the job got much more interesting; senior members of Congress serving on key committees became much more powerful.

Direct Election of Senators

The Seventeenth Amendment, also ratified in 1913, provided for the direct election of senators by the people rather than by the state legislatures. The change was considered consistent with a purer form of democracy. However, it also changed, if only subtly, the power of the states in the federal system. State legislatures were displaced by parties, as can be seen in the current era: States under the control of one party may elect senators of the opposing party such that state interests are not comparably represented in the Senate.

The Federal Reserve Bank

As discussed earlier, the country had experienced seemingly regular financial panics over the years – as had other countries. The one of 1907 was termed the "bankers panic" since its causes were determined to be, not the usual overleveraging of businesses and banks, "but a ruinous shortage of currency and inelasticity of credit. Only by hasty importations of gold from abroad and by resort to extra-legal forms of currency was business able to weather the crisis."[224] To deal with these kinds of crises, it became generally agreed that a national banking system of some sort was necessary. The Federal Reserve Act of 1913 created such a national system; all national banks were required to join regional banks, and

---

[224]   Samuel Eliot Morison, Henry Steele Commager, and William E. Leuchtenburg, *A Concise History of the American Republic*, 533.

state banks were permitted to join. In addition, the law authorized a new type of currency, Federal Reserve notes, designed to develop more elastic credit.[225]

Even though this move provided strong measures to prevent financial crises, those alone were no guarantee of success. Indeed, the Bank failed to address the country's needs at the onset of the Great Depression. Moreover, it later helped the government overspend by facilitating borrowing. As such, it became part of an arsenal to promote progressive ambitions. Its ability to create money led to a century of inflation; the purchasing power of a 2013 dollar was comparable to only five cents in 1913 dollars. That inflation, as some economists have noted, can be regarded as a hidden tax on society; savings were inexorably diminished in the service of income redistribution.

Franklin Roosevelt

Early on, Franklin Delano Roosevelt had similar views as Wilson regarding the Constitution's limits on federal power. Even during the Roaring Twenties, a time of rapidly growing prosperity under President Coolidge, in a 1926 address, "Whither Bound?" Roosevelt lamented the power of conservatives to thwart utopian programs espoused by liberals or radicals.[226] Roosevelt's subsequent presidency showed that he adhered to Wilson's belief that anything was constitutional if the president could convince Congress to go along.[227]

*　　*　　*

So, we have seen how the country's modernization led academics, writers, and political leaders to question the purposes and role of government. Even so, the protections of the Constitution remained intact for decades. What key legal

---

[225]　Ibid.

[226]　Mark R. Levin, *Ameritopia*, 199.

[227]　His early embrace of the progressive mindset was revealed more fully years later in his 1944 State of the Union speech, when he argued that "[n]ecessitous men are not free men." His mind free of constitutional limits, Roosevelt's logic led him to conclude that broad government intervention was needed to achieve his utopian goal of economic security. Specifically, he called for "a second Bill of Rights under which a new basis of security and prosperity can be established for all – regardless of station, race, or creed. Among these are: The right to a useful and remunerative job in the industries or shops or farms or mines of the nation; to earn enough to provide adequate food and clothing and recreation; of every farmer to raise and sell his products at a return which will give him and his family a decent living; of every businessman, large and small, to trade in an atmosphere of freedom from unfair competition and domination from monopolies at home or abroad; of every family to a decent home; to adequate medical care and the opportunity to achieve and enjoy good health; to adequate protection from the economic fears of old age, sickness, accident, and unemployment; and to a good education."

advances helped Progressives undermine those protections? How did the Supreme Court fail in its duty of protecting that Constitution?

REALIZATION OF THE PROGRESSIVE VISION

Despite the intellectual ferment and political agitation described above, the country went about its business and enjoyed unprecedented growth during the Roaring Twenties. However, all that was required for a renewed Progressive push was a popular trigger. This trigger took shape in the Great Depression, an opportunity for which Franklin Roosevelt's New Deal was ready and waiting.

Actions by Republican President Hoover and the Federal Reserve had inadvertently paved the way. In principle, there was little reason to believe that the downturn that began with the stock market crash of 1929 wouldn't be as short and self-correcting as the recession of 1919 had been. Indeed, within a year of the crash, the market and the economy had turned the corner. But a horrendous mix of political miscalculations ensued. Hoover, always predisposed to be a 'man of action,' got the ball rolling with the passage of the Smoot-Hawley tariffs and huge tax increases – both ill-considered and deeply harmful. Although all academic theory (David Ricardo) demonstrated the benefits of a comparative advantage in trade, the notion of protecting jobs by limiting imports was seductive. The hard reality was that high tariffs against foreign goods meant in turn, that foreign countries were not able to buy our goods. Moreover, other countries retaliated. After Smoot-Hawley, all global trade reduced sharply, to everyone's detriment.

However, the greater push to an unprecedented financial crisis can be traced to policies of the Federal Reserve Bank. It had sharply reduced the country's monetary base; the money supply contracted by 33% between 1929 and 1933 (to be followed by another fall in 1937-1938).[228] This contraction, in turn, induced substantial deflation: borrowers were increasingly unable to repay debts, which became evident in bank failures, mortgage foreclosures, and personal and corporate bankruptcies. Moreover, the Federal Reserve failed to be a lender of last resort to banks that were sound but illiquid to prevent their bankruptcies and thus avoid further shrinkage of the monetary base. Under such deflationary circumstances, an economy can only return to equilibrium and full employment if wages and prices are allowed to fall to match the reduced money supply. Neither of those things was about to happen under a New Deal government.

Recall from Chapter One that the Lockean principles of personal liberty and protection of property embrace the unarticulated wisdom underlying the FEO. Several features flow from these principles: limited government, low taxes, low

---

[228] James D. Gwartney et al., *Economics, Private and Public Choice* (South-Western Cengage Learning, 2008), 695.

governmental spending, and limited access for the government to intrude into the workings of the markets. The New Deal would stand all those principles on their heads, instituting high spending, high taxation, and monopolistic behavior through cartel-like rules and unionization.

At the onset of the Great Depression, the Constitution was intact; none of Hoover's actions departed from constitutional constraints. FDR, however, was far more ambitious to deploy unprecedented and unconstitutional means to bring the country out of the Depression as well as to pursue long-held progressive ambitions along the lines of Britain's and Germany's social insurance. For these greater ambitions to be realized, the enumerated powers of Congress had to be subverted somehow. Even Wilson's attachment to the federal system reserving most economic regulation to the states had to go.

In hindsight, it is clear that a new generation of political men came to power without an appreciation of the deeper wisdom of liberty and a free economy. They were driven by what Hayek termed a "fatal conceit" in their efforts to reorganize political and economic matters to their liking. They believed they could use government fiat to manage the forces of supply and demand to create jobs, reduce unemployment, raise prices for farmers, and reduce foreclosures and bankruptcies across the land. They passed a law or a regulation to attempt each of these outcomes directly without ever understanding how the pieces would come together.

So, for example, their efforts to mandate higher wages – through the minimum wage, by prohibiting wage reductions, or through aggressive unionization –actually reduced the demand for labor, keeping unemployment high. Attempts to stabilize high prices to benefit farmers and manufacturers reduced consumer demand.

As Richard Epstein notes, government actions to control prices and manage markets had all the earmarks of the creation of cartels to favor certain subgroups in society. Epstein comments:

> [Progressives'] tunnel vision let them focus their attention exclusively on the beneficiaries of their programs, be they union members or farmers, while taking no note of the adverse effects that their programs had on the parties excluded from the market or forced to pay the higher prices that the government policies maintained.[229] ... The workers whom the Progressives reflexively supported on matters of employment suffered under the agricultural regimes imposed to benefit dairy and wheat farmers, just as the farmers suffered from the legal regime that

---

[229]   Ibid, 72.

the Progressives adopted for labor unions. Neither error cancels
out the other. Rather, the two errors compound each other.[230]

Major intrusions into the economy included programs that raised taxes,
implemented Keynesian principles in government spending, aggressively favoring
unions over employers in a quasi-monopolistic fashion, and promoting national
social insurance schemes.

Regulating the Economy

Virtually all these initiatives required circumventing the Constitution's
enumerated powers of Congress. This time, however, amendments to the
Constitution were not considered. Notable specifics included the National
Industrial Recovery Act (NIRA) and the Agricultural Adjustment Administration
(AAA).

NIRA: The NIRA had ambitious goals: to drive prices up and to put
people back to work. It established the Public Works Administration to increase
government spending to spur the overall economy (very Keynesian), and it created
new labor rights based on the belief that better-paid workers will spend more
and thereby strengthen the economy. The most ambitious part of the Act was the
creation of the National Recovery Administration, which aimed to coordinate
whole industries and labor to reduce economic inefficiencies. The underlying
assumptions were that bigger is better and that industry, labor, and government
should work together to maximize productivity and efficiency. Business
representatives from each industry were invited to Washington to set production
quotas, prices, wages, working hours, distribution methods, and other mandates.
Firms that did not comply were fined, and in some cases, the owners were jailed.[231]
Prior to this, collusive behavior of this kind would have been prosecuted under
antitrust laws. The NIRA reduced competition, promoted monopoly-pricing, and
undermined the market process.

Broadly speaking, the NIRA authorized the government to curtail supply
with the aim of driving up prices. In addition, the terms of employment of some
twenty-two million workers were affected by its 557 basic codes. Of course, there
were unintended consequences. The forces of supply and demand in the context
of a reduced money supply reduced consumption as they reduced employment.
As will be discussed below, eventually, the constitutionality of the NIRA was
successfully challenged. However, before that happened, it had a disastrous
impact on the economy: Industrial production fell sharply – about 25% by the

---

[230]   Ibid, 74.

[231]   Ibid, 691.

end of 1933.[232] And while the country never again tried to create industrial cartels, the idea that the government could meddle with aspects of the economy remained.

AAA: While the NIRA dealt with industry, the Agricultural Adjustment Administration was created to address perceived problems in the farming sector. Here too, agriculture suffered from the deflationary impact of the Federal Reserve's monetary policy; in 1933, agricultural prices were only 40% of their 1926 levels. Because they failed to understand the true cause of the problem, the Administration was determined to use government fiat to increase farmers' purchasing power by artificially reducing supply. It did so by restricting the acreage that could be farmed and by slaughtering livestock by the millions (in 1933 alone, six million baby pigs were slaughtered and kept out of the market). Under price controls, the AAA attempted to keep the domestic price of wheat at $1.16 per bushel when the world price was $0.40.[233] This could only be achieved by major government intrusion in the market, which primarily involved limiting the amount of crops farmers could grow. In one instance, the government fined a farmer for producing wheat for his own use (to feed livestock). The farmer protested and the case made it all the way to the Supreme Court, which (incredibly) ruled in favor of the government.[234] However, in 1936, the Court ruled that the AAA as a whole was unconstitutional.

As summarized by Jay Weiser:

> In the economically illiterate hope that raising prices would increase incomes and restore prosperity, the New Deal cartelized agriculture. Landowners raked in subsidies for taking land out of production and destroying crops and livestock, which threw huge numbers of agricultural laborers, tenant farmers, and sharecroppers out of work, and made food and clothing more expensive.[235]

The New Deal had launched a major intervention in the economy to re-engineer free market price signals to its liking – i.e. to keep commodity prices and wages high to benefit workers and farmers and supposedly to reduce unemployment. These distortions of price signals, of course, could not be successful. Supply and demand were out of line, causing other participants in the economy to suffer. Industrial production plummeted by 25%, businesses and farms failed, and unemployment stayed high.

---

[232] Ibid.

[233] Richard A. Epstein, *How Progressives Rewrote the Constitution*, 66

[234] Ibid, 68.

[235] Jay Weiser, "Image of a Decade," *The Weekly Standard*, May 29, 2017.

According to Epstein:

> [Progressive legislation embodies] the unspoken but persistent preference for government monopolies over private competition… the various Agricultural Adjustment Acts … the manifold restrictions on labor markets running through the 1914 Clayton Act, the 1926 Railway Labor Act, the 1935 National Labor Relations Act, and the 1938 Fair Standards Act. They are all designed to restrict free entry and to empower certain preferred groups to gain monopoly profits in their relative market niches.[236]

Social Security

The economically most intrusive of the above programs eventually vanished due to court rulings or ineffectiveness. Nonetheless, other high-priority New Deal programs made it through. The most prominent of which was Social Security. For decades, Progressives had been eager to introduce government social insurance in the United States.

Social Security, or Old-Age, Survivors, and Disability Insurance (OASDI) was enacted in 1935 during Roosevelt's first term. That and the current amended version of the Act encompass several social welfare and social insurance programs funded by payroll taxes called the Federal Insurance Contributions Act Tax (FICA) and/or the Self-Employed Contributions Act Tax (SECA).

Roosevelt was influenced by and drew on the thinking of Progressives, notably Columbia University Professor Henry Rogers Seager, who wrote *Social Insurance: A Program of Social Reform* in 1910. Seager admired the compulsory programs instituted in the United Kingdom and believed that key features of those programs should be adopted in the United States through vigorous government action. However, he recognized that the American temper would resist such an approach, stating, "Only by a change of attitude and a change of heart on the part of the whole people can we hope to curb our rampant individualism and achieve those common ends which we all admit to be desirable but which are not attainable through our united efforts."[237] In other words, individuals should no longer buy their own insurance and engage in cooperative efforts; instead, a quasi-government monopoly should be instituted.

During the Great Depression, even though there was a natural demand for public assistance of various kinds, there was little call for compulsory old-age

---

[236] Richard A. Epstein, *The Classical Liberal Constitution* (Cambridge: Harvard University Press, 2014), 578.

[237] Mark R. Levin, *Ameritopia*, 226-227.

insurance. But Roosevelt recognized that people would feel a vested ownership in such a program once they had contributed taxes to it. Roosevelt has been quoted as saying, "With those taxes in there, no damn politician can ever scrap my social security program."[238] Still, Social Security was only passed through subterfuge involving cross-subsidies and inadequate pay-as-you-go financing that principally benefited the early beneficiaries.

Chapter Five will describe in more detail how embedded financial problems snowballed into the modern era. However, the central issue was that Social Security was sold to the public as an insurance system in which individual contributions are paid into a trust fund from which the individual earns future payments according to a formula. In fact, there is no fund of money; the trust only contains IOUs, and the formula for future payments was calculated politically and not by sound actuarial calculations. The system is simply pay-as-you-go: Current workers pay into the system and retirees make withdrawals from it. If the population of paying workers fails to grow quickly enough, more money will be withdrawn than paid in, stressing the overall national budget.

"Stimulative" Spending

In addition to the above efforts, the government attempted to stimulate the economy with spending along lines that would eventually be termed Keynesian. The intent was to help alleviate the immediate pain of widespread unemployment and to jumpstart economic activity in areas where the private sector was moribund. Two of the politically most visible efforts were the Works Projects Administration (WPA) and the Tennessee Valley Authority (TVA). These efforts were unprecedented for government, but still modest compared to modern-era spending.

The **Works Progress Administration** (renamed the **Work Projects Administration** or **WPA** in 1939) was the largest and most ambitious American New Deal agency. The stated goal of its public building programs was to end the Depression, or at least alleviate its worst effects, by providing millions with subsistence incomes. It employed millions of mostly unskilled men to carry out public works projects, reaching a peak employment of 3,334,594 people in November 1938. Its projects included constructing public buildings and roads, but also, much more modestly, employing musicians, artists, writers, actors, and directors in large arts, drama, media, and literacy projects.

The agency constructed a new park, bridge, or school in almost every community in the United States. The WPA's initial appropriation (in 1935) was $4.9 billion (about 6.7% of that year's GDP). Total expenditures on WPA projects through June 1941 totaled approximately $11.4 billion..[239]

---

[238]　Ibid, 230.

[239]　*Wikipedia.* "Works Progress Administration", accessed 9/14/2019.

The **Tennessee Valley Authority (TVA)** was a large-scale, highly visible effort to boost economic development in Appalachia, one of the most economically depressed regions of the United States. The corporation was created by congressional charter on May 18, 1933 to provide navigation, flood control, electricity generation, fertilizer manufacturing, and economic development to the Tennessee Valley. The centerpiece was low-cost electricity supplied by the TVA's network of twenty-nine hydropower facilities. That lower cost benefitted consumers and attracted new industry. However, this low cost was underwritten by government capital and the TVA's freedom from taxes. Its competition with private utilities drove a number of them into bankruptcy.

The question as to whether such an intrusion into the private sector was within the enumerated powers of Congress made its way to the Supreme Court in Ashwander vs. Tennessee Valley Authority, 297 U.S. 288 (1936). The Court ruled in the affirmative on the grounds that regulating commerce among the states includes regulating streams and that controlling floods is required to keep streams navigable. It was argued that electricity generation was a *by-product* of navigation and flood control and therefore could be considered constitutional. In his dissent, Justice McReynolds stated, "We should consider the truth of the petitioners' charge that while pretending to act within their powers to improve navigation, the United States through corporate agencies, are really seeking to accomplish what they have no right to undertake – the business of developing, distributing, and selling electric power." The case was really about whether government could "destroy every public service corporation within the confines of the United States."[240]

Ironically, while the government increased its spending to stimulate the economy, it simultaneously shrank the economy through higher taxes. Economic orthodoxy at the time aimed at achieving balanced budgets, though in retrospect we realize that such actions are counterproductive during a deflationary and contracting economy. To be sure, it was the Republican Hoover Administration, assisted by a newly elected Democratic Congress, that passed the largest tax increase in the country's history in 1932: Overall taxes were increased by 150% in one year, and the highest marginal rates from 25% to 63%. As a result, real output fell by 13% in one year, and unemployment[241] rose from 15.9% to 23.6%. In 1936, the Roosevelt Administration compounded this error by raising the top rate to 79%. Effectively, big investors could keep only twenty-one cents of each additional dollar they earned, which reduced business investments. Phil Gramm and Michael Solon summarize:

---

[240] Amity Schlaes, *The Forgotten Man: A New History of the Great Depression*, 271.

[241] James D. Gwartney et al., *Economics, Private and Public Choice*, 690.

As government assumed greater control, private investment collapsed, averaging only 40% of the 1929 level for nine consecutive years. League of Nations data show that by 1938, in five of six most-developed countries in the world industrial production was on average 23% above 1929 levels, but in the U.S., it was still down by 10%. Employment in five of the six major developed countries averaged 12% above the pre-Depression levels while the U.S. employment was still down by 20%. Before the Great Depression, real per capita GDP in the U.S. was about 25% larger than it was in Britain. By 1938, real per capita GDP in Britain was slightly higher than in the U.S.[242]

In the end, the New Deal efforts to artificially stimulate the economy came to little. Well into Roosevelt's second term in office, Treasury Secretary Henry Morgenthau, Jr. wrote in his diary, "We have tried spending money. We have spent more than we have ever spent before and it does not work ... We have never made good on our promises ... I say after eight years of this Administration we have just as much unemployment as when we started ... and an enormous debt to boot!"[243]

At no time during the eight years of the Great Depression did unemployment fall below 14%. It took the Second World War and a massive draft to reduce unemployment. According to a 2004 study by UCLA economists Harold L. Cole and Lee E. Ohanian, Roosevelt's policies extended the Depression by seven years. This study notes the obvious: During an economic slump, high wages and high prices run counter to the market's self-correcting forces.[244]

Roosevelt undoubtedly gained his reputation for ending high unemployment as a consequence of the Second World War. Of course drafting some sixteen million persons into the armed forces (comparable to around thirty million today) virtually eliminated unemployment. But this is hardly a possible solution for a peacetime economy in which workers want to be paid for their efforts with civilian goods and services.

*　*　*

Thus, in defiance of the Constitution, the New Deal launched an array of programs to reshape the economy. Meanwhile, where was the Supreme Court?

242　Phil Gramm and Michael Solon, "Why This Recovery is So Lousy," *The Wall Street Journal*, August 4, 2016, A11.

243　Mark R. Levin, *Liberty and Tyranny: A Conservative Manifesto* (New York: Threshold Editions, 2009), 87-88.

244　Ibid, 88-89.

THE SUPREME COURT

Recall from the previous chapter that the Constitution tasked the Supreme Court with protecting the powers and intent of the Constitution. In the *Federalist Papers*, Hamilton described the importance of an independent judiciary for maintaining the efficacy of the Constitution. Its duty is "to declare all acts contrary to the manifest tenor of the Constitution void. ... No legislative act, therefore, contrary to the Constitution, can be valid. ... A constitution is, in fact, and must be regarded by the judges, as a fundamental law."[245]

The Constitution was a Whig-inspired document designed to protect liberty, private property, and freedom of contract from the incursions of an overbearing state. Richard Epstein argues that the old Supreme Court (prior to the progressive assault) interpreted the Constitution along the lines of classical liberalism, balancing appropriate demands of the state against individual property rights. Government can use the power of eminent domain, but only for public use and with just compensation; regulation is permissible without compensation when it addresses the public health, safety, morals, or general welfare.[246]

The decisions of previous Courts upheld the liberty of the individual to pursue ambitions in the marketplace in ways congruent with the FEO. The government has a duty to free individuals to engage in market competition – to offer to do business with others, protected from fraud and the use of force.[247] Also, by the late nineteenth century, the Court supported government actions against monopolies in industries "affected with the public interest."

That tradition would have looked askance at usurped government authority to supersede free competition with government fiats that set prices and wages, to favor one class of economic actors over another, and to create quasi-governmental monopolies in key areas of the economy. So, for the New Deal's policies and programs to prevail, it would need to overturn both Supreme Court precedent and interpretations of the Constitution itself. To do so, it had to ignore the clear reading of the enumerated powers provision through a vague interpretation of the Commerce Clause.

The Commerce Clause (Article I, section 8, clause 3) empowered Congress to regulate commerce among the several states and with foreign nations – or, in a modern context, to establish a common market among the states. At that time, commerce referred to the economic transport of goods. The Constitutional Convention wanted to create a large common market that individual states could not undermine with parochial interests; it also sought to empower the new government to impose tariffs and embargos on foreign countries when necessary.

---

[245]   *Federalist Paper* no. 78.

[246]   Richard A. Epstein, *How Progressives Rewrote the Constitution. x.*

[247]   Ibid, 15.

The Convention had no intent to extend this authority to everything involved in manufacture and commerce, such as industry, agriculture, and labor, much less to more distant issues such as wages, prices, maximum hours, and unionization. We saw earlier that Wilson shared this view.

However, the New Deal and subsequent Courts chose a different interpretation. Overnight, the federal government gained the authority to regulate everything in the economy. Let's examine how the Court arrived at this position – the opinion that the interconnectedness of all aspects of the economy required equally broad regulation to implement the desired transformation of the country. In addition, growing wealth inequality was believed to justify overriding constitutionally protected rights of liberty, property, and contract.[248]

In 1935, the Supreme Court still defended constitutional principles. In a blow for private property rights, it overruled the Frazier-Lemke Act, which had limited banks' ability to repossess property. More dramatic and more significant was its unanimous decision in the Schechter case, which involved the application of the NIRA to a local poultry business in Brooklyn. The Court's decision rejected the authority of the NIRA; Justice Hughes stated that "defendants do not sell poultry in interstate commerce... Extraordinary conditions may call for extraordinary remedies. But the argument necessarily stops short of an attempt to justify action which lies outside the sphere of constitutional authority. Extraordinary conditions do not create or enlarge constitutional power."[249] This seemed to be a decisive moment. Afterward, Justice Brandeis told representatives of the president, "This is the end of this business of centralization, and I want you to go back and tell the president that we are not going to let this government centralize everything. It's come to an end."[250]

If only that had been true!

While this was the death knell for the NIRA, in just a few years, Roosevelt and progressive forces routed efforts to rein in federal authority. The goals the president laid out in his second Inaugural Address were undiminished in ambition. In this speech, he stated that men and women in the American republic would insist that every agency of popular government (including the Supreme Court) use effective instruments to carry out their will. Shortly thereafter, he announced his plan to simply ask Congress to increase the number of justices from nine to a figure as high as fifteen. For each justice who stayed on the court past the age of seventy, a new one would be added.[251] This was popularly known as Roosevelt's attempt to "pack the Court." The legislation was deeply unpopular and ultimately failed to pass Congress. Nonetheless, the president succeeded in intimidating

---

[248]   Ibid, 8.

[249]   Amity Shlaes, *The Forgotten Man*, 242.

[250]   Ibid, 243.

[251]   Ibid, 302.

the justices. And it was evident that, as justices retired, new judges who shared Roosevelt's views would be appointed. It was just a matter of time before the Supreme Court's defense of the Constitution crumbled.

By 1937, the shift was underway. In March, the Court supported Washington State's minimum wage law; whereas only ten months earlier it had struck down New York State's minimum wage law. Even the previous autumn it had refused to rehear the case.[252] Next, also in 1937, the Court ruled to uphold a National Labor Relations Act against a challenge that it lay outside the scope of Congress' federal powers to regulate interstate commerce. Epstein noted sarcastically that the Court's 1935 view of the reach of the Commerce Clause seemed to no longer meet modern conditions in 1937.[253]

While conflict over the government's role in the economy would continue, the Supreme Court's position had changed decisively by 1937. Epstein writes:

> But the 1936 term was distinctive in that it put to rest all the ongoing debates over federalism and individual rights that had raged in earlier years. The New Deal Court thus vindicated both expansive federal powers and limited protection of individual rights of liberty and property against both federal and state regulation.[254]

The federal government had usurped the role of the states and of private, voluntary action.

OVERALL ASSESSMENT

The Great Depression was a decade-long human tragedy, made unnecessarily long and severe by misguided government action. There was plenty of blame to go around: Hoover's policies, the Republican Congress, the New Deal (a Democratic President and a Democratic Congress), and the actions of the Federal Reserve Bank. Contrary to popular belief, the Depression was not caused by the stock market crash. The United States has had many similar crashes before and since, none of which had such dire consequences. Indeed, the stock market was snapping back in 1930 until misguided government programs such as the Smoot-Hawley Tariffs, tax increases, and inappropriate Federal Reserve policies led to the high levels of prolonged unemployment that characterized the Great Depression. There

---

[252]   Ibid, 308.

[253]   Richard A. Epstein, *How Progressives Rewrote the Constitution*, 66.

[254]   Ibid, 2.

is little reason to suppose that a policy like the one followed during the 1919 recession would not also have allowed the economy to self-correct.

One might argue that the whole Depression was simply the result of a series of well-intentioned errors. That approach, however, overlooks the opportunity for a deep learning experience. These errors were not random; they resulted from a deeply flawed worldview of liberty and the workings of the FEO. The Progressives saw the Depression as an opportunity to change the constitutional order to realize their utopian vision. In only two presidential terms, the Constitution ceased to offer effective protection of economic liberty and property.

The Progressives offered a Faustian bargain of the kind Madison feared; they offered Americans a mess of porridge in exchange for their birthright. Rather than a constitutional right to pursue happiness – to make the most of our innate talents and energy in life – we were to look to the larger community and the government for these things. The obvious negatives were dismissed: bureaucracy's inefficiency and risk averseness and the human tendency to freeload when possible, surely leading to high opportunity costs and unintended consequences.

Richard Epstein describes the main thrust of the progressive attack on the constitutional order as follows:

> Progressives attacked the two doctrines that most limited the scope of government power – federalism, on the one hand, and the protection of individual liberty and private property on the other. ... However grandly their rhetoric spoke about the need for sensible government intervention in response to changed conditions, the bottom line, sadly, was always the same: replace competitive processes, by hook or by crook, with state-run cartels.[255]

Indeed, some of the major progressive achievements became government-run cartels, including social security, Medicare, and public schooling. In recent decades, reforms have attempted to provide real competition to these cartel-like government programs: defined contribution retirement pensions through IRAs, medical savings accounts, and school vouchers – and all of these have been viciously attacked by progressive forces.

Setting aside the human costs of those policies for a moment, had the country learned the lessons of the Depression – that is, which policies work and which do not – Progressives' good intentions could be viewed more charitably. However, conventional wisdom (abetted by the U.S. educational system) teaches that Roosevelt heroically brought the nation out of the Depression, while the Harding

---

[255]   Richard A. Epstein, *How Progressives Rewrote the Constitution*, 52.

Administration is chiefly known for the Teapot Dome scandal and Coolidge for being a do-nothing president.

Moreover, the groundwork was laid for the continued erosion of the Constitution and weakening of the FEO. If the country had followed constitutional principles, it would have exited the Depression years earlier. The human cost would have been much less, and the nation would have avoided a plethora of additional programs that later led to a threat of insolvency. Indeed, the following decades saw the country doubling down on the failures of the New Deal. An overview of the costs will be presented in the next chapter.

CHAPTER 5

COSTLY GOOD INTENTIONS

"At root, the classical view of American constitutionalism examined all legal interventions under a presumption of error." – Richard A. Epstein[256]

"Every great cause begins as a movement, becomes a business, and eventually degenerates into a racket." – Eric Hoffer[257]

The abandonment of the constitutional protections described in the previous chapter unleashed behavior that has already cost us dearly and threatens to undermine future fiscal viability. It is essential to explain in detail how the federal government went down this path in order to understand the principles involved.

To that end, several points should be reiterated. First, the U.S. Constitution reflected lessons about mankind in government that had been learned over centuries. It implemented these lessons by granting the federal government only the powers that were essential to a strong country or that only the federal government could perform. At that point, history and knowledge of human nature made these conclusions compelling to Americans and others as well. For example, such a rationale also informed the Swiss, who created a national confederation around the same time granting their central government only the powers that could not be adequately performed by the cantons.

The inescapable reality is that a government with unlimited power to tax and unlimited power to dispense that money to electoral claimants faces little in the way of braking mechanisms to ward off improvidence. The U.S. Constitution as

---

[256]   Richard A. Epstein, *The Classical Liberal Constitution – The Uncertain Quest for Limited Government* (Cambridge, Massachusetts: Harvard University Press, 2014), 5.

[257]   Eric Hoffer, *The Temper of Our Time* (1967)

first written incorporates two effective brakes: the enumerated powers clause and the limitations on direct taxation. This clause simply did not permit the federal government to engage in unnecessary and ultimately highly problematic behavior. Before the Sixteenth Amendment was passed, the federal government could only tax individuals directly based on their presence in the census. In practice, this forbade progressive taxation and ensured that everyone would have to pay their own way. When *everyone* must pay their share, the electorate views spending and tax proposals with a more critical eye.

The prior chapter described the philosophical and political progressive forces that led to the abandonment of constitutional constraints. The chapter also showed how good intentions became the ingrained default condition of U.S. governance. To give the devil his due, this was all done for seemingly the best of reasons. Indeed, the chief uncertainties that have haunted man throughout history – bad health and old age – were now made the government's responsibility.

Why was this a bad thing? Is the adoption of a new form of government more than an academic consideration? After all, does it matter if social functions aren't optimally performed? As Adam Smith opined, there is a lot of ruin in every society. This can be seen as a cost of collective action; perfection is never a possibility, and some waste can facilitate social peace.

However, abandoning constitutional provisions accomplished nothing that could not have been done better by a combination of individual-effort and private cooperative systems. In the discussion that follows, keep two things in mind: Adam Smith's teaching about the light hand of government and Buchanan's criterion that state activity is justified only to remove external diseconomies that prevent individuals from accomplishing objectives through voluntary contractual relations with others. In the end, limited government is better for all concerned and does not endanger fiscal solvency, slow economic growth, or undermine personal self-sufficiency. A government that takes responsibility for tasks it is not suited to is not only less creative and more prone to value politics over empirical reality than the private sector, but also prone to one-size-fits-all approaches that limit competition. Without competition, everything becomes a racket; there is little real accountability for results when politics subvert fiscal discipline. To be sure, the populace is grounded in fiscal reality, and most programs include a façade of fiscal responsibility. But it is half-hearted; it leaves the door open to political meddling and is ultimately less than fully effective.

After the New Deal was passed, no aspect of human existence was protected from governmental interference, and the country had no shield against spiraling fiscal improvidence. To make that clear, this chapter will examine major governmental programs in the United States: Social Security, Medicare, Medicaid, student loans, and housing subsidies. The chapter will also examine other major progressive intrusions into the economy – education, housing, and general regulation of all sorts. These intrusions have vast present and future costs, betray their supposed purposes, reduce social capital, and generally smother the efficient workings of the FEO.

As in most things, the devil is in the details. This chapter will identify the intrinsic flaws of each program – indeed, the unavoidable shortfalls in most government programs – while indicating sustainable, free-market alternatives that would offer better returns and more stability. To help assess future prospects and dangers, this chapter will also tally these programs' contributions to growing economic instability.

A BASELINE OF INDIVIDUAL RESPONSIBILITY

To critique the shortfalls of the modern social democratic state, it is appropriate to consider other options to anticipate the question: compared to what? Must the federal government assume comprehensive social responsibilities for men's critical needs truly to be met?

What does history teach on this topic? We can intuit(as much as we might hope otherwise) that there are no free goods; the average person should not expect to receive more from the government than he contributes (and perhaps less after the bureaucratic state takes its share). Yet, to escape that siren song, we need confidence in an individual's ability to manage his or her own affairs in the modern world.

Empirical experience suggests that individuals are indeed capable of this. The histories of Britain and the United States contain numerous examples of individuals who met their own needs for pensions, healthcare, and education through collective non-governmental programs, in far poorer times than the present. Specifically, David Green's[258] research documents Britain's "friendly societies," which were the most important providers of social welfare during the nineteenth and early twentieth centuries.[259] One study found that, as early as 1801, there were about 7,200 friendly societies with around 648,000 adult male members in Britain. By 1911, when the national government passed the National Insurance Act, which quickly displaced the private initiatives, at least nine million individuals were already covered by voluntary insurance associations (primarily the friendly societies), and membership growth had been accelerating.[260]

These were not philanthropic organizations; they were mutual aid societies to

---

[258]   Founder and Director of Civitas, an institute for the study of civil society based in London. Palmer drew his work: David Green, *The Rediscovery of Welfare Without Politics* (London: Civitas, 2000).

[259]   Tom G. Palmer, ed., *After the Welfare State* (Ottawa, IL: Jameson Books, Inc., 2012), 55.

[260]   Ibid, 56-57.

which workers made regular contributions; they were then eligible for assistance when circumstances justified. The societies were managed by the participants, and peer pressure was an important tool for ensuring that members did not abuse the system.

A similar voluntary mutual aid system arose in the United States, as documented by David Beito.[261] He writes that, by 1920, eighteen million Americans belonged to fraternal societies; this amounted to about 30% of adults. During the late nineteenth and early twentieth centuries, many large orders built orphanages and old-age homes for members and their spouses.[262] Before the Depression, fraternal organizations dominated the health insurance market and effectively employed peer pressure to reduce participants' moral hazard.[263]

Mutual aid societies were also common and effective among immigrants and African-Americans. According to Beito, in the South, the "the total membership of the negro societies paying and non-paying, [was] nearly equal to the total church membership." For example, just one African-American order signed up over 30% of all African-Americans in the South. Other lodges provided a wide range of mutual aid services, including medical insurance, orphanages, employment bureaus, and homes for the aged. It has been estimated that in Chicago in 1919, African-Americans were the most insured ethnic group.[264]

The New York Commission on Old-Age Security estimated that 43% of elderly New York residents were self-supporting due to gainful employment, pensions, and savings and other forms of income, while families and friends supported another 50%. Less than 4% relied on public or private charity.[265]

To be sure, these programs were less universal than modern entitlement programs. But it was a far less affluent time, and there is no inherent reason why individual initiative and self-interest could not have enabled the programs to keep pace with growing prosperity. Moreover, these types of programs would likely have been far more cost-effective than the current state model due to their superior ability to minimize moral hazard.

This history of mutual aid societies illustrates the extended order of human cooperation at work. Without government intervention, entrepreneurs and individuals will seek each other out to get needs met. Also, when the goal is preserving individual liberty, these are precisely the areas in which individuals are freer and more likely to get their unique needs met through voluntary collaboration

---

[261]   Professor of history at the University of Alabama, Tuscaloosa. Palmer drew his work in *Critical Review*, Vol. 4, No.4 (1990), 709-736.

[262]   Palmer, *After the Welfare State*, 69.

[263]   Ibid, 72.

[264]   Ibid, 75-76.

[265]   Ibid, 71.

with others than by ceding their freedom of action to a bureaucratic central government.

Still, maintaining individual control entailed a high degree of personal responsibility. This is not universally realizable; many will make bad decisions or decisions that turn out badly in the absence of paternalistic governmental oversight. Moreover, many will fail to make any decision and eventually become a burden on the remainder of society. Nonetheless, as the experiences of other countries will demonstrate in later chapters, these concerns can be addressed without undue government intervention and without quasi-monopolistic governmental enterprises.

Moreover, once the demand for fiscal prudence is transferred from the individual to the government, there are no obvious ways to make key economic tradeoffs among the chief material and service needs such as consumption, healthcare, old age, education, and housing. Then every session of Congress becomes a tussle to politically decide how much of these things the country requires. In the long run, there is little political accountability for bad decisions. Since the government can borrow and has wide latitude not to make economic tradeoffs, the debates always demand more spending for the children, the poor, the old, and so forth.

These are not just economic matters; they are questions of liberty and of how we lead our lives. A common denominator among the major entitlement programs is, as Mark Levin put it, "politicians establishing permanent societal changes by using the law to seize the individual's sovereignty and transfer control to the administrative state."[266] Progressives urged these changes to create a utopian version of society in place of the Lockean version bequeathed by the Constitution.

A review of the specifics of major programs will show how they diverged from economic reality and the arguments used to support them. This review will demonstrate that these programs are not actuarially sound, that they fail to attain their stated goals, and that there are obvious alternatives that would be superior and would better align with the FEO.

SOCIAL SECURITY

This section, like the following reviews of other social programs, will demonstrate that Social Security was created in the Progressive template, in thrall to politics rather than economics, which is a prescription for failure.

---

[266]   Mark R. Levin, *Ameritopia: The Unmaking of America* (New York: Threshold Editions, 2012), 235.

Origins

Despite a tradition in which most individuals saved their own money to provide for themselves in old age, along with investing in private insurance or other cooperative efforts, politicians saw an opportunity to address human insecurity while making workers dependent on the state and thereby sympathetic to a given political party. As discussed in the previous chapter, the first national initiative giving the government these responsibilities was undertaken in Germany under Bismarck, the "Iron Chancellor." He pioneered the social-welfare state through a series of compulsory insurance schemes for accidents, health, disability, and old age that were enacted in the 1880s. Even though he was a staunch conservative, he justified his programs, which he termed "State Socialism," on grounds of political expediency. He stated, "Whoever has a pension for his old age is far more content and far easier to handle than one who has no such prospect."[267]Similar considerations influenced Franklin Roosevelt when he promoted the Social Security program in the United States.

As discussed in the previous chapter, Roosevelt could draw on the thinking of U.S. Progressives, notably Columbia University Professor Henry Rogers Seager, who admired the British experience, but realized that American sensibilities were far different. He particularly desired the populace to curb "rampant individualism".[268]

This illustrates an intellectual sleight of hand popular with Progressives and pervasive in present-day political discourse. It juxtaposes individualism with 'the common good,' implying that individualists are selfish and run roughshod over the rest of the community. However, who really disputes that everyone necessarily relies on the larger community and must cooperate in various fashions. The question is why that reliance should be implemented through a central government rather than through the marketplace in the form of insurances or other voluntary collaborative efforts such as churches, mutual societies, and the like.

Despite progressive drumbeating, little movement in this direction occurred until the New Deal. Even during the Great Depression, when there was a natural demand for various kinds of public assistance, there was little call for compulsory old-age insurance. Nonetheless, this idea fit the New Deal utopian vision, and it seemed like good politics. Unfortunately, such motivations were not likely to create a program that made economic sense; as a rule of thumb, once decision-making is removed from the individual maximizing his options in the FEO, economics take a back seat.

Had the New Deal pursued its vision via free markets with some mix of compulsory IRAs or annuities that were actuarially sound, the economic impact

---

[267]   Tom G. Palmer, ed., *After the Welfare State*, 35.

[268]   Mark R. Levin, *Ameritopia*, 226-227.

would have been minimal, but such a plan would have lacked the political payoff Roosevelt expected. Professor Charlotte A. Twight wrote, "Social Security's history unfolded as a montage of political transaction-cost manipulation that included governmental use of insurance imagery, instrumentalism, cost concealment, information control and censorship, suppression of rival programs, and a myth of actuarial balance."[269]

Structure

The Old-Age, Survivors, and Disability Insurance (OASDI) program, the original Social Security, was enacted in 1935. That and the current amended version of the Act encompass several social welfare and social insurance programs.

Initially, the program appeared modest: It instituted a 1% tax on incomes up to three thousand dollars a year paid by employees and an additional 1% paid by employers, for a total of sixty dollars per year. Early on, few questions arose about sustainability; the system was pay-as-you-go, and even as late as 1950, sixteen workers were paying into the program for every retiree withdrawing. But this early light taxation was the camel's nose under the tent. Vote buying would ensure that the program expanded beyond its early design to eventually become unaffordable:

- 1935: The thirty-seven-page Social Security Act was signed on August 14, 1935.
- 1950: Benefits increased, and cost of living adjustments (COLAs) were made at irregular intervals; a 77% COLA was made in 1950.
- 1954: A disability program was added to Social Security.
- 1961: The early retirement age was lowered to sixty-two (with reduced benefits).
- 1965: Medicare healthcare benefits were added to Social Security – twenty million joined in three years.
- 1975: Automatic COLAS were mandated.

In few ways was this an insurance program. It was not actuarially assured, there were cross-subsidies – lower-income groups were subsidized by middle- and higher-income groups and individuals neither owned their contributions nor were guaranteed a formula-based pension since Congress could alter the payout formula at will. Furthermore, the accounts could not be left to heirs.

---

[269]   Ibid, 228, referring to Charlotte A. Twight, *Dependent on DC: The Rise of Federal Control over the Lives of Ordinary Americans* (New York: Palgrave, 2002), 62.

Not Insurance and Not Actuarially Sound

Social Security was sold to the public as an *insurance* system in which an individual's contributions are paid into a trust fund from which the individual earns future payments based on actuarial considerations. The problem is that no actual fund is generating income to pay the promised benefits. Workers' payments go into the general fund, and the government establishes a formula to determine how much should be paid out of that fund.[270]

The system is simply pay-as-you-go: Current workers pay into the system and retirees withdraw from it. If the government misjudges future working populations, GDP growth rates, inflation, or changes in longevity, it is unlikely that they will accurately judge future funds flows over many decades. This rosy scenario works only for a while. The bottom line, however, is that once the worker population fails to grow fast enough, revenue will fail to keep up with payments. In reality, the mismatch was dramatic. In its early days, the program's popularity grew because of a generosity that could only be achieved through subterfuge involving cross-subsidies and inadequate pay-as-you-go financing. But empirical reality, as it must, caught up.

Structural Flaws Emerge

The program has been actuarially unsound since its beginning, but by the time the problems became apparent, the politicians who created it were long gone. As the number of workers fell in proportion to retirees and with additional benefits promised, the pay-as-you-go system became increasingly unviable. The date when the 'trust fund' would be depleted loomed ever closer.

When did economic reality assert itself? In 1975, 1976, and 1977, the program ran deficits and projected that its reserves would be exhausted by the 1980s. In response, Congress enacted a large tax increase. That was not enough; within a decade, it was clear that the problem had not been fixed. Congress then passed new reforms in 1983, increasing the age of eligibility for benefits and increasing the payroll tax. Each time it moved to save Social Security, the government predicted future financial stability;[271] each time they were wrong. Today, the country still

---

[270] Social Security is funded through payroll taxes called the Federal Insurance Contributions Act Tax (FICA) and/or the Self-Employed Contributions Act Tax (SECA). Tax deposits are collected by the Internal Revenue Service (IRS) and are formally entrusted to the Federal Old-Age and Survivors Insurance Trust Fund, the Federal Disability Insurance Trust Fund, the Federal Hospital Insurance Trust Fund, or the Federal Supplementary Medical Insurance Trust Fund, which together comprise the Social Security Trust Funds. Disability insurance (DI) taxes of 1.4% are included in the OASDI rate of 6.2% for workers and employers or 12.4% for the self-employed.

[271] Michael Tanner, *Going for Broke* (Washington, DC: Cato Institute, 2015), 65.

faces a huge unfunded entitlement problem. In 2019, the Social Security tax on income rose to 12.4% for incomes up to $132,900. Adjusted for inflation, this represents an 800% increase from the original beguilingly modest maximum of sixty dollars. And the program is still not economically viable, as seen in the most recent projections.

Unfunded Entitlement Becomes Huge

In 2013, all Social Security programs except the retirement trust fund (OASDI) were already spending more than they brought in and were forced to make significant withdrawals from their respective trust funds to pay their bills.[272] The retirement (OASDI) trust fund reserves of $2.9 trillion (at the end of 2018) are expected to be depleted by 2035.[273] By law, when the trust funds have completely exhausted their assets, payments must be reduced to match the taxes paid by workers at that time (a projected reduction of about 23%).

Politically, of course, this will never be allowed to happen. Congress will explore all avenues to avoid cutting benefits. It may simply authorize the funds out of general revenues. This would ignore the original financial structure of Social Security and would squeeze funding for the myriad legitimate functions of government and/or lead to increased borrowing or higher taxation. That is the reality of the future's "unfunded entitlement" crisis – unaffordable promises that are not supported by anticipated funding. Currently, Social Security's unfunded obligations amount to $24.9 trillion (more than the total U.S. GDP).

Better Alternatives

As an insurance scheme, Social Security was wishful thinking. Now, there is virtually no politically acceptable way to raise payroll taxes to keep the program's payout promises. Of course, the shortfall may be made up by general revenues, but that is hardly insurance. The best solution going forward is to make the retirement system actuarially sound using financial mechanisms that should have been used from the beginning – assuming, of course, that the government should have gotten involved at all. Any system should be economically self-regulating and should not rely on the political decision-making of Congress to determine payouts.

---

[272] Total Social Security expenditures in 2013 were $1,360 billion dollars, representing 8.4% of GNP of $16,200 billion (2013) and 37.0% of total federal expenditures, which were $3,684 billion (including a $971.0 billion deficit). All other parts of the Social Security program – Medicare (HI), disability (DI) and Supplemental Medical (SMI) – are already withdrawing from their trust funds and are projected to go into deficit in about 2020 if the present rates of withdrawals continue.

[273] Social Security and Medicare Boards of Trustees, *Summary of the 2019 Annual Reports.*

A logical alternative would be Individual Retirement Accounts – a contributory but not fixed-benefit system. The funds could be invested in stocks or government bonds. While the stock portion could and almost surely would be exposed to market volatility, assuming forty years of working, even worst-case scenarios (based on past history) show workers better off than they are with present-day Social Security.[274] Moreover, the government's budget would not be exposed, and the stock portion of the funds would make capital available for investment in the productive economy. In addition, workers would own their accounts and would be able to pass those assets down to their heirs.

Reform?

One might think that, given the failures of the past and the dire prognosis for the future, the people would be clamoring for reform – but no. Roosevelt recognized that once people have contributed taxes to such a program they feel a sense of ownership in the program.

Although it offers an inferior financial deal for most recipients (except the poor since the benefits are skewed to lower incomes) and despite the projected shortfalls, the program is widely popular. Retirees depend on Social Security for a substantial portion of their income: 46% of married couples and 65.5% of unmarried persons over sixty-five receive more than half of their income from Social Security. Indeed, 42% of unmarried retirees rely on it for at least 90% of their income.[275]

No wonder that Social Security reform is considered the "third rail" of American politics. The elderly certainly won't countenance the removal of these benefits. Of course, a workable answer to the problem would be to maintain the program for all current beneficiaries and to give younger workers the choice of paying into Social Security or IRAs. This approach has been successful in other countries, such as Chile, which implemented such a plan to address a comparable problem. However, Chile did not implement these reforms until confronted with a major financial crisis. That may have to be the trigger for reform in the United States as well.

The United States did not need a federally administered Social Security system, and now that it has become dangerously entrenched, it will be hard to get rid of it. Other countries, including Singapore, Chile, Sweden, and Denmark, have moved away from government-funded pension entitlements to defined contribution investment accounts (IRAs).[276] Over time, these accounts have

---

[274]   Ibid, 77.

[275]   Ibid, 62.

[276]   James Bartholomew, *The Welfare of Nations* (Washington, DC: Cato Institute, 2016), 239-241.

provided higher benefits and become popular. Equally important, these changes have been implemented without the political drama that periodically emerges in the United States when such changes are proposed.

The inherent financial flaws in Social Security are also evident in virtually all the government's entitlement programs. As mentioned above, the unfunded future tab for Social Security alone is around $25 trillion. The other programs discussed below will add to that amount many times over.

HEALTHCARE

Healthcare is all too likely to become a critical service at some point in an individual's life, and it is often so expensive that it can threaten personal bankruptcy. So, it's only natural that people are acutely sensitive to the healthcare system and its financing; their elected representatives are attuned to that sensitivity. However, people are just as sensitive to the danger of losing their homes to fire, so they purchase actuarially sound fire insurance. Why should healthcare be different?

In the United States, the Progressives found vulnerability to medical expenses a potent source of votes, so they proceeded to create programs that further cemented the government's role as the (apparent) protector of the people. They have managed to promote this social vision even though there is little reason to believe that personal insurance, free-market solutions, and cooperative efforts can't meet those needs without heavy federal government intrusion. Yes, some safety net would be needed for those with low incomes, but that could be provided by states and local communities. If the central government is determined to get involved, as with Social Security, it should be via sustainable, actuarially-sound means.

As this chapter has already argued, politics cause any process to tend to over-promise and underpay, to implement ineffective oversight and cost control, and eventually to become unsustainable. The government thinks it can manage markets better than the FEO; the folly of this belief is evident in the unfunded entitlements for Medicare, Medicaid, and Obamacare, which dwarf those of Social Security.

The First Inadvertent Intrusion

The first major federal intrusion into national healthcare was inadvertent and had little to do with healthcare itself. During the Second World War, the government imposed stringent wage controls. Since industry and commerce still had to compete fiercely for workers and could not offer higher wages, they began to offer fringe benefits instead. These had monetary value but did not count as wages and were not taxed. Chief among these was health insurance. Over time, these benefits had substantial after-tax value and would be unaffordable for the average person (not receiving them via employment). Moreover, the insurance was not portable; if a worker lost their job, they lost the insurance.

A second shortcoming (which started out small but then grew) was that health fringe benefits morphed into prepaid healthcare rather than *insurance* against unaffordable calamities. Health insurance began to function less like other insurances such as house or automobile insurance. The cost of insurance policies rose accordingly, pricing many individuals out of the market outside states that allowed pure catastrophic insurance, which many states did not and still do not.

After the war, perhaps in the 1950s or 1960s, a sensible government would have evened the playing field by making all health fringe benefits taxable or by enabling all individuals to make all individual health payments tax free. But, instead, the government chose to develop more and more intrusive healthcare programs.

The Progressives would have preferred for the United States to adopt a single-payer system such as those in the United Kingdom and Canada; in such systems, individuals pay the government and the government runs most of the healthcare system. This has always been seen as one step too far in the United States, so the Left chose to move incrementally (using "salami" tactics, one small slice at a time).

The Federal Government Moves

In 1960, Congress passed the Kerr-Mills Act, which created a needs-based medical program designed to assist the *aged poor*. One might reasonably argue that this program did meet an unacceptable gap in an increasingly affluent society and did not represent a major federal intrusion into healthcare economics. It certainly did not come close to realizing the Progressive dream. That opportunity came just a few years later when Lyndon Johnson was re-elected in a landslide and progressive forces dominated both houses of Congress. In 1965, Congress passed and Johnson signed legislation creating the far more ambitious programs of Medicare and Medicaid.

Medicare

Medicare was poorly conceived from the outset; it was imagined as a "first-dollar" insurance plan that would define benefits and create a bureaucracy to determine payments. It was an open door for non-cost-conscious consumption, for light oversight, for fraud, and for inflexible bureaucracy. A signal of its disregard for economics came early. When Medicare was created in 1965, government actuaries estimated that the cost of Medicare A (the hospital portion) would amount to nine billion dollars by 1990. In fact, it was seven times higher – sixty-seven billion dollars.[277] More examples of this will be presented later: The Congressional Budget Office, in seemingly a congenitally-flawed fashion, frequently underestimates the cost of the Left's social programs (and underestimates the benefits of the tax reform favored by the Right).

By departing from the economy's natural supply and demand balance, these programs created much more demand for services in ways that stimulated an inexorable rise in healthcare costs that far exceeded inflation. Arguably, participants had greater access to healthcare without the threat of financial distress, which was the purpose of the exercise. However, they stopped acting as consumers since they could view the service as an essentially free good without considering their frequency of use or the price of services.

In 1970, as Medicare began ramping up, total spending on healthcare as a percentage of GDP was about 7%. By 2011, it had reached 17% ($2.7 trillion). There is evidence that this sharp rise in prices occurred because the government made healthcare a 'right' that was subject to government subsidies and price setting. In areas, however, where free markets operated, the constant-dollar prices of non-essential, elective services that are not covered by Medicare, such as LASIK, cosmetic surgery, and pet care, fell steadily during this period.[278]

Moreover, Medicare enabled the government to set prices by limiting reimbursement rates for doctors and hospitals. Given the convoluted ways of establishing prices and methods of cost reimbursement, it has become very difficult for individuals to comparison-shop for healthcare services. Healthcare policy analyst Avik Roy wrote:

> Price transparency seems like the kind of thing that everyone should be able to rally around. But you would be wrong. Pretty much everyone in the health-care world – other than the patient – has an interest in keeping prices opaque ... Most doctors and hospitals would rather not post their prices... Insurers don't like price transparency, because they view the rates they negotiate with hospitals and doctors as proprietary trade secrets that give them an advantage over their competitors.[279]

---

[277] Ibid, 51.

[278] Robert Sirico, *Defending the Free Market, The Moral Case for a Free Economy* (Washington, DC: Regnery Publishing, Inc., 2012), 134-135.

[279] Kevin D. Williamson, *The End is Near and it's Going to be Awesome* (New York: Broadside Books, an imprint of Harper Collins Publishers, 2013), 125.

To be sure, the United States enjoys the most advanced healthcare services in the world. But the funding mechanisms made less and less sense, and total spending was becoming unaffordable. In 2010, the CBO estimated that Medicare's unfunded obligations are twenty-five trillion dollars.[280] As of 2019, the Social Security and Medicare Boards of Trustees reported that the HI Trust Fund (Medicare Part A) will be depleted in 2026.[281]

Rather than address financing pragmatically, Congress chose to double down on dysfunctional government expansion into healthcare. When Democrats once again took the presidency and both houses of Congress, they enacted Obamacare. Polls regularly showed that the American people did not support a government takeover of healthcare. The vast majority was satisfied with its insurance programs and healthcare services, but it seemed this was of little consequence when weighed against the Progressive ambitions of the president and House Speaker/Nancy Pelosi. Demonstrably false arguments were employed, particularly claims that forty-seven million Americans lacked health insurance and therefore medical care. This was nonsense. It is true that, in 2006, the Census Bureau reported that 46.6 million residents in the United States had no insurance. However, 9.5 million of these were not citizens, seventeen million lived in households with incomes exceeding $50,000 a year (and could presumably purchase insurance), and eighteen million were between the ages of 18 and 34. Most of these were in good health and *chose* not to purchase insurance. Moreover, at that time, about 50% of the non-elderly population who lost insurance regained it within four months.[282]

Given the lack of popular enthusiasm, the president found it politically necessary to dissemble to Americans, promising that this legislation would reduce healthcare costs for individuals and for the country as a whole, and that individuals would be able to retain the policies and the doctors of their choice (since they obviously liked what they had).

Affordable Care Act

The Affordable Care Act (aka Obamacare) approach to government policy attempts to place healthcare, which represents one-sixth of the U.S. economy, into a regulatory straitjacket. It requires all individuals to have health insurance; it mandates the minimum coverages[283] included in health insurance; it requires businesses of a certain size to provide insurance to employees (or pay a fine); it sets up health review panels to identify cost-effective treatments to be covered by

---

[280] Mark R. Levin, *Ameritopia*, 232.

[281] Social Security and Medicare Boards of Trustees, *A Summary of the 2019 Annual Reports.*

[282] Mark R. Levin, *Liberty and Tyranny: A Conservative Manifesto* (New York: Threshold Editions, 2009), 107.

[283]

insurance; and it sets limits on the amounts some doctors will be reimbursed. One analysis of the legislation by Peter Ferrara of the Heartland Institute estimates that the legislation establishes more than 150 new bureaucracies, agencies, boards, commissions, and programs that "are empowered to tell doctors and hospitals what is quality healthcare and what is not, what are best practices in medicine, how their medical practices should be structured, and what they will be paid and when."[284] In a country that has the best research institutes and medical schools in the world and during a time of rapid change, such bureaucratic arrogance is mind numbing.

The legislation also enables price distortions. It provides for massive government subsidies to those with average or below-average incomes while requiring the young and healthy to substantially subsidize the old. Thus, policies that subsidized others became more expensive through premiums and added high deductibles, a poor deal for the young and healthy. Many chose to pay the statutory penalty rather than buy into poor-return policies.

This program will ultimately add substantially to government deficits. When the legislation was passed, a Congressional Budget Office estimated that projected costs would not contribute significantly to the budget deficit. However, this estimate was misleading as it relied on procedures that allowed the analysis to count ten years of contributions to be offset by only six years of costs.[285] A more realistic analysis shows that Obamacare will add trillions of dollars to the U.S. deficit in the long term.

At the end of the day, the root of the problem is the government's attempt to make healthcare an entitlement rather than part of a free economy in which individuals make tradeoffs for economic needs and respond to free market price signals.

Other Options

A more sensible approach would be to make health insurance more like *insurance* rather than prepaid healthcare; in other words, to model it after home owner insurance and to include significant deductibles. This would vastly reduce administrative expenses, make fraud much easier to detect, and encourage patients to be much more careful consumers. In other words, individuals should cover all routine expenses and only use insurance for catastrophic losses. Experience has shown that catastrophic health insurance can be affordable (perversely, many states don't allow it to be sold alone). Moreover, competition should be built in to the system as much as possible. For example, the government could provide vouchers as a benefit to allow healthcare consumers to shop around for the insurance that best meets their needs while keeping insurance programs competitive.

---

[284]   Ibid, 238.

[285]   Michael Tanner. *Going for Broke*,(Washington, DC: Cato Institute, 2015) 141.

As an example of an approach involving true insurance and market competition, George Shultz cites Singapore:

> [It] has required health savings accounts and price transparency since 1984, and even the poor who get government support are motivated to spend carefully. According to World Bank figures, the total public and private spending on healthcare in Singapore is 4.7% of their GDP compared with 17.9% in the U.S. The outcomes and healthcare facilities in Singapore are among the best in the world. ... Finally, we should encourage public and private neighborhood health clinics, which are spreading rapidly and can dispense healthcare inexpensively.[286]

Or the United States should be contrasted with Germany another, perhaps more comparable, Western country, which spends 11.3% of its GDP on healthcare, far less than we do.[287] As discussed earlier, Germany led the way in a central government nationalization of health insurance. But like Switzerland, much insurance is in private hands, with healthy competition and is actuarially sound. In particular, Germany does not suffer from an ineffective bureaucracy with responsibility divided between federal and state entities that do a poor job in pricing and in monitoring costs. Most importantly, as a result there are no trillion-dollar unfunded future entitlements. The Krankenkassen (the health insurance entities) are obliged to maintain financial reserves; in 2017 the German system had an Euro18 billion surplus.[288]

In the U.S., financial reality will make fundamental change inevitable. According to the 2014 *Annual Report of the Boards of Trustees of the Federal Hospital Insurance and Federal Supplementary Medical Insurance Trust Funds*, Medicare reported shortfalls that year in Parts A, B, and D that amounted to $274.9 billion. These funds are projected to continue to pay out more in benefits than they collect in taxes by relying on past surpluses in the Medicare Trust Fund to cover the shortfalls. It is projected that the surplus will be exhausted by about 2030.[289] Long-term forecasts show a total of $47.6 trillion in unfunded liabilities. More troubling, if the reforms in reimbursement rates envisioned in those projections are not implemented, the liabilities could be significantly higher.[290]

---

[286] George P. Shultz, "How to Get America Moving Again," *The Wall Street Journal*, August 9-10, 2014, A11.

[287] James Bartholomew, *The Welfare of Nations*), 66.

[288] *Wikipedia, Healthcare in Germany.*

[289] Michael Tanner, *Going for Broke* (Washington, DC: Cato Institute, 2015), 90-91.

[290] Ibid, 96.

Medicaid

Medicaid is included in this discussion not because it is a badly designed federal intrusion into insurance like Social Security and Medicare, but because it is a badly designed form of social welfare that adds to the huge unfunded entitlement crisis ahead. In reality, it is a means-tested welfare program financed jointly by the federal and state governments. It was created in 1965 to provide medical assistance to eligible needy persons: the elderly, the disabled, and poor children and their parents. The federal government provides a substantial part of the financing and a set of national guidelines. The states set eligibility standards, determine the services to be provided, and set payment rates for providers.[291]

The program can well be regarded as part of the "safety net" society should provide for those unable to provide for themselves. However, is this the best way to achieve those ends? Ultimately, unaffordable costs and poor outcomes suggest otherwise. The more the government strays from realistic economic incentives that help control costs, the more unnecessarily costly a program will become – especially under the pressure of politics.

For example, over time, Medicaid eligibility expanded from truly needy, well-defined populations to include others based on income thresholds, transforming the program from welfare to income redistribution. This change was announced with the creation of Obamacare, making all individuals with incomes below 138% of the poverty level eligible for Medicaid. This is clearly a far cry from the initial limited purpose of a safety net and represents a major intrusion into what was the domain of private insurance; this move also made the program a greater burden on federal and state budgets.[292]

All the problems of politically constructed programs shielded from competitive market forces manifest in Medicaid: poor outcomes, poor-quality care, inaccurate payments, and fraud. Medicaid beneficiaries have poorer health outcomes than those with private insurance: A University of Virginia study found that Medicaid patients are 13% more likely to die than those with no insurance at all and 97% more likely to die than those with private insurance.[293] These outcomes can be traced in part to the shift from insurance to bureaucratic regulation and price setting. States reimburse doctors below market rates and require onerous paperwork; as a result, a significant number of physicians refuse to accept Medicaid patients.[294]

In addition, the government cannot detect and control waste and fraud as

---

[291]   Michael Tanner, *Going for Broke*, 115.

[292]   Ibid, 118-120.

[293]   Ibid, 126.

[294]   Ibid, 125.

well as private insurance companies – it simply doesn't have the same financial incentives. The states administer the program, but the federal government pays for most of it, so the administering states bear few of the costs and capture little of savings that would follow from more rigorous administration. The Inspector General of the Department of Health and Human Services said, "Everywhere it looks the Office of Inspector General continues to find fraud." A Harvard study estimated that improper payments could amount to eighty-five billion dollars a year.[295]

While Medicaid is not among the "unfunded entitlements" described above, projected obligations associated with the program will add considerable uncertainty to the country's precarious financial future. In 1970, total federal and state spending on Medicaid was only $5.1 billion. By 2014, it was more than $430 billion.[296] This will grow substantially as more states buy into Obamacare. So, what was originally a welfare program for fourteen million people in 1970 had metastasized to enroll fifty-eight million in 2014 and is on course to grow further still.[297]

This is surely a case of unbridled political good intentions at full throttle!

*　　*　　*

So, one can see that American politics abuse public programs to promise more social entitlements than the government can afford. This occurs largely because of utopian sentiment, belief in the beneficence of government, and a departure from the discipline of competitive market forces.

EDUCATION

The field of education – primary, secondary, and post-secondary –is another area where utopian sentiment has run amok, both in financial terms and in failed pedagogical ambitions.

Public education occurs on the local level where spending levels in light of other community needs and educational results can be best evaluated. Why should the federal government play a role in local education at all? Proponents argue that students in lower-income communities will be shortchanged. Yet there is ample evidence that some states spend relatively less on education but perform better than the richest states. It's not the money; it's how you do it. Moreover, there is little evidence that the federal government knows more about education simply

---

[295]   Ibid, 127.

[296]   Ibid,118.

[297]   Ibid.

because it is bigger. Schools everywhere have access to best practices through schools of education and national associations.

Nonetheless, in 1979, the federal government created a Department of Education. The initiative was all sentiment; there is precious little evidence that national bureaucrats have more insight into pedagogy and research than educational practitioners. But since they held the purse strings, they were given the opportunity to attempt to establish national standards, to push for national excellence.

Perversely, the demand created by the insertion of federal spending has allowed the cost of education to the students themselves to expand much faster than inflation, distorting educational programs and burdening students with loans to trouble their future while adding to the country's debt. With all that government spending, citizens could expect to see the consumer costs of education decline, especially because of the new possibilities afforded by the computer age. However, the current educational model shows no signs of lower costs or improved results; indeed, the opposite is true.

This section will show how a progressive, utopian approach in the field of education has contributed substantially to the country's coming economic predicament without providing any evident benefits. The following sections offer an alternative model that aligns with the FEO in contrast to the problematic progressive vision.

An FEO Model for Education

The importance of education is self-evident in virtually all modern societies, whether developed or developing. Enhanced social capital contributes to society by increasing productivity, and it is in the interests of the general population. This reality is so compelling that people will find a way, with or without government. Indeed, two centuries ago, before the British government took over education in 1880 by making education compulsory, 95% of fifteen-year-olds were already literate thanks to voluntary education provided by families, churches, charities, and the private sector – that is, due to spontaneous development within the FEO.[298]

Matt Ridley relates several examples of contemporary spontaneous order in modern Africa and India. Three of these (in Africa) were reported by James Tooley. In Ghana, a teacher built a school with four branches. He taught 3,400 children and charged fifty dollars a term but provided scholarships to those who couldn't afford it. Tooley reports that Somaliland had two private schools for every state one. In Lagos, where government officials and representatives of aid agencies all but denied the existence of low-cost private schools, 75% of children in fact attended such private schools. The poor spent 5% to 10% of their earnings

---

[298]   Matt Ridley, *The Evolution of Everything: How New Ideas Emerge* (New York: Harper Collins Publishers, 2015), 177.

to educate their children.[299] In Hyderabad, India, Ridley found an association of five hundred private schools that catered to the poor, who paid the equivalent of about one English pound a month. Free State schools were available, but the quality of the private schools was clearly superior.[300]

The lesson here is that parents *will* educate their children and *will* seek out the best alternatives available to them. Competition produces excellence and reform.

What compelling reason is there to distort a spontaneous system in which individuals' needs are met? One leading argument is that the government's formidable taxing powers can ensure that educational resources are available to all –that no child need be left behind. This, however, begs the question of how government's resources can best be used to achieve that end. For example, indirect alternatives that do not involve government monopolies, such as vouchers, can also help ensure this end. When confronting the shortfalls of the government system, rationally, we should strive to use public funding to harness the extended order rather than displace it.

That has not been the way of much of the world; virtually all modern societies have taken the route of public schooling run by the government. Since no money is without strings, governments invariably establish standards and means of accountability; the outcome is ubiquitous local school boards along with federal and state regulations. Over time, these have produced conventional, politically-correct curricula, value conflicts, lawsuits, unruly classrooms, and innovation-stifling, unionized teachers. Rather than harnessing innovation, flexibility, personal competence, and ambition, the system produces lockstep results and slows innovation.

The sad reality in the United States is that, in education as in Social Security and healthcare, the government has placed itself in a role that it does not perform well.

In a representative government, however, such sub-par performance does not continue for long unless someone is benefitting from it – someone politically powerful. The biggest beneficiaries of the current model of public education, of course, are the unions, which obtain high pay, high pensions, expensive health insurance, and job tenure for their members. They collect dues from their members so as to help elect the officials that determine these benefits. In the field of education, we can clearly see how noble sentiments have eventually become a racket in one of great causes foreseen by Hoffer.

This section will consider how poor the educational outcomes have been in primary and higher education and how this contributes to problems in our financial future.

---

[299]   Ibid, 182-183.

[300]   Ibid, 181.

Primary and Secondary Education

In some areas, especially within cities, primary and secondary education in the United States has become a disgrace. At vast expense, it has shortchanged the young; in many ways reducing rather than enhancing social capital. Moreover, the iron grip of unions is endangering the future financial stability of many states because of inadequately funded future pension liabilities. This section will argue that none of the shortfalls would occur under a public regime of free choice and competition.

The following section will explore the background to this picture: the explosion of costs, the macro-failures in light of the system's own goals, the obvious indicators of failures within the schools themselves, and the simple (but politically challenging) ways to remedy the situation.

High Expenditures, Poor Results

The United States devotes a considerable share of its income to education: in 2017-2018, all institutions spent some $1.4 trillion; in 2015-2016 state and local governments spent a total of $985 billion; and the federal government in 2017 budgeted $228 billion.[301] In 2015, the United States spent 35% more per student on elementary and secondary education than the average of countries in the Organization for Economic Cooperation and Development (OECD). At the post-secondary level, the U.S. spent 93% more per student than average.[302]

Despite these high expenditures, U.S. fifteen-year-olds rank fourteenth in the world in reading skills, seventeenth in science, and twenty-fifth in mathematics.[303] A more telling shortfall of American education can be seen in the rates of functional illiteracy after completion of education. Astonishingly, 16.6% of U.S. children are left functionally illiterate.[304]

Yet this need not be the case. Other countries have achieved lower illiteracy levels: Shanghai's is 2.9%, Hong Kong's 6.8%, and South Korea's 7.6%. To be sure, these superior results are not the result of dramatically better public education. In South Korea, for example, parents spend a staggering amount on private "shadow education."[305] In the United States as well, the children of parents who are willing and able to spend their own money on schooling also

---

[301]   National Center for Education Statistics, "Digest of Education Statistics", 2019.

[302]   National Center for Education Statistics, May, 2019.

[303]   Kevin D. Williamson, *The End is Near and It's Going to be Awesome* (New York: Broadside Books, an imprint of Harper Collins Publishers, 2013), 156.

[304]   James Bartholomew, *The Welfare of Nations*, 92.

[305]   Ibid, 105.

perform well: Illiteracy rates at private schools are just 3.1%, compared to 19% in government schools.[306] So, clearly, we can do better.

This nationwide outcome is not some anodyne "shortfall"; it borders on tragic. Functional illiteracy is connected to crime, unemployment, poverty, and unmarried parenting. James Bartholomew mentions some statistics:

> Fifty percent of the chronically unemployed are not functionally literate.

> Two-thirds of students who cannot read proficiently by the end of the fourth grade will end up in jail or on welfare. Sixty percent of young black men who drop out of school land in prison by their thirties.[307]

Of course, the United States has many superior schools, but all too many students are left behind. While numerous reformers have attempted improvements, they generally evade the obvious: The problem is systemic and institutional; it is not a matter of not knowing how to educate. A century ago, the nation's schools did a pretty good job of teaching the basics despite having to teach many immigrant children who did not speak English at home. The key to education is clearly teachers who are substantively grounded in their academic disciplines, who can learn educational techniques from accomplished peers, and who can teach motivated students in disciplined classrooms. A principal will quickly identify the effective teachers. But in a monolithic structure fashioned by unions, principals are shackled to the detriment of the children.

Crippled by political correctness, the country is unwilling to address problems of student motivation and classroom discipline, so it throws money at the problem instead. A teacher from Washington, DC offers some insights:

> The dirty little secret of American education is that not only do half of students in high-poverty high schools drop out, but most of those who graduate ... operate at about the fifth-grade level in academics, organization and behavior. ... Of my ninth-graders last year, only 10% were present in class more than three days a week, and a full 50% attended two days a week or fewer... As a result, I thought it remarkable that a mere 68% of my ninth graders failed – which, by the way was typical across the ninth grade in the math department.

---

[306]   Ibid, 116.

[307]   Ibid, 97.

> Instead of insisting that students retake failed courses and actually work, the school system allows students to take Credit Recovery or equally bogus summer-school courses. Thus students "age-out" of middle school with second-grade skills and "D-out" of high school courses they rarely attend.

> In Credit Recovery, students who have failed a semester-long course attend a special class after school for a few weeks and magically earn credit for it – without taking a mastery exam.[308]

In another example taken from New York City: "the vast majority of students at more than 40 public schools … had received passing report-card grades, but less than a fifth could pass the statewide math and English exams in grades three to eight. In an especially egregious school, every student received a passing grade, but only 7 percent could pass the state English exam".[309]

Studies describe how often classroom discipline has collapsed, teachers have resigned, and principals have been unable to withstand threats of lawsuits and politically correct forces. Jason L. Riley[310] reports on the Obama Administration's wrong-headed approach to school discipline. Observing that black students were disproportionately suspended for disciplinary reasons, the Education Department sent a letter to school districts warning them to do something about this disparity – in other words, to stop suspending so many disruptive black students or risk becoming the subject of a federal civil-rights investigation. Reports from around the country reflected a sharp decrease in discipline. A Chicago teacher said her school became lawless. Given the potential importance of schools for inner-city students and given the importance of discipline is to the effectiveness of schools, how could the administration have come up with such a counterproductive approach to education?

A just solution would (again) relate to parental choice: Parents who prefer to minimize the chances that their children will be suspended could send their children to one school, while parents who prioritize sound discipline could send their children to another.

Naturally, this situation is demoralizing to the teachers themselves. They are forced to make do to keep their jobs. Even worse, the power of the unions

---

308   Caleb Rossiter, "How Washington, D.C. Schools Cheat Their Students Twice," *The Wall Street Journal*, December 1, 2012, A13.

309   Rafi Eis, "The Conservative and Progressive Theories of Education", *National Review*, November 25, 2019, 46.

310   Jason L. Riley, "An Obama Decree Continues to Make Public Schools Lawless," *The Wall Street Journal*, March 22, 2017.

prevents the system from ridding itself of incompetent teachers. New York City, for example, pays thousands of teachers not to teach.[311]

Politics

Once the public sector made public education a quasi-monopoly, it was only a matter of time until teachers unionized so they could control the terms of their employment – and their retirement. To be sure, city councils and state legislatures control these terms, but the unions spend substantial amounts to support candidates that will agree to union demands. Very few politicians are willing to take the unions on.

This demonstrates that the human predatory instinct outlined in Chapter Two is at work among "public servants" such as teachers. They demand job protection even in the face of incompetence and financial remuneration beyond all financial rationality. Just as unions have bankrupted entire industries in the United States – steel, airlines, automobiles – because of unwillingness to recognize that their pay demands threatened their employers' viability, so do teachers' unions ignore the financial peril they place their states and localities in.

Illinois, Connecticut, and New Jersey are good examples of the threat posed to state finances by future pension obligations. In 2017, Moody's Investors Service estimated that the state of Illinois confronted future pension obligations of $259 billion in a year that the entire state budget was about $36 billion.[312] According to *The Wall Street Journal*, pensions consume about a quarter of the general fund; the State Universities Retirement System the prior year received funding at levels comparable to that of all higher education. *The Journal* paints a similar picture in other states. In Connecticut, pension contributions have doubled in the last seven years, and retiree health benefits make up 20% of the state budget. In New Jersey, in 2017, pension payments had doubled over the prior two years and were expected to triple over the next five.[313] According to the Federal Reserve, nationwide, states and localities are short some $4.2 trillion in assets to meet promised future commitments.[314]

Unwilling to confront the unions or address the obvious problems of non-competition in education, politicians simply avoid the facts, play on voters' heartstrings about the importance of children, and pretend to do something by commissioning studies and implementing national motivational schemes. This approach has been taken for decades by both parties and all presidents. One

---

[311]   Kevin D. Williamson, *The End is Near and It's Going to be Awesome*, 164.

[312]   "In Illinois, Long-Term Problems Still Loom," *The Wall Street Journal*, July 6, 2017, A3.

[313]   "Blue State Budget Breakdowns," *The Wall Street Journal*, July 5, 2017, A16.

[314]   "Public Pension Funds Miss Their Mark", *The Wall Street Journal*, August 7, 2019, A2.

opaque program after another is foisted on the educational establishment. It began with the creation of the Department of Education in 1979; next, a blue-ribbon panel commissioned by President Reagan to address low test scores prepared a report called "A Nation at Risk: The Imperative for Educational Reform." In 1990, President George H.W. Bush launched a school reform plan called America 2000 to raise standards. (He wanted to be known as "the education president.") Shortly thereafter, President Clinton instituted Goals 2000 to improve test scores. This was followed eight years later by President George W. Bush's No Child Left Behind, which was designed to raise academic standards. And at the time of this writing, the country is pursuing Common Core Standards.

To illustrate the futility of these approaches, one can look at Obama's initiative, the School Improvement Grants Program, which funneled seven billion dollars to schools between 2010 and 2015. Individual schools could receive up to two million dollars per year if they adopted one of the Obama Administration's improvement measures. Secretary Arne Duncan set a goal of turning around 1,000 schools a year for five years. A study released in January 2017 disclosed that *zero improvement* was found in the schools receiving the money.[315]

All of this is the standard political kabuki dance of politicians trying to show that they care while avoiding taking on powerful special interests. Kevin Williamson captures it well: "The poor, the black, and the Hispanic are the worst served by the system, while the elite exits through the escape hatch to private schools. That this is done in the name of fairness, democratic idealism, equality, social justice, and other such high-minded miasma suggests a cynicism that is startling in its depth and subtlety."[316]

It is all too clear why presidents such as Clinton and Obama send their children to private schools. And it's not just presidents – half the public schoolteachers in Philadelphia enroll their children in private schools. There should be public outrage against the hypocrisy of politicians who trade on public sentiment and then pervert the system to value teachers' unions and public-sector bureaucracies over the needs of children.

Obvious Remedies

At this point in the chapter, it should be self-evident that education is another field that functions best when the spontaneous order can function freely. Since learning and instruction evolve constantly, schools can learn from one another facilitated by professional organizations that share best practices. Exams that measure performance should be added to this model to keep everyone honest. With such a system, new insights or advances in educational techniques would

---

[315]   *Washington Post*, January 21, 2017, A6.

[316]   Kevin D. Williamson, *The End is Near and It's Going to be Awesome*, 153.

spread quickly through the profession and schools of education. We don't need a Department of Education to somehow discover "the best way to educate"; schools themselves, when free to do so, will quickly emulate their most successful peers.

This suggests that empowering parents and enhancing competition among schools is the key to reform. Parents are not fooled, as can be seen in the popularity of magnet schools, charter schools, and leading private schools. Smart people will find a way to get educated.

The answer to the problem is, of course, simple, but because of union politics, it is not easy. Every school principal should have the funding and authority to hire and to maintain discipline, and then he should have to compete for students with other schools.

Teachers' unions, guided by their vested interest, have fought charter schools vociferously with arguments that range from the specious to the outrageous. Although no controlled studies support it, they claim that charter schools are ineffective or point to a few that have adopted misguided approaches (which is inevitable when one permits "a hundred flowers to bloom"). Yet many examples demonstrate the efficacy of charter schools. In DC, 90% of charter-school students go on to college; this is fifty points higher than the rate for public school students.

A definitive study of charter schools in New York City counters union claims that charters' superior performance has to do with "cherry-picking" students rather than intrinsic superiority. The study followed two groups of similar students; most were poor, black, or Hispanic; all of their parents were motivated and applied to enroll them in charter schools. One was fortunate enough to win the random lottery that granted access, and the other was not. The students were tracked for six academic years. The charter school students gained an average of 3.6 points in math test scores per year for a total of 30 points over six years; they gained 2.4 points per year in English for a total gain of 23 points. (A score of 650 points indicates proficiency, and a score of 685 indicates good performance.)[317]

Eva Moskowitz (the founder and CEO of Success Academy Charter Schools) reported the results of New York State tests: "In central Harlem ... the number of students meeting rigorous, Common Core math standards has more than doubled since 2013 – from 1,690 to 3,703. Students attending charter schools account for 96% of that growth. Results for English language arts are similarly inspiring." She further notes that the students in the best charter schools outperform the city's most affluent students in both math and reading.

Parents know this. In Harlem, 14,000 students applied for entry via the lottery system; only 3,000 spots were available. Across the entire city, 48,000 students

---

[317]   James Bartholomew, *The Welfare of Nations*, 112-113.

are on charter school waitlists.[318] Unbelievably, the city's politicians, in thrall to the unions, restrict the growth of charter schools.

Opponents argue that charter schools siphon money away from the public schools. Well, yes; that's the nature of competition. However, this does not mean that public schools get less money per student. Moreover, since charter schools use less money per student, society gains superior performance at a reduced cost.

In one recent bizarre move, unions enlisted Obama's Justice Department to attack Louisiana's scholarship program on the grounds that it violated a forty-year-old desegregation order, even though 90% of the beneficiaries were black students for whom the scholarship presented an opportunity to leave their failing public schools.[319]

Despite the vociferous resistance of the teachers' unions and their enablers in the Democratic Party, change is inevitable. After decades of failure in many school districts, pressure from parents will out. The proper solutions are to empower parents, free schools to fire teachers, and establish effective classroom discipline and competition among schools. Other countries, even those with social democratic governments that were once in thrall to utopian notions about the power of government to transform society, have come to see the power of these ideas.

James Bartholomew reports on such a change in Sweden:

> Private companies have turned out to be the driving force behind the burgeoning number of free schools in Sweden. Free schools currently account for 10% of schooling in Sweden ... and 25% in Stockholm. One welcome result has been open competition between different educational ideas. ... With this mushrooming of free schools, power lies with the parents to decide which kind of school will prosper. ... The competition is intense."[320]

A similar approach was instituted in New Zealand in the early 1990s when that country faced both a financial crisis and unacceptable student performance.[321] Maurice McTigue reports how a few key reforms transformed the performance of New Zealand's primary and secondary education; parents were given authority

---

[318] Eva Moskowitz, "Test Scores Don't Lie: Charter Schools are Transformative," *The Wall Street Journal*, August 24, 2017, A15.

[319] Allysia Finley, Interview with Kevin Chavous, "On the School-Choice Barricades," *The Wall Street Journal*, September 6-7. 2014, A13.

[320] James Bartholomew, *The Welfare of Nations*, 115.

[321] Maurice McTigue, "Making Government Accountable: Reform Lessons from New Zealand", speech to the Mercatus Center, George Mason University.

over each schools' board. Moreover, parents could choose any school for their children, private as well as public. The results were speedy and dramatic: in 1987 New Zealand's' school performance lagged the average of its international peers by 15%; three years after the reforms, it was 15% ahead. Notably, the improvements occurred in disadvantaged areas that had had particularly weak results previously.

Higher Education

U.S. higher education poses a different picture than primary education. There is plenty of competition, but also dysfunctional federal involvement. To be sure, the United States has the best universities in the world. They undertake leading-edge research; talented individuals from around the world strive to attend them, and a larger percentage of the U.S. population attends college or university than that of any other country. So, does U.S. higher education really represent another example of good intentions run amok?

Indeed it does. Despite good intentions, the United States spends far too much on higher education, contributing still more to the country's future financial problems, and it still fails to meet the needs of too many of the students. The lack of a sensible economic balancing mechanism distorts the resources consumed and the financial burden placed on students.

Although many private and state institutions compete for students and resources, the field of education does not contain the price competition and increasing efficiency observed in all other service industries. Something perverse is happening, something that can be partially traced back to the government, if perhaps in a different way than in the prior examples. In particular, we can look to the government's over-promotion of the idea that higher education is for virtually everybody, combined with high-octane grant and loan programs. These two factors have vastly increased the demand for higher education, allowing educational institutions to grow without the competitive pressures normally seen in the private sector.

As related by Richard Vedder, before the federal government began to participate significantly in higher education financing, from around 1840 to 1978, inflation-adjusted tuition grew merely 1% a year. After the institution of major federal support programs, it grew at triple that pace. At the time of this writing, some $158 billion is spent each year on student aid and government-backed student loans; as of 2019, the federal student-loan portfolio reached an amount of $1.5 trillion.[322] This is a burden to many students and will contribute to the government's coming financial difficulties. That the loans are a burden – at least for the students for whom higher education has not sufficiently improved earning

---

[322]   "The Great Student-Loan Scam", *The Wall Street Journal*, August 21, 2019, A14.

capacity – is clear: A majority of borrowers at over one thousand institutions have repaid nothing in the three years following graduation, and the number of debtors over sixty has quadrupled in a decade.[323]

However, all this money has not improved educational performance. There are few indications that universities have used modern technology to improve instruction. Even worse, they have failed to complete their traditional mission. Economists Robert E. Martin and R. Carter Hill wrote that "completion rates declined, grade inflation increased, students spend less time studying, adult numeracy/literacy rates declined, and critical thinking skills did not improve." University spending on administration has increased; between 1987 and 2012, colleges added 517,636 administrators and professional employees, public colleges now have two non-academic staffers for every full-time, tenure-track faculty member. Universities try to outdo one another in non-core areas by constructing fancy new buildings and sports facilities.[324]

These results, of course, are counterintuitive. It seems safe to assume that the creators and administrators of government programs and of higher education have the best of intentions. However, the Law of Unintended Consequences seems to be at work. Too many young people are attending institutes of higher education, and the government makes it too easy for them to finance that education.

First, the government has exceeded any justifiable goal of improving the nation's social capital. Governmental education policy should seek to develop the country's social capital as much as needed to meet economic and civic needs in economically sensible ways. However, we have overdone education due to a misguided sense of egalitarianism. Because the best jobs are only open to those with advanced degrees, fairness requires (or so the thinking goes) that everyone should have access to higher education. In our highly egalitarian society, degrees have come to define status; individuals without advanced degrees feel *déclassé*. As a result, many students try and fail to obtain degrees at great financial cost. In the end, too many gain a personal sense of failure.

There are two problems with federal involvement in education. First, the federal government mindset becomes elitist; and, second, it is tailor-made for utopian thinking, not to mention political correctness. The elites define a "desirable" world based on their own experience and conclude that a university education is universally desirable; it creates cultured individuals who are poised to maximize their earnings. However, experience demonstrates that this vision is unrealistic. Expensive higher education requires more abstract thinking skills and esoteric knowledge than the average person can utilize effectively. The inevitable

---

[323]   Richard Vedder, "How to Beat the High Cost of Learning," *The Wall Street Journal*, February 16, 2017, A15.

[324]   Charles J. Sykes, "Clinton's Bailout for the College-Industrial Complex," *The Wall Street Journal*, August 23, 2016.

result is that many students incur huge expenses for an education that they will not use in the jobs they eventually take.

Rather than pursuing a misplaced ideal vision in an effort to improve young people's self-esteem, we should pursue a vision in which each and every one of us can maximize their inherent competences and receive a broad cultural inheritance and pride in citizenship in much more financially sensible ways.

The government simply should not promote the message that anyone without a college degree is a relative failure. European countries handle this better; there, a significantly smaller percentage of the population attends college or university. These countries recognize that higher education is (or should be) designed to help students master a profession or gain the knowledge necessary to do research or pursue a career in academia. This is simply not everyone's cup of tea. To be sure, it is in everyone's interest to teach all students critical thinking, clear writing skills, and cultural awareness. However, this should not require four years of college.

Europeans, notably the Swiss, Germans, and French, take a more pragmatic and less romantic approach. For example, secondary schools are more rigorous than in the United States. It is a mark of achievement in Germany and France to earn an *Abitur* from a Gymnasium or a *Baccalaureat* from a Lysee. Those graduates have gained the critical thinking and writing skills they need to enter the economic world or a professional program.

That might be too radical a change for the United States. But Charles Sykes suggests "supporting alternative education options – such as two-year and three-year degrees, certification for professions that don't require a bachelor's degree, or Massive Open Online Courses."[325] Alternatively, we might consider something like Germany's well-established apprentice program, which imparts high-tech skills in tune with students' interests. Such skills can be for many much more valuable to society than a university degree. Importantly, these highly skilled students earn better incomes than liberal arts majors, who often end up in jobs that don't require a college diploma.

Moreover, in the United States, a sensible economic mechanism is needed to control financing. Such a mechanism would help students assess whether years of higher education will pay off for them or not. It could also incorporate terms that would incentivize students to study harder and graduate sooner. Easy money has led them deeply into debt, affecting their long-term financial well-being and adding substantially to the country's future debt loads.

---

[325]   Ibid.

HOUSING

Progressives pushed their way into pensions, healthcare, and education, so it was inevitable that housing would come to their attention as well. Why do we even have a Department of Urban and Housing Development? Can individuals not even be allowed to decide whether to rent or buy a home? Apparently not! However, let's set aside that agency's budget, regulations, and intrusion into the housing market and examine one startling case study. In this example, sentiment endangered the nation's fiscal health due to the pursuit of a decades-long utopian ambition to increase home ownership, especially among minorities.

In 1995, the Clinton administration issued its National Home Ownership Strategy, which aimed to "lift America's homeownership rate to an all-time high by the end of the century." It pressured banks through the Community Reinvestment Act, which required all financial institutions to measure and report their progress against public goals to increase mortgage lending to minorities. HUD worked with the Mortgage Bankers Association to find ways to provide low-income borrowers better access to financing through *reduced underwriting standards*. Fannie Mae and Freddie Mac, the dominant lenders in the secondary market (who operate with an implicit government backstop), primed the mortgage market by creating artificial demand for risky subprime mortgages. It was risky because banks were pressured to reduce down payment requirements and because of new "flexible underwriting criteria."

These were not suggestions. Earlier, the Fed had threatened lenders by reminding them of their legal obligation to *remedy* discrimination. It demanded that they consider lower down payments, lower FICO scores, and undocumented sources of income as *fairer* ways to finance low-income home buyers. The program worked as intended, sort of – the percentage of U.S. homes purchased with low down payments surged in the next decade. In addition, in the United States (unlike in many other countries), homeowners are protected from "full recourse" by lenders; in other words, they can walk away from home repayment obligations without risk to their other possessions.[326] What could go wrong?

It all exploded in the fiscal crisis of 2008. The cascading sequence began with a bubble in housing sales and prices, followed by increased defaults, collapsing prices, bank runs, and bank failures. The government was on the hook for trillions of dollars to stabilize the economy and restore growth. Real estate prices fell 30%, lenders lost $320 billion, bank withdrawals totaled $1.5 trillion, and the Lehman Brothers, Bear Stearns, AIG, Washington Mutual, and Wachovia all declared bankruptcy. Furthermore, the government started running unprecedented budget

---

[326]   Edward Conard, *Unintended Consequences: Why Everything You've Been Told About the Economy Is Wrong* (New York: Portfolio/ Penguin, 2012), 170-173.

deficits in excess of one trillion dollars a year..[327] And, of course, there was the personal anguish caused by millions of foreclosures on borrowers who should not have been sucked into this disaster in the first place.

Did anyone take responsibility? Was anything learned? One theme of this book addresses the adeptness of Progressives to create false narratives that prevent accountability and preclude learning. In this case, although the policies were indubitably Democrat ones put in place during the Clinton Administration, the house of cards fell while Bush was President – so, voilà, the entire fault was his. Furthermore, with a new Democrat President and a Democrat Congress, the Congressional Committee on Oversight and Government Reform glossed over the central importance of the above events and focused on things like accounting errors, bankers' bonuses, and sales of imprudent mortgages. The public was left with the impression that Wall Street was at fault.

Another time-honored political tool is the introduction of new regulations that will supposedly prevent reoccurrence of a problem to soothe the electorate. Such regulations usually have little to do with the past crisis, but they do allow politicians to achieve other long-sought goals. In the immortal words of White House Chief of Staff Emmanuel Rahm, it was a crisis too good to waste (by failing to further progressive goals). In this case, the crisis led to the Dodd-Frank legislation, which will eventually lead to some 25,000 pages of regulations – the largest increase in banking regulations in history.

The crisis chiefly involved only twenty institutions (who danced to the government's tune); none were mainstream commercial banks. Why, questions Richard Kovacevich, are six thousand banks being punished for something they didn't do? He notes that the management of commercial banks now spend most of their time and resources on compliance, regulatory changes, and litigation. Since 2008, banks have spent $275 billion on legal expenses, which translates into a reduced lending capacity of five trillion dollars.[328] Moreover, large banks may have more than one hundred regulators with an average of fifteen years of experience. They did not spot problems before the crisis. In another supposed reform, independent board members (who often lack specific experience in the industry) who meet one day a month are expected to be accountable for these commercial banks' failings.[329]

Financial decisions regarding housing should be left to the FEO; the government should focus on transparency and protection against fraud.

---

[327]   Ibid, 162, 165, 177.

[328]   Per Minouche Shafik, deputy Governor of the Bank of England, *The Wall Street Journal*, October 21, 2016.

[329]   Richard Kovacevich, September/October 2014, "Cato Policy Report," 11.

REGULATION

The desire to regulate others to protect ourselves against exploitation or to induce others to behave morally (according to our standards) has always been integral to human nature. We're not talking about admonitions of the Ten Commandments here, but more bureaucratic intrusion.

Earlier examples demonstrated that societies have been willing to shackle the FEO with "fair prices," regulated exchanges, and "fair wages" and more, allegedly to ensure that individuals will not be taken advantage of. Examined closely, these ideas can be seen to have a Medieval provenance. Medieval Europeans attempted to impose "social justice" through a highly stratified system of fair prices, a socially stratified population, restrictions on tradesmen, and requirements for apprentices. However, an underlying practical goal was to prevent competition (which gained the support of the guilds). Of course this societal construct had the unintended consequence of producing stagnant, stultified economies. This kind of thinking has never entirely left our culture, although its modern iteration has been driven by a utopian desire to do good rather than as earlier to establish a religious state.

A key virtue of the U.S. Constitution as written is that it limits such impulses to the state level by restricting the federal government's authority to meddle in the economy. As late as the beginning of the twentieth century, as we saw in the last chapter, even Woodrow Wilson argued against the federal government usurping domestic and business relationships that were in the undisputed field of state law.

Indeed, it seems that a regulatory mindset was not part of the independent American worldview. De Tocqueville observes that, during the early years of the republic, individual Americans were largely free of government intrusion into their liberty: "[T]he secondary affairs of society have never been regulated by authority and nothing has hitherto betrayed its desire of even interfering in them."[330] He also notes that no bureaucratic authority even existed to enforce interference, and this was all to the good. However, he also foresaw democracy's vulnerability to administrative despotism even when an autocracy was unlikely. Chapter Two noted his observations about the slippery slope of good intentions that, over time, lead to a society in which "a[bove this race of men stands an intense and tutelary power, which takes upon itself alone to secure their gratifications and to watch over their fate."[331] Now, two centuries later, after a century of progressive ascendency, we are well on our way to this fate.

So, both the Constitution and U.S. tradition once opposed federal micromanagement of the economy, but this is no longer true. This conclusion is not to argue that the federal government has no regulatory role. Richard Epstein argues

---

[330]   Alexis de Tocqueville, *Democracy in America*, I (New York: Mentor Books, 1956), 271.

[331]   Ibid, I, 303.

that common law precedent, on which the Constitution is silent, justifies regulation when required to protect "safety, health, morals and the general welfare."[332] Protecting the people's physical safety, as the Center for Disease Control and the Food and Drug Administration do, is justification enough. However, once the door is opened to the justification of good intentions limited only by vague cost/benefit principles administered by the do-gooders themselves, the whole economy becomes captive to the "Administrative State." Effectively, as in the cases discussed previously, few limiting principles come into play. The so-called societal benefits derived from such regulations are difficult to measure and escape public scrutiny because they seem to be well intentioned.

The following sections will provide an overview of the avalanche of regulatory actions in the last century, the costs they have imposed on the American people, and their contribution to the nation's future fiscal pain.

The Regulatory Embrace

In *Ameritopia*, Mark Levin illustrates the extent of federal regulation:[333]

> **Homebuilding:** Federal rules set standards for insulation, gypsum board, treated lumber, windows, pipes, ventilation ducts, flooring paint, etc. Home builders must comply with the Clean Air Act, the Clean Water Act, the Endangered Species Act, the Resources Conservation and Recovery Act, the Toxic Substances Control Act, and the National Historic Preservation Act.

> **Inside the home:** The federal government regulates washing machines, dryers, dishwashers, dishwasher detergents, microwave ovens, toilets, showerheads, heating and cooling systems, refrigerators, freezers, furnace fans and boilers, ceiling fans, dehumidifiers, light bulbs, certain renovations, fitness equipment, clothing, baby cribs, pacifiers, rattles and toys, marbles, latex balloons, matchbooks, bunk beds, mattresses, mattress pads, televisions, radios, cell phones, iPods and other digital media devices, computer components, video recording devices, speakers, batteries, battery chargers, power supplies, stereo equipment, garage door openers, lawn mowers, lawn darts, pool slides, etc.

---

[332] Richard Epstein, *The Classical Liberal Constitution* (Cambridge, Massachusetts: Harvard University Press, 2014), 15.

[333] Mark R. Levin, *Ameritopia*, 217-222.

Automobiles: Federal mandates set standards for automobiles' engines, bumpers, headrests, seat belts, door latches, brakes, fuel systems, windshields, side-door guard beams, and energy absorbing steering columns. The biggest mandates, of course, are the requirements for average fuel economy and for the blending of biofuels into gasoline. (These sorts of things were introduced during the energy crises in the 1970s, they are surely moot now thanks to low oil prices and the great success of fracking.)

The workplace: Federal rules affect wages, taxes, health benefits, pension benefits, working conditions, environmental conditions, human resources, union elections, financial practices, and record keeping. Even vending machines on the premises are regulated.

Regulations in the workplace are so pervasively onerous that they deserve a more detailed listing, particularly as they affect the ability of new small businesses to form and thrive. *Ten Thousand Commandments*[334] provides a partial list of generic regulations (in contrast to those specific to industries such as mining, agriculture, trucking, or finance):

- Fair Labor Standards Act (regulates overtime and minimum wage
- Social Security matching and deposits
- Medicare, Federal Insurance Contributions Act (FICA)
- Military Selective Service Act
- Equal Pay Act (forbids sex discrimination in wages)
- Immigration Reform Act
- Federal Unemployment Tax Act
- Employee Retirement Income Security Act
- Occupational Safety and Health Act
- Polygraph Protection Act
- Civil Rights Act (regarding discrimination)
- Americans with Disabilities Act
- Age Discrimination Act
- Older Workers Benefit Protection Act
- COBRA (continuation of medical benefits upon termination)
- Health Maintenance Organization Act
- Veterans' Reemployment Act

---

[334] Clyde Wayne Crews, Jr., *Ten Thousand Commandments: An Annual Snapshot of the Federal Regulatory State, 2012 Edition*, Competitive Enterprise Institute, 31.

- Family and Medical Leave Act
- WARN Act (sixty-days written notice of a plant's closing)

Consider as well the area of food; originally, regulation in this domain was justifiable on the grounds of health and safety. But, given authority, regulators *will* regulate –until they establish a nanny-state. Certainly, obesity is a health concern. But doctors and the whole health profession have gotten that message out. Will governmental hectoring of the food industry really do a better job? Levin describes the government's lack of restraint in this area:

> Indeed, not just food, but food labeling and packaging are subject to extensive federal regulation. New mandates require food labels to "disclose net contents, identity of commodity, and name and place of business of the product's manufacturer, packer, or distributor." Labels must also include the presence of major food allergens. Certain terms like "low sodium," "reduced fat," and "high fiber" must meet strict government definitions. The federal government has defined other terms used for nutritional content including "low," "reduced," "high," "free," "lean," "extra lean," "good source," "less," and "lite." ... The food industry will also face ... federally recommended nutrition labels and federally recommended nutritional criteria for foods making "dietary guidance" statements."[335]

George Will highlights the pettiness of the tyrannical nanny-state. With good intentions, Congress authorized programs subsidizing student lunches. Very well. With that foot in the door, however, federal administrators began dictating the content of those lunches. And, in a final act of pettiness, they prescribed forms of cupcakes that could be sold at school fundraising activities.

This account is not intended to argue that many of the above objectives are not inherently good. But why does the federal government have to be involved? The food industry is incredibly competitive. Businesses seek out niche customers who prefer organic or gluten-free foods. Publications such as *Consumer Reports* investigate extensively. Organizations such as the Heart Association collect substantial donations to get the word out about nutritional issues. Anyone who has had a recent physical has probably gotten good advice regarding food. Even if the government contributes something extra to this information, is the cost justified? Levin notes that the total federal budget for regulating nearly all aspects of food, from production to consumption, exceeds the entire country's net farm income.[336]

---

[335] Mark R. Levin, *Ameritopia,* 220.

[336] Ibid, 222.

In addition, consumers can receive guidance from the Better Business Bureau, consumer-product reviewers, and "list-serves," and has access to the tort system to address injury; these systems spontaneously discipline the market. It is also problematic when government intrudes in favor of special interests to reduce competition whether in legal advice, taxi services, funeral practices, or hair braiding. Reduced regulation has great potential to spur increased productivity. For example, studies in the United Kingdom have found that on a variety of matters such as welfare benefits, housing, and employment, non-lawyers generally outperformed lawyers in terms of serving low-income clients. The study concluded that specialization and not professional status was the best predictor of quality.[337]

The Financial Burden

An implicit measure of the burden that regulation imposes on the country is the *Federal Register,* which lists all the regulations flowing from congressional action. The register now comprises 235 volumes with six- or seven-point type that occupy seventeen feet of shelf space.[338] In 2018, it was 63,645 pages long. The driver of growth is the number of new rules made final: in 2018 the administration issued 3,368 rules, a rate of eleven for every law.[339]

What are the costs associated with these attempts to reach utopia? Economic actors pay compliance costs; stifled innovation represents another cost; the government incurs enforcement costs; the leviathan *Federal Register* creates legal costs; and the loss of liberty has psychic costs.

These regulations are not suggestions – they require hiring systems, product designers, compliance officers, and lawyers. Economists Nicole V. Crain and W. Mark Crain estimated that, in 2008, the average cost to businesses per employee amounted to $8,086 (more for smaller firms), and for the entire country, regulatory costs amounted to $1.752 trillion, or about 11.7% of the U.S. GDP.[340]

A study by the Mercatus Center used a model that goes beyond direct regulatory costs to examine the impact of regulations on firms' investment choices. It examined a twenty-two-industry dataset with data from 1977 through 2012. It found that the distortion of investment choices linked to innovation reduced economic production, slowing the GDP growth rate by some 0.8%. Over time, this is a tremendous impact. The study estimated that, if regulations had remained at

---

[337]   Deborah L. Rhode and Lucy Buford Ricca in the May issue of the *Fordham Law Review,* reported in *The Wall Street Journal,* Sept. 26, 2014, A13.

[338]   *The Wall Street Journal,* interview with James Taranto, Aug. 2-3, 2014, A9.

[339]   *The Washington Times,* "No Big Dent Made in Annual Cost of Federal Regulations", May, 8, 2019.

[340]   Clyde Wayne Crews Jr., *Ten Thousand Commandments* 2, 7.

1980 levels, the economy would have been 25% larger than it was in 2012.[341] In that context, it is amusing to read the current explanations of economists on the Left who claim that the historically sub-par economic recovery from the 2008 crises is due to some mysterious, now-permanent decrease in productivity.

Even with this expansion of legal oversight and increase in the number of compliance officers, prosecutable transgressions arise. According to the Heritage Foundation, "Scores of federal departments and agencies have created so many criminal offenses that the Congressional Research Service (CRS) [the research arm of Congress] ... admitted that it was unable to even count all of the offenses. The Service's best estimate: tens of thousands."[342]

Politicians justify vast amounts of regulation by claiming it protects citizens' health and shields them from fraud. But really, how did populations manage to feed, clothe, and transport themselves before this awesome nanny state came into being? Can the average American not comparison-shop? Does one truly believe that corporations seek to defraud customers or cut corners at their expense unless the government micromanages virtually all economic transactions? Maybe he or she does, after a century of subjection to progressive demonization of business. However, the customer still must ask whether the resulting adjustments merit their negative effect on the economy and *his share* of those costs (opportunity costs) – that is, whether thousands of dollars lost per year really justify this protection.

And aside from the cost, what about our liberties? The regulatory state has become a fourth branch of the U.S. government that operates arbitrarily and autonomously – that is, it is free of specific congressional authorization. This opens the door to arbitrary regulations because Congress often passes vague legislation that allows regulatory agencies broad options for interpretation. Arbitrary regulation is usually upheld by the courts, which defer to the agencies' actions (derived from the Chevron U.S.A., Inc. v. Natural Resources Defense Council, Inc. decision by the Supreme Court).[343]

Regulation in Action

The above section provided a broad overview of the magnitude of the U.S. regulatory state, but the reader may well find this narrative dry or "bloodless"; it does not illustrate how these costly, stultifying effects play out in everyday life. *The Wall Street Journal*[344] gave a pithy account of the sweeping impact of the

---

[341] Mercatus Center, George Mason University, "Research Summary: The Cumulative Cost of Regulations."

[342] Brian Walsh, "Over-criminalization: An Explosion of Federal Criminal Law," Heritage Foundation, April 27, 2011.

[343] Adam J. White, "Betraying the Constitution," *The Wall Street Journal*, June 30, 2014, A9.

[344] "If You're Riding Through Hell ...," *The Wall Street Journal*, July 15-16, 2017, A12.

regulatory state on the country's efficiency and effectiveness, both of which are harmed by increased costs to the taxpayers and by government pandering to leftist special interests such as unions and extreme environmentalists. The account deals with the New York City area, a citadel of Progressivism. Burgeoning costs are shown to be the result of the delays, inefficiencies, unnecessary add-ons, and the union cost structure mandated by the feds.

The latter is especially onerous. The 1931 Davis-Bacon Act requires public projects receiving federal funds to pay prevailing wage rates (largely determined by unions); it also sets inefficient work rules that stipulate how many and which workers must perform specific tasks. Moreover, the Federal Transit Act requires grant recipients to protect workers against a "worsening of employment conditions." Practically, this means that agencies cannot contract out services, reduce benefits, or lay off workers. No wonder that costs skyrocket. From 2005 to 2017, the MTA's labor costs (60% of its expenses) jumped by 80%. Its costs for pensions and healthcare doubled. The cumulative impact of these burdens is demonstrated in the following examples:

- The Hudson tunnel retrofit was originally estimated at $7.7 billion; that increased to thirteen billion dollars one year later because of an environmental impact statement. The Federal Railroad Administration and New Jersey Transit had to deal with twenty-nine agencies in order to issue the nineteen required permits. Some cost-drivers were defensive contracting to avoid lawsuits, such as blocking views of the construction with aesthetic fabric, and transplanting marsh-pennyworth plants. Construction is to begin in 2019 and will take at least seven years.
- New York's Metropolitan Transportation Authority spent forty-five years and $4.5 billion to build the two-mile long Second Avenue subway line.
- In 1999, the East Side Access project to bring Long Island Railroad trains into Grand Central was estimated at $4.3 billion, but the MTA now expects it to be completed by 2023 at a cost of $10.8 billion.

These aren't isolated examples. Senator Dan Sullivan wrote that while the 1,500-mile Alaska–Canadian Highway once took about eight months to build, new U.S. highway construction projects now take between nine and nineteen years from initial planning and permitting to completion of construction (per a U.S. Government Accountability Office (GAO) study). It took four years to construct a new runway at the Seattle-Tacoma Airport, and it took fifteen years to get the permits.[345]

Bret Stephens provided some equally alarming national averages from a World Bank Survey: "Eight years ago [2008], 40 days were needed to get a construction permit, now it's 81. When President Bush left office, it took 300 days to enforce a contract. Today: 420. As for registering property, the cost has nearly quintupled since 2009, to 2.4% of property value from 0.5%."[346]

A perennially popular theme on the campaign trail is that the country must upgrade its infrastructure, which of course always requires more funding. But examples like those listed above exist everywhere. Obviously, the system is not designed to meet the needs of the citizenry quickly; rather, it is designed to overspend, cause delays, and pander to special interests.

Another minor, but telling, example of the egregious overreach of a regulatory agency was the suit that the EPA brought against John Duarte, a California farmer. Duarte had bought land to plant wheat but had not obtained a permit from the EPA. Why would he have to? Our Kafkaesque system concluded that plowing would affect water runoff. Because the EPA was given the authority to protect "navigable waters" under the 1972 Clean Water Act, they believed they could regulate this farmer because his rainwater might flow into a nearby creek and eventually into a river. Incredibly (in deference to the regulators), the courts ruled for the government. At the time of this writing, Duarte must pay a $2.8 million fine and buy mitigation credits that may cost thirteen million dollars.[347]

Imagine that: the administrative state has been granted such authority that it can arbitrarily determine that natural rainwater runoff from a farm somehow endangers the environment, and failure to comply with their diktats could drive a farmer into potential bankruptcy.

Reform?

Obviously, the regulatory state must be reined in, which only can be done by Congress. But it suits Congress on many levels not to do so. Instead, Congress prefers to legislate good intentions but leave the onerous costs and restrictions to the regulatory agencies to keep their own hands clean come election time. Still, political pressure has forced Congress to appear to deal with the problem. For example, agencies are now required to do cost–benefit analyses before imposing regulations that would cost more than ninety-nine million dollars to implement. This has brought a measure of transparency to the issue and has helped analytic

---

[345]   Dan Sullivan, "How to Put Building Permits on a Fast Track," *The Wall Street Journal*, December 5, 2016, A21.

[346]   Bret Stephens, "Doomed to Stagnate?" *The Wall Street Journal*, December 20, 2016, A21.

[347]   Tony Mecia, "Plowed Under," *The Weekly Standard*, August 21, 28, 2017, 10.

studies such as those cited above. Nonetheless, agencies have more than enough room to maneuver free of meaningful restraint, particularly regarding benefit calculations, as they are virtually the sole judges of the outcome.

Good intentions reign; liberty, property rights, and economic common sense suffer.

Unfortunately, once regulation reaches gargantuan proportions, it defies oversight. Regulators will regulate or lose their jobs. Many businesses accept regulations because of the economic disadvantages they impose on competitors (see the above discussion of the regulatory burdens on new startups). As Mancur Olson's work shows, all societies have a natural dynamic of growing regulation, which then significantly slows economic growth. This condition seems to be a form of entropy in human societies.

It seems likely that the problem cannot be addressed with a scalpel; it requires sweeping reform, something like New Zealand's sunset laws on regulations that require them to be updated and reconciled periodically (to be discussed in Chapter 7). More recently, President Trump has ordered agencies to delete two old regulations before imposing a new one.

THE FUTURE TAB

It will be seen in the next chapter that other countries with similar dynamics (a representative government prone to overpromise and make bad choices) were forced by fiscal circumstances to make major reforms. The United States, however, is still sleepwalking toward this fate.

The stakes are enormous and growing. Michael Tanner outlines the contours of the unfolding crisis.[348] The first issue is the unbalanced budget. The U.S. budget has run deficits of half a trillion to over a trillion dollars every year for the last decade, and the national debt has reached around eighteen trillion dollars, not much less than the entire GDP. This amounts to a debt of $56,496 for every man, woman, and child in America. Furthermore, this snapshot does not include the future tsunami of promises to spend on the "entitlement programs" of Social Security, Medicare, and Medicaid. Discounting the future cost estimates of the first two programs into current dollars, Tanner estimates that Social Security faces a shortfall of $24.9 trillion and Medicare a shortfall of forty-eight trillion (an optimistic view) to eighty-nine trillion dollars. Medicaid, which is funded differently on an annual basis, will add significantly to the financial tab. Federal Medicaid costs are expected to double to $576 billion by 2024, and Obamacare could add $1.3 trillion during the same period.

Jagadeesh Gokhale's book *The Government Debt Iceberg* puts those sums

---

[348]   Michael Tanner, *Going for Broke* (Washington, D.C.: Cato Institute, 2015), 5, 172.

into a larger perspective. He calculates "the fiscal imbalance" – the difference between promised spending and government revenues –implied by these entitlement promises. He estimates an imbalance of $91.4 trillion. This amount, if financed at the long-term average interest rate, implies an annual accrual of $3.3 trillion – amounting to 21.2% of the annual GDP. Financing this amount could require the government to double taxes, a politically improbable solution.[349]

*　　*　　*

Clearly the country at large has not even recognized this problem, much less come to terms with it. Still, the evidence of progressive failure keeps accruing. The discussion on education illustrated the kinds of fiscal pressure created by tax-and-spend governments in Illinois, Connecticut, and New Jersey. In California, cities like San Bernardino, Stockton, and Mammoth Lake have recently slid into insolvency. Like Detroit, Michigan in recent times, Chicago's fiscal prospects do not look very promising given its unfunded public pension liabilities. More recently, Congress has had to impose a control board on Puerto Rico when it was unable to make bond payments because of decades of government profligacy.

So, where has a century of progressive ascendency left us? We're in a deep fiscal hole that grows by the day, with a political establishment that is too hapless and too much at loggerheads to deal with it. At the same time, the cost of progressive programs and their pervasive regulations have increasingly strangled the country's capacity to generate wealth, which is crucial to meeting those obligations.

It is evident that the progressive worldview has failed. Its all-important sentiment and good intentions are no match for empirical reality. Its inclinations are so invariably wrong-headed that one could say that it possesses a reverse Midas-touch: a talent for destroying rather than creating wealth.

LESSONS AND IMPLICATIONS

This chapter relates the harm that progressive utopianism has done to the United States in the twentieth century. It shows how Progressives were carried away by what Hayek terms a *fatal conceit*: the belief that the government can solve problems better than free people exercising their rights under the FEO, and that its narrow good intentions are superior to the distributed wisdom of the citizenry. That arrogance has left us with an enormous bill for the next generation, a probable financial crisis, and an uncertain future for our way of life. Let's

---

[349]　JagadeeshGokhale, *The Government Debt Iceberg*(London: The Institute of Economic Affairs, 2014), 137, 140.

summarize what we can learn from the failures of the progressive reign and consider some implications for the future.

Lessons

This chapter distilled lessons from the progressive experience of the last century. The failures described here were not bad luck or random mistakes; they were inevitable results of that worldview and the consequence of abandoning constitutional restraint. Some highlights are:

- The FEO is the best way to meet people's needs for food, housing, healthcare, pensions, and education. It did so in the past and can do so again. To be sure, some people will always require a social safety net, but that reality should not be the tail that wags the body of the entire economy. Moreover, this civic assistance should not be the domain of the central government, which is too distant and too bureaucratic to provide it effectively and efficiently.
- The intended beneficiaries of government programs receive a poorer deal than they would under the FEO, which would enable them to purchase insurance or engage in cooperative ventures with others.
- The government lacks the private sector's built-in economic regulator that requires the operations of individual enterprises to make economic sense. Such a regulator should require that the use of resources or funding at least be balanced by the products or services provided; in the marketplace an enterprise must show a profit in competition with alternative uses of those resources.
- In the private sector, inefficient or less-than-optimal models are quickly punished by bankruptcies, but government programs rarely admit mistakes; rather, they double down with public spending when problems emerge. We have seen above how the major entitlement programs became increasingly unbalanced and insolvent, in turn threatening the country with insolvency.
- Since the government can levy taxes and print money, government programs lack an effective control mechanism. Everything becomes a matter for special interests, factions, and politics. Once an entitlement program is unleashed from true actuarial considerations, it will escape financial rationality as those in the United States surely have. Moreover, government monopolies are always less efficient and more vulnerable to moral hazard than free markets.
- Beyond the specifics, when so much of the national income flows through government hands, overall growth suffers, which means that everyone

is poorer in the long term. The government is less flexible and less innovative than the private sector. It also requires a huge bureaucracy to handle taxation and to prevent inevitable fraud in programs that are managed by procedure rather than the face-to-face engagement that would be the case in extended families, churches, and most local governments.

- Today, a regulatory nanny-state is strangling economic growth, as outlined by Mancur Olsen. The impenetrable maze of regulation has become a kludge[350] afflicting us all.

- This is not a matter of accepting sub-par government performance as a price of social peace. As events have unfolded, there is no longer a viable tradeoff. The country's solvency is at stake, and in a financial crisis, it will surely be the poor who suffer the most – the poor who are the intended beneficiaries of this government largess.

- Progressives have left an enormous tab to be paid by the next generations, one unlikely to be honored.

This is the price of a philosophy that ignores Aristotle and Madison; that cavalierly allows government to escape its constitutional leash.

Future Implications

As the economist Stein stated: If something can't go on, it won't. In this case, our only obvious options are effective default or total reform. If business goes on as usual, these promises won't be kept. Kevin Williamson summarizes:

> There are basically three ways in which the federal government can go about not paying its obligations. One is by explicitly defaulting on creditors ... The second is "monetizing" the debt and entitlement liabilities, which means artificially creating money ... and nominally paying those benefits in increasingly worthless dollars... The third is implicitly defaulting on taxpayers, eliminating the entitlement programs as we know them.[351]

Clearly, it would be better to free the economy of its shackles as soon as possible to recharge economic growth. Increased prosperity would better position us to address these bills as they come due. Indeed, we could partially reduce the

---

[350] An older engineering term: A ludicrous assortment of incompatible and unworkable components.

[351] Kevin D. Williamson, *The End is Near and It's Going to be Awesome*, 105.

magnitude of the unfunded entitlements now. Stephen Moore writes that if we could restore average GDP growth to the historic average of 1974-2001 (1% a year more than it is), then in twenty-five years, the economy would be about eight trillion dollars larger than it would otherwise be. That is a big number that could solve many problems.[352]

However, one can say with some certainty that, without a sea change in the electorate and fundamental changes in how Congress conducts its affairs, the more positive outcome simply will not happen. Reform would be no small thing. Indeed, it would entail discarding a century of failed progressive ideas and, to a significant degree, returning the country to our constitutional heritage, leaving the government far smaller.

This would be an achievement of historical import. The last two chapters of the book outline what it would entail: the political worldviews that need to shift (Chapter Nine) and the major changes needed in our governmental institutions (Chapter Ten).

However, before we examine these options in more detail, it would be useful to examine the examples of some other countries – both good and bad – to help light the way.

---

[352]   Stephen Moore, "Growth Can Solve the Debt Dilemma," *The Wall Street Journal*, April 26, 2017, A17.

CHAPTER 6

CAUTIONARY EXAMPLES OF REPRESENTATIVE GOVERNMENT

"Aristotle identifies a commonwealth as the exercise of power by a majority – but a virtuous majority, respecting the lawful rights of all classes; in its deviations democracy is rule by the crowd, for the benefit of the dominant majority."[353] – Russell Kirk

"[P]ossession of political power through universal suffrage ... forces the political rule of the bourgeoisie into democratic conditions, which at every moment jeopardizes the very foundations of bourgeois society."[354] – Karl Marx

The earlier chapters discussed how mankind learned how to deal with governmental predation to allow the FEO to flourish under a light hand of government. To be sure, this was accomplished through trial and error, occurred in relatively few countries, and was not written in stone. Still, it was one of the preeminent achievements of humankind. The challenge was to address the potential flaws in pure democracy identified by Aristotle by checking the passions and power of majoritarianism while adequately representing the people and enabling individual liberty to flourish. Without adequate restraints on spending, borrowing, and taxation by the majority, the FEO stagnates and can be smothered.

---

[353] *The Roots of American Order* (Washington, DC: Regnery Gateway, 1991), 90.

[354] Ibid.

Chapter Three described the awesome achievement of the U.S. Constitution. The next chapter will discuss a few – a very few – other countries that have successfully addressed the same challenges. However, more countries than not have failed to do so. Without adequate constitutional restraints, majoritarianism under pure democracy is inevitably improvident and ultimately unstable. Ambitious politicians simply cannot resist well-intended but flawed spending schemes. Alexander Fraser Tyler, an eighteenth-century economist from the University of Edinburgh, opined that democracy "can only exist until the voters discover that they can vote themselves largesse from the public treasury."[355]

These tendencies are so powerful that, as the last two chapters demonstrated, they successfully undermined a few critical constitutional protections in the United States, leaving the country with alarming and perhaps unpayable debts for the future. Moreover, since the problem derives from human nature itself, it appears everywhere it is not deliberately checked – indeed, it is virtually a textbook result. All free countries need to take these lessons to heart. The universality of these tendencies can readily be observed in case studies from around the globe.

All the examples discussed below describe countries that modernized and experienced explosive improvements in living standards under an FEO initially supported by a protective oligarchy of landowning and financial interests who controlled legislatures that limited suffrage only to those who paid the bills. Despite its success, this model was changed due to pressure from an increasingly more educated, prosperous population. Suffrage was made universal so that governments would become truly representative, consistent with individual liberty. This transformation occurred with amazing speed in a number of countries during a few decades at the beginning of the twentieth century. Unavoidably, those events brought these countries – virtually all *Western* countries – face to face with Aristotle's concerns about pure democracy. His concerns proved to be well founded.

The common political dynamic drove events in numerous countries along amazingly similar paths: Prosperity was followed by deviations from the predicates of the FEO. The latter generally involved offering widespread economic *rights* that went beyond fiscal reason; attempting to transform society along utopian lines akin to Hayek's fatal conceit; taxing, borrowing, and manipulating markets through interest rates, currency controls, fixed prices, banking regulation, and other methods until the government ran out of money and could no longer borrow more. The end of this path is usually fiscal crisis, bankruptcy, high unemployment, and spreading misery.

Country case studies bring home the immediacy of those general conclusions; eight case studies will be presented in this chapter. However, they are divided into two dissimilar groups: (1)countries that are still struggling with fundamental

---

[355]   *Wikipedia*, Alexander Fraser Tyler.

unresolved problems – Greece, Italy, Argentina and Brazil and (2) countries who faced a fiscal crisis and eventually successfully re-grounded their FEO –Sweden, New Zealand, Canada, and Chile. The contrast between these groups will highlight the importance of the predicates of the FEO for reform. The countries in the second group will serve a dual-purpose: offer cautionary examples in this chapter, but becoming potential role models in the next.

Moreover, the latter group can serve to provide context to a popular belief that Sweden, and others somehow represent a valid "third way" between Capitalism (aka the FEO) and hard socialism as ways to organize society. As will be demonstrated, that view is not supportable. When those countries fully indulged the third way, it led to fiscal crisis. Only by reform to a stronger FEO-construct was stability restored. To be sure, Sweden is an attractive society characterized by a relatively large welfare state and safety-nets, but it is attainable only by first nurturing the predicates of the FEO. And, it comes with a trade-off: more sluggish growth and eventually lower standards of living for everyone when the size of government remains unduly large and intrusive.

COUNTRIES THAT DEVIATED FROM THE FEO AND ARE STILL STRUGGLING

Greece

Greece provides the most telling example of the pitfalls of representative government in the absence of appropriate constitutional safeguards or a supportive political culture. This example is unique because of the economic milieu created by its entry into the European Union, which facilitated borrowing and minimized the traditional penalties for overspending. The outcome is a dramatic example of an opportunistic political establishment prone to overpromise and overspend to buy votes, promote good intentions, and feather their nests without pushback from the markets. Market feedback, which would normally be seen in currency exchange rates, was rendered inoperative by Greece's use of the Euro. In addition to its institutional flaws, the country suffered from a credulous electorate that is culturally out of tune with the Protestant ethic and is suspicious of business, entrepreneurship, and most of the requirements for a smoothly functioning FEO.

To be sure, the outcome was not foreordained; a century or more ago, Greece had many characteristics common to strong commercial and entrepreneurial economies and contained many self-help civil institutions. However, Greece followed a path common to modernizing countries: rapid growth followed by profligate spending, which in its case was aggravated by the environment of the EU.

Historical context

Greece's history includes early times of promise, but societal changes after the First World War paved the way to hostility towards the FEO.

Classical and ancient Greece

Classical Greece was known for the prowess of its traders and the prosperity of commercial city-states such as Athens. While these traits were less evident after Greece lost its political autonomy, those values were not extinguished. Moreover, at the beginning of the twentieth century, when Greece was still part of the Ottoman Empire, its local governance showed all the signs of responsible, practical institutions. According to Antonis Kamaras:

> [C]ommunities in the trading cities of Alexandria, Odessa, Salonika, Smyrna, and Trieste, already had a long history of running their own school systems, hospitals, and orphanages. ... That system worked. Through local and communal organization, by the mid to late nineteenth century, the Greeks were one of the most prosperous and dynamic groups in Southeast Europe.[356]

This outcome was consistent with the Greeks' long mercantile history and was promising for the development of an FEO.

Modern Greece

After the First World War, however, a central administrative structure took over communal institutions, and powerful new national party machines displaced local elites who had successfully served as administrators. For example, in Greece's second-largest city, Salonika, schools, hospitals, and other institutions were nationalized, and local trustees were replaced by centrally appointed bureaucrats. Likewise, the responsibility for funding these institutions passed to the central government. The long-terms effects of this can account for much of the country's recent crisis. Long-established, autonomous local elites were displaced by a new group of people adept at managing a rent-seeking relationship with the state:

> The new local leaders joined national parties and then worked to build up party machines by distributing state largesse. Not a

---

[356] AntonisKamaras, "The Origins of the Greek Financial Crisis – Letter from Thessaloniki," *Foreign Affairs*, December 13, 2011.

> single region or city of note mobilized its resources in pursuit
> of economic success, based on international competitiveness.
> Instead all major localities channeled central government
> resources into patronage. The central government, which was
> dominated by the same parties, was an energetic accomplice.[357]

Even so, the post-Second World War era began with great promise: From 1950 to 1973, the Greek economy grew by an average of 7.7% per year, second in the world only to Japan.[358]While this early growth included a degree of deficit spending, large public deficits became a notable feature of Greece's social model only after the restoration of democracy in 1974, which marked the end of spectacular growth.

Democracy was restored with the removal of a right-leaning military junta. The new government wanted to bring "disenfranchised" left-leaning portions of the population into the economic mainstream. The Greek Constitution contains little in the way of checks and balances to restrain such populist impulses. Indeed, it implies that the government's role supersedes the functioning of the FEO. For example, Article 106(1) of the Constitution states:

> The State shall plan and co-ordinate economic activity in the
> country in order to consolidate social peace and protect the
> general interests with a view to achieving the development of all
> the sectors of the national economy. It shall take the necessary
> measure for the exploitation of the national resources in the
> atmosphere and the subterranean and under-sea deposits and for
> the promotion of regional development with special emphasis
> on strengthening the economy of mountainous and other areas
> and the islands.

In order to accomplish this, successive Greek governments regularly ran large deficits to finance public-sector jobs, pensions, and other social benefits. Prior to 1980, public debt only amounted to about 25% of GDP, and the government borrowed primarily to invest. But, with the advent of a socialist government in 1981, external borrowing was used to boost consumption. By the end of the 1980s, debt had reached 80% of the GDP. The spending trend continued even under subsequent conservative governments as they contended for votes.[359]

The expansion of the public sector corresponded with the decline of the

---

[357]   Ibid.

[358]   Graham T. Allison and KalypsoNicobidis, ed., *The Greek Paradox: Promise v. Performance* (Cambridge, Mass.: The MIT Press, 1997), 43.

[359]   Georgios P. Kouretas, *The Greek Debt Crisis: Origins and Implications.*

private, reducing the Greek economy's competitiveness and dramatically reducing manufacturing and industrial production. That decline was primarily caused by the governmental policy of taxing productive sectors and transferring those funds to the public. It was abetted by stifling regulation and wrongheaded public attitudes towards free markets.

Favoring the public sector, the government paid government employees higher wages than they would receive in the private sector. This disparity encouraged workers to seek public-sector jobs where payment was not linked to productivity. The EU-16 report on public spending and employment shows that, from the 1995 to 2005 period, Greece's highest increases in growth were in public spending and public administration.

World Bank indices also indicate that Greece presented entrepreneurs and startup businesses with bureaucratic obstacles. This had the added downside of increasingly corruption (Greece is ranked109[th] in the world for ease of starting a business). Unfortunately, these policies are also supported by public attitudes. For example, a European Commission Entrepreneurship's Survey published in December 2009 demonstrates the negative attitude of Greeks towards entrepreneurs and entrepreneurship. Agreement with statements such as "Entrepreneurs think only about their wallets" and "Entrepreneurs exploit other people's work" was even more common than in communist China.[360]

Entry into the EU Accelerates Profligate Behavior

The trajectory created by expanding government, vote-buying, and an electorate suspicious of the private sector was not notably different than that of a host of other countries around the globe (several of which will be examined in this chapter). However, economic stabilizing forces probably would likely have brought the fiscal spree to an earlier end if they had been allowed to take effect. Since the rest of the world will not subsidize profligacy, artificial happy times come to an end when a country can no longer borrow on viable terms.

Corrective forces common to all such national circumstances act along several lines. If spending is sustained by high rates of taxation, the economy will ultimately stagnate and shrink, forcing political change. If spending is supported by a central bank's money creation, inflation will set in and the currency will lose value, making borrowing difficult. If it is primarily supported by borrowing, interest rates will rise, the currency will fall, and the country will no longer be able to borrow from foreign sources. The system will ultimately correct, although the process may be painful. But what happens when these natural forces are forestalled artificially? The answer can be seen in Greece's experience.

Entering the European Union and adopting the euro gave Greece a multi-year

---

[360]   Ibid.

reprieve from the consequences of its misgovernment. Greece's ability to borrow improved dramatically upon its adoption of the euro. As Greece entered the euro zone, interest rate spreads between Greek and German ten-year government bonds fell drastically, from 1,100 basis points in early 1998 to about 100 basis points one year before Greece adopted the euro. After Greece adopted the euro, these spreads fell to as little as ten to thirty base points at the end of 2007.

Greece's economy and borrowing levels made up too little of the euro zone to impact the euro, so Greece could continue borrowing because banks saw little risk of currency devaluation. Usually cautious, banks apparently disregarded the moral hazard of a country borrowing beyond its means. Much of the profligate behavior was disguised, but it was also without precedent. In addition, banks probably calculated that, in the event of default, other EU governments would come to the rescue.

EU member states were not oblivious to the potential moral hazard, so they tried to erect protective barriers before allowing countries to adopt the euro. Euro zone countries had to commit to keeping annual governmental deficits below 3% of their GDP and to keep accumulated deficits below 60% of GDP. Greece pledged to do so, but given ongoing political pressure to spend and the lack of internal pushback, it was very unlikely that it would honor that pledge. Moreover, since the European Union put no teeth in the requirement, Greece simply took the easy way out with a mixture of deceit and slight-of-hand.

Able to borrow freely at low rates of interest, Greece accelerated its borrowing and spending habits. Initially, the Greek GDP grew significantly; between 1999 and 2004, government expenditures increased by more than 50%, and GDP increased by 23%. Indeed, after entering the European Union, Greece initially enjoyed a relatively high per-capita income on this borrowed money.

However, this was unsustainable since this growth was accompanied by unusually low business competitiveness. From 2001 to 2009, inflation and wage increases exceeded average increases in the rest of the euro zone. Greece's competitiveness, as measured by consumer prices, declined by 20%; measured by unit labor costs, it declined by 25%. One red flag was the country's huge current trade account deficit, which was sustained by borrowing.[361] But the natural corrective forces that would curb most independent countries, such as bank failures, sovereign default on debt, and currency devaluation, were temporarily held at bay. Had it not been part of the Eurozone, Greece's feckless behavior would have required it to borrow at interest rates far higher than those offered to fiscally responsible countries such as Germany.

Since no one was paying close attention neither the banks, nor the EU Parliament in Brussels, nor the International Monetary Fund – it's easy to understand why the import of Greece's behavior went unremarked as long as

---

[361]   Ibid.

174

it did. Actions by several successive Greek governments enabled the nation to continue spending and to hide its actual deficit from the European Union. The European Statistics Agency sent ten delegations to Athens at regular intervals. These delegates were tasked with improving the reliability of the statistics regarding the Greek national account, but they failed to uncover the true picture. Finally, in January 2010, the Statistic Agency issued a damning report accusing Greece of falsified data and political interference. For example, at the beginning of 2010, it was discovered that, since 2001, Greece had been paying banks hundreds of millions of dollars in fees for arranging transactions that hid the nation's actual level of borrowing. Most notable was a cross-currency swap in which billions of Euros of Greek debts and loans were converted into yen and dollars at a fictitious exchange rate to hide the true extent of Greece's loans.[362]

Ultimately, the problem grew too large and too unsustainable to hide. It became known that, from 2005 to 2009, Greece's structural deficit, which supported the illusion of prosperity, had grown steadily, from 6.7% to 19.1% of GDP. These spending policies pushed the gross government debt-to-GDP ratio to its 2011 apex of 170%. A significant amount of this was spent on public-sector compensation, which rose by 39% in real terms from 2003 to 2009, and pension increases, which were accentuated by the growing number of retirees.

In February 2010, a new government admitted to previously using a "flawed statistical procedure" and revised the 2009 deficit from the previously estimated 6% to 8% to an alarming 12.7% of GDP. Further revisions using Eurostat's standardized method showed it actually to be 15.7% of the GDP, the highest deficit by far for any EU country in 2009.

Greek debts had grown too large to be serviced by the country's anemic economy. Interest rates for Greek borrowers shot up, curtailing the country's ability to borrow further and eventually leading to sovereign and banking defaults on debt.

This example dramatically demonstrated the unsustainability of this spend-and-borrow system designed for a bloated public sector. Key metrics illustrate this: From its 2008 peak, Greece's economy contracted by more than 23% (retracing the unsustainable growth on borrowed money when entering the euro zone). Unemployment rose to 27.5% in December 2013, and youth unemployment rose to 60%. Greece's financial institutions were threatened, as was its membership in the European Union and the euro zone. The EU and international institutions intervened with two bailouts and a default that permitted a 50% debt write-down. In exchange, Greece had to agree to substantial public-sector reforms, more effective tax collection, some privatization of public property, and other fiscal adjustments.

A society grown accustomed to public largesse did not accept austerity

---

362   *Wikipedia. Greek Government Debt Crisis*

easily; there were numerous protests and violence in the streets. At one point, verdicts by Greek courts, such as the decision that the public-sector wage cuts are unconstitutional, will likely attenuate the efficacy of reforms. Moreover, other efforts to balance the books are likely to slow the economic growth needed to bring Greece back to economic viability. For example, in January 2011, the Greek government increased the standard value-added tax (VAT) to 23%. New taxes on gasoline were introduced, and in 2014, a new property tax that aims to raise $3.5 billion per year was imposed.[363]

While higher taxes and spending limits are crucial to shrink the deficit, ultimately the country has to be able to grow its way out of debt by creating a more productive economy. This seems problematic given the electorate's head-in-the-sand approach to the causes of Greece's predicament and the cultural lack of support for free markets. The *Index of Economic Freedom* rates Greece's economy as "mostly unfree," commenting on "Greece's worsening competitiveness and political volatility. Bold policy actions are needed to restore fiscal sustainability, enhance labor market flexibility, and tackle systemic corruption."[364]

Many Greeks viewed these problems as someone else's fault. After all, they are good people who just want what other prosperous countries have. Somehow, it must be the fault of the Germans with their Teutonic rigidity, their desire that loans be paid back. Some even blamed the crisis on the German occupation during the Second World War fifty years earlier. Denial is a powerful force.

Italy

Italy experienced the pattern of economic development that occurred in virtually all the world's developed countries: an extensive period of rapid growth in which the FEO was allowed to function, followed by a time when representative governments succumbed to spending and regulation on behalf of special interests. Examining this pattern through the predicates of the FEO helps explain Italy's current economic stagnation, falling productivity, and high unemployment rate.

Italy saw exemplary economic progress after the Second World War. It was a major manufacturer and exporter in the 1950s and 1960s; labor markets were flexible, productivity was high, and bureaucracy was relatively small. Then, as in other countries, factions in the parliament undermined the foundation of Italy's excellent post-war recovery and prosperity. They did so by increasing government spending and implementing a regulatory straitjacket designed to protect those

---

[363] "Europe's Fiscal Crisis Revealed: An In-Depth Analysis of Spending, Austerity, and Growth," Heritage Foundation Special Report on Europe, June 6, 2014.

[364] Terry Miller and Anthony B. Kim, *2016 Index of Economic Freedom: Promoting Economic Opportunity and Prosperity* (The Heritage Foundation and *The Wall Street Journal*, 2016), 215.

who already had jobs and had prospered by giving union laborers quasi-monopoly powers.

Annual government expenditures rose to 50% of the GDP. This spending was funded by years of borrowing, leading to a public debt totaling 127% of the GDP, the second highest in the European Union. Despite all this borrowing, taxes were also high, amounting to 43% of the GDP.[365] Recall that the more of the GDP the government consumes, the lower the average rates of growth. Italy fits that picture: In 2014, its economy had shrunk for five years at a compound rate of 1.4%, and unemployment was over 10%.[366]

However, it is in the area of worker regulation that Italy excels in stifling its economy. According to a Heritage Foundation study, in the early 1970s, the Italian government responded to inflation and recession by introducing a slew of strict labor regulations that gave unions more power to represent workers. Labor costs skyrocketed, and Italy's productivity shriveled, along with its share of the export market.

At the same time, rather than freeing the private economy, the government effectively made public employment a social benefit for the unemployed and a tool of political patronage. According to the same study, the efficiency of Italy's bureaucracy suffered, and tax increases paid for more unemployed workers portrayed as government employees. Together, these rigid labor rules and bureaucratic growth have produced the second-worst business climate in the developed world.

The Wall Street Journal provided an overview of Italy's condition:[367]

- Regulated professions such as lawyers and pharmacists consistently beat back efforts to break their cartels.
- Powerful bureaucrats bog down the implementation of new laws for years.
- Red tape is one factor that deters business from growing. Esselunga, the supermarket chain, says it scaled back plans for new stores after frustrating experiences involving building permits and other permissions ... In 2012 British Gas PLC threw in the towel on a 500€ million gas import terminal in southern Italy after struggling for over a decade to get the necessary permits.
- Routine contract disputes take more than three years on average to resolve in court – and much longer if there are appeals. ... At the end of 2012, there was a backlog of 9.7 million cases.

---

[365]   *2014 Index of Economic Freedom*, Italy, 251-252.

[366]   Ibid.

[367]   "Italy Struggles to Find its Way Back from the Crisis," *The Wall Street Journal*, A12. Note that everything quoted is from the article, but the order of points has been changed.

- Former Premier Mario Monti tried to inject more free-market competition in service sectors. Striking taxi and truck drivers, railway workers, pharmacists, lawyers and gas station owners protested his overhaul attempts and lobbied parliament to water them down. Even the weakened measures that passed into law have often made little difference [about five hundred laws had been passed but not implemented].
- Fear often lies behind the unions' defense of the status quo. Redundant blue-collar workers might never find jobs again in Italy's sclerotic jobs market.

The *Wall Street Journal* also notes that the 2,700-page labor code governs employment in exquisite detail, basically creating a dual system in which older workers benefit from the full force of the law, including restrictions on laying off, firing, or disciplining employees, while the remainder (mostly young workers) make do with temporary, freelance, or itinerant work. Businesses are so hesitant to hire that the official unemployment rate stands at 12% and half of Italy's young are unemployed. The World Economic Forum's 2014–2015 assessment of labor market efficiency ranked Italy 141 out of 144 countries.[368]

When Greece's economic crisis increased scrutiny of other European countries with shaky fiscal policies, Italy promised reform in the form of austerity. As is unfortunately not unusual in those circumstances, 'reform' meant raising taxes to reduce deficits, rather than reducing spending. Higher taxes (as discussed earlier) reduce economic growth, thus producing less revenue than expected and making further growth and potential revenues less likely.

According to Heritage, despite government ministers' claims that Italy embarked on a new age of austerity in July 2010, annual government spending decreased only slightly below pre-austerity levels from mid-2011 to mid-2012, and it has not fallen any further since then. On the other hand, taxes are now higher than before austerity; they have increased 57% more than spending has decreased. Attempts to liberalize Italy's rigid labor market have been unsuccessful, and Italian bureaucracy has not changed appreciably. In Italy, austerity has meant tax increases but little change in the size of government.[369] One result of resistance to change is that Italian households' disposable incomes have fallen.

So, a country can live beyond its means for years, but eventually the bill comes due.

---

[368] *The Wall Street Journal*, "Italy's Economic Suicide Movement," October 27, 2014.

[369] Europe's Fiscal Crisis Revealed: An In-Depth Analysis of Spending, Austerity, and Growth," Heritage Foundation Special Report on Europe, June 6, 2014.

Argentina

Argentina is a prime example of a country that grew wealthy quickly by aligning with the FEO, only to see subsequent representative governments sap its wealth and strangle wealth creation.

In 1853, in a promising beginning, the dictator Rosas was ousted. Argentina was blessed by the institution of a new constitution that incorporated FEO principles: the division of governmental powers, freedom of religion, support of private property and free trade, encouragement of immigration, foreign investment, and rule of law. This enabled it to rapidly develop its fertile pampas to produce grain and cattle while investing in the postal service, telegraph, railways, and ports.[370] With a relatively unburdened free market, Argentina underwent a half century of rapid growth now known as its Golden Age.

Indeed, by 1910, its GDP comprised half of all Hispanic America's GDP, and Argentina's economy was ranked tenth in the world with a per-capita income surpassing those of France and Italy.[371] The landed and business elites created favorable economic conditions similar to those set up by Whigs in Great Britain at the beginning of the Industrial Revolution. Indeed, these conditions were similar to those of most developed countries during their periods of most rapid growth (including Sweden, which will be discussed below). Nonetheless, as Marx noted, representative government will always be subject to populist pressures for universal suffrage. Argentina was no different. At virtually the same time as Great Britain, the United States, and Sweden, it altered its constitution to broaden the electoral franchise (lacking institutional checks like the U.S.). That was all it took for the country to regress economically.

The historian Carlos Rangel comments that after a populist government was elected in 1916, "Oligarchic democracy became chaotic democracy, full of inner contradictions, demagogical, ineffectual, incapable of holding in check the factions and the forces of disintegration..."[372] Rent-seeking, vote buying, and cronyism played leading roles.

Ineffectual representative government led to political instability characterized by military autocracy alternating with renewed parliamentary government. Both, however, were influenced by special interests of one kind or another: favored groups that supported the military on one hand and populism on the other. Little progress was made towards renewing the FEO that characterized early Argentina.

---

[370] Jose Ignacio Garcia Hamilton, "Historical Reflections on the Splendor and Decline of Argentina," *Cato Journal*, Vol.25, No.3 (Fall 2005).

[371] Ibid.

[372] Carlos Rangel, *The Latin Americans: Their Love-Hate Relationship with the United States*, 240-241, in Lawrence Harrison, *Underdevelopment is a State of Mind* (New York: Madison Books, 1985), 108.

Growing statist interventions into markets included rent control and marketing boards to regulate the production of meat, cereals, and other products. State intervention accelerated after Juan Peron came to power in 1946; he nationalized electricity, gas, and telephone utilities, as well as railroads and broadcasting. As is typical in populist regimes, rather than recognizing the errors of policy, he took more extreme measures to retain power. These included printing excess money, which led to inflation and eventually price controls. To retain power and facilitate extra-legal measures, he replaced the judges of the Supreme Court of Justice with "friendly" judges, abolished the freedom of the press, and jailed opposition leaders.[373]

Despite these desperate measures, a failing economy led to popular unrest and Peron's ousting in 1955 by a military coup. As was typical throughout Latin America, military coups might restore social stability, but, except in Chile, these military governments lacked a political philosophy compatible with free markets and liberty, so they invariably brought more corruption and oppression rather than reform.

By the late 1980s, inflation hit an annual rate of nearly 5000%. President Alfonsin resigned, calling the country "ungovernable." Hope arose when the new President Menem undertook key reforms in macroeconomic policies: He pegged the peso to the U.S. dollar, launched a major privatization program, and opened Argentina's highly protected economy.[374] He also dropped marginal tax rates; the top rate in 1984, 64%, was reduced to 30%.[375] From 1991 to 1998, the Argentine GDP grew by 6% a year, creating optimism at home and abroad that Argentina was finally getting its economic house in order.

These steps were necessary but insufficient. Because of tenacious resistance of special interests, the government continued to carry out profligate policies. Brink Lindsey notes that government spending rose from 9.4% of the GDP in 1989 to 21% in 2000.[376]

Vote buying led to pervasive featherbedding, particularly at the state level. For example, in the province of Tucuman:

> The public sector... serves primarily to enrich politicians and fund patronage jobs. Out of a formal work force of some 400,000, there are nearly 80,000 provincial and municipal government employees and another 10,000 federal government workers.

---

[373] Jose Hamilton, "Historical Reflections."

[374] Mary Anastasia O'Grady, The Americas: "Don't Blame the Free Market for Argentina's Woes," *The Wall Street Journal*, May 30, 1997, A19.

[375] David R. Henderson, *The Wall Street Journal*, March 29, 1996, A11.

[376] Brink Lindsey, Op-ed, *The Wall Street Journal*, January 9, 2002

> Elected officials siphon off small fortunes for themselves: The annual salary for provincial legislators is roughly $300,000.
>
> Tucuman is by no means noteworthy for such abuses. In the impoverished province of Formosa on the country's northern border, about half of all formally employed workers are on the government payroll, and many show up only once a month – to collect their paychecks."[377]

In 2001, Transparency International ranked Argentina fifty-seventh out of ninety-one nations in terms of corruption.

The weight of unaddressed structural problems overwhelmed the benefits of the new reforms. The government had not addressed the problems of huge bureaucracy, high levels of corruption, an intrusive regulatory regime, and a system of subsidizing special interest groups. As the costs of unaddressed problems mounted, the government took steps that are all too common for countries in such situations: It increased taxes and borrowed heavily from abroad. The house of cards fell in 2002 with a run on the banks. Under a new president, Argentina devalued the peso by 75%, defaulted on the terms of its public debt, and essentially confiscated bank deposits (by paying them off in devalued pesos rather than according to their contractual dollar status).[378] At the time of this writing, in 2014, Argentina has not repaid its debts and has been largely cut off from international lending and much investment.

Argentina's per-capita GDP was once comparable to France's; now is only 56% of France's GDP,[379] and Argentina continues to stagnate.

Brazil

Brazil followed the same pattern of rapid economic expansion under a FEO followed by populist-like governments that exploited its wealth for electoral purposes, followed in turn by economic upheaval.

For example, during a sixty-eight-year period, from 1920 to 1988, Brazil's GDP grew at an average of 6% a year, surpassed only by Japan. Importantly, more of Brazil's growth was industrial than that of the rest of Latin America. Due to the energies of large entrepreneurial immigrant groups, notably Germans and Japanese, industrial production increased at an average annual rate of 11% from

---

[377] Ibid.

[378] Guillermo M. Yeats, *The Roots of Poverty in Latin America* (Jefferson, North Carolina: McFarland & Company, 2005), 108.

[379] *2016 Index of Economic Freedom.*

1930 to 1940 and at an average annual rate of 9.9% from 1965 to 1980.[380] Because of these robust periods of growth, Brazil's overall economic performance in the twentieth century eclipsed that of all other Latin American countries, even oil-rich Mexico and Venezuela.[381]

But Brazil has no constitutional brake on utopian temptations. On the contrary, that country's Left embraced a constitution embodying "positive rights." The Brazilian Constitution guarantees the allocation of a certain minimum of government revenues to education. Health assistance must be available to all Brazilians, with a requirement that regional governments dedicate at least 12% of revenue to healthcare. Minimum levels of basic welfare and pensions were specified as well.[382]

Inevitably, these utopian goals led to high taxes, heavy regulation, and over-protectionism. Indeed, Brazil had been rated among the least free nations in Latin America according to *Economic Freedom of the World*, 1975-1995. The resulting problems became glaring; for twenty years, from the mid-seventies to the mid-nineties, Brazil experienced little economic growth. Per-capita income fell to an annual average of only 0.6% throughout the eighties, even as government spending on goods and services grew steadily and inflation became endemic, hitting triple-digit rates annually.

Corrective action was essential; under the leadership of Henrique Cardoso, Brazil's Minister of Finance, it took the form of the Real Plan in 1994, which provided monetary discipline and privatized some industry. Inflation was brought under control, and growth resumed. Two years after implementing these reforms, he was elected president.[383]

This was all to the good, but it was not enough. As in other countries, factions and special interests limited reforms to half-measures. The central state remained paramount. More ominously, a populist government under President da Silva followed Cardoso. Then, predictably, public debt increased from sixty billion dollars in 1994 to $370 billion in 2002; it is now over two trillion dollars.[384]

At this writing, spending by Brazil's local, regional, and national governments amounts to 41% of its GDP. The country's deficit amounts to 10% of the GDP, a level that has been seen to smother investment and economic growth. Moreover, the constitution and popular temper weaken efforts to bring this spending under

---

[380] Lawrence E. Harrison, *Who Prospers: How Cultural Values Shape Economic and Political Success* (New York: Basic Books, 1992), 35.

[381] Ibid, 28.

[382] William W. Lewis, *The Power of Productivity* (Chicago: The University of Chicago Press, 2004), 278.

[383] David Landes, in Lawrence E. Harrison and Samuel P. Huntington, *Culture Matters: How Values Shape Human Progress* (New York: Basic Books, 2000), 6.

[384] *2016 Index of Economic Freedom*, 129.

control. For example, pursuant to the "positive rights" guaranteed by government, Brazilian men typically retire at age fifty-four and women at age fifty-two; public pensions have increased from 3% to 7% of the GDP. Most other aspects of public life suffer. In 2019, 45% of the federal budget goes to pensions; only 2.8% is used to build and maintain public schools, hospitals, and roads or to pay for police, sanitation, and other infrastructure.[385]

Not surprisingly, at this writing in 2016, the country is again experiencing inflation, high unemployment, recession, and economic crisis.[386] So, while Brazil has seen periods of reform over the last century, the profligate progressive eras have overwhelmed the efforts made during those times.

COUNTRIES THAT ENCOUNTERED FISCAL CRISES BUT LATER REFORMED SUCCESSFULLY

The following four examples – Sweden, New Zealand, Canada, and Chile – experienced similar pressures of representative government to those seen in the problematic examples described above. These also fell prey to spending and regulation that eventually led to a fiscal dead-end. That pattern reinforces the conclusion that, without constitutional restraint, representative government tends towards unstable profligacy. But these examples are especially important, because, as will be discussed in the following section, they all discovered ways to return to a reinvigorated FEO.

Sweden

Sweden followed the fiscal trajectory discussed above; the details were perhaps different, but it was subject to the same societal and electoral dynamics. A century and a half ago, it evolved from a monarchical government to a parliamentary government, but slowly and with institutional protections against unrestricted popular representation. Much like other countries in that era, including Great Britain, Japan, Argentina, and the United States, landed and commercial property and capital interests were intent on keeping essential power in the hands of those who would pay the bills. Under a limited electoral franchise, proper constitutional limits were not so important.

After the 1865 parliamentary reform, the First Chamber (of a bicameral legislature) was indirectly elected from provincial and municipal councils.

---

[385] "Brazil Set to Tackle Pensions Overhaul," *The Wall Street Journal*, July 9, 2019, A16.

[386] Ruchir Sharma, "Impeachment Won't Save Brazil," *The Wall Street Journal*, April 19, 2016, A13.

Members had to meet wealth and income requirements. The members of the Second Chamber were directly elected, but they, too, had to meet income requirements. Rapid economic growth ensued.

In an increasingly well-to-do country, however, electoral change became unavoidable. In Sweden, as in other representative democracies, government would not be seen as legitimate until it truly represented the people. Consequently, in 1921, suffrage was extended to include women. Much later, on January 1, 1975, a new constitution providing for a directly elected unicameral legislature went into effect. This constitution limited the king's authority to ceremonial duties and discarded the checks and balances provided by a bicameral legislature.

Until these changes were implemented, Sweden, benefitting from its free-market origins, became increasingly prosperous. It relied on raw materials such as timber and iron ore but also benefited from a growing export industry involving globally competitive companies such as Volvo and Erickson. Although it increasingly pursued a social-democratic vision, Sweden was careful to nurture business, especially exporters, even as it raised taxes and spending. Sweden policies used a unique, almost corporatist approach characterized by two key features. First, the central Labor Union (LO) collaborated with a unified business council to reach agreement on most labor matters with limited input from the government. Consequently, there was much less labor strife than in other industrial nations. Second, while Sweden instituted high taxes in general (income taxes and value-added taxes), it taxed business and capital formation relatively lightly, which in turn nurtured growth. The implicit paradigm was that global companies such as Volvo and Erickson would generate wealth while enlightened bureaucrats drew on that wealth to build the "people's home" through welfare spending.

However, without real restraints or economic understanding politicians overreached in attempts to win votes. By the early 1970s, the industrial sector was becoming relatively smaller, and there were concerns about Sweden's trade balance. Moreover, the government kept growing as a share of the GDP; it doubled from 1960 to 1980 and peaked at 67% in 1993.[387] During this period, Sweden, which was prosperous and had highly developed social programs, was viewed as a prototype for a "third way" of government between "raw capitalism" and socialism. As overspending picked up speed, Olof Palme, the Prime Minister, stated that "the era of neo-capitalism is drawing to an end. It is some kind of socialism that is the key to the future."[388]

In line with that, the public sector grew relative to the private sector's large exporters. The public sector's share of total employment went from 20% in

---

[387]   *The Economist*, "Northern Lights," February 2, 2013.

[388]   Ibid.

1965 to 38% in 1985.[389] Even so, unemployment grew. To cover growing budget deficits, the government resorted to more foreign borrowing and higher taxes. The marginal tax rate for the average worker rose from 35% in the 1960s to 65% in 1976.[390] Inflation rose (to 15% annually in 1980), and the krona was devalued several times. Consequently, as the economy became less robust, the two decades after 1970 were a period of relative decline – Sweden had been the world's fourth richest nation in 1970; in 1993, it was only the fourteenth.[391]

Something had to give. Unfortunately, as is usually the case, politicians will not take sufficient corrective action in fiscal matters without a crisis, and certainly those who benefit from fiscal policies will not do so. How did Sweden recognize the need for change? This knowledge dawned slowly.

While political parties took notice of the growing problems and stagnation, they undertook few serious reforms until few options were left. Some early modest steps werein the 1970s: The budget was kept under control and credit policy was tightened. In 1976, when the non-socialist parties got their first chance in decades to form a government they focused on economic problems, but even then, no fundamental changes were implemented. "On the contrary, the nonsocialist Cabinet was eager to show that the Social Democrats were wrong when they claimed that the welfare state would be wrecked."[392] Given that Sweden had some of the highest direct taxes in the world, tax reform was an obvious idea, but was resisted by the Social Democrats.[393] Nonetheless, due to sensible private-sector policies, the economy eked out continued growth until the 1990s.

Unfortunately, that growth was achieved not through reform but through greater regulation and government distortion of economic incentives, a method that could only be effective for a short while. For example, the government controlled the quantity and price of credit; it favored exporters but harmed other sectors of the economy. At the same time, the government stopped borrowing from foreign markets to fund deficits in efforts to maintain a currency peg (the international exchange value of the krona). This kept domestic interest rates high and foreign rates low, leading the banks (as opposed to the government)to borrow low from foreign markets and lend to the government, effectively transferring the foreign-exchange risk from the government to the banks. (If the krona peg slipped

---

[389]   "On the Resolution of Financial Crises: The Swedish Experience," Federal Reserve Bank of Cleveland, Policy Discussion Paper No. 21, June 2007, 2.

[390]   Ibid.

[391]   *The Economist*, "Northern Lights," February 2, 2013.

[392]   StigHadenius. *Swedish Politics During the 20th Century: Conflict and Consensus*(Trelleborg: The Swedish Institute, 1997), 124.

[393]   Ibid, 138.

substantially, the banks would owe considerably more than they had borrowed since their debts were denominated in foreign currencies.)[394]

In addition, relaxed controls on domestic borrowing led to a housing boom; it was also fueled by bank lending, which depended on foreign borrowing. The boom turned into a speculative bubble, and household outstanding debt increased rapidly. (This was not too dissimilar to the 2008 financial crisis in the United States.)

Rising levels of foreign borrowing made the currency peg unsupportable. Sweden had to allow the krona to fluctuate freely in value against other currencies, which resulted in their loans, which were fixed in other currencies, growing as measured by the krona. The housing boom collapsed, real estate prices dropped by 25%, the banks' nonperforming loans mushroomed, and Sweden's largest banks began failing. The unforgiving nature of the crisis became evident in the autumn of 1990 when a major finance company declared insolvency; this led to problems throughout the financial services industry. In 1991 and 1992, Swedish banks had to take write-downs and loss provisions of some one hundred billion kronor – equivalent to the entire banking system's total equity capital.[395] The state took over much of the banking sector to resolve the failed banks' debts; this was similar to the United States' creation of the Resolution Trust Corporation in 1989 to resolve the debts of the failed Savings and Loan banks.[396]

This wholesale crisis forced the political establishment finally to seriously consider reform. That story will be related in the next chapter, which examines the steps various countries have taken to maintain or restore economic health.

New Zealand

Like Sweden, New Zealand traveled down the road of social democratic good intentions; it also saw a similar outcome.

New Zealand's adoption of the elements common to social democracies began with the Liberal government of the 1890s, expanded significantly with the first Labour government of the 1930s, and continued with subsequent governments, even those of the more conservative National Party. The utopian philosophy governing New Zealand politics over decades has been summarized by Boston and Holland:

> The State had an active and major role to play in the nation's
> economic affairs, in the promotion of social justice and in

---

[394]   "On the Resolution of Financial Crises: The Swedish Experience," Federal Reserve Bank of Cleveland, Policy Discussion Paper No. 21, June 2007, 3.

[395]   Ibid, 142.

[396]   Ibid, 3-6.

the betterment of the human condition. Not merely did this include measures for correcting market failures, it also involved State provision of goods and services, the detailed regulation of economic activity (including decisions on production and pricing), the redistribution of income, and the supply of welfare benefits for those in need. Correspondingly, the role of the market as an allocation mechanism was diminished and the legitimacy of market outcomes called into question.

Coupled with this advocacy of an activist State was the quest for economic stability, security and certainty. At the macroeconomic level this found practical expression in the vigorous pursuit of Keynesian-type demand-management strategies and the maintenance of a fixed exchange rate ... Such policies were supported with guaranteed prices for agricultural commodities, various kinds of subsidies and incentives to the export sector, the maintenance of a substantial level of border protection for domestic manufacturing, the tight control of capital markets, strict limits on foreign ownership, and a highly regulated labor market. ... [even in the face of negative consequences, the goal was] that the costs of economic adjustment were spread throughout the community, and that full employment was maintained – even at the price of substantial foreign borrowing.[397]

Decades of this political approach necessarily smothered the working of the FEO, leading to an increasingly sclerotic economy and eventually a financial crisis in the early 1980s. Left and Right governments alike had good intentions but lacked a coherent economic theory, so they resorted to *ad hoc* intervention in the economy to correct the unintended consequences of past interventions, holding to the arrogant belief that political manipulation of the business cycle was superior to free markets.

In such circumstances, everything economic becomes intensely political. As a result, special interests (factions) assumed an unusually dominant role. These included the Federated Farmers, the Producer Boards, the Manufacturers Federation, and the Federation of Labor. According to Boston and Holland:

Almost inevitably this process resulted in a large political constituency with a vested interest in resisting change:

---

[397]   Jonathan Boston and Martin Holland, *The Fourth Labour Government: Radical Politics in New Zealand* (Auckland: Oxford University Press, 1987), 3.

> manufacturers sought to maintain existing levels of protection;
> unions strove to preserve, if not improve, the real wages of their
> members; and farmers demanded Government action to defend
> their incomes in the face of rising input costs and falling export
> prices.[398]

On the macroeconomic level, again according to Boston and Holland:

> The results could be seen in the country's relative economic
> decline, slow rate of growth, poor adjustments to external supply
> shocks and adverse terms of trade, high levels of inflation, an
> increasing level of distribution dissent, the growth of structural
> unemployment, and mounting international indebtedness.[399]

That indebtedness became the impetus for reform because government subsidies and income redistribution could only be sustained by foreign lenders. This led to high debt loads, a falling currency, and demands by foreign lenders for higher rates of interest, all of which made the model increasingly unsustainable.

In a 1994 speech, John Wood, who had been a deputy secretary of Foreign Affairs, provided a useful overview of New Zealand's condition at the time as well as the comprehensive nature of the reforms it eventually implemented.[400] He noted that New Zealand had escaped the ravages of the Second World War and, at the time of the Korean War, was among the five wealthiest countries in the world. However, by the late 1970s, it had nearly fallen to twentieth. Because of the policies described above, its national debt was approaching third-world proportions; it had a top tax rate of 66%; and from 1975 to 1983, the economy barely grew while unemployment went from 0% to 5%.[401]

So, New Zealand became an object lesson of the downsides of disregarding the predicates of the FEO and of social democracy itself (not that other countries were paying any attention). In line with the continuing theme of this chapter, New Zealand's case illustrates that only dire necessity can motivate free-spending politicians to act.

The unanticipated surprise was that New Zealand's political class was not only capable of learning but also of taking the lesson to heart. Moreover, it was the leftwing Labor Party that initially implemented the reforms that led to a world-class achievement; this will be examined in the next chapter.

---

[398] Ibid, 4.

[399] Ibid, 5.

[400] John Wood, "New Zealand: A Blueprint for Economic Reform," Heritage Foundation HL 531, June 16, 1995.

[401] Ibid.

Canada

Canada did not experience a fiscal crisis to the same degree as the other countries described here. This was partly because it found solutions much sooner than the other examples. Nonetheless, Canada was subject to the same pressures to overspend as the others and also suffered diminished economic growth.

Like the other examples, in its early history, Canada leaned towards classical liberal beliefs. It kept tax rates low to compete with the United States for investments and immigrants. Specifically, Wilfred Laurier, the prime minister from 1896 to 1911, favored spending restraint, low taxes, free trade, and civil liberties. Canada did not significantly deviate from such policies until Pierre Trudeau's leftist administration in the 1960s. Trudeau followed the course set by social democrats elsewhere – he expanded social programs, levied higher taxes, nationalized businesses, and set trade barriers. Federal spending as a share of GDP rose from around 16% to almost 25% from the mid-1960s to the mid-1980s, on top of provincial government spending. This was accompanied by high inflation.[402]

These policies had the same negative results seen in other left-of-center governments – increased debt, slowed growth, and lower levels of employment. Unlike New Zealand and Sweden, which were forced to institute abrupt reforms, Canada's reforms were implemented gradually over a decade or so. Initially, these reforms were spurred by sluggish economic performance at home and influenced by Reagan's positive reforms in the United States and Thatcher's in the United Kingdom. In the second half of the 1980s, Canada's central bank adopted a goal of price stability, and the government cut selected tax rates, privatized a number of major companies, and entered into a free-trade agreement with the United States.

Ultimately, however, these market reforms were insufficient to stem growing spending and debt levels that left the economy sluggish and vulnerable. Concomitant with a recession in the United States, a severe recession hit Canada in 1990, causing the GDP to fall more than 3% below its peak; employment fell alongside it. Even though the GDP stabilized and began a slow recovery, employment kept falling through 1991 and 1992. Yet the country maintained high levels of spending (federal and provincial); total expenditures exceeded 50% of the GDP, and in 1995 gross public debt exceeded the GDP for the first time.

Fortunately, the Canadian government finally recognized the failings of their social-democratic ways and – without a full-blown crisis as in Sweden and New Zealand – launched various reforms. These will be discussed in the next chapter along with the other heartening examples.

---

[402]   Chris Edwards. "We Can Cut Government Debt: Canada Did," *Cato Policy Report*, Vol. 34, No.3, May/June 2012.

Chile

Like Argentina, after gaining its independence, Chile was ruled by an oligopoly of landed and commercial interests. It experienced many decades of growth by developing its copper and nitrate resources and agricultural products. By 1900, Chile's per-capita income, while only three-quarters of Argentina's, was twice that of Brazil and more than those of Columbia, Mexico, and Peru.[403]

However, also like Argentina, in the new century, suffrage was expanded and Chile's economic growth flagged, again due to the familiar combination of unstable governments and statist economic policies. The middle of the twentieth century, a forty-year period, was characterized by constitutional government in which the government swung between leftist parties, including Communists and Socialists, to those on the right, notably the Christian Democrats. All of them lacked free-market principles and followed the nostrums of most Latin American parties, pursuing policies of spending, import substitution, and state involvement in the economy. The predictable results were chronic inflation and generally low growth during those years.

However, this lengthy dysfunctional pattern did not lead to crisis until the election of Salvador Allende in 1970, an event that signaled a hard left turn in Chilean politics. He was elected by a bare plurality of the vote (36.6%), yet his government embarked on a program of radical populism, attempting to redistribute wealth, expropriate American copper companies, nationalize Chilean private companies (150 in 1971), and vastly increasing spending on welfare, subsidized housing, healthcare, and education. This sharp political turn resulted in a still sharper economic decline as business investment dried up, foreign exchange reserves ran out, and inflation hit 500% per year in 1973. Equally importantly, the government's legitimacy was undermined as rule of law weakened when the government looked the other way as squatters took over private property. Social unrest grew.

As Parliament was clearly unable to deal with the unrest, the military intervened – as it often did in other Latin American countries. Unlike elsewhere, however, this produced some unexpected positive outcomes reinstituting the FEO; these effects will be discussed in the next chapter.

*   *   *

The narrative in this chapter has illustrated the unhappy common tendencies of representative governments that lack constitutional restraints to pursue utopian goals that undermine the FEO and eventually result in stagnation or

---

[403]   Lawrence E. Harrison, *The Pan-American Dream* (Boulder, Colorado: Westview Press, 1997), 154.

crisis. Fortunately, given human ingenuity and humans' ability to adapt, general tendencies need not determine a country's fate. Indeed, a number have learned from their mistakes and have implemented impressive reforms after crises, from which others can in turn learn.

In addition, there are others who had constitutional bulwarks that enabled them from the outset to avoid the most egregious effects of those tendencies. Both groups are the subject of the next chapter; they provide lessons that should be taken to heart.

CHAPTER 7

COUNTRIES ALIGNED WITH THE FEO

"The *Economic Freedom of the World* rating is a measure of the extent to which countries rely on private ownership and markets rather than the political process to allocate goods, services, and resources."[404]

Chapter Five demonstrated the problems faced by the United States when it departed from the predicates of the FEO by undermining constitutional protections. Chapter Six demonstrated that such patterns of mis-governance are all too common because of how human nature plays out under representative government. However, Chapter Three showed that human intelligence and creativity enable us to limit our darker (or at least self-defeating) impulses to craft stable, working governments that keep such impulses in check; this is what the U.S. Constitution was originally designed to do.

The hapless impasse in the current U.S. government strongly suggests that significant reform will be needed if the country is to successfully address the fiscal problems that lie ahead. The ongoing theme of this book is that such measures will be required to bring the United States back into alignment with the principles of the FEO. However, the U.S. is not alone in this endeavor. We can draw on the experience of others – even if special interests, much of academia, and the mainstream media choose to avert their eyes. Therefore, this chapter will consider the experiences of others who have dealt successfully with similar problems or, even better, have managed to avoid them.

---

[404] James Gwartney and Robert Lawson with William Easterly, *Economic Freedom of the World 2006 Annual Report* (Canada: The Fraser Institute, 2006), 5.

Two categories of foreign experience suggest measures that can invigorate the FEO at home. The first are countries whose governmental designs kept them aligned with the FEO and helped them avoid fiscal crises; the second are those who started down the wrong road, learned their lessons, and reformed. Both kinds of experience contain a host of useful lessons. This chapter identifies methods other countries have used to check utopian impulses, overambitious central governments, unaffordable spending, and encroachments on individual liberty.

Since there is a close link between the principles of the FEO and the countries ranked high in the *Index of Economic Freedom,* this examination will pay particular attention to the highest-ranked countries. The examples fall naturally into three types: Some use a form of federalism to provide checks and balances; some achieved high rankings due to strong, enlightened leadership; and some have made the parliamentary form of government work through determined reform. While there is no universal elixir of reform, they are all examples of successful incorporation of the central elements of an FEO.

One common dominator of the examples is that they have all either avoided or overcome the singular weakness of representative government – its tendency to overpromise benefits and impose regulations supporting special interests. Another common denominator that is much more difficult to define is cultural: The examples share a tradition of the Protestant Ethic; that is, all the leading examples are Germanic, Scandinavian, or English or are colonial offshoots of England. This makes sense because, as discussed in Chapter Three, England led the way in the evolutionary development of representative government. The populations in most of the examples inherited that evolutionary development. Outliers include Hong Kong and Singapore, which benefitted from the example of British governance but whose traditional cultures are largely Confucian, and Chile, which is essentially Hispanic but has many citizens of European descent.

The examples are grouped as (1) federal republics that incorporate institutional checks and balances – Switzerland, the Netherlands, and Germany; (2) countries that benefitted from strong, principled leadership – Hong Kong and Singapore; and (3) countries with reformed parliamentary governments – Sweden, New Zealand, Canada, and Chile.

FEDERAL REPUBLICS

Chapter Three described how federal republics (such as the United States) evolved. A roughly similar dynamic produced federal republics elsewhere, notably in Switzerland, Germany, and the Netherlands. While the experiences of these federations do not reveal a cure-all for governmental breaches of the FEO, they do demonstrate ways to corral the worst excesses. An implicit conclusion is that effective checks by subsidiary political elements (e.g., states, cantons, Länder, or provinces) can limit utopian overreach by the central government. Indeed, it appears that these subsidiary elements can help limit the problematic aspects of representative government: huge deficits, massive national debt, and impossible entitlement programs. However, none of the examples described here has an ideal FEO. For example, in many of these countries, central government spending comprises too much of the GDP, which (as we have seen) reduces growth rates. But none have the fiscal imbalances – a portent of crisis – seen in the United States today.

Switzerland

The Swiss government highlights one of this book's principal themes: the utility of distrusting strong central government and maintaining a political structure that protects against its overreach. This approach has given Switzerland a relatively light touch of government that makes it a leading example of nations preserving a robust FEO. What is the source of this philosophy of vigilance, what governmental features are used to implement it, and how did the nation's politics and economic promise unfold as a result?

Historical background

The Helvetian Confederation was formed from an alliance of cantons that agreed to protect one another against larger powers like the French Bourbons on one side and the Hapsburg Empire on the other. At that time, it consisted of a notably heterogeneous collection of political entities. The confederation had to pragmatically address these entities' mutual suspicion to pursue the larger goal of security and liberty. The numerous cantons included Protestants and Catholics, as well as a range of cultures that mirrored their native languages: German, French, Italian, and Romansch. At a time when religious passions ran high (as manifested in ruinous wars), these cantons were decidedly unwilling to submit their sovereignty to a political system that might allow some to become overbearing. The initial confederation, which lasted for centuries, required consensus on all matters requiring mutual action. Like the United States' Articles of Confederation, this arrangement facilitated common defense but little else.

But institutional change did come. Initially, it was externally imposed by Napoleon's creation of a unitary state, which disbanded after his defeat. Afterwards, even though some cantons (the "radicals") wanted to transform the confederacy into a Napoleonic-like *unitary* state, the resistance of others (mainly the Catholic members) prevented that outcome. Eventually, however, in 1848, the desire for a common market led the Diet to adopt a new constitution establishing a *federal* rather than a unitary state. At first, the new federal government was given only a few enumerated "competences" and the cantons retained control of all other political matters. In 1874, another new constitution broke down economic barriers among the cantons by introducing freedom of commerce and trade, as well as freedom of residence.[405] Nonetheless, the cantons ceded to the central government only matters that could not be effectively handled locally: defense, foreign affairs, currency, and so forth.

The underlying rationale was not dissimilar to that motivating the U.S. Constitutional Convention. The federal government was limited by checks and balances, especially by juxtaposing subsidiary entities (states/cantons) against a central government. The two nations had a similar republican form of government as well: In Switzerland, the people's direct votes were channeled through representatives in the National Council, the legislature's lower house; the Council of States, which was the upper house, directly represented the cantons themselves (just as, initially, U.S. Senators were elected by state legislatures).

However, Switzerland differed from the United States in important ways. In particular, Switzerland more pointedly limited the central government's power constitutionally.

Swiss Constitutional Limits

The most recent Swiss Constitution, which was adopted by public referendum on April 18, 1999 and has been in force since January 1, 2000, contains the following provisions:

Article 43a, Principles for the Allocation and Fulfillment of State Functions
    (1) The Federation only undertakes tasks that the Cantons are unable to perform or which require uniform regulation by the Federation.
    (2) The collective body that benefits from a public service bears the costs thereof.
    (3) The collective body that bears the costs of a public service may decide on the nature of that service.

Article 47, Autonomy of the Cantons
    (1) The Federation preserves the autonomy of the Cantons.
    (2) It leaves the Cantons sufficient functions of their own and respects their organizational autonomy.

---

[405]   Hanspeter Kriesi and Alexander H. Trechsel, *The Politics of Switzerland, Continuity and Change in a Consensus Democracy* (Cambridge: Cambridge University Press, 2008), 2-3.

Article 126, Budget
    (1) The Federation holds its expenditures and revenues in the long term in equilibrium.
    (2) The maximum amount in the estimated budget of total expenditure to be granted depends, considering the economic situation, on the estimated revenues.
    (3) With extraordinary financial need the maximum amount of Paragraph (2) above may be appropriately increased. The Federal Parliament decides on such an increase according to Article 159(3)c.
    (4) If the expenditure shown in state budget (*Staatsrechnung*) exceeds the maximum amount in Paragraphs (2) and (3) above, the excess expenditure has to be compensated during the following years.

Article 128, Direct Taxes
    (1) The Federation may levy a direct tax:
          a.   of at most 11.5% on the income of natural persons.
          b.   of at most 8.5% on the net proceed of legal persons.

So, not only does the Swiss Constitution take the enumerated-powers approach of the original U.S. Constitution, but it also places a fiscal halter on the government. On the other hand, as will be discussed, recognizing that times and needs change, the Swiss Constitution was designed to be easier to amend than the U.S. one.

Institutional Structure

This institutional design promoted cautious government through (1) a collaborative executive function and (2) two types of institutional checks and balances.

The Swiss president serves a one-year term of office and is drawn from a seven-man Federal Council, who are drawn from members of the Parliament. Each member of the Council leads a governmental department; collectively, they constitute an effective executive arm. This arrangement allows more executive function than might be expected due to a principle of "non-hierarchy": Once a decision is made, each Council member commits to defending it. This differs significantly from most parliamentary systems in which typically, members of the majority party in Parliament head up ministries and can be removed from those positions by the dominant party. In Switzerland, however, Parliament appoints members to the Council for four-year terms and cannot remove them during that period.[406] Furthermore, tradition (though not constitutional provisions) requires that four different parties – the Liberals, the Christian Democrats, the Social

---

[406]   Ibid,76.

Democrats, and the Swiss People's Party – be represented among those seven Council members.[407]

It should be self-evident that the weak Swiss presidency does not lend itself to the exertions of ambitious men. Recall Wilson's outsized ambitions as the United States started down the Progressive road: "The president is at liberty, both in law and conscience, to be as big a man as he can. His capacity will set the limit; and if Congress be overborne by him … it will be from no lack of constitutional powers ... but only because the president has the nation behind him, and Congress does not." There would be none of that in the Swiss Republic.

Moreover, experience has shown that the inclusion of all the major parties in the Federal Council tempers partisanship and disunity, albeit at the cost of speed. While this structure has significantly slowed change, where change has occurred, it has been more prudent and less sweeping, than, for example, in the United States, where strong leaders supported by supermajorities in Congress allowed the unfortunate introduction of Social Security, Medicare, and Obamacare.

Institutional checks and balances arise from a bicameral legislature. The cantons participate directly in one of the legislative houses; the other gives the people a direct voice. The Swiss system also incorporates a much-used referendum process. Therefore, both the cantons and the people have direct means to slow the legislative process or even reverse outcomes. The number of actors, the Federal Council, parliament itself, the cantons, and public referenda, have, according to Kriesi and Trechsel, transformed a "plebiscitary democracy" into a "negotiation democracy"; it takes an average of five years for an initiative to receive a final vote in Parliament.[408] More dramatically, it is estimated that the optional referendum alone is responsible for delaying the introduction of new social insurance schemes by an average of fifteen years.[409]

Amending the Constitution

Yet, in one key respect, change is easier in Switzerland than in the United States: Constitutional change can be achieved through a "double majority" formed by the votes of the cantons together with a referendum, an outcome that has been achieved on relatively numerous occasions. Still, it is not easy.[410]

In the United States, of course, constitutional change is far more difficult; it requires *super-majorities* in both Houses of Congress as well as in the states. This feature was designed to create stability and to slow changes to the form

---

[407]   Ibid.

[408]   Ibid, 115.

[409]   Ibid, 162.

[410]   Kriesi and Trechsel, *The Politics of Switzerland*, 34-35.

of government. However, as seen in Chapter Four, when U.S. political forces became impatient with constitutional limitations, they chose to simply ignore the Constitution (presumably the worst of outcomes in terms of the rule of law). To be sure, at the onset of the progressive era, the United States did do the hard work of amending the Constitution (such as when income taxes were implemented). However, the ambitions of the New Deal led Roosevelt and the Democrats to simply abandon that constitutional requirement.

In contrast, Switzerland adhered to its constitutional procedures. As they found it necessary to increase the power of their federal government, each additional "competence" was subject to national debate and the referenda process. Appropriately, although these measures sometimes failed, the Swiss were eventually able to adopt measures similar to those of other modern representative governments, including old-age pensions and universal healthcare. However, due to Swiss tradition and caution, they approached these issues more slowly and prudently than the United States or other countries discussed in the prior chapter.

How has this form of government played out? How did they handle the big-ticket items of pensions and healthcare that most threaten the United States' fiscal future, and how does the country fare in general as measured by the predicates of the FEO?

An Assessment

If Adam Smith was correct that a light hand of government in economic matters is a prerequisite for prosperity, Switzerland should be expected to perform well. This turns out to be the case. In the *2014 Index of Economic Freedom*, Switzerland was ranked fourth in the world. It particularly excels in the elements of the FEO: rule of law, regulatory efficiency, and open markets.[411] In addition, the World Economic Forum's *Global Competitiveness Index* has ranked Switzerland first in the world for many years running.[412] Its openness to entrepreneurship has been the engine of prosperity. For example, in proportion to population, Switzerland has four times as many Fortune 500 companies as other leading countries.[413] At the same time, small and medium-sized companies make up 70% of the Swiss economy and, according to Breiding, punch well above their weight competitively.[414]

All in all, the country enjoys sound finances (modest government debt and no threatening unfunded entitlements), a sound currency, low unemployment, and

---

[411]   *Index of Economic Freedom*, Switzerland.

[412]   *The Wall Street Journal*, September 27, 2017, B11.

[413]   R. James Breiding, *Swiss Made: The Untold Story Behind Switzerland's Success* (London: Profile Books Ltd., 2013), 7.

[414]   Ibid, 11.

a high standard of living. Its federal form of government provides an important counterexample to the view that representative government need be undone by unfounded good intentions and ambitious politicians. Its system of checks and balances has effectively hindered the growth of well-intentioned but misguided initiatives that have sprung up in other democracies.

Most importantly, unlike the United States, Switzerland dealt with the universal issues of healthcare and pensions prudently, in keeping with tradition and with an FEO. The slow process for adopting new competences does not permit the introduction of grandiose, economically impossible schemes. While in the United States, this can occur when one party enjoys a monopoly on power, in Switzerland, it is first necessary to change the competences of the federal government via constitutional amendments, which require the "double majority" described above.

Just as in all modern democracies, Swiss political forces on the Left, particularly the unions and the Social Democrats, pushed for ambitious social programs. Fortunately, Swiss culture, traditions, and the slow deliberation required by the political system produced a process more in tune with the FEO (not to mention basic economics) than was the case in the United States.

For example, in Switzerland, health insurance was initially handled primarily by civil society, as was once the case in the United States and Britain. Insured persons paid premiums to mutual societies. So when the country moved to make insurance more universal, the consensus process preserved the strengths of the traditional system; most importantly, it continued to fund healthcare through insurance rather than a prepaid system. One result is that healthcare costs are only 11% of the GDP in Switzerland; in the United States, they are 17% (and are still inadequately funded).

Swiss legislation on pensions came later, in 1948 and 1984. Here, too, earlier traditions of civil society were influential: Because "voluntary collectivization of provision had preceded state interventions by decades and mutual societies or unions had built up extensive institutional networks of their own, they tended to resist any takeover by the state and to oppose compulsory arrangements."[415]

By retaining the best traditions of civil society and employing sound principles of insurance, Switzerland's national debt remains modest, and the nation has no looming unfunded entitlements like those in the United States. According to R. James Breiding, "[n]o other developed country has avoided burdening future generations with large debts or fostering illusions among its people about meeting pension and healthcare costs."[416]

Beyond those two issues, Swiss studies show that "direct democracy puts

---

[415]   Kriesi and Trechsel, *The Politics of Switzerland*, 159.

[416]   Breiding, *Swiss Made*, 1.

the brake on public expenditure and on public debt. The citizens appear to be generally … more frugal with public resources than their political elites."[417]

Nonetheless, in some respects, the Swiss experience has been less stellar than one would expect based on its governmental system. To be sure, its financial stability is unsurpassed; it seems very unlikely that the country could ever face the potential insolvency (or at least default on sovereign debt) faced by many other European countries and perhaps in time the United States itself. However, Switzerland's economic growth rates and standard of living are lower than one might expect from its macroeconomic and political systems, particularly since it avoided the devastation of the First and Second World Wars.

Contrast Switzerland with another highly ranked country in the Index, Singapore. In 2014, Singapore's GDP per capita was 30% higher than Switzerland's, and its compound growth over the previous five years was about three times higher.[418] Closer to home, while the Swiss standard of living exceeds the EU average, it is barely higher than that of Ireland, which was a poor country until a few decades ago. What can account for this disparity?

One factor is that Switzerland does not adhere closely to all the key factors of the *Index of Economic Freedom*, especially not in the areas of government size and spending. In this regard, Switzerland is similar to Scandinavian countries, which protect the private sector to generate wealth but then drain some of that wealth to fund social welfare, even at the cost of GDP growth.

In Switzerland, as elsewhere, once a foundation for wealth had been created, political forces wanted more redistribution. Since the 1970s, the Swiss welfare state has mostly caught up with other representative governments, becoming more generous and universal. For example, since the 1970s, Swiss transfer payments have increased almost twice as much as the OECD average.[419]

A second possible explanation for the economic drag lies at the cantonal level of government. Cantons and municipalities have fostered protectionism for agriculture, trades, and small business. So the regulatory drag described by Mancour Olson and discussed in earlier chapters affects the country as a whole, although it is implemented on a lower level of government.

Equally important, the cantons add substantially to taxation; the federal corporate tax is just 8.5%, but when combined with canton taxes, the total can reach 24%.[420]

Thus, the Swiss population, while enjoying enviable prosperity, suffers under

---

[417]   Kriesi and Trechsel, *The Politics of Switzerland*, 161.

[418]   Terry Miller and Anthony B. Kim, *2016 Index of Economic Freedom: Promoting Economic Opportunity and Prosperity, Singapore, 383 and Switzerland*, 407.

[419]   Kriesi and Trechsel, *The Politics of Switzerland*, 156.

[420]   Terry Miller and Anthony B. Kim, *2016 Index of Economic Freedom: Promoting Economic Opportunity and Prosperity, Switzerland*, 408.

some of the same slow growth and relatively high prices (undermining standard of living) that have occurred elsewhere, notably in Japan.

All in all, the Swiss experience still sheds light on Aristotle's concerns about the dangers of democracy and majoritarianism, dangers inherent in human nature that cannot be wholly eradicated. Central governments can be checked constitutionally, but subsidiary elements remain subject to these universal dysfunctional pressures. The great virtue of federal states, however, is that this model introduces the element of competition, which can act as the long-term regulator on state actors. Those with the soundest policies prosper the most, the others lag behind until they reform.

In short, Switzerland provides an alternative model of consensus government that produces fiscal stability and protects citizens in many ways from financial risk. However, it grows more slowly than some other highly-ranked systems.

The Swiss example suggests that the chief virtue of federal states is their incorporation of a healthy mistrust of a strong central government, competition among sub-entities, and mechanisms to slow major social changes that have economic dimensions. Grueling national debate helps ensure that good intentions mesh with empirical reality.

Other Examples of Federal States

The above discussion devoted a great deal of space to the Swiss form of federalism because it may represent the purest form of a federal government in the world today. This makes it easier to extract conclusions from experiences related to specific features of that federalism and to contrast its outcomes with those of the United States, which was once another example of a strong federal system, as discussed at length in Chapter Three.

The examples below will not be discussed in as much detail since they contain fewer features of federalism than the Swiss model and are therefore less relevant to the current discussion. Nonetheless, there are some striking similarities in the outcomes of Switzerland, Germany, and the Netherlands.

Germany

Germany is a democratic federal parliamentary republic. Federal legislative power lies in the *Bundestag*, the lower house of parliament, which is made up of representatives elected directly by the people; and the *Bundesrat*, the upper house, which represents the *Länder*, Germany's sixteen regional states.

The chancellor (comparable to a prime minister) leads the ruling parliamentary coalition and is the effective head of government; the president, the head of state, plays a primarily ceremonial role. The chief feature of German federalism is twofold: The states (the *Länder*) retain constitutional rights (like the U.S. states and the Swiss cantons). They can use the Bundesrat to check the Bundestag. Indeed, the delegates in the Bundesrat are not independent but are instructed how to vote by the federated states' governments.

Above all, the German constitution emphasizes the protection of individual liberty in an extensive catalog of human and civil rights. It divides power between the federal and state governments and between the legislative, executive, and judicial branches. Institutionally, the Bundestag is more powerful than the Bundesrat because it has the initiative to introduce legislation. In practice, however, the Bundesrat's agreement is often required in the legislative process because legislative initiatives must be passed by the Bundesrat before the Bundestag can vote on them. When the Bundestag and the Bundesrat disagree, a conciliation committee is formed to find a compromise.

In larger matters of constitutional import, the Bundesrat must approve all legislation that affects policy areas in which the law grants the Länder concurrent powers and in which the Länder must administer federal regulations. Constitutional changes require two-thirds majority approval in both houses, which empowers the Bundesrat to veto constitutional change.

However, Germany has fewer checks and balances on the federal government's power than Switzerland or the United States. For example, the Bundesrat has an important checking function but does not have the standing of the Swiss upper house, which is equal with the Diet, nor does Germany have a referendum process.

As a result, the German government is more activist because of the chancellor's inherently strong position and the far speedier legislative process. However, like Switzerland, the German federal system protects the rights of the Länder and provides them with important checking powers in the Bundesrat.

Whether due to this federal form of government or cultural similarities, Switzerland's and Germany's economic outcomes in the post-war era have been remarkably similar: rapid economic growth followed by an increase in social programs that significantly slowed that growth. However, unlike those in the United States, those social programs were fiscally prudent, so Switzerland and Germany have sound currencies, modest national debt, and no dangerous impending unfunded entitlements. Still, their growth has slowed since the expansion of social programs.

After the Second World War, Germany saw vigorous growth, which was initially nurtured by a robust FEO; the country has maintained a consistently high ranking in the *Index of Economic Freedom*. The immediate post-war era policies were exemplary as means to produce wealth and widespread prosperity. Thanks to the staunch leadership of Chancellor Konrad Adenauer and Economic Minister Ludwig Erhard, Germany ignored the conventional economic thinking evident in the U.S. New Deal and British socialism.

For example, as soon as a new German government was in place after the war, Erhard devalued the mark to produce a sound currency. He then took action to eliminate rationing and most elements of the previous comprehensively controlled economy. Even though British economists of the Labor government predicted disaster, these decisions led to two decades of *Wirtschaftswunder* (an economic miracle).[421] Under the following two decades of Christian Democratic rule, German unemployment was non-existent. In fact, Germany had to import large numbers of guest workers to meet the demands of an economy at full throttle.

However, the same pattern seen in many representative democracies emerged in Germany as well as the Left pushed for the state to play a larger role in the economy. The election of the Social Democrats led by Brandt in 1969 marked a turning point. Thereafter, even under subsequent Christian Democrat administrations, government spending and unemployment rose. At the same time, regulation added to economic drag with measures such as minimum wage, rent control, and *Mitbestimmung*, which required corporate boards to include labor representation.

Recall the discussion in Chapter Two referencing Mancour Olson's analysis of the economic drag of regulation on an economy – that is, the dynamic whereby small, concentrated interest groups are likely to form and use lobbying to influence the democratic political process to their ends. One of his case studies was post-war Germany. He shows how a fresh start gave Germany an opportunity to grow without the baggage of previous regulations: "In Japan and West Germany, totalitarian governments were followed by Allied occupiers determined to promote institutional change and to ensure that institutional life would start almost anew." As a result, he argues, in the first two decades after the war, Germany had not developed the degree of regulatory complexity and scale of government that characterized older governments. His analysis predicts that countries starting from scratch will eventually accumulate more distributional coalitions that adversely affect their growth rates; unfortunately, this proved true in Germany.[422]

As a result, in the post-war years, Germany's standard of living rapidly approached that of the United States, but now, after years of social spending and regulation, the German GDP is 84 % of that of the U.S.[423] The population is forgetting the "miracle" in favor of a less-demanding social democracy. British

---

[421]   Consistent with Labor's wrong-headed economics, Britain maintained rationing and capital controls well into the 1950s – along with a stagnant economy. Worse, just as with the economic shortfalls of America's New Deal, there were few signs that the British government had learned anything until years later under Margaret Thatcher.

[422]   Mancur Olson, *The Rise and Decline of Nations* (New Haven: Yale University Press, 1982), 76.

[423]   Terry Miller and Anthony B. Kim, *2016 Index of Economic Freedom: Promoting Economic Opportunity and Prosperity, Germany,211 and the U.S. 441*

authors John Micklethwait and Adrian Wooldridge of *The Economist* write: "The percentage of Americans who believe that success is determined by forces outside their control has fallen from 41% in 1988 to 32% today; by contrast, the percentage of Germans who believe it has risen from 59% in 1991 to 68% today."[424]

However, as in the Swiss case, credit must be given to the Germans' fiscal prudence in their social policies, some of which must be attributed to the checks and balances of their federal form of government. Germany ranks eighteenth in the *Index* and has moderate governmental debt and no looming entitlement problem. This is partly due to the structure chosen for many of their social programs. Health insurance, while universally mandated like the Swiss, is financially sound and produces excellent outcomes for the cost of about 11% of the GDP (in contrast to 17% in the United States).

In short, the Germans adhere for the most part to the predicates of the FEO, aside from relatively high government spending that, along with regulation, slows growth below optimum rates.

The Netherlands

The modern Netherlands originated as the States General in the fifteenth century. This was an assembly of all the provincial states of the Burgundian Netherlands. In 1579, during the Dutch Revolt, the States General split in two, with the Northern Provinces replacing Philip II as the supreme authority of the Dutch Republic in 1581. Like the thirteen colonies that would become America, this disparate group of Dutch provinces had to find the political means to cooperate effectively in a long and grueling war of independence.

The Union of Utrecht (1579) laid down the constitutional framework: The separate provinces would act "as if they constituted only a single province [but] each province and the individual cities, members and inhabitants thereof [would] each retain undiminished its special and particular privileges, franchises, exemptions, rights, statutes, laudable and long-practiced customs."[425]

In subsequent centuries, the form evolved. It was a republic from 1581 to 1806, a constitutional monarchy beginning in 1815, and a parliamentary democracy beginning in 1848.[426] The balance of power between the provinces and the central state would remain. Today, the Netherlands combines a parliamentary representative democracy with a constitutional monarchy and a decentralized

---

[424]   George Will, *The Washington Post*, October 10, 2004.

[425]   Andre Holenstein, Thomas Maissen, and Maarten Prak, eds., *The Republican Alternative: The Netherlands and Switzerland Compared* (Amsterdam: Amsterdam University Press, 2008), 53.

[426]   It was also briefly a kingdom (1806-1810) and part of France (1810-1813) during the Napoleonic Wars.

unitary state. The major political institutions are the monarchy, the cabinet, the States General (parliament), and the judicial system.

Checks and balances in the Dutch system are somewhat different than those in the other examples because the Netherlands is a constitutional monarchy rather than a pure federal republic. Accordingly, power is less separated than in the earlier examples; the constitution divides legislative power between the States General and the government (the king and the cabinet). However, this arrangement provides a check on the States General not unlike the check that the American president places on Congress.

For example, constitutionally, the king or queen is the head of state and plays a role in the formation of government and in the legislative process. Without his or her co-signature, a law is invalid. The monarch is also the *ex officio* chair of the Council of State, which advises the cabinet on every piece of legislation and is the final court for administrative law.

In addition, while the Netherlands is a constitutional monarchy, it shares a critical feature of federalism with the other examples: the parliament is bicameral. The Dutch parliament, the States General, consists of a lower house (or Second Chamber) and an upper house (or First Chamber), also referred to as the Senate. Both houses discuss proposed legislation and review of the actions of the cabinet. The Second Chamber has the right to propose or amend legislation; the First Chamber can only accept or reject legislative proposals but cannot amend them or initiate legislation. So, the First Chamber, which represents the provinces, acts mainly to check legislation. Its members are elected indirectly by provincial councilors just after the elections of the provincial councils via a system of proportional representation. This election method reflects the historical roots of the First Chamber as a representative body of the different regional entities that formed the Netherlands. Moreover, this quasi-federal structure explicitly leaves certain powers to the provinces, which are responsible for spatial planning, health policies, and municipal finances.[427]

In practice, the Dutch government produced a responsible, stable, but slow-growing economy similar to that of Switzerland, although it first had to suffer missteps similar to those of Sweden and New Zealand discussed in the previous chapter. Similar to New Zealand, the Dutch welfare state had established one of the most extensive social security system in the world by the early 1980s. It faced the same economic forces that burdened so many faltering representative governments, ultimately producing a crisis when spending rose sharply, leading to high unemployment rates and poor economic growth. In the early 1980s, unemployment rose to over 11% and the budget deficit to 10.7% of the national income.

The Dutch saw the need for reform sooner than other representative governments that went down the same path. The Christian Democrat Appeal

---

[427]   *Wikipedia*, "Government of the Netherlands."

(CDA) and the Peoples Party for Freedom and Democracy (VVD) and the CDA and Labor Party (PvdA) formed center-right and center-left coalitions that reformed the Dutch welfare state to bring the budget deficit under control and create jobs. Social benefits were reduced, taxes lowered, and businesses deregulated. Gradually, the economy recovered, and the budget deficit and unemployment decreased considerably.[428]

After this economic rollercoaster and the subsequent reforms, the Netherlands now enjoys a rank of fifteen in *The Index*. Like Switzerland and Germany, it ranks high on most elements of the FEO: high rates of entrepreneurship, free institutions, and sound economic policy. But, like the two other examples, it falls short in the area of government spending: The overall tax burden makes up 38.7% of gross domestic income, and public expenditures amount to about half the GDP.[429] That and regulation combine to produce relatively sluggish growth.

*　　*　　*

A common element among the federal states discussed above is that they grew out of confederacies that faced external adversaries but were wary of ceding too much power to their diverse compatriots. The Swiss cantons had confessional and cultural differences; the Dutch provinces had disparities in wealth and confession; South Germans and small German principalities were suspicious of Prussia; and in the American colonies, small states distrusted large ones. All of these smaller entities worried about power imbalances but also about the possibility of exploitation arising from a universal propensity for freeloading. It is simply human nature for groups to try to take advantage regardless of written pledges.

Consequently, these federations arose in a state of vigilance reinforced by institutional checks and balances. For the most part, the new states avoided grand crusades and maintained a tradition of negotiation that produced prudent social change, economic health, and political stability.

However, not all these results can be attributed to federalism *per se*. All the countries in these examples shared important cultural inheritances – notably Roman traditions that the law emanates from the people and rulers are subject to tradition and law, as well as a Protestant ethic encouraging personal responsibility in life. Certainly, it is not possible to disentangle these factors from any analysis of why these countries chose the social and economic policies that they did.

---

[428]　Ibid.

[429]　*The 2014 Index of Economic Freedom.*

CITY-STATES WITH STRONG LEADERSHIP

Two countries – or rather city-states – lead the *Index* rankings in sound economic policies that optimize the extended order: Hong Kong and Singapore. Hong Kong did not develop these policies organically through a representative government but as a result of enlightened colonial leadership. Singapore inherited a parliamentary system from British tradition but benefitted from an unusually strong leader and one-party governments for several decades. In both cases, enlightened leadership produced dramatic and illuminating economic performance.

Hong Kong

Hong Kong, which is ranked first in the *Index*, established an optimal form of the extended order by escaping the propensity of twentieth-century representative governments to overspend and over-regulate. As Richard Rahn notes, at first, as a British colony, Hong Kong had an ideal benevolent autocrat. The British provided a common law legal system, strong private property rights, competent and honest judges, an uncorrupt civil service, low tax rates, free trade, and minimal economic regulation.

In addition to benefitting from the inheritance of classical liberalism enjoyed by British colonies, Hong Kong serendipitously experienced a particularly apt administration—one devoted to more classically liberal economic policies than Britain's own government at home. Sir John Cowperthwaite, who was Hong Kong's financial secretary from 1961 to 1971, epitomized libertarian leadership. He had this latitude because Hong Kong was a colony with a limited representative government and the United Kingdom did not involve itself much with the details. Following free-market principles, Cowperthwaite balanced budgets, lowered taxes, kept markets open, and opposed efforts to regulate and direct the movement of capital in Hong Kong. In his view, "in the long run, the aggregate of decisions of individual businessmen, exercising individual judgment in a free economy, even if it is mistaken, is less likely to do harm than the centralized decisions of a government, and certainly the harm is likely to be counteracted faster." He deterred efforts to get the government to favor one line of development over another or one industry over another.[430]

As a result, the cost of government to business and society was minimal. Milton Friedman estimated that Hong Kong's direct government spending in 1996 comprised less than 15% of national income, compared to 40% in the United States (and much more in Western Europe). The costs of regulation absorb another

---

[430] Nancy DeWolf Smith, "The Wisdom that Built Hong Kong's Prosperity," *The Wall Street Journal*, July 1, 1997, A14.

10% of national income in the United States, while in Hong Kong, that amount is negligible.[431] During a period of rapid growth (1950-1997), it had all but closed the per-capita income gap with the United States. As a result, even though Hong Kong has no natural resources (other than a good harbor), economic freedom created a prosperity that has allowed that population to achieve a standard of living comparable to that of the United States and almost twice that of France. It also enjoys the highest life expectancy in the world and stands near the top in most indices of human development.[432]

While the example of Hong Kong is surely *sui generis*, it demonstrates the power of sound policy. However, this form of government may not be transferable to other cases. As Aristotle noted long ago, without representative government to control them, benevolent autocracies tend to become less benevolent with time.

Singapore

Singapore, which was a sparsely populated island when it was ceded to the British East India Company in 1819, eventually came completely under British control. Like Hong Kong, it benefited from British rule of law and grew rapidly, attracting a large Chinese population along with many Malays. After the Second World War, the city was part of a newly independent Malaysia, but it became an independent republic with a parliamentary system in 1965. In Singapore's system, the parliament's legislative agenda is determined by the cabinet.

While its structure was like that of other governments, Singapore's experience unfolded differently. Perhaps this was due to a unique culture. While it followed a dynamic common to many de-colonized countries by essentially having one-party rule (by the People's Action Party), the results were uncommonly successful. In terms of the predicates of the FEO, the one-party and the strong leader were enlightened. For over thirty-one years (until 1990), the government was led by Lee Kuan Yew.

To be sure, outsiders were critical of some of his methods: It is commonly believed that, to maintain power, his government (among other things) freely employed libel and defamation laws against political opponents in ways unlike most democratic governments. Nonetheless, Singapore is one of the world's few instances in which a one-party system provided the political stability necessary for investment and growth without also creating a corrupt predatory state.

Singapore's economic performance has been extraordinary. After gaining independence from Malaysia in 1965, it had a small domestic market and high levels of unemployment and poverty. Seventy percent of Singaporeans lived in

---

[431]   David L. Littman, *The Wall Street Journal*, op-ed, May 28, 1998.

[432]   Richard W. Rahn, "Hong Kong's Miraculous Progress," *The Washington Times*, September 2, 2014, B1.

badly overcrowded conditions, and a third of its people squatted in slums on the city fringes. Unemployment averaged 14%, GDP per capita was US$516, and half of the population was illiterate. These discouraging beginnings did not hold the country back. Singapore's sound economic policies produced real growth that averaged 8% per year from 1960 to 1999.[433] By 2018, its GDP per capita had surpassed that of the United States:64.6 thousand U.S. dollars versus $62.8 thousand.[434]

Those successful policies were largely in tune with the predicates of the FEO as well as the key elements of the *Index*. Indeed, Singapore ranks second, just behind Hong Kong, in the *Index*.

However, in one notable exception, Singapore's policies and programs are more paternalistic than Hong Kong's and more like the democracies discussed previously. In Singapore, the government actively facilitates welfare, pensions, and healthcare for all its citizens. However, it has managed to do so in a unique way that aligns with the FEO, thereby achieving results superior to those of virtually all other developed countries. All individuals are required to pay 20% of their earnings into a Central Provident Fund. This money is used for several purposes, including retirement, education, healthcare, and home purchases.[435] However, these programs are actuarially sound and have not hampered growth or threatened economic stability. A few examples can demonstrate why this is so.

The government reflects the population's self-reliance ethic, which is like that once prevalent in the United States. For example, citizens do not receive welfare from the government if their families can help them instead. Applicants for assistance must list all members of their household, along with their occupations and incomes. Government assistance is temporary and recipients must agree to a plan to become self-reliant, which usually involves government-assisted training.[436]

Another telling example is the pensions provided through the Central Provident Fund. Everyone must pay into the program, but individuals can pick fund managers and investments, similar to investors in IRAs in the United States.[437] This system encourages a sense of self-reliance, is transparent, and is fully funded – all the things that the U.S. Social Security system is not.

Healthcare incorporates insurance and market competition. Singapore's programs have required health savings accounts and price transparency since 1984, and even the poor who receive government support are motivated to spend

---

[433]   *Wikipedia*, "Singapore."

[434]   *2019 The World Bank Group: World Development Indicators.*

[435]   *Economic Freedom of the World 1997*, 165.

[436]   James Bartholomew, *The Welfare of Nations* (Washington DC: Cato Institute, 2016), 48-49.

[437]   Ibid, 238-239.

carefully. How so? Patients use their own money and are encouraged to shop wisely in a competitive market. They pay from medical savings accounts and their own pockets; fees for visits to a general practitioner and normal prescriptions are out-of-pocket. Everyone is also required to pay into a Medisave account, as are employers. Individuals decide how the money is used; it is theirs and they can bequeath it to heirs.

Everyone in Singapore is covered under this healthcare plan. The government does provide subsidies for the poor who cannot manage to pay for healthcare any other way. However, recipients of this program must demonstrate need; there are no entitlements here.[438]

The payoff is in excellent healthcare and affordable prices. According to the World Bank, total public and private spending on healthcare in Singapore is 4.7% of the GDP, compared to 17.9% in the United States. Despite this enormous disparity in expenditures, Singapore's life expectancy is the third highest in the world and higher than that of the United States.[439]

The above examples describe other solutions for precisely those areas in which the United States has constructed poorly designed social programs that are not economically sound and that threaten the country's future financial stability. The key differences are the extent to which individual liberty and personal responsibility are emphasized rather than ongoing political entanglements in program operations that benefit one faction or another. The power of the FEO could not be more evident than in the example of these two countries. Just removing the deadweight of expensive entitlements from the national budget improves growth.

Thus, Singapore offers many lessons regarding how the United States could address its economic problem along the lines spelled out in the *Index*. Singapore demonstrates that some representative parliamentary systems can avoid the weaknesses prevalent in others. However, it is difficult to pinpoint unique features that account for this outstanding performance. Perhaps it was the fluke of (unsustainable) inspired, quasi-authoritarian leadership, or perhaps it was the culture of self-reliance, neither of which is replicable. However, this example does dramatically illustrate the policies that work.

*　*　*

The next countries to be discussed are also governed by parliaments but, unlike Singapore, they lost their way economically, only to find it again when unsustainable systems forced them to do so. Examples of their unexpected reform can inspire many other possibilities.

---

[438]   Ibid, 67-68.

[439]   World Health Organization, *Life Expectancy 2015*.

REFORMED PARLIAMENTARY GOVERNMENTS

Chapter Six showed how parliamentary governments almost uniformly responded to universal suffrage with overspending and overregulation, usually to the point of financial crisis. Without constitutional restraints, political pressures from special interests drove the political process in these directions. This next section shows how several countries took the necessary steps to reform their ways. Their efforts had much in common and form a template for other fiscally imprudent nations, notably the United States.

Sweden

As previously discussed, by the early 1990s, Sweden could no longer borrow on reasonable terms after years of foreign borrowing made the currency peg unsupportable. Sweden then had to float the krona, causing its banks to face higher foreign interest rates. In turn, the housing boom collapsed, real estate prices dropped 25%, nonperforming loans mushroomed, and Sweden's largest banks began failing. In 1991 and 1992, Swedish banks had to take write-downs and loss provisions equivalent to the banking system's total equity capital.[440] The state took over much of the banking sector to resolve the debts of the failed banks.

Action Taken

With dramatic evidence of failed economic policies and little hope they could continue, after the 1991 elections, a moderate-led government with Carl Bildt as prime minister introduced major reforms to restore fiscal balance and shore up the principal elements of the FEO. The government lowered taxes (the wealth tax and taxes on income from capital)and promoted free enterprise by selling the state's share in thirty-four companies. To balance the budget, they reduced public spending from 67% of GDP in 1993 to 49% today. Several actions contributed to this. An unaffordable defined-benefit pension system was converted to a defined contribution system (similar to IRAs in the United States). This was done without all the invective seen in the United States whenever modifications to Social Security enter the political debate. They also reduced the cost of services by paying the private sector to provide them through a universal system of school vouchers and competitive contracts for private companies to provide state-funded health services and care for the elderly.

As part of these reforms, Sweden also imposed an expenditure ceiling and tightened the budget financing process. It joined the European Union, which

---

[440]   Ibid, 142.

broadened the export markets but also compelled businesses to maintain a high degree of competitiveness.[441] Counter-intuitively (to the American Left anyway), despite their goal of balanced budgets, they did not raise taxes but rather *cut* the marginal tax rates by twenty-seven percentage points and scrapped taxes on property, gifts, wealth, and inheritance.[442]

Aftermath

The country was put on a sound financial footing. The budget shifted from an 11% deficit in 1993 to a surplus of 0.3% in 2010; public debt fell from 70% of GDP to 37% over the same period. Economic and productivity growth were restored, averaging 2.7% and 2.1%, respectively, during the same period.[443] This was significantly superior to the average performance of EU countries.

Professor Olle Kranz produced a dramatic graph showing how Swedish per capita income in relation to other industrialized countries varied during three eras: prior to the welfare state, during the welfare state, and following the reforms discussed here.[444] The key findings are summarized in the following chart.

**Swedish Per-capita GDP Relative to the
Average of Other Advanced Nations**

Free Market Era	Welfare State Era	Reform Era
1890-1950	1950-1995	1995-2010
Rose from 60% to 110%	**Fell from 110%to 90%**	**Rose from 90% to 100%**

This data clearly demonstrates that Sweden went from being a relatively under-developed country in 1890 to one whose per capita GDP exceeded that of other developed countries in just 60 years (by 1950). Forty-five years of welfare-state policies caused Sweden's relative position to drop by 20 percentage points so that its relative GDP lagged other developed countries by 10 percent. Then 15 years of reform resulted in Sweden's GDP rising to match the average of other advanced countries.

Moreover, Sweden came through the 2008 recession in better shape than most of Europe. Swedish Finance Minister Anders Borg not only reduced welfare

---

[441]   "Europe's Fiscal Crisis Revealed: An In-Depth Analysis of Spending, Austerity, and Growth," *Heritage Foundation Special Report on Europe*, June 6, 2014.

[442]   "Northern Lights", *The Economist*. February 2,2013.

[443]   Ibid.

[444]   Dan Mitchell, "The Rise and Fall (and Rise) of Sweden", International Liberty, November 14, 2016.

spending, but also pursued economic stimulus through a permanent reduction in the taxes that included a twenty-point reduction in the top marginal income tax rate. At the same time, Sweden benefited from strong export revenues and steady domestic demand. As a result, the country's economy has grown even more, helping Sweden shrink its debt as a percentage of GDP rapidly over the past decade.[445]

Nevertheless, Sweden undertook these reforms without disowning its social democratic roots; it maintained high level of government-funded social services in line with their political ideals but rested those services firmly on the foundation of a free economy. The important point is that the FEO is a healthy generator of wealth to support social welfare. Still, there is a trade-off; when the government consumes a high share of the GDP in service of social democratic norms, economic growth, which could eventually benefit everyone, diminishes. So, while Sweden outperformed EU countries (5-year compound growth rate of 2.4%), it did less well than top-ranked Hong Kong (3.7%) and Singapore (6.4%).[446]

Because of relatively sluggish growth, Sweden has somewhat of a job-creation problem. Before the crisis in the early 1990s, around 80% of the population between the ages of sixteen and sixty-four was employed. By 2012 that figure was only 75%. This lack of jobs afflicts large sections of the country's population, including immigrants, young people, and the disabled. The inability of these outsiders to benefit from Sweden's economic growth could lead to long-term social problems and segregation. Sweden's housing and labor markets are still more or less unreformed and retain outdated regulations favoring those who already have houses and jobs.[447]

Nonetheless, given their political norms, Sweden did an impressive job of righting the economic ship through free-market policies.

New Zealand

As described in Chapter Six, New Zealand was the "poster child" for failed good intentions followed by a financial crisis. The nation's history gave little reason to expect it, but the New Zealand government found a way to institute splendid reforms across the board that were in tune with the FEO.

---

445   "Europe's Fiscal Crisis Revealed."

446   Terry Miller and Anthony B. Kim, *2016 Index of Economic Freedom: Promoting Economic Opportunity and Prosperity, Hong Kong 229; Singapore 381; and the U.S. 441*

447   Ibid.

Political Underpinnings

After decades of social-democratic governance, New Zealand had little choice but to make extensive changes. Of course, like others such as Argentina, it could have defaulted on its sovereign debt and tried to muddle through. But New Zealand had a different culture and benefited from the contemporaneous experiences of the United States under Ronald Reagan and Great Britain under the policies of Margaret Thatcher, both of which undertook major fiscal reform that had swift positive results. A remarkable feature of New Zealand's reforms is that they were undertaken under the aegis of a leftist Labor government. Where did they find the political and moral wherewithal?

According to John Wood, New Zealand benefitted from three critical preconditions for reform:

> First, in 1984 there was an acute sense of crisis in the country at large. Second, there was a consensus among New Zealand's professional leadership, both public and private sector, that drastic and comprehensive change was necessary, that no single interest group should be immune from change or should be permitted to dictate the agenda. An intellectual basis for change was provided by a key group of officials in the Treasury, drawing in part on their exposure to academic debate in the United States. …Third, there was a realization that no one else was going to help us. There was no fairy godmother out there willing and able to shore up our currency, extend our debt raising capacity, or anything else. We were in trouble, in part of our own making. We had to get out of it ourselves.[448]

So, change came under the banner of the Fourth Labor Government following the 1984 elections. The government was able to move rapidly due to several favorable features of New Zealand's governance: a unicameral parliament, a powerful executive, and a competent, non-partisan public service. New Zealand's leadership seized the moment. Boston and Holland cite Mancur Olson's analysis of failing nations: The political entrepreneur who is willing to tackle vested interests and challenge outmoded ideas in the face of a faltering economy and rigid institutions can receive a high return.[449]

---

[448] John Wood, "New Zealand: A Blueprint for Economic Reform," Heritage Foundation HL 531, June 16, 1995.

[449] Jonathan Boston and Martin Holland, ed., *The Fourth Labour Government: Radical Politics in New Zealand* (Auckland: Oxford University Press, 1987), 10.

Reform

The election of New Zealand's Fourth Labor Government in July 1984 introduced broad changes in the nation's approach to the welfare state (almost as though it were following an FEO-based script for success).[450] John Wood summarizes the reforms in key areas.[451]

International Finances: The foreign exchange crisis underway at the time of the change in government required speedy, coordinated action. The new government massively devalued the currency, free-floated the exchange rate, lifted controls on foreign exchange, and comprehensively deregulated the financial sector.

Domestic Finances: Wage and price controls were eliminated, the financial sector was liberalized (allowing new banks to open among other things), and the tax system was reformed – marginal rates were simplified and reduced. Over time, other legislation reinforced these reforms. The Reserve Bank Act of 1989 enhanced the independence of the Reserve Bank and stipulated that the bank's main function, for which the governor would be held personally responsible, was maintaining price stability within a 0% to 2% annual increase. The Fiscal Responsibility Act of 1994 set medium-term objectives that included reducing net debt to between 20% and 30% of the GDP and reducing government expenditure to below 30% of the GDP.

Trade: New Zealand dramatically established a free-trade regime by opening its market to imports and international competition. At first, tariffs were reduced to one-third of what they had previously been, and after the conclusion of the Uruguay Round, New Zealand unilaterally announced a further series of tariff reductions in textiles, clothing, and footwear. Today, over 90% of all imports enter New Zealand free of any quota, duty, or other restriction.

Subsidies: In another set of key moves to open the economy to competition, subsidies to industry were reduced; this included automobiles and shoe manufacturing and, more importantly, agriculture. Farm production and processing accounted for nearly 12% of New Zealand's GDP, and the majority of this was exported, earning 60% of total export revenue. New Zealand's greatest comparative advantage in trade was in agriculture, and it made little overall sense for the rest of the economy to subsidize it, especially at an unsustainable 30% of output, which was the case in 1984. One year later, almost all subsidies were gone, and the rest went soon after. It was not a painless process – market land values fell by 22% from 1982 to 1988 – but only about 1% of farmers went out of business.

Farmers adjusted rapidly to liberalization by becoming more innovative and more responsive to markets, allocating their resources more efficiently and

---

450   Ibid, 1.

451   John Wood, "New Zealand: A Blueprint for Economic Reform."

developing new markets. For example, the sector moved away from traditional pastoral farming, where most subsidies were once directed, into a range of areas such as horticulture, forestry, and cattle. Farmers' real net incomes have returned to the level prevailing in the early 1980s.

Private Sector Reforms: As John Wood summarized:

> In 1984, the government adopted the principle that the state should not be involved in any activities that could be more efficiently and effectively run by the private sector... The first step was corporatization through the State Owned Enterprises Act of 1986, which involved getting enterprises run on a commercial basis, freeing them from government red tape, putting a private sector board in charge, removing political interference, requiring them to make a profit. Areas of fundamental change included telecommunications and coal mines.

Telecommunications was corporatized in 1987 and privatized in 1990. Government funding for capital investments is no longer needed, and the industry's profits contribute to government revenue. Exposed to competition, this sector became more efficient and profitable. Telecom New Zealand once had had 26,500 employees; in 1994, it had 9,300. In the process, it transformed an antiquated technology to a modern system that was 97% digital and was rated second-highest in the World Competitiveness Report.

The corporatization of the Coal Corporation had a similar result. After seeing net losses in twenty of the previous twenty-two years, in its first year of corporatization, it increased production while cutting staff in half, thereby making a profit.

Public Sector Reform: Much of the public sector, from education to forestry, was reformed through privatization, vouchers, and financial efficacy tests. Public-sector employment decreased from 88,000 people in 1984 to 36,000 ten years later.

Welfare Reform: The government reduced the value of benefits and targeted them more precisely, including means testing to ensure assistance was directed to those most in need.

In addition to these specific areas, the government tackled regulation reform. According to Maurice McTigue[452], New Zealand suffered from a stultifying morass of regulations occasioned by old and new laws, often outdated and contradictory (a phenomenon common to most countries as analyzed by Olson

---

[452]   Maurice McTigue was a 10-year member of the New Zealand parliament and served as a Minister in the reform government.

and as discussed earlier in the section about post-war Germany). The reform government systematically rewrote laws to consolidate and rationalize them, while at the same time recasting the regulations they spawned. It was a multi-year effort with public-input, which produced streamlined laws, a fraction of the prior size and far easier to comprehend.[453]

Politically, it was critical for these reforms to work and to endure, and this, in turn, required broad bipartisan support. Fortunately, the reform process took place under two different governments representing the major parties in New Zealand; from 1984-1990 under a Labor government and from 1990 onwards under a National government.

Results of Ten Years of Reform

In 1994, in the speech referenced above, John Wood provided a snapshot of the results of this comprehensive reform.[454] At that time, New Zealand was ranked ninth in the OECD in the World Competitiveness Report and first in the world for competitive business environment.[455]

For the first few years, as the nation adjusted to these wrenching changes, growth was mediocre – but there was growth. With the benefits of reform in place, New Zealand's economy picked up the pace to 5% annual GDP growth that at times exceeded 6%. Inflation held below 2% – the second-lowest in the OECD. The government also balanced its budget: In 1984 the deficit was 9% of the GDP; in 1994 there was a *surplus* of over 4%. Public debt, which was nearly 52% of GDP in 1992, fell to 38% in 1994. Government spending was 41% of GDP in 1991 and fell to 34% in 1994. Meanwhile, New Zealand's manufacturing base flourished: Total exports of all goods increased by 5% in 1994, and exports of manufactured goods increased by 7%.

These were awe-inspiring results. Equally inspiring was the lack of backsliding – in 2014, New Zealand ranked fifth in the *Index*. However, as argued in the previous chapter, without constitutional restraint, it is impossible to eliminate the tendency of parliamentary representatives to buy votes, even if the debate is informed by dramatic empirical results. Incredibly, in the 2014 elections, the Labor Party revived the old leftist playbook about income inequality by proposing higher capital gains taxes and a higher minimum wage. The center-right National Party campaigned on continuing the reforms with added tax cuts

---

[453] McTigue, Maurice. "Making Government Accountable: Reform Lessons from New Zealand", speech to the Mercatus Center, George Mason University.

[454] Ibid.

[455] *World Competitiveness Report*, issued annually by IMD World Competitiveness Center.

to keep the economy going. Reassuringly, they crushed the Labor Party, which received only 25% of the vote.[456]

Canada

The previous chapter showed how years of spending and regulation, together with inadequate reform, brought Canada to a period of low employment, slow growth, and precarious finances in the early 1990s. A severe recession hit in 1990, causing the GDP to fall more than 3% below its peak and employment to drop below 60% of the working-age population. Meanwhile, the government (federal and provincial) continued to spend at a record pace: Total government spending was over 50% of the GDP. In 1995, gross public debt exceeded GDP for the first time.

Political pressure for more extensive reform (in contrast to previous modest attempts) grew, notably from the Reform Party, a new political party that emerged in the provinces. However, it was the Liberals, who gained power in the 1993 national elections, who heard the message and promised fiscal restraint. At first this seemed unlikely. But, like New Zealand's left-of-center Labor Party, the Liberals carried out difficult spending cuts with dramatic results.

To be sure, their first budget, in 1994, contained only modest cuts; but then serious reductions were undertaken. In the next two years, federal spending was cut by a full 10%. These cuts were real, not the phony cuts often made by American politicians (i.e., reductions in the forecast growth of spending rather than actual spending). Defense, unemployment insurance, subsidies to agriculture and business, and aid to provincial governments were cut. For the next three years, spending growth was held to about 2% a year. The federal share of the GDP gradually fell from 22% in 1995 to 17% in 2000; it continued to decrease in subsequent years and reached its lowest level since the 1940s. The Canadian government has had a balanced budget every year since 1998 (except during the worldwide financial crisis of 2008) and government debt has fallen to 33% of the GDP.

In addition, in the 2000s, Canada cut tax rates: The capital gains tax fell to 14.5%, and the federal corporate tax rate fell from 29% in 2000 to 15% in 2012. Despite the cut in rates, revenues did not decline. In fact, tax revenues rose as a percentage of GDP. Moreover, in other major reforms, the government began to shift the Canada Pension Plan from a pay-as-you-go system to one that is partially funded and solvent for the foreseeable future.

Just as in New Zealand, Sweden, and other countries, austerity cuts helped rather than harmed economic growth. These reforms launched a fifteen-year boom

---

[456] *The Wall Street Journal*, Editorial, September 22, 2014, A16.

in which unemployment fell from more than 11% in the early 1990s to less than 7% a decade later.[457]

And just like those other countries, Canada placed high (sixth) in the 2014 *Index* rankings, once again demonstrating the power of the FEO.

Nonetheless, like Switzerland, Germany, and the Netherlands, Canada has not escaped the spending pressures representative governments often experience. The country still has a large welfare system, particularly in healthcare; federal personal income tax rates are still relatively high; and some of the provinces continue to have high budget deficits.

But Canada has demonstrated an amazing capacity for reform.

Chile

Chile, like the other examples discussed above, implemented unsustainable economic policies and reached a point of no return. It also found a way back – not via parliamentary reform but through an authoritarian military government. Yet the specifics of its reform were similar to the others discussed here.

After the political crisis discussed in the previous chapter, the military took over under the leadership of General Pinochet, temporarily ending the forty-year period of constitutional government. Remarkably, this *junta* differed from others on the continent. Rather than establishing an authoritarian regime based on statist economic principles and cronyism, Pinochet presided over a transformation of the economy similar to that achieved by other economically successful autocratic regimes, such as Lee in Singapore, Chiang Kai-shek in Taiwan, Park Chung Hee in South Korea, and Francisco Franco in Spain. He brought in experts from the "Chicago School," a leading proponent of free markets and libertarianism, to launch reforms. Chile slashed the budget deficit, instituted a sound monetary policy, lifted price controls, eliminated market subsidies, privatized more than three hundred firms, and cut tariffs.

These dramatic reforms, implemented during the untimely circumstances of the oil shocks of the 1970s that threw much of the developed world into recession, had high short-term social costs. Chile's domestic demand fell by 25%, and unemployment rose to 15%. But with the aid of further reforms in the early eighties and a revived world economy, the economy improved steadily.[458] Sound macro-economic policies and structural reforms had a big payoff. According to the *Index*, Chile has been a model of economic performance for Latin America since the beginning of the 1980s.[459] Thereafter and until 1994, aside from a

---

[457]   Ibid.

[458]   Lawrence E. Harrison, *The Pan-American Dream* (Boulder, Colorado: Westview Press, 1997), 161-162.

[459]   *2001 Index of Economic Freedom*, 125.

recession in 1982 and 1983, Chile's economic growth has remained between 6% and 10% per year. Inflation was down to 8.4% in 1994 and the unemployment rate was under 5%, one of the lowest rates among the world's less-developed countries. Chile weathered the worldwide economic crisis of 1997 better than other Latin American countries and resumed economic growth.

In a political development parallel to those of Taiwan, South Korea, and Spain, once the economy had been transformed and begun to grow, power was returned to a constitutional government. Since then, Chile has held several free elections that resulted in peaceful transfers of power between parties. But electorates have short memories, and leftist ideas always have allure. Despite a highly successful track record– Chile tripled its real income in three decades and achieved the greatest social mobility on the continent (per a 2013 World Bank Study)[460] – socialist parties have been elected and re-elected.

As Mary Anastasia O'Grady reports, Chile's Socialist President Michelle Bachelet has backtracked under the banner of reducing inequality – a fixation of the Left everywhere. The Socialists increased taxes on capital and consumption to soak the investor class in an attempt to reduce inequality. Figures from Chile's central bank demonstrate the inevitable dampening effect of this move on investment and growth: Investment fell 12.3% in the last quarter of 2013 and 5.5% and 8.21% in the first and second quarters of 2014.[461]

However, this backtracking does not diminish the power of Chile's example of reform. It is the nature of representative government to alternate between parties with different worldviews. Progress rarely follows a straight line. Despite this retreat from FEO principles, the 2014 *Index* ranks Chile seventh worldwide and first in Latin America. Once in place, a strong FEO can tolerate many mistakes.

THE UNITED STATES

Despite the dispiriting gridlock of the American government's attempts to address its future economic problems, the United States does have a notable past record of reform in these matters. Indeed, it compares well with the countries discussed in this chapter. In particular, the economic history of the United States provides three dramatic examples of the power of the right kind of reform: namely, the Harding/Coolidge Administration, the Truman Administration, and Reagan's 'supply-side' reforms.

Chapter Four described Harding's and Coolidge's approach to the recession that followed the First World War: spending and tax-cut policies that led to the

---

[460]   Mary Anastasia O'Grady, "The Chile 'Miracle' Goes in Reverse," *The Wall Street Journal*, November 3, 2014.

[461]   .Ibid.

Roaring Twenties. Equally dramatic and productive were the reforms of the Truman Administration in the aftermath of the Second World War. Stephen Moore summarizes the policy measures and results of the latter. At the war's conclusion, government spending was quickly and dramatically reduced, from 41% of GDP in 1945 to less than 15% in 1947. Tax rates were cut and price controls lifted; the Keynesians of the day predicted a depression. To be sure, there was a brief eight-month recession as the economy adjusted, but then it soared. In the first two years, private investment rose by 28.6% and then 139.6%, replacing government spending. At the same time, following wartime austerity, personal consumption grew by 6.2% in 1945 and 12.4% in 1946.[462]

Most recently, the United States benefitted from Reagan's 'supply side' reforms: a monetary policy that greatly reduced the inflation rate and a fiscal policy that sharply reduced tax rates to spur investment. These reforms, despite some backsliding under Bush and Clinton, produced twenty-five years of strong growth.

So, it seems that the United States can do what is necessary to address growing fiscal imbalances. However, to paraphrase St. Augustine regarding finding virtue: just not yet.

*   *   *

LESSONS AND INSIGHTS

There is no mystery here. Every country described in this chapter followed virtually the same playbook to a comparable positive end. The *Index* provides simple 'how-to' steps. It is not ignorance but always political will (or the lack thereof) that determines the outcome.

Some insights on finding political will emerge from this and the prior chapter; some are now intuitively obvious, others inferential.

1. Limited suffrage, broadly based on economic interests of land, commerce, and industry, tend to produce a FEO that establishes the basis for a country's wealth. However, given the modern empowerment of the individual plus the need to give government broad legitimacy among the people, suffrage had to be broadened. The obvious question in doing so, how to avoid Aristotle's majoritarian dilemma?

2. The leading countries of the *Index,* Hong Kong and Singapore, which attained the best practices compatible with a robust FEO, did so thanks to

---

462   Stephen Moore, "How Did the Great Depression Actually Run Its Course?" *The Washington Times*, October 13, 2014, B3.

unique circumstances that provided strong enlightened leadership – but without institutional structures that would ensure a continuation. So their exemplary experience is probably not transferrable to others in that form.

3.   More widely applicable is the experience of representative governments such as Switzerland and the early United States who distrusted too strong a central government and provided only enumerated powers to it. This is probably the surest way to institutionally ensure a robust FEO. Even then, as seen in U.S. history, it can only be effective while the people honor that constitutional construct and vigilantly protect it.

4.   More numerous examples of effective representative government include those based on principles of republican federalism. Allowing constituent entities like states, cantons and provinces to retain key rights and establishing an upper house to directly represent their interests in a bicameral system seems to provide a key check on dysfunctional majoritarianism.[463]

5.   Representative government can work without constitutional restraint or a federal structure, but (presumably) only if the people are culturally 'virtuous' (in an Aristotelian sense).[464] Examples of this include countries where majoritarianism led to financial difficulty but representatives found a way (and the political support) to right the ship. This is common in countries with unicameral legislatures that lack the check of an upper house. Such countries almost universally find themselves in fiscal difficulty. Yet the party controlling parliament has wide leeway to pursue their ambitions for good as well as ill. The countries that succeeded in reforming clearly benefitted from a positive learning curve. Was there a common denominator? Well, yes: an *inescapable crisis*, an awareness of what had worked elsewhere, and a *stable polity*. Unfortunately, as seen from the large array of countries discussed in the *Index*, more countries than not seem unable to benefit from such a learning curve.

In summary, the experience of the last century or so seems to validate Aristotle's view that democracy without institutional restraints eventually reveals

---

[463]   While the case is not developed in this section, there is a strong suggestion that key errors were made in constructing post-war governments for Iraq and Afghanistan. These are countries riven with tribal and religious divisions, generating deep mutual suspicion. These seem like places in which culturally uniform provinces should have become the basis for a republican rather than a parliamentary structure.

[464]   Importantly, in the examples presented here – or, more broadly, in the countries in the top ranks of the *Index* – we have found no examples of countries that do not have a cultural foundation in either the Protestant ethic or Confucianism (the list might be stretched to include Ireland and Mauritius, but one was governed by Great Britain for centuries and the other was a British colony). All countries have the capacity to learn from experience; it may simply take longer for some than others.

critical fault lines, especially when power slips from the landed, commercial, and industrial classes to forms offering universal suffrage. At the same time, the positive examples in this chapter suggest that Aristotle's workable mix of governing forms can be achieved when popular democracy is checked within a federal-structure offering guarantees of property and individual rights.

In the not distant future, these lessons will become highly relevant to the circumstances facing the United States. Business as usual will not be an option (as it wasn't for Sweden, New Zealand, and others). Very likely, a sea-change in values, new policies, and limited but key institutional change will be required. On the positive side of the ledger, the United States has done it before – three times in the last century – and, presumably, can again rise to the occasion. Moreover, as seen above, it can benefit from the experience of other countries and it has the advantage of the "roadmap" provided by the *Index*.

The next three chapters will outline the hurdles to be faced, and the ways in which these might be surmounted.

CHAPTER 8

THREATS TO THE FREE EXTENDED ORDER: SENTAMENTALITY VERSUS EXPERIENCE

"If we were to apply the unmodified, uncurbed, rules of the micro-cosmos (i.e., of the small band or troop, or of, say, our families) to the macro-cosmos (our wider civilization), as our instincts and sentimental yearnings often make us wish to do, we would destroy it. Yet if we were always to apply the rules of the extended order to our more intimate groupings, we would crush them. So we must learn to live in two sorts of worlds at once."[465]– Friedrich von Hayek

"I believe that it is easier to establish an absolute and despotic government amongst a people in which the conditions of society are equal ... if such a government were established amongst such a people, it would not only oppress men, but would eventually strip each of them ... of the highest qualities of humanity."[466] – Alexis de Toqueville

The book's first chapters have shown how humans organized social affairs to create prosperous, advanced civilizations in the form of robust FEOs. In contrast, Chapters Four through Six illustrate why and how governments have repeatedly

---

[465]   W.W. Bartley III, ed., Hayek, F.A. *The Fatal Conceit: The Errors of Socialism*, 18.

[466]   Alexis De Toqueville, *Democracy in America* (New York: Mentor Books, 1956), 306.

ignored this history to pursue some "greater wisdom," resulting in immense unintended consequences at a cost to us all. Progressive forces continue this attack on all fronts, which is astonishing given the mountains of evidence that are increasingly available to us. Indeed, the collapse of the Soviet Union made many believe that we could put such arguments behind us. Adding to that experience, were other non-communist social democratic countries, notably New Zealand and Sweden, which were forced to reform dramatically. There is probably not a single country in which full implementation of leftist policies has not led to tears. The good intentions behind leftist alternatives do not counterbalance the fiscal and human costs they incur. That should have been the end of the story: Populations should by now have learned the lessons from experience.

Alas, much of the political establishment at home and abroad has not accepted these lessons. The Left remains in denial and continues to fight reform while arguing for even more dysfunctional policies[467] –and it still wins elections. However, considering looming fiscal problems, resignation about human nature is not the answer. Rather, it is urgent to counter those views, and a two-pronged approach is needed: We must highlight the fallacies of progressive arguments (the subject of this chapter) while providing a robust defense of the FEO (the subject of the next).

To give the mainstream U.S. Left its due, its heart is good and its intentions admirable, indeed utopian. The problem is that, collectively, it has failed to understand the societal evolution that began in medieval times and makes the FEO possible; nor has it understood the principles and institutions that evolved in parallel to check governmental predation and enable personal freedom under a representative government. Understanding how the Left's value system is out of sync with the dictates of the FEO because it is mired in an atavistic set of values is the beginning of wisdom.

Friedrich von Hayek's introductory quote pinpoints the heart of the matter. While free markets are clearly the best tool for furthering the material well-being of all humans, human nature does have other important sides and other needs that should be considered in the broad management of society and the design of government. For example, what if critical human values suffer in an imperfectly conceived societal pursuit of material prosperity? What if free markets produce "unfair" results; what if the poor lag behind; what if a lack of "social justice" destabilizes representative government? Do answers to these questions override the predicates for an optimally functioning FEO?

Not really, if attaining those other social objectives is the end goal. Countries with an FEO thrive, while those that prioritize values opposed to the FEO suffer materially *and* also fail to achieve the goals associated with their alternative

---

[467]   Two socialists, Bernie Sanders in the United States and Jeremy Corbyn in the United Kingdom, bring to mind the Bourbons of France, who, as was said, learned nothing and forgot nothing.

values. Understanding this dichotomy is essential to resolving the political debate that continues to confound and debilitate our country – indeed, all countries. Such an understanding can come from recognizing the origins of the contending value-sets.

Atavistic values are instinctual as well as still essential in many aspects of our lives; they make us human and support our psychological well-being by strengthening family and communal ties. Still, the societal evolution that allowed modern economies to function as they do required that additional new values in other areas of society evolve and take root. This may present apparent cognitive dissonance, but most of us have learned to balance them appropriately. However, the Left has not; it truly believes that re-imposing archaic values on free markets via government fiat will enable those markets to function more fairly and benefit us all. Historical economic evidence is, of course, at odds with these views. Nonetheless, their arguments can be seductive to the unwary and appealing to the average person who cannot parse them knowledgably.

To clarify the philosophical contest, the chapter first examines how values supporting the FEO evolved over centuries from an atavistic foundation, then parses the arguments of the Left which attempt to resist the conclusions evident in that evolutionary outcome.

THE EVOLUTION OF FEO VALUES

The desire to help our fellow man goes back to prehistory, was essential to human survival in tribal life, and remains part of who we are. Indeed, the behavior corresponding to such values is probably genetically ingrained. Such values are so robust they persist even where they produce dysfunction in the evolved, complex modern world. An understanding of original and evolved value-sets and how to reconcile them is essential to understanding the FEO and finding a way forward.

Original values entail a strong human instinct for virtuous cooperation, which predates civilization and can be observed in other primates as well. The simple reality is that no individual can survive for long on his own; he needs a group for defense, a society for cooperation, and exchange to obtain the necessities of life. Indeed, some groups considered ostracization or expulsion from the group to be a death sentence. Trust and a sense of mutual obligation were prerequisites for survival, for collective defense, and for the division of labor and trade.

For this system to function properly, values had to be inculcated that ensured cooperation while limiting freeloading. Cultural systems used peer pressure to establish a "moral" community in which "right" coincides with group welfare and "wrong" with self-serving acts at the expense of other members of the group.[468] This was accompanied by an acute sense of fairness in mutual exchanges.

David Sloan Wilson cites the work of several researchers who have attempted to show how such moral systems align with a specialized, genetically evolved cognitive architecture that includes features of conformity. One researcher, Ellickson, demonstrated how people spontaneously establish, enforce, and largely abide by social norms in the absence of a formal legal system.[469]

Spontaneous values served mankind well in small tribal communities where everyone knew everyone. However, clear-cut values became more problematic as societies grew, strangers entered the picture, and trade became essential. Yet from the beginning, commerce was suspect even though it benefits all parties and is in accord with the economic laws of comparative advantage and consumer surplus. The average person retained an intuitively suspicious view of trade because the intrinsic value of foreign goods was unknowable and because some merchants grew relatively wealthy, which alone was suspicious to the tribal mindset. Yes, everyone benefited, but was it "fair"?

It may not have been fair in an egalitarian sense, but disparities in wealth were nonetheless essential to the growth of civilization. The merchant and the middleman, who often grew wealthy without being seen to produce anything, were actually being compensated for planning, for investing capital in inventory, for providing transport, and for taking risks – all work that was invisible to the average person. Since they didn't know any better, societies looked down on trade and tried to control prices and wages in the name of fairness; they tried to preclude the payment of interest on seemingly "sterile" money. Moreover, they did not recognize that the accumulation of wealth in relatively few hands created capital that could be invested in expanded production eventually benefitting all.

This tension between suspicion of wealth and the desire for the things that trade brought occurred in all cultures that grew into empires– the Islamic, Indian, Chinese, and Japanese empires. Even as goods became more available and prosperity increased modestly (at least for the elite), traders and moneymen continued to be suspect, and the institutions that finance trade, enable the accumulation of productive capital, and protect property rights were not understood and were even considered unjust. Hostile viewpoints were pervasive and even enforced through religious doctrine.

The medieval church's scholastic teachings created an elaborate metaphysical structure to justify traditional atavistic viewpoints. According to Karl Pribram "A hierarchical social order was established by a range of definitions which started with the standard duties for Christians in general." The Church strove to create

---

[468]   David Sloan Wilson, *Darwin's Cathedral – Evolution, Religion, and the Nature of Society* (Chicago: The University of Chicago Press, 2003), 22.

[469]   Ibid, 27.

metaphysics based on 'universals' so as to provide a logical basis for ancient and still prevailing values: communal responsibility, sharing, and fairness in transactions.[470] More specifically, the church's views of social cohesiveness and economic relationships among individuals reflected a distrust of personal initiative, emphasized charitable values over the acquisitive instinct, and disapproved of most instruments of impersonal financial transactions. Catholic theology is still caught in the instinctual undertow, as evidenced by Pope Francis's statements condemning inequality as the root of social evil and arguing that the problems of the poor should be radically resolved by rejecting the absolute autonomy of markets and financial speculation.[471]

Similarly, even today, Quranic values oppose the *ruiner*, the selfish individualist who jeopardizes the moral integrity of the Muslim community. Not only did all past cultures contain the same visceral antagonism towards merchants and wealth accumulation, but they all shared a predisposition to prize collective action over that of the "greedy" individual. Since our early existence, the appeal of the collective has maintained its influence over the human psyche in good and not-so-good ways. As Hayek argues, this is good because it reflects our commitments to extended family, to our communities, to our nations in patriotism, and to a host of charitable activities in civil society. The negative side of these values attempts to undermine the impersonal operational principles of modern economies as represented by the FEO.

Despite emotional resistance, however, economic evolution found ways to bypass atavistic sentiments to generate values that promoted trade, protected wealth, and found more efficacious ways to deploy capital. These ways included innovative instruments and institutions, such as money, banks, contracts, and courts to enforce contracts. In the West, usually in *unseen ways*, new worldviews acknowledging the utility of modern commerce and enterprise partially displaced value systems that had once been universal. As trade and a money-based economy spread, transactions had to become more impersonal, *less sentimental*, and increasingly indifferent to specific needs of the individual. Counter-intuitively to most, individuals benefit significantly from such systems overall, if not necessarily in all individual transactions.

The importance of new ways was not immediately evident because, as Hayek argues:

> Neither all ends pursued, nor all means used, are known or need
> to be known to anybody, in order for them to be taken account of
> within a spontaneous order. Such an order forms of itself. That

---

[470]   Karl Pribram, *A History of Economic Reasoning* (Baltimore: The Johns Hopkins University Press, 1983), 6.

[471]   *The Washington Post*, June 19, 2015, A1.

rules become increasingly better adjusted to generate order happened not because men better understood their function, but because those groups prospered who happened to change them in a way that rendered them increasingly adaptive. This evolution was not linear, but resulted from trial and error, constant "experimentation" in arenas wherein different orders contended. Of course there was no intention to experiment – yet the changes in rules thrown forth by historical accident, analogous to genetic mutations, had something of the same effect.[472]

Adam Smith also perceived the undirected spontaneity of the economic process, such as when the market signals shortages through the mechanism of prices, indicating where a given amount of effort can be most fruitful. He argues that as individuals endeavor to maximize their own income, they ineluctably increase the income of the nation as well, as though "led by an invisible hand to promote an end which was no part of his intention."[473]

In so doing, individuals learned to function in expanding circles of mutual trust, expecting that others would keep their commitments in ways not seen in earlier societies or, indeed, in many less-developed countries today. Productive activity was increasingly freed to be shaped by basic economic forces, such as supply and demand, comparative advantage, and free market prices, rather than by governmental fiat. As advanced societies progressed, they became increasingly more powerful, wealthier, and more liberated from atavistic peer pressure as they relinquished old ways for new in the public arena.

Nonetheless, while many members of modern society have learned these new, more productive ways experientially rather than by examining evidence and applying a process of reason, most have not developed a unified worldview of why these ways are necessary. The central reason is, as Hayek recognized, that the FEO came into being (over the last few centuries) faster than human instincts evolved to accommodate it. Thus, instincts still favor the communal helping hand over the unsentimental dictates of the extended order, which relies on arm's-length contractual transactions that are oblivious to personal circumstances. Those living in the productive arena of the extended order are accustomed to *not* treating one another as neighbors, rather adhering to rules of private property and contract instead of solidarity and altruism.[474]

---

[472] Hayek, *The Fatal Conceit*, 20.

[473] David Boaz, *The Libertarian Reader: Classic & Contemporary Writings from Lao-Tzu to Milton Friedman* (New York: The Free Press, A Division of Simon & Schuster, 1997), 261 (taken from Adam Smith, *The Wealth of Nations*)..

[474] Hayek, *The Fatal Conceit*, 13.

In adapting to the demands of freer, more complex, and demanding economies, societies have had to learn experientially how to empower the individual, rely on less personal contractual ties, constrain authority, and live with the uncertainties and the give-and-take of free societies. Seen in this light, the human species made a quantum leap in its collective capabilities by developing new social systems and adopting new values appropriate to those systems.

COUNTER-VIEWS OF THE LEFT

Despite a thousand years of evolutionary change, the modern Left continues to embrace atavistic values, because it "just feels right" and still resonates with much of the electorate. Most modern-day attacks on free markets can and should be viewed as a regression to a medieval sensibility. The essence of their political movements, their professed philosophy, and their day-to-day arguments is that government is responsible for ensuring fair economic transactions, that free markets are suspect, and that reliance on spontaneous development in the face of need is also morally suspect.

The hold of atavistic values, even when clearly counterproductive, is not to be underestimated. In *A Conflict of Visions*,[475] Thomas Sowell analyzes the underlying structure of this value debate in a way that enables us to track the ongoing clash between medieval world views and those of the extended order. Supporters of the FEO understand that there are practical limits on a government's ability to reorder the natural outcomes of free exchange without costly unintended consequences. The Left, on the other hand, sees no natural limits on the government's intention to do good. Indeed, not only is the government capable of so much more, but Progressives argue that it has a moral obligation to do so. According to this belief, society's most intelligent and beneficent members should lead the way. The views of two promoters of this philosophy – William Godwin and John Rawls – are illustrative.

William Godwin

An early articulation of such views is found in William Godwin's "Enquiry Concerning Political Justice," published in England in 1793. Sowell writes:

> Where in Adam Smith moral or socially beneficial behavior could be evoked from man only by incentives [inherent in the operation of the "invisible hand"], in William Godwin's

---

[475] Thomas Sowell, *A Conflict of Visions: Ideological Origins of Political Struggle* (New York: Quill, William Morrow and Company, 1987), 23.

[view], man's understanding and disposition were capable of intentionally creating social benefits. Godwin regarded the *intention* to benefit others as being "of the essence of virtue," and virtue in turn as being the road to human happiness.[476]

Chapter Four described how this belief took on new force and urgency at the turn of the twentieth century as science and government became capable of a broader scope of action.

Moreover, in this view, morality is of such overriding importance that empiricism should be disregarded when it contradicts morality. Indeed, Godwin argued that experience was greatly overrated and that the wisdom of the ages was largely the illusions of the ignorant.[477] Godwin defined the two groups as "persons of narrow views" and those with "cultivated" minds.[478] According to Godwin, we need to infuse "just views of society" into "the liberally educated and reflecting members" of society, who in turn will become "guides and instructors" for the rest of society.[479] These views are still evident two centuries later in modern 'political correctness'.

John Rawls

More recently, John Rawls's first book, *A Theory of Justice*,[480] revitalized the idea of the social contract, articulating and defending a detailed vision of egalitarian liberalism that he calls "Justice as Fairness." His reasoning is based on two principles. The first addresses the essentials of a constitutional structure and holds that society must assure each citizen "an equal claim to a fully adequate scheme of equal basic rights and liberties, which scheme is compatible with the same scheme for all." Very well; the U.S. Constitution is based on the concept of equal rights.

His second principle, however, addresses aspects of the basic structure that go beyond equal opportunity to equal outcomes, arguing for the distribution of opportunities, offices, income, wealth, and in general social advantages. He argues that income disparity is an accident of natural endowment and the contingencies of social circumstances. He writes that life's inequalities are "undeserved" and

---

[476]   Ibid, 23.

[477]   Ibid, 43.

[478]   Ibid, 44.

[479]   Ibid, 46.

[480]   John Rawls, *A Theory of Justice* (Cambridge, Massachusetts: Belknap Press of Harvard University Press, 1971).

called for redress, suggesting that talent be treated as a "collective asset."[481] He also articulates a liberal-egalitarian socio-economic position, suggesting that social and economic inequalities should be resolved for the benefit of the least advantaged members of society. He concludes that social justice demands deep reforms in existing societies and that the government must remedy inequalities, even those attributable to different individual capabilities.

This is quite a Kantian categorical imperative: Morally, society must redress nature's random distribution of attributes among men. It is the opposite of the libertarian stance that individuals can self-actualize in a free environment.

How does Rawls arrive at this vision? His concepts are not grounded on empirical principles; they are derived from abstract reasoning. He postulates a thought experiment in which participants establish just rules for society behind a "veil of ignorance," without knowing what position they themselves would hold in that society. Logically, in such a case, most individuals would consider equal distribution to be a reasonable starting point. Therefore, logically, a society that produces unequal outcomes must be unfair (though his logic allows inequality to the extent that deviations are permissible that make some better off as long as no one is worse off).[482]

This presumably means that the government could lay claim to one's talent as well as one's wealth. It is difficult to envision the degree of social engineering required to redress the balance between individuals with vastly differently endowments from nature. This is not far from the Marxian adage: "From each according to his talents, to each according to his needs."

While Rawls' reasoning may be logically coherent given his postulates, it considers only one aspect of human nature. No one makes political decisions behind a veil of ignorance, and virtually everyone works for their own self-interest. To be sure, if we all entered a world that contained existing wealth to which our claims were unknown, we would opt for fair distribution of that wealth. But, of course, that does not correspond to reality and begs the question of how wealth is produced and the motivations and laws conducive to the growth of wealth.

There have been a number of communal attempts to live under Rawls-like principles, including Robert Owen's in England, the early Jamestown settlement, and the early Plymouth colony – and they provide a record of failure. Few will work sixty-plus hours a week primarily to benefit others.

In addition to impairing economic ambition, enforcing such a regime would imperil individual liberty. Every spontaneous individual action in mutually beneficial transactions would come under the eye of an omnipresent government, which might prefer another outcome for politically inspired reasons. A coercive

---

[481]   Ibid, 164.

[482]   *Internet Encyclopedia of Philosophy*, "John Rawls."

government hand would be present in every aspect of our lives, quickly leading to a totalitarian state.

A more realistic thought experiment is surely the one rooted in experience proposed by James Buchanan, which was discussed in Chapter One. Assuming that individuals already have wealth and a position in life, what powers can they safely cede to the government to protect their property and liberty while reducing externalities in society?

The above are modern comprehensive articulations of values intended to govern society. However, they are rooted in the Middle Ages, in the idea that government is a necessary tool for enforcing fairness and social justice.

PARSING UTOPIAN ARGUMENTS

These attacks on the FEO rest on assumptions: that the government can produce better results than free markets, and that even if it can't, the overall results will be more just if it tries. Such endeavors to achieve "fairness,""social justice" and "caring for the poor" are presented without useful metrics and thus are highly subjective. Consider some current views espoused by the Left. One is that, while free markets may produce wealth, it is unfairly concentrated in the top 1% at the expense of broader social goals such as individual mobility and opportunity and the well-being of all classes. Moreover, given these negative factors they believe that an unfettered FEO eventually leads to other undesirable social and fiscal outcomes. While these arguments may be appealing at some level, a deeper examination highlights their inapplicability.

Fairness and Social Justice

The Wall Street Journal quotes Shelby Steele from his book *Shame*: "Liberalism in the twenty-first century is, for the most part, a moral manipulation that exaggerates inequality and unfairness in American life in order to justify overreaching public policies and programs."[483] Indeed it is; because inequality is a fact of life, it is patently obvious and an electoral target of opportunity.

The leftist critique highlights the uneven distribution of wealth, but not why it is so. Taken by itself, "fairness presumes some *a priori* foundation for what is actually a value judgment. When a mother cuts a pie for her children, the implicit criterion is that she should cut equal slices. If the material wealth of the world were simply made available to its inhabitants without the requirement of labor, fairness would imply some equal distribution (see Rawls's argument above).

However, these views run counter to one implicit principle of fairness:

---

[483]   *The Wall Street Journal*, March 11, 2015, A13.

Fairness is attained when you have been promised something and you get it; unfairness is when the agreement is arbitrarily violated. In that light, fairness can only be determined against some rules of the game. Societies establish such rules in widely different ways depending on their prior cultural evolution. In a free society, in which government maintains rule of law and effectively prevents fraud, overall results cannot logically be defined as unfair. Certainly, outcomes can then be characterized as unlucky or personally tragic, but not unfair. Moreover, personal attributes that produce wealth, such as talent and the desire to work hard and take risks, are simply not distributed equally in the population, and this will always produce disparate results. Surely those who create the most wealth will be better recompensed than those who do not. That is the essence of "fairness" in free-market societies: being compensated according to one's contributions to society (playing by the economic rules). Rawls's counterargument is that life unfairly distributes intelligence, creativity, talent, vigor, determination, and health. So it does.

Given the differences in human endowments among individuals, place any group of individuals in a *de novo* set of circumstances, and inequalities will develop rapidly. Consider the example of the settlers of the North American English colonies: Within a generation or two, most of the population built family farms, while crafts and professional classes arose in the towns. Disparities in capability and work generated wealth inequalities in short order; hardly the result of class oppression.

This is equally true today, where examples like Gates and Zuckerberg abound. Given economic rules that establish a "flat playing field" based on individual liberty and private property rights, who would not justifiably expect to find wealth disparities among the following groups?

- Incarcerated individuals
- Single parents on welfare
- Individuals who have not finished high school and work part-time
- Laborers working full-time
- Two professional middle-income wage earners
- A middle-income worker who saves and carries out a side activity such as investing in real estate
- A professional in law or medicine who has devoted eight or more years to higher education, foregoing earned income all that time
- Creative innovators working under uncertainty whose work creates great value for the economy
- Financiers who take personal risk by directing capital to the most productive uses and reap the results of being right (and the losses if they are wrong)

- One-of-a-kind entertainers and sports figures who receive seemingly outlandish compensation (usually for brief periods)

Presented in this way, the inevitability of economic inequality is intuitively obvious. So, how can an argument for redistribution of income plausibly be made? Typically, these arguments target the wealth of the top 1%. This exploits the average person's unfamiliarity with wealth creation at those levels. The average person can recognize the value added by, for example, physicians, inventors, entrepreneurs, and entertainers, but seldom that added by those in highest tiers of banking, Wall Street, and corporations. However, a moment's reflection should show why talent responsible for the deployment of billions in capital to its most productive uses would be well remunerated. Nevertheless, the average person does not do so and as a result, the individuals in the top one percent are easy targets for demonization. This is a close analog to the medieval mindset that traders were suspect because the value they added was not immediately apparent.

Another medieval cheap shot is to accuse high earners of the sin of "greed," of wanting more than they "need." If the production of the targeted class's wealth is veiled and the owners are greedy, why shouldn't the government try to extract their wealth to benefit others? The answer is, of course, the other side of the fairness coin: The owners have earned it, and the hopeful recipients haven't. Personal ambition, the desire to make the most of one's abilities, to work to ensure against life's uncertainties, and to provide for one's progeny, is not greed. This mindless, medieval attack by the Left was evident when Reagan's "supply side" economic program brought the country out of years of stagflation and produced a decade-long boom that significantly benefitted *every* income class. The Left, dismissed the results as that of a "decade of greed."

To the contrary, true greed is motivated by envy of others' achievements and attempts to wrest unearned benefits from others. It is those who wish to exploit the producers of wealth that benefits everyone that are greedy. Ambition, hard work, creativity, investing, and producing wealth is not evidence of greed.

And, of course, setting fairness aside, exploiting the wealth of others is eventually self-defeating. The wealth of the top percentage of earners contains the "seed corn" of new entrepreneurial investment that generates jobs and rising tax revenues. As noted by John Maynard Keynes: "It was precisely the inequality of the distribution of wealth which made possible those vast accumulations of fixed wealth and of capital improvements ... [These], which, to the great benefit of mankind, were built up during the half century before the war could never have come about in a society where wealth was divided equitably."[484]

---

[484] John Maynard Keynes, *The Economic Consequences of the Peace* (New York: Harcourt, Brace and Howe, 1920), in Edward Conard, *Unintended Consequences, Why Everything You've Been Told About the Economy is Wrong* (New York: Portfolio/Penguin, 2012), 91.

A prosperous extended order both depends on and produces inequality. Surely, some inequality where *all* are better off is more desirable than more equal relative poverty. If everyone plays by commonly accepted rules and coerces no-one and all of society grows wealthier as a result, the mere fact of unequal income distribution has little intrinsic meaning. The Left's ambition to achieve "social justice" implies an intrusive government that limits individual freedom and forcibly reorders what would be the spontaneous order of the FEO. Investment would flag in favor of short-term consumption, economic growth would slow, and, in the long run, every class would be poorer. This is the real-world tradeoff: There are no free lunches, positive rights must be funded by someone, individuals are unlikely to get more from the government than they contribute, and individual needs are better met through the choices of free markets than by one-size-fits-all government programs.

Nonetheless, modern Progressivism has succeeded in making the abstraction of income equality an alluring motivator for overbearing political action.

Correcting the Imperfect Outcomes of the FEO?

While some on the Left might concede the FEO's power to produce material wealth, they have concerns about potential problems that might result in social pathologies or eventually sap the FEO's strength if the government does not actively intervene. For example, given the inevitability of uneven wealth distribution, is there a danger that the FEO will create a class-based society, in turn encumbering income mobility and preventing individuals from achieving self-actualization?

Avoiding a Class-based Society

Harvard professor Seymour Martin Lipset presents an example of leftist concerns regarding class in *Political Man*.[485] He views politics as a modern offshoot of the Marxist contest between the proletariat and the privileged classes. In this struggle, the working classes attempt to gain their "rights" from the wealthy in a continuing struggle over the distribution of national income.[486]

It all came down to class struggle. He characterizes the growth of democracy as a process in which "freedom of organization and of speech, together with universal suffrage, were necessary weapons in the battle for a better standard of living. ... The upper classes resisted the extension of political freedom as part of their defense of economic and social privilege."[487] He states that in every modern

---

[485]   Seymour Martin Lipset, *Political Man*(London: Heineman Educational Books Ltd, 1969).

[486]   Ibid, 83.

[487]   Ibid, 127.

democracy, conflict among political parties is a democratic translation of the class struggle.[488] He quotes Robert MacIver: "[T]he conservative right has defended entrenched prerogatives, privileges and powers; the left has attacked them. The right has been more favorable to the aristocratic position, to the hierarchy of birth or of wealth; the left has fought for the equalization of advantage or of opportunity, for the claims of the less advantaged."[489]

This may be considered to be a dated formulation of the perceived social order drawn from America of the mid-twentieth century. The ideas of aristocratic positions and hierarchy of birth hardly resonate today. Yet the idea has persisted and currently appears in the form of "white privilege," transforming it into a minorities-versus-white contest rather than a class contest. In either event, the Left characterizes the protection of property rights as *defending entrenched prerogatives, privileges, and powers.*

It is to the advantage of Marxists and the Left to see struggle where there is none. There is no such thing as a laboring *class* (which implies a unified view and unity of purpose as well as something immutable), rather, there are individuals who trade their labor for money where they find it most advantageous. Later they may become small businessmen, and via IRAs and mutual funds, part of the so-called capitalist class.

However, might the FEO unfairly trap lower classes in an inferior position? Might it impair social capital because of sub-par opportunities that limit income mobility? In a separate attack, the Left contends that, without government control, capital formation and investment will be less than ideal. In this light, inherited wealth over time and the advantages that high-income parents bestow on their children are suspect. In their eyes, to avoid such outcomes, the government should provide an equal start for all (way beyond the vast sums already provided for free public education).

But do disparate earning levels and inherited wealth really create a "class-based" society under an FEO (in contrast perhaps to some other countries)? Historically, there is little evidence for this in the United States. From a generational perspective, wealth is a fleeting family advantage. Each larger new generation divides inherited wealth, causing it to attenuate because of consumption and bad luck, as well as because genetic ability tends to gravitate back towards the mean over several generations. The adage says, "The first generation makes it; the second generation maintains it, and the third generation blows it."

Today, the Vanderbilt and Rockefeller families, which held great wealth over a century ago, can hardly match the wealth of Gates, Buffet, Bezos, and Zuckerberg. New wealth is continually arising from the fields of technology, finance, entertainment. Even in the corporate world, position has a way of eroding;

---

[488]   Ibid, 220.

[489]   Ibid, 222.

the entropy of life extends to corporations as well. Very few companies listed on the Dow Jones a century or more ago are there today; indeed, many of them have gone bankrupt.

Promoting Income Mobility

Despite these well-known examples, the Left remains fixated on income mobility. It ignores evidence that it is the free-wheeling nature of the extended order that provides opportunity for those with talent and social capital, not some illusory government attempt to achieve absolutely equal educational and economic starting points.

Clearly study, hard work, talent, and enterprise are rewarded – as they should be – in a society where wealth is increasing and individuals can rise according to merit. As remarked by Arthur Brooks of the American Enterprise Institute: "[M]ost who benefit from freer markets are the have-nots: those without inherited wealth, prestigious credentials, social or class advantages – in other words, people whose only hope for a better life is a social order that will reward their hard work and enterprise."[490]

The proof is seen in outcomes in countries with an FEO. There is little evidence that economic mobility is impaired or that income classes become ossified under an FEO. To see this, one must consider the ranks of the rich and poor over the span of a lifetime: Relatively few experience long-term poverty in a dynamic economy. In fact, the ranks of the rich and poor change continuously over time, demonstrating much more income mobility than is commonly perceived.

One survey by the Treasury Office of Tax Analysis,[491] for example, reviewed representative taxpayers over a ten-year period (1979-1988) to track their progress through income quintiles:

> In no quintile was the turnover less than 33% during the decade. In the bottom three, at least 66% of the occupants changed quintiles, generally trading up. ... What about those who started the decade in the bottom quintile? Sixty-five percent moved up at least two quintiles during the decade. Similarly, a large fraction of the most affluent in the highest quintile will move down within a comparable space in time. Thus, when we are students, or just out of school, we'll probably be in the lowest quintile. In our peak earning years, we will be in one of the two top quintiles, and in retirement, we will likely fall again.

---

[490] Arthur Brooks, *The Wall Street Journal*, July 11-12, 2015.

[491] "Income Dynamics," *The Wall Street Journal*, June 16, 1991, A1.

Moreover, *all* those quintiles have grown steadily in absolute terms over the last two centuries. In the United States, even the relatively poor own their own homes and have automobiles and the most modern of electronic appliances. None of the conditions that spurred social democracy a century or more ago exist in any meaningful way today. Indeed, according to Phil Gramm and John F. Early, if government transfers are taken into account, poverty incidence is only about 2 percent.[492] Granted, there is still suffering – some are homeless or caught in the welfare system – but there are programs that offer them food, shelter, and education. The chief point is not to ignore ways to help those still in poverty, but that such measures should not subvert the wealth generating capacity of the economy, which benefits everyone,

Far better would be to address some of the remaining root causes of poverty; for example, the persistence of an "underclass" that is fairly stable and perhaps even growing. This phenomenon has little to do with the lack of opportunity for mobility. It has to do with a growing segment of our culture in which the youth do not adopt past prevailing cultural values. Following those historic values, if an individual finishes school, works, marries, and then has children, the odds are high that they will prosper and move up the income scale. Single parenthood, on the other hand greatly raises the probability of staying in poverty. A National Longitudinal Survey of Youth showed that 53% of millennials who had failed to complete these steps were poor, but the poverty rate dropped to 31% for those who completed high school, 16% for those with a diploma and a full-time job, and 3% for those who married before having children.[493]

For most people with life experience, these results are intuitively obvious. Yet American academia rejects them as "bourgeois" or even as a manifestation of "white supremacy." This dismissive attitude supports several, perhaps unconscious, goals: It removes the need to hold those who suffer the effects of dysfunctional behavior accountable; it blames these outcomes on the system (the FEO); and it removes the need to address tough problems based on empirical findings.

Such sentiment equates 'caring' with government money and government intervention, of which there has been plenty since the 1960s. African-American incomes and entrepreneurship were rising rapidly in the United States until the "War on Poverty" began. Since then, trillions of dollars have been expended in that "war," yet the proportion of the population defined (a subjective dollar amount of annual income) as poor is virtually unchanged. Government spending and activist intervention have largely failed to move the needle. Nonetheless, the Left

---

[492]   Phil Gramm and John F. Early, "Americans are Richer than We Think" *The Wall Street Journal*, August 22, 2019.

[493]   Wendy Wang, "The Sequence is the Secret to Success," *The Wall Street Journal*, March 28, 2018, A17.

wants more of the same, such as offering everyone a government income at age eighteen to reduce inequality and poverty (or the need to work).

Avoiding FEO Stagnation

Other analyses from the Left argue that the FEO has an innate entropy that requires government intervention to prevent the economy from ossifying. For example, in *Capital in the 21ˢᵗ Century*, French economists Thomas Piketty and Emmanuel Saez argue that, in modern market economies, private returns on capital investment are systematically higher than the growth rates of income and output, and that this difference explains the increase in inequality. Since only a fortunate few derive their income from capital, the authors are led to conclude that capital divergence is natural and inexorable and that the only effective correction is highly progressive taxes on investment income and wealth, preferably on a global basis to forestall capital flight.[494]

Phil Gramm and Michael Solon demonstrate that this conclusion contradicts the experience of the last three decades and could only have been reached by cherry-picking an extraordinarily limited data set. For example, Piketty and Saez argue that in the Reaganomics economic boom, the rich got richer, the poor got poorer, and relatively few Americans benefitted. However, a study published in the *Southern Economic Journal* that used a much broader set of economic inputs demonstrates how misleading these conclusions were: The bottom quintile of Americans experienced a 31% *increase* in income from 1979 to 2007, rather than the 33% *decline* found by Piketty and Saez; the second quintile's income rose by 32%, not 0.7%; and the middle quintile's rose by 37%, not 2.2%.

These are dramatic differences; what could account for them? Gramm and Solon point out that Piketty and Saez only looked at pre-tax cash market incomes. They failed to consider taxes; employer health insurance and retirement benefits; Social Security, Medicare and Medicaid benefits; capital gains from the first $500,000 on the sale of a home, and changes to small business taxes established by the 1986 reform. The influence of the latter particularly distorts the results in the Piketty-Saez report. They highlight an apparent 44% increase in the income of the top 1% in 1987. However, that jump was a consequence of different income reporting due to the previous year's tax legislation. Individuals began to report business income on their personal returns rather than via a small business return – their income had not changed at all.[495]

Aside from these analytical errors, the study embraces the fallacy that income inequality itself slows growth. Importantly, it ignores Keynes's observation that

---

[494]   Christopher DeMuth, "Capital for the Masses," *The Wall Street Journal,* April 8, 2014, A15.

[495]   Phil Gramm and Michael Solon, "How to Distort Income Inequality," *The Wall Street Journal,* November 12, 2014, A15.

new capital investment comes (and has always come) from capital accumulated by those in higher income brackets. A more quantitative take is seen in a World Bank study of OECD members. This study shows that the five countries with the most income inequality grew nearly five times faster than the others from 2011 to 2013.[496]

The study by Piketty and Saez was received positively partly because of circumstances: years of exceptionally slow growth under the Obama administration, which were excused based on "secular stagnation." Perhaps capitalism had reached a point of diminishing returns under the existing rules and needed reform, and perhaps that reform should be conducted along the lines suggested by Piketty and Saez. Unfortunately for that view, two years of FEO-friendly policies of deregulation and tax reform under the Trump Administration bumped growth closer to U.S. historic levels.

There is no credible evidence that free markets cause the poor to get poorer or lead to stagnant growth that could be improved by government intervention.

Environmentalism – Bypassing Economic Arguments

Without credible empirical arguments for attacking the superiority of the FEO, how else can Progressives argue for medieval values of fairness? Perhaps they find arguments in movements to "save all of humanity" in ways that displace the FEO; ways that require placing all key economic decisions in the hands of the elites. For example, they could become even more atavistic than the medieval church by tapping prehistoric values such as the worship of Mother Earth (Gaia).

Environmentalism fits the bill. It has a good pedigree; originally, it addressed real, severe problems in ways that benefited everyone by improving health and maintaining an attractive, sustainable environment. The original pragmatic form of environmentalism aimed at correcting the imbalances that had accumulated from rapid industrialization and the ubiquitous use of automobiles. Rivers were noticeably polluted, and the skies of major metropolitan areas were filled with smog. Political pressure led to the creation of the Environmental Protection Agency (EPA), whose mission was to develop clean air and water standards, with enforcement mechanisms, to protect the nation's health. These efforts were undeniably successful – rivers were cleaned up, the air over cities grew vastly healthier, automobile emissions became a tiny fraction of what they once were, and incidental to government action, the United States became more forested than it had been for a century or more.

These results were the undisputed positive outcome of appropriate government

---

496   Mathew Schoenfeld, "The Mythical Link Between Income Inequality and Slow Growth," *The Wall Street Journal*, June 15, 2015, A17.

intervention in the economy. From a libertarian perspective, the government was taking action to protect citizens from the externalities of other citizens' behavior and posed no threat to the FEO. This, however, fundamentally shifted when the EPA moved from sound cost/benefit analyses to align with activists who were adamantly opposed to fossil fuels and nuclear power. This transition became overt under the Obama Administration when the EPA issued draconian regulations in a "War on Coal" and federal agencies slow-walked permitting for traditional energy projects in favor of more expensive renewables.

The ideological arm of the environmental movement wanted far more than a clean environment to protect citizens' health. It believed that, in addition to cleaning up the environment, we needed to change our entire way of life. This movement was convinced, despite evidence to the contrary, that growing populations and growing economies constantly using more natural resources were ultimately unsustainable, and indeed a threat to human existence. The beginnings of this ideological movement can be seen in E.F. Schumacher's book *Small is Beautiful*, a call for smaller institutions, a move back to the land, the adoption of simpler technologies, and societies that are more "people-oriented."[497]All of this is in contradiction to the spontaneous order produced by individual desires.

However, this thinking, which appeals primarily to the already well-off elites, spread internationally. International conferences such as the Club of Rome trumpeted alarms about the overconsumption of natural resources. Popular books such as Paul Ehrlich's *The Population Bomb* warned about overpopulation. All these arguments concluded that governments, domestic and international, needed to rein in the FEO in order to save humanity.

This alarmism overlooked more important empirical trends. Most notably, economic growth is the most effective way to slow population growth and clean up the environment. In virtually all developed countries, population growth has fallen to sustainable or even sub-maintenance levels. In effect, prosperity means greater health, lower infant mortality, and less need for individuals to have many children as insurance for their own old age. Moreover, stronger economies provide the financial wherewithal for extensive pollution control. Ironically, the unintended consequences of the action proposed by these alarmists would be the least effective way of achieving their goals.

Environmentalist arguments about natural resources proved equally fallacious. First, current knowledge about the available resources is limited. Second, human ingenuity in exploiting existing resources and using them more effectively is constantly improving. A telling example is a famous wager that Julian Simon and Paul Ehrlich made in the 1970s. Simon bet Ehrlich that through

---

[497]   E.F.Schumacher, *Small Is Beautiful: Economics as if People Mattered* (Canada: Harper Collins Publishers,1974).

human ingenuity in the use and substitution of materials and through improved exploration-science, resources would become more and more available rather than less. He bet Ehrlich one thousand dollars per commodity that *any* ten commodities selected by Ehrlich would be more plentiful and cheaper two decades in the future. The wager was agreed, and two decades later, Ehrlich had to pay up on every one of the commodity bets. The distributed wisdom of the extended order easily defeats the effective intelligence of a small alarmist elite. Twenty years later, the environment was far cleaner, general health better, population growth substantially more moderate, and natural resources still plentiful.

By the early 1990s, the alarmist techniques of environmental ideologists had lost their efficacy. Something dramatically new would be required to rally the population to their cause, something like a threat of *global warming*. Some scientists had noticed that global average temperatures had been rising since about 1970 and that this coincided with increasing levels of CO_2 in the atmosphere. Scientists also determined that the CO_2 molecule in the atmosphere *could* have an effect of trapping heat. Computer models were built using this hypothesis to forecast rising temperatures coincident with rising CO_2 levels. If true, this danger would need to be tracked. After testifying before Congress in 1988, James Hansen of NASA became a prominent voice warning about the imminent danger of rapidly rising temperatures. He testified without agency approval; years later it was revealed that his testimony was staged and deliberately alarmist to catch the attention of the public and policymakers.[498]

This message has been on the front pages of newspapers for a quarter of a century, even though close monitoring of temperatures has discredited the underlying hypothesis. While CO_2 levels have continued to climb, statistically, the planet has barely warmed further for two decades after the peak recorded in 1998. Virtually all the projections of increasing temperatures made at the beginning of the twenty-first century failed to materialize.[499]

Moreover, considering natural variability, the hypothesis was problematic to begin with. Over the last two thousand years, global temperatures have naturally cycled. The Roman warm period was followed by a cool stretch during the Dark Ages, then another warm period during which Greenland was settled, followed by the Little Ice Age, followed by gradual warming over the last three centuries. Over the last hundred years, the planet has warmed a bit more than one to two degrees, entirely consistent with cyclical variability and hardly enough to justify the hysteria promoted by "warmists."[500] Virtually all of the alarmism is based on computer forecasts that tightly link rising temperatures with rising levels of CO_2

---

[498]   Marc Morano, *Climate Change* (Washington, DC: Regnery Publishing, 2018), 23-24.

[499]   University of Alabama – Huntsville (UAH) Satellite-Based Temperature of the Global Lower Atmosphere (version 6.0)

[500]   Al Gore's film *An Inconvenient Truth* is a prominent example.

in the atmosphere. Yet those models fail to explain three decades of cooling that occurred from 1940 to 1970. Dixy Lee Ray discusses numerous natural phenomena that are not well understood or considered by the models such as: sun-spots, cosmic radiation, the earth's shifts in relative position to the sun, and so forth.[501]

Environmentalists, however, are not ready to throw in the towel. Their arguments have strayed in a slippery fashion to recast the problem as one of "climate change" (which is never defined in a measurable way). International conferences still have ambitions to redo international energy production and redistribute income from the developed to the undeveloped world. Their larger goal, rarely clearly articulated, is to upend the FEO. Indeed, Christiana Figueres, who led U.N. efforts to forge a new international climate treaty in Paris (December 2015), told reporters the previous February that the real goal was "to change the economic development model that has been reigning for at least 150 years." In other words, according to Lamar Smith, a central objective of these negotiations is the redistribution of wealth among nations and giving governments iron control over their economies.[502]

*   *   *

All these leftist critiques of the FEO amount to a call for larger, more intrusive government to correct some postulated, but empirically unsupported, moral, social, or structural problem.

Dismissing Empiricism in Favor of Good Intentions

In light of the above, what can committed Leftists, utopian re-distributionists, do to challenge society's reliance on free markets? Expediency could argue for denying the use of empiricism in these matters– for denying the relevance of facts, data, and analyses, for valuing good intentions over empiricism and shifting the argument from economics to morality.

While the language of the well-intended Left has evolved, its reactionary mindset reproduces not just the values of the medieval church but also its self-righteousness. Unable to deal objectively with fiscal policy, it demonizes opponents, arguing that those who oppose even the most poorly designed government action to relieve suffering or economic inequality must be morally deficient.

For example, attempts to bring major entitlements into realistic economic bounds are characterized as a lack of caring. Attempts to keep the budget in balance are used to call conservatives the servants of Wall Street or the top 1%. Attempts to optimize tax rates to avoid counterproductively overtaxing the

---

[501]   Dixy Lee Ray with Lou Guzzo, *Trashing the Planet* (Washington D.C. Regnery Gateway, 1990), 38.

[502]   Lamar Smith, "The Climate Change Religion," *The Wall Street Journal*, April 24, 2015, A11.

investor class are characterized as shielding the rich from paying their fair share. Virtually any redistributive program can, in their minds, be justified on the grounds of helping the poor or achieving fairness.

The last resort of such arguments is that utopian sentiments have never yet been implemented properly, so there is no conclusive evidence against them. The belief endures that the right elite leadership and education could help human nature become less "selfish" and more "focused on others" so that leftist policies *could* work. The record, however, shows that virtually all unfettered attempts to pursue utopian goals have failed or, as in the case of the Soviet Union, have had catastrophic results.

Another line of attack is to cast doubt on empiricism itself by criticizing the metrics employed to measure human well-being. While some of these arguments are pretty much limited to academia, they animate the committed Leftist. These views argue that support of the FEO is a result of a social construction or that truth in these matters is inherently undiscoverable.

Deconstructionists fall into this camp. They reject the so-called rationalist bias that has dominated Western thought since the time of Plato in favor of a method of "reflective attentiveness" that discloses the individual's "lived experience" in the context of power relationships and personal "construction" of truth and world views.

Paul Boghossian presents a full-scale critique of such philosophical attacks. He summarizes the deconstructionist view:

> According to this core idea, the truth of a belief is not a matter of how things stand with an "independently existing reality," and its rationality is not a matter of its approval by "transcendent procedures of rational assessment." Rather, whether a belief is knowledge necessarily depends at least in part on the contingent social and material setting in which the belief is produced (or maintained).
>
> This is a *social dependence* conception of knowledge. … if a belief's being knowledge is always a function of the contingent social setting in which it is produced, then it looks as though it could very well turn out that what is knowledge for us is not knowledge for [some other cultural group].[503]

Thus, any claim to knowledge is reduced to a relativistic statement.

He describes a related concept, the "doctrine of equal validity," which

---

[503]   Paul Boghossian, *Fear of Knowledge – Against Relativism and Constructivism* (Oxford: Clarendon Press, 2006), 6-7.

maintains that there are many radically different, yet "equally valid" ways of knowing the world, and science is just one of them.[504] These views, of course, tend to undermine the power of empirical evidence.

In this way, the deconstructionist camp exploits a vulnerability in arguments defending the FEO that was identified by von Hayek: Its evolutionary development is veiled by centuries of trial and error and is nowhere engraved in stone. Derrida targets this vulnerability by arguing that the veiled history of these values reduces their legitimacy and suggests that they are therefore an artificial construct of society's power centers. In response to this assertion, my previous book, *Free People, Free Markets: Their Evolutionary Origins* shows that it is indeed possible to trace its evolutionary development revealing the origins, strengths, and validity of the FEO.

Richard Epstein discusses other potential dangers of such philosophic attacks.

> Quite simply, the rule of law requires a degree of linguistic clarity that allows for the articulation of any set of comprehensible rules, regardless of their content, which others can choose to obey or disobey. ... this view is in opposition to a universal theory of language that is systematically skeptical of the linguistic building blocks of every legal rule, or worse, selectively skeptical of the clarity of any legal rule that its theorists oppose on substantive grounds.[505]

Once the possibility of objective truth has been dismissed, many underpinnings of the FEO, including key terms in the Constitution (such as property; commerce; freedom of speech; and legislative, executive, and judicial power) become subject to deep and inescapable definitional ambiguities.

Supporters of the FEO, on the other hand, might simply dismiss deconstructionist relativist views in favor of those of Confucius. His views, expressed thousands of years ago, still ring true:

> Clarity and honesty of thought and expression were the first lessons of the Master ... obscurity of thought and insincere inaccuracy of speech seemed to him national calamities. Confucius argued the importance of defining one's terms, of not allowing wishes to discolor the facts and determine the conclusions, and of impartially investigating the nature of things.[506]

---

[504] Ibid, 2.

[505] Richard A. Epstein, *Design for Liberty* (Cambridge: Harvard University Press, 2011) 14-15.

[506] Will Durant, *Our Oriental Heritage*, 668.

Dismissing Past Experience

In addition, in an effort to shutdown debate, the Left undermines learning from experience. It supports false narratives, disguises the magnitude of the economic progress that has occurred, delegitimizes the outcomes, and hides the wellsprings of that progress. Examples include the nineteenth-century myth of the "Robber Barons"; the economy's spontaneous recovery from the 1919 recession; the failure of the New Deal to bring the country out of the Depression; the nation's spontaneous recovery from a wartime economy in 1946; and the successes of supply-side policies under Kennedy in 1964, under Reagan in 1982, and under Bush in 2003.

This approach has largely succeeded in public discourse because the long feedback loop demonstrating the effects of government policies means that the electorate learns very slowly. Moreover, politicians have little incentive to speed this process. Indeed, politicians' ideological rigidity and natural aversion to accountability tend to ensure that things must be very serious before the government acknowledges the need for radical change. It seems that history and analysis alone are not up to the task.

*   *   *

Despite a record in which (by absolutely every metric of human well-being) lifestyles have improved dramatically over generations and even just over decades, the FEO is attacked as uncaring and non-egalitarian, because society could do so much more for the human condition if it really tried. Indeed, it is seen as having a moral imperative to do so. If we must abandon key elements of the constitutional/economic model bequeathed to better meet the needs of the people and achieve greater social justice, so be it. Ultimately, the philosophic debate between such views and those who support FEO-values comes down to arguments based on intuition and sentiment on one hand, at which the Left excels, against those of experience and scientific analysis, at which they don't.

This issue is not merely academic; there is much at stake if the United States is to correct its governmental pathologies and alarming fiscal imbalances to restore the vigor of the FEO. This chapter has attempted to deconstruct the arguments of the progressive Left. Still, if a vigilant electorate is to be energized, a *positive alternative* must be articulated and made readily available. The next chapter, therefore, will outline a positive manifesto for the FEO. It emphasizes libertarian values of personal liberty, the protection of private property, trust in distributed human intelligence, and distrust of strong central government.

CHAPTER 9

AFFIRMING THE FREE EXTENDED ORDER

"If you don't stand for something you'll fall for anything." – Attributed to Alexander Hamilton

"Be assured that freedom of trade, freedom of thought, freedom of speech, and freedom of action, are but modifications of one great fundamental truth, and that all must be maintained or all risked: they stand and fall together."[507] – *Edinburgh Review*

So far, this book has described the marvelous rise of the FEO in much of the modern world, an emergence that involved extending inherited value-sets and confronting unrelenting ideological threats. Unfortunately, as economies grew more modern and sophisticated, so did the forces that would exploit their wealth. The previous chapter described the political and philosophical assault that has been launched against the FEO. While the FEO's impressive results should – and to a large extent do – speak for themselves, more is needed; free markets, liberty, and the rules of representative government call for comprehensive affirmation.

Accordingly, this chapter presents an argument for those who want to preserve and advance the evolutionary heritage represented by the FEO. The argument has two parts. First, it summarizes the superiority of the FEO to any other known political model; then, it lists the touchstones that support and define the FEO.

---

[507] 77 *Edinburgh Review*, (1843), 224; quoted in Viner, *supra* note 21 at 55 n.41. (Epstein, *The Classical Liberal Constitution*, 651).

THE SUPERIORITY OF THE FEO

Earlier chapters provided numerous examples demonstrating the superiority of the FEO and the costs incurred when a country departs from its predicates. However, to offer a more complete defense this chapter will distil those lessons so as to connect the dots. Moreover, the FEO's superiority as a structure for society is seen not only in material advances, but also in its ability to restrain governmental predation under representative democracy, and is the optimal setting for individual self-actualization.

Produces Affluence

The proof is in the pudding. As shown in Chapter One, a country that governs in accord with the precepts of the FEO creates more wealth than other nations and enjoys everything that wealth makes possible: education, health, a cleaner environment, and so forth. While there is not yet an indisputable mathematical model that fully characterizes the FEO, economic theory supports its elements. The predicates of the FEO are known, and correlating a country's performance with those predicates is a straightforward task. It then becomes clear that the success of different countries is not random; it occurs in those that adhere to most of the principles of the FEO.

Macro-data

As noted in Chapter One, several analyses published annually allow a country's performance as measured by certain predicates to be tracked; these include *The Index of Economic Freedom* (the *Index*) and *The Economic Freedom of the World, Annual Report* (the *Report*). They draw on assessments of countries' policies and institutions to measure how countries organize and deploy labor and its capital, as seen in private property rights, the rule of law, the ability to efficiently raise and deploy capital, sound macro-economic policies, openness to innovation and competition, and entrepreneurial tradition. The assessments are quantitative (e.g., the proportion of GDP spent by the government) and qualitative (e.g., how well the country adheres to rule of law or protects private property).

In all the criteria, freedom is the common denominator. The *Report* examines "the key ingredients of economic freedom: personal choice, voluntary exchange coordinated by markets, freedom to enter and compete in markets, and protection of persons and their property from aggression by others."[508]

The *Index* considers virtually the same factors; its ten metrics (listed in Chapter One) provide quantitative measurements of the FEO's manifestation.

---

[508] James Gwartney and Robert Lawson with William Easterly, *Economic Freedom of the World 2006 Annual Report* (Canada: The Fraser Institute, 2006), 5.

The close correlation between affluence and a high ranking in these measures is illustrated in the figure below, which shows the per capita GDP (purchasing power parity) for each ranked group of nations in the 2016 *Report*.[509] The freer a nation is according to these metrics, the wealthier it is likely to be, with the caveat that a country has to do most things right. Countries categorized as "mostly unfree," which adhere to only some of the necessary policies, fare as poorly as the countries categorized as "repressed."

Unfortunately, most countries fail to adhere to these precepts of economic freedom. For example, in the *Index* (2016), of the 178 countries assessed, thirty-eight are "free" or "mostly free" (in general, they adhere to most of the factors), fifty-four are "moderately free," and eighty-six are "mostly unfree" or "repressed."

This data is readily available across the globe, yet governments in the lower rankings routinely ignore the lessons and interfere with the market for a host of sentimental and/or predatory reasons, creating coerced or unfree economies. Obviously, some governments do this because they are kleptocracies, but others do it because of misguided sentiment that blinds them to the lessons of the FEO. The most common of these views were discussed in the previous chapter: They challenge the efficacy of the market, claim that the market ignores important human considerations, or argue that "market failures" exist that only governmental action can correct.

Such views, contrary to the FEO, prompt government intervention to reorder the natural outcomes of free markets through taxation, tariffs, and regulation in the pursuit of more politically desirable results. This entails a high opportunity cost. However emotionally powerful non-FEO considerations might seem, they fail to achieve their goals because they are economically dysfunctional.

Case Studies

While the close correlation between economic performance and adherence to FEO predicates is analytically convincing at the macro-level, specific examples can be even more compelling – knowing specifically what has and hasn't worked keeps one grounded in reality.

The most dramatic positive example is Singapore, which was discussed in Chapter Seven. At the conclusion of the Second World War, the U.S. GDP was equal to half the planet's, and its standard of living was the envy of all. Singapore (not yet an independent entity) was an impoverished city with no natural resources at the southern tip of the Malayan peninsula. After gaining independence, Singapore adopted policies that adhered to virtually all the precepts of the *Index*. Today, its standard of living is higher than that of the United States. Admittedly,

---

[509]   Terry Miller and Anthony H. Kim, *2016 Index of Economic Freedom: Promoting Economic Opportunity and Prosperity* (The Heritage Foundation and *The Wall Street Journal*), 2016.

culturally and politically, Singapore is *sui generis*, but its successful policies certainly act as a beacon for all who wish to transform their economies.

Equally important are the examples of countries that had grown wealthy by adhering to the precepts of free markets and liberty but were beguiled by Hayek's fatal conceit – the belief that beneficent government could outperform the FEO. This temptation in representative governments is almost universal. Earlier chapters presented case studies of several such countries that undermined the foundations of prosperity only to hit a fiscal wall, but then turned things around by following almost a textbook set of remedies corresponding to the metrics discussed in the previous section.

New Zealand's example is probably most telling. For decades, its governments pursued utopian goals counter to the principles of the FEO, until the system simply ceased to be financially viable. Finally recognizing that reality, a new government shifted policies virtually overnight, after which inflation fell, the currency stabilized, and vigorous growth took off. One could say that New Zealand's efforts are the 'gold standard' of reform.

Other case-studies demonstrating the severe downside of ignoring the conclusions of the *Index* and the *Report,* while not discussed in this book, can be seen on the front pages of newspapers everywhere. Notable are Venezuela and Cuba. Both went down the path of hard-socialism with disastrous results. Venezuela, once the wealthiest Latin American country in terms of GDP per capita is now among the poorest, with suffering evident throughout its society. Similarly, Cuba, once having the third highest GDP per capita in the Western Hemisphere, is now among the poorest.

Past U.S. Experience

The United States' experience provides a host of lessons for what works and what doesn't. Notably:

- In response to the serious recession of 1919 that followed the First World War, the Republican administration chose to let the economy self-correct, which it speedily did.
- In contrast, in response to the stock market crash and early depression of 1929, both the Hoover and Roosevelt Administrations opted for massive government intervention – spending, tariffs, and regulation. This extended hard times until 1940, and, as the Treasury Secretary's diary noted at the end of these interventions – nothing seemed to work.
- At the end of the Second World War, when sixteen million citizens were in the armed forces and a third of the economy served the

military, the country quit the war-economy cold-turkey by returning these resources to the private sector. The Left prophesized major dislocations and depression if there were not continued government intervention. Their advice was rejected, and the economy boomed.

- On a number of subsequent occasions, in defiance of leftist protests, presidents have reduced the government's fiscal hold on the private sector with reductions in tax rates, each time producing a boom: Kennedy did this in 1962; Reagan did it in 1982 with the Supply Side Revolution; Clinton reduced capital gains rates in 1998; and Bush reduced tax rates in 2003.

Those who limit themselves to the mainstream media are unaware of this history and therefore ignorant of its lessons: namely, that limiting government intervention in the economy has been shown to produce the most rapid economic growth, which benefits every income stratum.

Chapter 1 laid out the empirical reasons to expect these results, namely that a light hand of government that allows free play of human distributed intelligence, spontaneous economic development, and economic laws of comparative advantage, consumer surplus, supply/demand, and clear price signals produces the most effective outcomes.

However, there are other reasons why the FEO, given human nature, offers a better model for organizing society than does large government.

Offers Narrower Scope for Mis-governance

Keeping government small in itself simply limits opportunities for mis-governance. Utopian schemes are less likely to be entertained in the first place (recall Epstein's caution about the presumption of error). Moreover, it constricts the impulses for unnecessary regulation. First, it counters the universal tendencies researched by Mancur Olson: "The behavior of individuals and firms in stable societies leads to the formation of dense networks of collusive, cartelistic, and lobbying organizations that make economies less efficient and dynamic and polities less governable."[510] In addition, it limits a drift to a regulatory state that burdens individuals and the private sector without adequate congressional oversight as was discussed in Chapter Five. Also, adhering to a philosophy of small and limited government alleviates somewhat the phenomena behind Lal's conclusion that "A universal feature of polities is the ubiquitous predatoriness

---

[510]   Mancur Olson, *The Rise and Decline of Nations* (New Haven: Yale University Press, 1982), cover flyleaf.

of the State."[511] There are simply fewer opportunities for predation under a constitutionally constrained government.

Finally, limited government provides far fewer opportunities to undermine individual liberty. Indeed, as John Trenchard and Thomas Gordon wrote:

> Liberty, the source of all the fruits of civilization and human happiness, is ever liable to suffer the aggressions and encroachments of government, of power, the source from which war, tyranny, and impoverishment ever flow. Power always stands ready to conspire against liberty, and the only salvation is for the public to keep government within strictly limited bounds, and to be ever watchful, vigilant, and hostile to the inevitable tendencies of government power to encroach upon liberty ...[512]

Aside from those negative aspects, government simply cannot match civil society and the private sector in efficiency, effectiveness, and innovation, because it experiences less in the way of competition and accountability.

Promotes Competition

The central reason for relatively inefficient government programs is the lack of meaningful competition – evident in Social Security, Medicare, Medicaid, and most public education, all quasi-monopolies. The discussion of healthcare, pensions, and education at home and abroad (Chapters Five to Seven) show that these need not be run by the government to the extent they are in the United States. The government might require residents to have health insurance or a pension plan, as is the case in Singapore, Germany, and Switzerland, but the execution should be left to the private sector, which works in an actuarially sound way that includes competition among insurance agents and providers

A micro-level view of the economy demonstrates why individual actors and the private sector are likely to use resources more efficiently than the government. Properly crafted health insurance is superior to Medicaid; charter schools outperform public schools when serving students of the same socio-economic strata; IRAs are superior to Social Security; and infrastructure constructed via competitive bids not bogged down by convoluted regulations and in thrall to unions would be far cheaper than under the current arrangements. Moreover,

---

[511]   Deepak Lal, *Unintended Consequences* (Cambridge: The MIT Press, 1998), 16.

[512]   James Ostrowski, *Progressivism: A Primer on the Idea Destroying America*(Buffalo, New York: Cazenovia Books, 2014),95, in Murray N. Rothbard, *Conceived in Liberty*, Vol. I, 693.

when governments are assigned an overwhelmingly large role, potentially superior options are crowded out, undermining the reforming powers of competition.

Bureaucracies are invariably less innovative and nimble than entrepreneurs because they tend to prefer one-size-fits-all designs and because they are too risk-averse – in bureaucracy, mistakes are punished more than successful innovations are rewarded. As von Hayek argues, the best elite minds cannot compete with the distributed intelligence of the people. *Competition* among institutions, not the weak accountability of bureaucracies, is the best protection against economic predation and inefficiency.

Not only are government programs relatively inefficient, but, in serving special interests the government foists regulations on states and cities that propagate inefficiency elsewhere. Ongoing attempts to fix the terms of labor, require wage controls, favor certain industries, favor unions (which have high direct costs and infamous work rules), and institute protectionism in agricultural sectors increase inefficiency throughout the economy.

Aligns with Oversight and Accountability

If government functioned as it is presented to the electorate – if it were held strictly accountable for the taxpayer dollar via congressional oversight hearings, the inspectors general, the Government Accountability Office, and presidential commissions – then there might be a presumed learning curve for overcoming shortfalls. By and large, however, this is not the case.

To be sure, most government workers do their jobs; fraud, when it occurs, is discovered by oversight entities. Similarly, agencies can be said to do their jobs based on certain metrics; for example, they issue checks punctually and accurately. The more important issue arises when government programs fail to achieve their larger missions – that is, when the original design was flawed for meeting the country's needs.

In that light, oversight functions too often as a façade to protect the status quo and preserve the positions of special interests. Chapter Five provided some examples of parties that shifted responsibility for crises and supported false narratives. Politicians may mandate cost-benefit analyses, but recent decades have shown that thumbs are placed on the scale – for example, the monetary value of "social benefits" is highly elastic. One is hard pressed to find an example of any government program that has ever been eliminated or sharply curtailed because of inferior performance.

Even more perverse, when government programs obviously falter in meeting their goals, the usual cry is for still more resources. Medicare and Medicaid face looming financial problems because of bad business models, yet the government solution was to double-down with Obamacare. Schools don't perform to standard, so politicians want to throw more money at an already resource-rich system. An unavoidable reality is that government programs are sustained by politicians who bear no direct costs in the outcome, whereas when private enterprises use resources inefficiently, they lose money and eventually fail.

*   *   *

Of course, the government performs many necessary tasks that help keep us safe and healthy. It does tasks that go beyond the capacities of individuals and civil society – in precisely the areas that Buchanan says it is appropriate to cede some individual freedom of action to the government. But political vigilance is essential to keeping government functions within these bounds, because special-interest factions will always push governments to expand in their favor. Chapter Five illustrated how these tendencies played out under the public radar in the United States over the last century when government escaped the constitutional leash.

Taken as a whole, this expansion has produced what has been termed a "swamp": unproductive but lucrative activity made possible by government regulations, lobbying, and litigation. These create a maze of legislation, virtually impossible for the average voter to monitor and thus difficult to reform through the political process. It is not a random outcome that a disproportionate number of the most affluent counties in the United States are in the Washington, DC metropolitan area. It is even more common for the government to support special interests by tweaking the rules of the game– that is, by influencing free, contractual, honest exchanges in the marketplace via taxation and regulation.

There is no real surprise here: Madison foresaw the temptations and possible outcomes. He helped craft a checks-and-balances plus enumerated-powers solution that worked tolerably well for a long while. But as we have seen, government has slipped its leash. What standards should be applied as the leash is re-imposed? Writ large it is this: The central government's primary role is to protect against aggression, domestic and external; to enforce contracts; to protect the public's health and safety; and to establish the "rules of the road." Federal regulation should not be used to impose the government's views on how to do something in opposition to the private sector's "best practices".

Enhances Individual Liberty and Social Capital

Not only is a robust FEO the best way to generate affluence – benefiting all classes – and to constrain predatory factions in politics, but it is the economic system most in keeping with the ideals of a free people. Limited government married to principles of individual liberty goes hand-in-hand with greater social capital: more creative, self-actualized, and energetic individuals who are free and able to pursue happiness. In this context, more of the citizenry will seek to maximize their talents rather than expecting government assistance to reach their life goals.

This, of course, was our colonial heritage: a Lockean, Whiggish view that evolved from several centuries of British experience. It placed a premium on all forms of individual liberty and on the importance of protecting private property against predation. The colonists also inherited views of personal responsibility and morality that prepared them to realize the opportunities of a new life on a new continent. These views reflected (in part) austere strains of Protestantism such as Calvinism, Presbyterianism, and the Dutch Reformed Church, all of which emphasized a life of achievement and demanded truth-telling, hard work, deferred gratification, saving, investing, and living up to one's commitments. Economically, these values enhanced individual social capital and reduced transaction costs throughout the economy. Colonial society had little patience with a "victim mentality," with misbehavior justified by the argument that "everyone does it," or with organized attempts to extract wealth from those who had produced it.

Prior to the onslaught of Progressivism, most of America adhered to a Protestant ethic: hard work, discipline and frugality, combined with the belief that individuals succeed due to ability, self-reliance, and perseverance in the face of hardship. In short, they had to be "self-made." Of course, that fit with the inescapable reality of settling a frontier society that offered few alternatives to self-reliance.

In effect, by now reaffirming the FEO, we reaffirm a specific cultural set of values: an emphasis on character, which was stronger in our early years, as well as broader libertarian values of life, liberty, and the pursuit of happiness. These values define an individual's view of himself as well as his attitude towards government. Self-reliant individuals, who probably comprise the vast majority of the population, can generally do better for themselves than with one-size-fits-all government programs. Rather than using government as the middleman, experience has shown that the inescapable vicissitudes of life are best addressed by a system in which each individual strives first to maximize his own success through foresight and hard work, purchases insurance in case of bad luck, and allows a small circumscribed government (preferably at the local level) to help those truly unable to cope.

An updated expression for "life, liberty, and the pursuit of happiness" might be: "The desire to do as well as you can in life, to develop your potential and expect to be rewarded for it, to provide your family with the greatest possible opportunity for self-improvement, and to do that on your own without depending on the state."[513]

---

[513]   Janet Daley, *The Telegraph*, May 9, 2015, in *The Wall Street Journal*, May 11, 2015, A13.

Contrast worldviews of the individual in the FEO with those in Progressivism:

- The FEO keeps wealth generation in individual hands, embedded in man's distributed intelligence subject to market forces. Individuals have competitive options and need not depend on an opaque political process, which they inevitably perceive to advantage others over themselves.
- Progressivism encourages an entitlement mentality; positive rights are bestowed by the state through programs that lack meaningful competition and are implemented through a political process that unavoidably becomes a contest among rent-seeking special interests, breeding dissatisfaction and distrust throughout society. Progressivism chains the individual with regulation, lack of choice, and societal discord fueled by group-identity politics and political correctness.

Widespread acceptance of the FEO will produce a 'virtuous circle': The more individuals look to themselves and distrust big government, the fewer opportunities for predation, waste, and inefficiency will exist on the national level, and the faster affluence and social capital will grow. Moreover, counter-intuitively, an FEO can be the best way to meet the needs of all citizens when it incorporates 'safety nets' for those unable to cope.

Produces a Sounder Safety Net

There are better ways than many proposals of the Left to meet the needs of the poor, but they lack the emotional satisfaction of immediate spending proposals or grandiose social programs on the national level. The core of the argument for the FEO is that, while indeed many individuals (but a small percentage of the population) need assistance, it should be delivered in ways that don't undermine the prosperity of the entire society, which benefits everyone. Assistance must avoid moral hazard by claimants on the one hand and bureaucratic inefficiencies that tend towards larger government on the other.

Society's primary goal should be to establish policies and institutions that grow the economy and make everyone better off – wealth must be created before it can be redistributed. A subsidiary goal, informed by experience with unintended consequences, freeloading, and an understanding of human nature, suggests that welfare should primarily be the domain of local governments, extended families, civil society, churches, and philanthropic organizations. These groups are operated by those closest to recipients and are therefore best able to judge actual need and eventually empower recipients to return to a productive role in the FEO. The example of Singapore described in Chapter Seven illustrates one way this can be done.

TOUCHSTONES

That is the broad philosophy. Day-to-day vigilance can benefit from understanding an array of touchstones grounded in empirical reality and adherence to liberty in all its forms. Unlike abstractions such as democracy or capitalism, properly defined, the FEO is empirically real – its structure and the results of its precepts are measurable. Most individuals should be able to grasp the underlying principles of the FEO, much as they understand that the earth is round and revolves around the sun. Just as a few astronomical observations and simple principles make the case for the solar-centric view, the metrics of the *Index* can do the same for the FEO.

Moreover, an understanding of the FEO as the vanguard of an evolutionary process in which societies gradually learned to organize their social affairs more effectively – became more 'fit' – leads to an appreciation of one of humankind's greatest collective achievements. Mankind had to retain essential instincts from his prehistoric antecedents while learning new behaviors that would be compatible with a modern world. The result is a marvel of human learning and adaptation that meshes innate atavistic instincts (communal, sentimental, and jealous) with the values of an extended order of cooperation (hands-off, distant, and a wider circle of trust). The recurring theme in that evolution is the widening of individual freedom in responsible mutually beneficial forms.

Accordingly, the FEO is not some random collection of precepts to be accepted or discarded by the political winds of our time. They constitute a collective whole that has evolved over time because the elements organize society better. There may be no 'blueprint' carved in stone to guide everyday understanding, but the elements (see Chapter One) can be traced through time (see Chapter Three); we can observe how they first came into use and their utility was proven.

To defend the FEO is to defend its predicates: the principles of liberty, private property, free markets, and rule of law.

Liberty

The first and most important touchstone of the FEO is liberty. George H. Smith, author of *The System of Liberty*, wrote that liberty is not simply a means but also an end in and of itself. In this light, according to Lord Acton, a liberal is a person whose "pole star is liberty" – one who deems those things right in politics which, taken all round, promote, increase, and perpetuate freedom; and who deems those things wrong that impede it. This led to the belief that individuals have the natural right to use their bodies, labor, and justly acquired property as they see fit, as long as they respect the equal freedom of others.[514] This is

---

[514]   *Cato Policy Report*, July/August 2013, 13.

who we once were as a society; such views informed the American Declaration of Independence and the U.S. Constitution. Liberty is the indispensable social element that unleashes the benefits of human action.

While Progressives might give lip-service to this principle, they encroach upon it at every turn in pursuit of utopian ends. For example, they want to abridge free speech through government-enforced spending restrictions for elections; they promote politically correct views; they want to curtail personal choice in pension and health plans; they want to control companies directly or indirectly to counter "market imperfections"; they want to tell bakers how to decorate cakes so as not to offend favored groups; they want to encroach on property rights for trivial issues like standing water; they want to seize property to benefit favored groups and take ever larger fractions of one's income.[515]

Private property

While liberty gives individuals the latitude to pursue entrepreneurial ends, property rights provide the essential material means. John Locke's view was that "[t]he great and chief end of men uniting into commonwealths, and putting themselves under government, is the preservation of their property. ... the supreme power cannot take from any man any part of his property without his own consent."[516] At that time, *property* entailed much more than physical assets; it encompassed one's right to use and enjoy the benefits of one's ideas and efforts.

Moreover, private property, because it allows the owner discretion regarding the use of his assets, creates multiple competing economic centers. As Tom Bethell points out:

> [P]eople can benefit from their own industry and insulate themselves from the negative effects of others' actions. ... The industrious will reap the benefits of their industry, the frugal the consequences of their frugality; the improvident and the profligate likewise. They receive their due, which is to say they experience justice as a matter of routine. *Private property institutionalizes justice.* [517]

Indeed, in contrast to the Left's loose use of the term justice, he notes that "the act of justice is to render what is due," which in turn requires pre-agreed rules.

Chapter One provided some supporting rationale for this view. It demonstrated

---

[515]   See Chapter Five for examples.

[516]   Bertrand Russell, *A History of Western Philosophy* (New York: Simon and Schuster, 1945), 632.

[517]   Ibid, 162.

that allowing owners discretion regarding the use of their assets creates multiple competing economic centers that make the most of distributed intelligence and spontaneous order. Another beneficial aspect is that, when property rights and their associated income are secure, individuals can contest government encroachment on their liberty in the courts as well as through the political process. When those rights are not protected, the weak suffer as well, because they are least politically well-connected.

In summary, the institution of private property lends operational meaning to liberty by enabling individuals to live and act without governmental sanction. It frees the individual from dependence on the whims of the state and makes free exchange possible. That recognition accounts for its inclusion as the Fifth Amendment to the U.S. Constitution, which states that the government may not, without compelling necessity, override the outcomes of free exchange. In other words, the government may not take property without compensation, nor may it invalidate contracts.

Free Markets

Another touchstone for guarding the FEO is keeping markets free. To reiterate earlier points, the FEO relies on private-sector investment to direct capital to its best uses without inefficient governmental second-guessing. However, the government must provide security, the rule of law, and sound currencies, and it must promote competition to enable the system to function optimally. Finding the appropriate boundary between these two principles is the essence of sound government. Chapter One listed the criteria that the *Index* and the *Report* use to measure the freedom of countries' economies. Each criterion should be included on a checklist that citizens use to evaluate government proposals. Specifically:

- A financial system should facilitate the accumulation of capital through savings and a free flow of that capital through investors and intermediary institutions such as banks. It also needs to allow for returns on capital commensurate with the risk taken, protect capital under the rule of law, and permit capital to flow in the most productive directions.
- A free market should not inhibit the free play of supply and demand, which generates clear price signals for producers and consumers. Rising prices encourage new production and discourage consumption; falling prices have the reverse effect.
- Open competition ensures that economic enterprises utilize the full mix of resources to meet consumer desires more efficiently than their competitors, at the risk of becoming less profitable or

unprofitable. This criterion should equally apply to government programs.

- Free trade with other countries should be encouraged to maximize the benefits of comparative advantage.
- The system should work to minimize externalities (costs) due to regulation and uncertainty. These can include costs due to unsound currencies, wasteful regulation, political instability, and crime.
- Direct government intrusion in economic activity should be minimized. Since it lacks the constant pressure of competition and the penalties the market imposes on mistakes and bad policy, the government tends to employ resources less productively than the private sector.
- The tax burden should be minimized consistent with providing *essential* government services. Taxing commercial activity discourages it, and taxation takes financial resources out of the hands of the more productive sectors and places them in the hands of a less productive government.
- Starting new businesses should be relatively easy and quick.

In short, in a healthy FEO, human productive impulses have a range of opportunities and a supportive environment in which to act on them. When the government places a heavy tax on productive behavior, distorts price signals, undermines economic rights, increases uncertainty, redirects capital, discourages innovation, and places regulatory hurdles on new enterprises, economic growth languishes. While such encroachments are frequently justified by some apparent greater social good, unintended consequences have repeatedly demonstrated the weakness of such arguments. Focusing on the paramount importance of liberty, property, and free markets ultimately produces greater benefits than all the random tinkering of politicians because it produces the most robust extended order.

Rule of Law

An equally important touchstone is vigilance regarding the rule of law. Chapter Three showed how the concept of rule of law underpins personal liberty because it means that both rulers and ruled are equally subject to the law. Beyond that, the clear, predictable, and unbiased application of the law is essential to the free functioning of the FEO. This reduces transaction costs and the costs of legal uncertainties. Moreover, courts need to be held accountable for applying the law according to text, legislative action, and precedent, not according to subjective views of what is "just."

* * *

In summary, liberty, property rights, free markets, and the rule of law can be the polestars that guide citizens through the thicket of ungrounded sentiment used by those who prefer a different outcome to the FEO. These values should be brought to bear whenever the government wants to curtail economic liberty, including individuals' use of their energy, time, property, and their freely entered economic transactions.

FROM UNDERSTANDING TO ACTION

This worldview and set of arguments may by this point in the book seem self-evident. Nonetheless, even a casual observer of the political scene can spot its vulnerabilities. Many, if not most, politicians simply don't care. As mentioned in the second chapter, all they care about is winning votes. That was Aristotle's concern about democracy two and a half millennia ago. Chapter Three limned the process whereby mankind fortunately came upon ways to counter the weaknesses of the democratic model through the insights of men like Montesquieu and Madison. Centuries of experience have shown that constitutional restraints rather than relying on the virtue of leaders provide the only effective solution.

Imagine the eventual payoff of a system that can draw on these insights to put the United States' fiscal house in order. At the least, crisis and political instability would be averted. In addition, this could bump long-term growth rates back to their historical average after the sluggish growth of recent decades. The added kicker is that these steps would fully energize human distributed intelligence to take full advantage of the computer revolution and artificial intelligence, which promise a new age on the order of the Industrial Revolution.

Shifting to this mindset and undoing the mistakes of the previous century will entail heavy political lifting. At the moment, it seems impossible due to partisan deadlock and the absence of real leadership. Nevertheless, inaction will likely soon cease to be an option. The looming fiscal entitlement time bomb will probably provide the catalyst for fundamental reform, which will require finding a way back to the spirit and form of the Constitution as first ratified.

What this might entail specifically is the subject of the next chapter.

CHAPTER 10

STRENGTHENING THE FREE EXTENDED ORDER AND THWARTING A CRISIS

"… there is nothing more difficult to arrange, more doubtful of success, and more dangerous to carry through than initiating changes in a State's constitution. The innovator makes enemies of all those who prospered under the old order, and only lukewarm support is forthcoming from those who would prosper under the new."– Niccolò Machiavelli[518]

"In the last resort, too, the returns to political entrepreneurship from trying to change the institutional and political rules in favor of better economic performance may become so great that the changes are made."– S. Brittan[519]

"Only a crisis – actual or perceived – produces real change. When that crisis occurs, the actions that are taken depend on the ideas that are lying around. That, I believe, is our basic function: to develop alternatives to existing policies, to keep them alive and available until the politically impossible becomes the politically inevitable." – Milton Friedman[520]

---

[518] Niccolò Machiavelli, *The Prince* (Harmondsworth: Penguin Books, 1973), 51; in Jonathan Boston and Martin Holland, eds., *The Fourth Labour Government, Radical Politics in New Zealand* (Auckland: Oxford University Press, 1987), 11.

[519] S. Brittan, *The Role and Limits of Government: Essays in Political Economy* (Hounslow: Maurice Temple Smith, 1983), 238; in Jonathan Boston and Martin Holland, eds., *The Fourth Labour Government*, 10.

[520] Milton Friedman (2009). *Capitalism and Freedom*: Fortieth Anniversary Edition (University of Chicago Press, 2009), 14.

The prior chapter presented the empirical basis and political philosophy underlying the FEO, which has brought unprecedented benefits to much of the world. Despite the evidence, it is under attack; chief among the attacks has been a century-long assault by U.S. Progressives. To be sure, the U.S. still benefits enormously from a robust FEO. Nonetheless, the U.S. could be so much better off; but now, because of living way beyond its means and borrowing enormous sums from the future, it is likely to become much less so. Repelling those attacks and reinvigorating the FEO-precepts constitutionally and programmatically would give us the means both to address our fiscal problems and restore us to earlier paths of rapid growth. This chapter considers how that be made to come about – however unlikely it may now appear.

The impetus for reform will almost certainly begin with a more widespread recognition of the nation's fiscal improvidence, demonstrated in annual budget deficits, ballooning national debt, a growing debt-service burden, slower growth, and the financial erosion of the Social Security and Medicare systems.

Epstein sums up the impact of bad policy and poorly constructed national programs:

> [E]pic mistakes in constitutional and political judgment have long-term adverse effects on the power of a nation to regenerate and recreate itself. So long as the progressives continue to embrace policies that first tolerate and then encourage the massive expansion of transfer payments off an ever-decreasing productive base, they will also reinforce the economic and political risks.[521]

Astonishingly, despite the track record, the Left is still feeling its oats. Their candidates have been promoting national healthcare for all, free college tuition, government-guaranteed jobs and other extremely expensive ideas. They also want to increase taxes on the top income levels, sapping new investment and virtually ensuring that economic growth flags to the point that fiscal problems become unmanageable. At some point, we will no longer be able to borrow trillions of dollars a year at affordable rates– it is precisely the path followed by other countries with representative governments and leftist ambitions.

An "emperor-has-no-clothes" moment will come, and it will become clear that the system is not working; that the programs on which much of the population depends are being critically weakened. The key thrusts of reform will have to be the implementation of ways that can address out-of-control spending – and unaffordable future entitlement promises on one hand, while also reforming Progressive policies and programs that sap the vitality of the FEO. Effective

---

[521]   Richard A. Epstein, *The Classical Liberal Constitution*, 581.

reform will entail smaller government, major reshaping of entitlement programs, much less regulation, more federalism, greater emphasis on personal liberty, the protection of private property, and a Supreme Court committed to the rule of law. Moving along this path, the country will have to revisit the role of the Constitution whose features intended to keep central government limited were undermined.

We can draw some optimism from ways in which the American people have in the past experienced major shifts in political outlooks in relatively short periods of time. Indeed, our system of government presupposes a confidence in the longer-term wisdom of the people – however, misguided they may be in any given election.

The remainder of this chapter identifies how lines of potential reform might unfold in the United States. The conclusion of this book is that *any* solution (short of financial default or inflationary devaluation of claims) to our future fiscal problems will have to involve strengthening elements of our FEO; essential for accelerating economic growth sufficiently to enable us to meet our liabilities. Two broad possibilities are:

- The country re-establishes the predicates for a robust FEO spurred by a political sea-change, perhaps akin to a "Third American Revolution", and Congress simply does its job in the spirit of the original constitution, without additional amendments.
- Exigent circumstances demand that the Constitution be amended to restore its earlier efficacy.

REGROUNDING THE FEO VIA A SEA-CHANGE IN ATTITUDES

The solution to the country's problems – as was the case for other countries discussed in Chapter 7 – is simple if not easy. The simple aspect is to limit the role of the Federal Government in the functioning of the FEO congruent with the spirit of the U.S. Constitution as originally created, drawing upon the essence of federalism, constitutional checks and balances, and the Bill of Rights.

In the United States today, enough of these features remain admirably intact, aside from the Enumerated Powers Clause and some checks and balances that are not fully performing as intended. Restoring the Enumerated Powers Clause may be beyond us, but there are other constitutional features that can be used to restore a semblance of that function.

While the necessary actions are straightforward, the politics are enormously complicated because too many factions and their representatives are invested in the current dysfunctional system creating a political deadlock between forces of FEO-reform and Progressive special interests. This impasse is unlikely to be broken in a meaningful way absent an epiphany in the electorate; a sea change that then is translated into election results.

A Sea Change

Reform adequate to the challenges presupposes changes in the electorate evident in worldviews and accompanying political values. Perhaps it is not so much a matter of inducing change but of allowing values already in the citizenry to emerge with effect. There have already been ripples of such possibilities; most polls indicate widespread distrust of government, and unexpected political forces have over recent decades emerged, such as Ross Perot in the nineties, the Tea Party in the 2000s, and Donald Trump's "Make America Great" campaign.

Nonetheless, if they are to meet the national need these ripples must eventually coalesce into a wave of reform comparable to what has happened from time to time in America's past.

Previous Waves of Reform

Historically, meaningful, relatively swift changes in public attitudes have been a consequence of major shifts in value systems, often religiously inspired. Illustrative examples include the 'Second American Revolution', the events leading to the Civil War, and the Great Awakenings.

The Second American Revolution

What Gordon Wood characterizes as the "Second American Revolution" is a vivid example of how imbedded values can lead to major change. He writes:

> ... the electoral victory of the Republicans in 1800 ... brought, in the eyes of many Americans, the entire revolutionary venture of two and a half decades to successful completion.... He [Jefferson] and his Republican party took over the presidency and both houses of the Congress in 1801 with a worldview that was fundamentally different from that of the Federalists [notably John Adams and Alexander Hamilton].[522]

Consider the events that led up to the election of 1800. The framers of the Constitution had carefully given the new central government powers that would

---

[522]   Gordon S. Wood, *Empire of Liberty* (New York: Oxford University Press, 2009), 276.

remedy the obvious shortcomings of the Articles of Confederation in a way acceptable to the states and in accordance with values of individual liberty. Nonetheless, ratification of the Constitution was a close thing. The people of virtually every state were suspicious of central government, especially regarding taxation and the use of the military. In every such case, Madison and others reassured them that they had nothing to fear because the Constitution only provided Congress with *enumerated powers*. Moreover, throughout the rocky ratification process, commitments were made regarding amendments to the Constitution that would reinforce those principles for the future. And, in short order, Congress passed the Bill of Rights; Amendments Nine and Ten emphasizing the restricted nature of the powers granted to the central government.

With the people reassured, the Federalists won large majorities in the first Congress, getting the new country off to a sound start. Nonetheless, there were overt signs that the government was not adequately honoring the enumerated powers, such as its creation of a U.S. Bank and passage of the Alien and Sedition Act. Jefferson raised the alarm and brought the main body of the country with him to win the election of 1800. The Anti-federalists (the Republicans of the day) then gained large majorities in both houses of Congress; the Federalists never regained majority power. The limited government model was preserved.

The takeaway is this: The people successfully transmitted their set of values to new representatives when the prior government was no longer seen as acting congruent with them; they can do so again. Unfortunately, a contemporary Jefferson seems to still be in the wings.

The Civil War

While the circumstances leading to the Civil War were very different from those described above, the lessons are similar. Prevailing civic values were increasingly hostile to slavery, but the existing political parties were not up to the task of translating those values into political action. As a result, in short order during the 1850s, a new party – the (modern) Republicans – was created, greatly weakening the Democrats and ousting the Whigs. This allowed the nation to finally confront the issue of slavery. Moreover, at that juncture, the nation had a Lincoln to lead the way.

Of course, it also required a civil war to eliminate slavery from our midst, but the shifting moral imperative of the times was the first step that made it all happen.

Religious Movements

Aside from politics, the United States has experienced several widely-based religious movements, such as the First and Second Great Awakenings. The first occurred during late colonial days when new schools and colleges were founded; the second began around 1795 and lasted until 1835. These changes were mostly centered in a new evangelical movement, but they provided powerful support for social reform.[523] To be sure, religious fervor differs considerably from political passion. Nonetheless, such events illustrate the power of ideas to create and motivate social reform.

Value Changes for the Modern Era

This book argues for society to turn its back on Progressivism and encourages a moral renewal congruent with the needs of the FEO. Such changes must emphasize individual liberty, which has a long heritage and a healthy place in our collective psyche. After all, the main thrust of a thousand years of societal evolution has been to liberate the individual as a free – and responsible – actor to maximize the functioning of the FEO. This has cultural and personal components. Society must encourage it and individuals must relish it. They must have confidence in their capability to act in their own self-interests to realize their ambitions and actualize their talents. An optimal FEO requires intellectually tough individuals who can use their freedom effectively and remain vigilant against the encroachment of government.

Prevailing developments of the last century have gotten it precisely backwards by attempting to increase, rather than decrease, individual dependence on government. Regaining our collective footing will require a philosophical bulwark against ongoing attacks on the extended order: consisting of our heritage from the Enlightenment and the Protestant ethic, which define individual morality, and a continuing suspicion of strong central government.

Due respect must be paid to the numerous positive social changes of the last century (inappropriately associated with Progressivism) that benefit the FEO. These include new values associated with the full acceptance of African-Americans, women, and gays in all aspects of society. In evolutionary terms, erasing negative views and removing ways in which society hobbled these groups allows them to self-actualize and to make a full contribution to society. The Left misapplies the lesson of these advances by using their past suppression to justify making them perpetual wards of the state rather than liberated, autonomous individuals. This is insupportable, and common sense should eventually show these groups the superior wisdom of an FEO-approach.

Part of protecting the FEO is managing the predatory side of human nature, requiring a healthy wariness of attempts to use sentimentality to override empiricism. Appropriate vigilance involves addressing moral hazard, propensities

---

[523]   Samuel Eliot Morrison, Henry Steele Commager, and William E. Leuchtenburg, *A Concise History of the American Republic* (New York: Oxford University Press, 1977), 220.

to game the system, freeloading, and adverse economic incentives. Explicitly recognizing the ineradicable predatory side of human nature – which exists even in a representative government – is simply realism.

In short, the people will have to be brought to see that a belief in liberty, freedom, and the right to the fruit of our own labors align not only with empirical findings but also with a prosperous, self-actualized life; that these values lead to results far superior to those promised by progressive sentiment.

It is impossible to foresee in detail how such an American course correction might unfold. Indeed, timing and circumstances are everything. However, when something can't go on, it won't, and once the people believe that the center cannot hold, they will be prepared to leave autopilot and consider other options more seriously.

Will adequate responses result from a virtuous rebirth that allows problems to be resolved by the current system, or will dramatic constitutional change induced by a fiscal calamity that forces us out of the status quo be our fate?

A GRADUAL CONSERVATIVE POLICY/ INSTITUTIONAL PATH

How might a gradual – but decisive shift in political values in a still-divided nation occur? Presumably, such a change would be induced by widespread recognition that budget deficits, accumulating debt, and especially the financial inadequacies of Social Security and Medicare must be addressed. The electorate would see that the status quo is unsustainable and the system is unstable; politicians would see the potential electoral payoff of reform; and the old dysfunctional arguments would lose their electoral appeal.

Under the current political arrangements, gradualist reform would presuppose the finding of minimum common ground and then an understanding of essential substantive reforms.

Finding Common Ground

Reform will undoubtedly require up-ending the hold of special interests. In the abstract, this entails wide recognition that, over the last century, the sheer bulk of interdependence costs are higher than necessary. Buchanan notes "ultimately the hope for some 'improvement' must lie in the mutual consent of the special interests themselves for constitutional changes which will act so as to reduce the excessive costs that discriminatory legislation [considered as a whole] imposes on all groups over time." However, they will not do so unilaterally and independently.[524] It will require an across-the-board package where most give up some of a vested advantage for the greater good.

Along these lines, again according to Buchanan:

> [W]e can also be somewhat optimistic, over the long run, regarding the prospects for securing some genuine improvements in political organization. If, in fact, the organization of special interests has advanced to the point at which no one interest can expect, in the long run, to secure differential advantage, the way may be open for some changes in the organizational rules themselves. Each interest group will, of course, turn every effort toward improving its own position, within the limits of the prevailing rules; but if, in fact, all interests come to recognize that the external costs involved in this continuous struggle of interests are excessive, all might agree on some changes in the rules that allow such behavior to take place.[525]

When things are sufficiently dire, all parties will have a political incentive to appear to be constructive.

Buchanan also wrote that "… the discussion points toward the derivation of a logical basis for constitutional contract, a basis which involves the demonstration that all members of a community secure gains when rights are defined, when rules imposing behavioral limits are settled, and when enforcement institutions are established."[526] According to Buchanan: "Any multiparty exchange that captures potentially realizable surplus can conceptually secure the unanimous approval of all participants (in positive-sum games, all players can gain)."[527] Seeking unanimity, or at least a super-majority, suggests that reform be kept focused on modifying the rules of the game rather than on attacking partisan positions.

While the Left is likely to be distrustful, if things become sufficiently dire, they might well perceive the benefit in appearing constructive. Moreover, in one sense, political wars are never won forever; change is acceptable when there is reasonable assurance that the parties will have appropriate opportunities to continue their battles later if they haven't ceded critical strategic positions. At the moment, this seems unlikely. Yet the Labor Party in New Zealand achieved this feat.

In such a case, reform might work to the advantage of either major party.

---

[524] James M. Buchanan and Gordon Tullock. *The Calculus of Consent – Logical Foundations of Constitutional Democracy* (Ann Arbor: The University of Michigan Press, 1965) 291.

[525] Ibid, 290-291.

[526] Ibid, 168.

[527] James M. Buchanan, *The Limits of Liberty: Between Anarchy and Leviathan, 41.*

However feckless our representatives might be, they are masters at reading the political tea leaves. A majority could well shift from intransigence to saying that they always recognized the problems but disagreed on the details (hypocrisy and cynicism are the mothers' milk of politics). There is, after all, a pot of political gold awaiting successful political entrepreneurs.

There have in the past been significant examples of bi-partisanship to deal with substantial national issues: Democrats made common cause with the Republicans for civil rights legislation in the 1960s and for a substantive reform of Social Security in 1983 (which, unfortunately, was actuarially inadequate). There were later inconclusive signals that the Congress and President were prepared to deal with serious Social Security concerns. President Clinton was said to have been ready to consider further reform of Social Security just before he was sidetracked by impeachment. President Bush also raised that prospect (albeit to deafening silence from Congress).

The operative question will be: Can transformative reforms be identified that are acceptable to enough parties for a super-majority to coalesce? The constellation of emerging factors has promising features. For example, workable solutions have been road-tested elsewhere, are straightforward, and have modest costs.

However, to rise to the challenge, changes would need to be rationally coherent, entailing: new policies, reformed institutions, and a supportive Supreme Court.

Policy

An understanding of the FEO drawn from the empirical description in Chapter One and the philosophy in Chapter Nine provides a roadmap for dealing with pressing problems and for realizing a future of rapid growth. Actually, relatively few fixes could address the most pressing of our problems: entitlements, the tax burden on investment, and the regulatory state; those do not require dramatic constitutional change.

The potential payoff from comprehensive reform is readily illustrated, as shown in a chart published in *The Washington Times*.[528] The chart illustrates the power of a robust FEO in addressing the country's fiscal challenges. Three percent annual GDP growth (corresponding to relatively smaller government, limited spending, and light regulation) can produce over the longer-term a declining federal debt as a percentage of the GDP. With a 3% rate of growth, many ways to put our fiscal house in order become possible. However, if the government continues unreformed with current policies that ignore the predicates of the FEO, the recently more typical growth rate of 1.9% annually will lead to more

---

[528]   Stephen Moore and Louis Woodhill, "Avoiding Fiscal Armageddon," *The Washington Times*, November 19, 2018, B3.

borrowing, higher debt, an inability to meet our commitments, and ultimately an inability to borrow from others, à la Greece.

The most favorable outcome will entail more than damage control; it would require widespread reforms. Again, the key elements include enhanced competition in all spheres of public life, smaller government, less regulation, and strengthening the role of the states.

The most promising areas of reform, which are eminently possible, are described in the following sections.

Reforming Entitlements

In theory, reforming entitlements is straightforward, and it has been road-tested by other countries that avoided utopian, government-knows-best approaches. Evident workable solutions include: Transform Social Security to a defined contribution system; turn healthcare into competitively priced insurance rather than prepaid care; simplify the tax code as in the supply-side revolution; and revamp regulations as New Zealand did. It is simplicity itself: Big-ticket items are handled by individuals through the insurance-mechanisms of civil society. The examples of Switzerland and Singapore are most illuminating. IRAs can take pensions out of the hands of politicians; healthcare can be financed through true private insurance programs.

The numbers shout out the opportunity. Medical costs as a proportion of the U.S. GDP, is currently about 17%[529]; Singapore's is a mere 4%, and Western European countries such as Switzerland, Germany, and the Netherlands get by with about 11% of GDP. Yet health outcomes in all these countries are comparable or superior to those in the United States. How much would it boost our economy to reduce the take of these programs by perhaps 6% of GDP and to eliminate the huge, unaffordable future entitlement payments?

For Social Security, we could follow the lead of other countries, such as Chile, Great Britain, and Sweden; they have shifted from defined benefit programs to defined contribution programs without political upheaval. Chile's reform is a case in point: Individuals could shift to individual defined contribution accounts or keep their existing memberships in a government-run defined benefits program. Most shifted to the new version, benefited mightily from the country's growth, and were happy with the result. If individuals can choose between staying with the current arrangements or shifting to a new contributory system, there is no rational reason why Social Security reform in the United States must remain "the third rail" since it will likely be better and stronger than before.

The Left would have to relinquish an effective campaign issue that plays on people's insecurities. But there may well be other ways for them to play the

---

[529] "Diagnosing Health Care's Hidden Costs", *The Wall Street Journal*, August 1, 2018.

electoral-game. Moreover, projections of growing entitlement deficits show that all other discretionary programs will be squeezed substantially. The Left will soon see that none of its other cherished social goals can be pursued without entitlement reform. This, along with the need to stabilize fiscal matters overall, might open the door to Democratic cooperation.

Rationalizing Regulation

Experience here and abroad (notably in New Zealand) shows how national economic growth can be nudged onto the 3% growth curve by restraining and reforming regulations. Indeed, as discussed in Chapter Five, regulatory costs in 2011 amounted to $1.752 trillion, or about 11.7% of the U.S. GDP.[530] Just lifting unnecessary regulation, as done in New Zealand for example, could boost the GDP by several percent. Recently, at home, at the beginning of his Administration, Trump made a beginning by ordering the elimination of two pieces of regulation for every new one.

The metastasizing administrative state principally relies on three factors: the allure of good intentions, the acquiescence of the courts (which seem content with any rational basis, as noted in the discussion of the Chevron precedent in Chapter 5), and the manipulation of cost-benefit analyses by administrative agencies.

The entire mindset of the government needs to shift. Regulation is essential for many health and safety objectives, but not because the government is generally wiser than the private sector. Richard Epstein suggests that government intrusion be viewed with a presumption of error. Is the federal government really better at managing industry and commerce than the states and a competitive private sector? Moreover, bureaucratic analyses serving agency ambitions are easily biased toward good intentions as the intended benefits become more abstract and intrinsically immeasurable.

Epstein argues that, rather than deferring to administrative decisions, the courts should try to enforce a sound government approach to finances that protects positive-sum government programs but strikes down negative-sum projects in which regulation is a disguised system of wealth transfer. He states that "both private property and liberty of contract in their separate ways have as their minimum condition blocking forms of government action that shrink the overall size of the pie. Toward that end, it becomes appropriate to strike down legislation that prevents gains from trade in consensual arrangements."[531]

In addition, he concludes that the modern adminitrative state has become arbitrary and capricious as a result of open-ended legislation combined with the courts' peculiar deference to administrative agencies in their interpretation of

---

[530]   Clyde Wayne Crews Jr., *Ten Thousand Commandments* 2, 7.

[531]   Richard A. Epstein, *Design for Liberty* (Cambridge: Harvard University Press, 2011), 131.

legal language. He is especially critical of recent healthcare and financial system regulations; new regulations run to hundreds of pages and allow "ambitious social agendas [to] introduce massive amounts of administrative discretion that are inconsistent with the rule of law."[532]

Revamping Institutions and Procedures

Conceivably, the political hurdle in achieving the above could be lowered by modifying the ways in which the will of the people is transmitted to their representatives as well as how the representatives respond. Are there structural institutional ways to reduce partisanship and have greater weight given to the needs of the country? Present-day political discussion suggests that modest tweaks to the system could provide beneficial shifts in the political dynamic.

Insight into that question can be gleaned from failure to adhere to the terms of the original Constitution and/or to ways in which that Constitution was not able to adequately anticipate dysfunctional political performance. For example, the Constitutional Convention did not foresee a highly-partisan two-party system, career politicians, a Supreme Court no longer policing the Constitution in these matters, changes in the selection of senators, and Senate rules.

Promising areas of reform relate to how the will of the people is expressed institutionally. Some changes under this rubric include modifying procedures for electing representatives, strengthening federalism by increasing state-power relative to the federal, and reforming the Senate to better reflect the needs of the states rather than political parties and to minimize its tendency towards "minority rule."

Election Procedures

First, as a hypothesis, let us consider that the current hyper-partisan system in the United States is a consequence of a party system that was not envisioned by the founders, although it is painfully in keeping with human nature. Is it possible that the expression of the will of the people is distorted by this system? The problem likely does not arise from bad congressmen, who are merely reading their political bases. However, perhaps the system design unduly encourages a hard partisanship not fully reflective of the broader electorate.

Originally, Madison hoped that the distribution of a multitude of interests throughout a large republic would check individual factions as they attempted to use the state to gain advantage over others. In hindsight, that feature was probably inadequate to the task. For example, this approach could not foresee the emergence of a two-party system, which is the natural outcome of first-over-the-finish-line

---

[532]   Ibid, 189.

elections. Moreover, human nature is demonstrably prone to an "us-versus-them" approach, whether in politics or sports teams.

As true as this may be, virtually all polls show that the electorate is not locked into a fifty-fifty division along hard partisan lines. Perhaps 30% to 40% adhere strongly to one party and the same percentage to the other, leaving a sizeable middle that can go either way but is far from radical. Presently, this middle drifts from one side to the other based on "hot button" issues pushed by the parties.

Perhaps the electoral system can be modified to encourage coalition building and the election of representatives more concerned with national needs than their own careers, for example through term limits, the reduction of gerrymandering, reforming the Senate so it reflects the views of the states rather than of political parties, and reforming how the Senate conducts its business.

These would modify how Representative-nominees are selected within the states. Two methods currently under consideration that could reduce extreme partisanship are: reducing gerrymandering and a implementing a primary process that nominates the top two candidates, regardless of party.

Gerrymandering is a process in which election districts are drawn in ways to ensure that a given party will receive a majority of the votes in that district. A major downside of this is that primary elections tend to be won by the most partisan candidate that excites the base because the population makeup eliminates the need to appeal to a moderate middle in the subsequent general election. Districts that better reflect diverse populations are more likely to be moderate.

In a second approach, allowing two candidates from the same party to win the primaries (especially in states that heavily favor one party) would increase the likelihood that the less extreme of the two candidates would win the general election since they could draw votes from members of the opposition party (for whom no candidate would run).

The jury is out on these reforms, but at least attention is being given to the phenomenon.

Some other reforms designed to shift representatives' motivations would require constitutional amendments. These changes involve term limits and the method of senator selection. They will be discussed later in the section on possible constitutional amendments.

Invigorated Federalism

Other institutional changes that would help the United States return to the tenor of the Constitution might reinvigorate federalism by encouraging the states to play a greater role in balancing the central government. Unfortunately, due to the amount of federal money that is passed on to the states, they have so far tended to be easily bought off from contesting federal over-reach. For example, most recently, many states have bought into the bad idea of Medicaid expansion, because – for the first years – the federal government picks up much of the tab. But it is clear that expanded Medicaid is not the way to rein in medical costs; furthermore, when this federal largess shrinks, it will pressure those states' budgets.

However, there have been signs that some states are seeking to protect their rights from the federal government. Fred Barnes reports on the reinvigorated role of states' attorneys general in resisting federal overreach. He draws from Ken Cuccinelli's (Virginia's prior attorney general) book *The Last Line of Defense: The New Fight for American Liberty*. Fred Barnes writes that in 2013, twenty-five Republican state attorneys general were resisting federal expansion at the expense of the states. They champion federalism, the Tenth Amendment, states' rights, and a defanged federal government. In those years, they blocked the EPA from overreaching regarding air and water pollution enforcement, forced federal mining authorities to refrain from attempting to wrest mining authority from the states, and intervened to halt the National Labor Relations Board from barring Boeing from setting up production in South Carolina, which is a right-to-work state. Also, while they failed to stop Obamacare in the Supreme Court, they managed to limit Medicaid and neutralize the use of the Commerce Clause to expand the reach of the federal government.[533]

The Wall Street Journal noted in another significant case, twenty-six attorneys general and business lobbies asked the DC Circuit Court of Appeals for a stay while the judiciary considered the legal merits of the EPA's finalized Clean Power Plan, which ordered states to reorganize their energy systems from power plants to electric outlets. The EPA's own models showed that utilities would have to shed 223 coal-fired plants in 2016 alone. Some rural non-profits may go under. The 2,000-page proposal was conjured up from a sub-section of a thirty-eight-year-old statute about best systems of emissions reduction (traditionally meant to be systems like scrubbers). Such a claim of new authority with no limiting principle would naturally expand over time. Oklahoma [then] Attorney General Scott Pruitt grounded his counterargument in the Supreme Court's anti-coercion doctrine, which teaches that the feds cannot commandeer sovereign state resources.[534]

Also, despite the Supreme Court's defense of the Affordable Care Act, because of pushback from states, it did reverse part of the Obamacare Medicaid expansion on the basis that it "violates the Constitution by threatening States with the loss of their existing Medicaid funding if they decline to comply with the expansion" (National Federation of Independent Business v. Sebelius.)[535]

State resistance of the progressive model can also be part of the

---

[533]   Fred Barnes, "The Last Redoubt," *The Weekly Standard*, July 22, 2013.

[534]   Per the *Wall Street Journal* editorial, October 30, 2015.

[535]   Michael D. Tanner, *Going for Broke*, 121.

FEO-invigoration toolkit, but only if the political will to do so is there. At the time of this writing, conservatives control a majority of the fifty states, and in many of them, more conservative policies demonstrate the superiority of their approach to governance over that of the most progressive-states. Indeed, these are the states that are most growing economically and in population, while the states that favor Progressivism grow more slowly.[536]

Senate Self-reform

Despite hopeful signs, major change is more likely in a parliamentary system than in our federal republic, which has powerful checks and balances generally designed to slow change. That is particularly true of the Senate. That body has become the chief block of legislation of all kinds, and presently, substantial reform is possible only with a supermajority. As some wag expressed it: 'The Senate is where legislation is sent to die.'

To be sure, the U.S. Senate was designed to frustrate ill-considered change emanating from the fleeting passions of the electorate and to protect states' and minority rights. Its constitutional structure enables it to do this by checking the president and the House of Representatives. Moreover, since it represents entire states rather than electoral districts and its members have longer terms of office than representatives in the House, in theory, senators can make decisions more dispassionately. However, over the years, the Senate has decided that it needed to hobble its own functionality to protect minority rights even more than established by the Constitution. Indeed, it has voluntarily chosen operational procedures that hamstring all sorts of ordinary legislative functions. The chief sources of operational dysfunction are twofold: the filibuster and the power granted to individual senators, which allows one person unparalleled leverage to frustrate Senate action. An understanding of the Senate's arcane system is veiled from the average citizen but can be understood through examining the standing rules of the Senate.[537]

These rules were designed to promote deliberation by permitting Senators to debate at length and by precluding a simple majority from ending debate when they are prepared to vote to approve a bill. In the abstract, this is an admirable feature designed to protect a person-of-principle's ability to make themselves fully heard and to prevent precipitous action by the chamber. The practical outcome, however, is that the right of extended debate permits filibusters that can be brought

---

[536] USA.com, American Community Survey 2010-2014. Texas ranked 4th and Florida ranked 6th vs. Connecticut (37th), New Jersey (38th) and Illinois (44th) in population growth rates.

[537] Congressional Research Service, "The Legislative Process on the Senate Floor: An Introduction", Valerie Heitshusen, Specialist on Congress and the Legislative Process, Updated July 22, 2019

to an end only if the Senate invokes cloture, usually by a vote of three-fifths of all Senators. Even then, consideration of proposed action can typically continue under cloture for an additional 30 hours.

This situation obviously can result in the Chamber being unable to conduct its affairs efficiently, even in many instances not at all. In effect, the Senate's standing rules place greater emphasis on the rights of individual Senators—and, therefore, of minorities within the Senate – than on the powers of the majority. To get much of anything accomplished requires 'work-arounds'. In most cases, alternative arrangements require the unanimous consent of the Senate—the explicit or implicit concurrence of *each of the 100 Senators*. Specifically, the Senate relies on unanimous consent agreements every day for many purposes—purposes great and small, important and routine.

In managing the affairs of the Senate, the majority leader essentially must poll all of its members before taking up a matter. If one senator withholds consent, he is implicitly threatening extended debate on the question of considering the bill. Senators may do so because they oppose that bill or because they wish to delay consideration of one measure in the hope of influencing the fate of some other, possibly unrelated, measure. Senators can even place a "hold" on a bill; the majority leader will not even make such a unanimous consent request if there is a hold on a bill.

These circumstances open the door to petty coercion on unrelated matters, e.g., provide an earmark for a senator's constituency or else the government's business on the matter comes to a standstill.

These maneuvers accounted for the disgraceful backlog in the Senate's confirmation process regarding judges and appointments to government agencies. While there are exceptions to the use of the filibuster such as on final budget matters, as a practical matter the Senate has not completed its work on authorization and appropriation bills in years (whereas the House operating under different rules routinely does). This failure to govern properly is a chief contributor to the government's annual fiscal deficits. For example, when budgets cannot be passed through a disciplined process, the government is kept open by desperate, last-minute continuing resolutions in which votes are bought and no serious cuts contemplated. It is an insidious phenomenon that ratchets expenditures higher every year.

This dysfunctional state of affairs is justified as protecting minority rights. However, one would think that the purpose of a Senate vote is to establish a majority point of view in most matters. If a minority of 40% can routinely frustrate the majority, impasse results. Arguably, the Bill of Rights and the structure of checks and balances already in place provide necessary protections. The Senate's self-selected mode of operation is extra-constitutional and enhances senatorial egos more than it meets the country's needs. Establishing procedures by which a minority can frustrate routine action is not the same as protecting minority *rights*.

An obvious fix is for the Senate to reform its own rules to circumscribe the use of filibusters or more to the point the mere threat of a filibuster to delay its deliberations. In so doing it should explicitly preclude the ability of a single senator for any reason whatsoever to prevent the entire Senate from taking up new matters. The creators of the Constitution already specified cases for which they believed a supermajority was appropriate, such as approving treaties and amending the Constitution. Finally, largely invisible (from the electorate) senatorial prerogatives should be curtailed.

In addition to matters under the Senate's own rules, the country should consider the ways in which Senators are chosen so as to change their motivations – that is, to make them more directly responsible to their states, as originally intended by the Constitution. Clearly, when their allegiance is to the party rather than the state, senators' voting patterns change. Moreover, if senators were compelled to follow state interests, they would have less incentive to grandstand and filibuster.

Such changes would have a marginal effect on the ability to protect minority rights given checks and balances and the Bill of Rights. As Buchannan and Tullock argue in *The Calculus of Consent*, minority rights are well protected simply by the existence of a bicameral legislature in which the members of each house are selected from different constituencies: the House from small electoral districts; the Senate by entire states, which are more likely to take a holistic approach. The next section, which discusses possibilities for constitutional amendments, indicates how others have reached the conclusion that returning to a process of selecting senators according to the terms of the original Constitution is the best solution.

In any event, substantive reform is out of reach under the current system until a broad national change in values produces either supermajorities or more bi-partisanship. In addition, a supportive Supreme Court will be essential.

A More Conservative Supreme Court

A conservative Supreme Court could do much to build up federalism, enforce property rights and further competition by retreating from progressive constitutional interpretations, especially of the Commerce and Welfare Clauses of the Constitution.

Governing Principles

Richard Epstein argues that much of the major disarray of modern American life can be traced to Supreme Court jurisprudence, including:

> ... constant battles over debt limits and fiscal cliffs; uncertainty over key elements of the tax structure; massive overregulation of the most productive sources in society (health care and financial services); government-inspired brinksmanship in labor negotiations; and runaway redistribution programs that undercut the economic production that makes these programs viable. ...They are the ultimate consequence of the profound progressive break with the classical liberal tradition that was the guiding genius in the drafting and interpretation of the Constitution.[538]

He cites two types of long-term failures. First, explicit limitations on the government's power to tax and spend or to influence commerce have not been enforced. This has led to an unsupportable expansion of government power. Second, ingenious efforts to limit the guarantees of private property and economic liberty have been tolerated.[539] To these ends, the Supreme Court has managed to support Progressive ideas that are utterly without constitutional justification. According to Michael Greve, during the New Deal, "the Court discarded the premises upon which its federalism had rested – the intimate connection between federalism and individual liberty, the notion of enumerated federal powers, and the Court's duty and responsibility to police federalism's constitutional boundaries."[540]

Moreover, they did so without replacing the enumerated powers with any new firm philosophic principles of government, certainly none that were ever ratified by the people. Penumbras don't count. This left the country with the thin porridge of ideas that the complexity of modern life somehow meant that the Constitution was outdated, that the legislature should be given wide latitude, and *stare decisis* – that a decision, once made, should not be revisited. In contrast to the centuries of governmental evolution that discovered ways to reconcile human nature with sound self-government that eventually led to the Constitution, this was pretty thin stuff.

What one Court did *without constitutional principle*, another can surely reverse *on principle* when the times and popular sentiment are right. Certainly, a future Court with an FEO-mindset could shift course based on constitutional justification. Past judicial decisions should not be considered the last word *per se*. Notably, the Court has reversed itself on principle, for example regarding school

---

[538]   Richard A. Epstein, *The Classical Liberal Constitution – The Uncertain Quest for Limited Government* (Cambridge, Massachusetts: Harvard University Press, 2014), 569.

[539]   Ibid, 571.

[540]   Michael S. Greve, *Real Federalism: Why It Matters, How It Could Happen* (Washington, DC: The AEI Press, 1999), 16.

segregation.[541] Regarding past court decisions that should not be allowed to stand, Antonin Scalia suggested that several points be considered:

(1) whether harm will be caused to those who justifiably relied on the decision,

(2) how clear it is that the decision was textually and historically wrong,

(3) whether the decision has generally been accepted by society, and

(4) whether the decision permanently places courts in the position of making policy calls appropriate for elected officials."[542]

To this end, the Court could place greater weight on the spirit or tenor as well as the words of the Constitution. For example, at the time of ratification, it was clear that the country feared an overly strong central government. The single most consistent theme of the state ratifying conventions was the need to limit the central government's activities and to provide checks and balances to protect against factions in society and in the legislature. It shouldn't be that difficult for the Court to consider these antecedents in its decisions.

Other constitutional language that the Court can draw on is, of course, the protection of property rights, contracts, and due process of law found in the Bill of Rights. Epstein suggests also that progressive "positive rights" can be countered using the Privileges and Immunities Clause and the Equal Protection Clause.[543]

Epstein argues that legal arguments would benefit from an infusion of empiricism. For example, rulings based on private property rights and liberty of contract should seek to maximize consumer surplus and block government action that shrinks the overall size of the economic pie. Moreover, a strong just-compensation regime should be enforced to block negative-sum projects that should not be undertaken in the first place.

Role of the Court

A shift to originalist principles would have to be accompanied by a shift in the Supreme Court's mindset about its role. In recent years, the Court has ruled that anything goes if a rational basis test can be found, even if the decision substantively narrows the protection of individual rights. Moreover, individual rights can be further narrowed by the administrative state under a legal regime of deference to those agencies. Epstein recommends a shift to a "classical liberal proposition that all state action should be examined under a presumption of error,

---

[541] Brown v. Board of Education Topeka, 347 U.S.483 (1954) overruled Plessy v. Ferguson (1896)

[542] Antonin Scalia and Bryan A. Garner, *Reading Law: The Interpretation of Texts* (St. Paul, Minnesota: Thomson/West, 2012), 412.

[543] Richard A. Epstein, *The Classical Liberal Constitution*, 581-582.

which has led in turn to a broad recognition of individual rights that can be limited only by a strong showing of state interest in regulation."[544]

In this shift, Conservatives will themselves have to revisit their vision of the role of the Court. Epstein argues that, as long as conservative justices cloak themselves in the language of judicial restraint on structural and economic issues, they will not address the legislative and administrative excesses currently in place at the federal and state levels. Their policing of the Constitution will then amount to little.

It is important to note that such a shift in mindset would merely be a return to the Constitution's presumption of the rule of law. According to the Constitution, the Court's role is only to interpret cases in light of existing law, not to support sentiments that the justices happen to hold more dear. In the words of Alexander Hamilton:

> The judiciary ... can take no active resolution whatever. It may be truly said to have neither FORCE NOR WILL, but merely judgment... there is no liberty, if the power of judging be not separated from the legislative and executive powers... The complete independence of the courts of justice is peculiarly essential in a limited Constitution ... [whose] limitations ... can be preserved in practice no other way than through the medium of the courts of justice, whose duty it must be to declare all acts contrary to the manifest tenor of the Constitution void. Without this, all the reservations of particular rights or privileges would amount to nothing.[545]

As others have noted, the history of the last century has revealed a very different Court: one that follows the election returns. It is reluctant to counter the expressed will of the people or their representatives in the legislature in any dramatic fashion. To an extent, this is understandable, but the Founding Fathers expected the Court to be of firmer character— it should ensure the rule of law, police the boundaries of the provisions of the Constitution, and avoid becoming captive to the two other branches of government.

Political realism suggests that new election cycles and more conservative justices will be required before a significant change in mindset is institutionalized. However, one justice, Clarence Thomas is already there. As Myron Magnet writes: "Clarence Thomas is our era's most consequential jurist ... During his almost three decades on the bench, he has been laying out a blue print for remaking Supreme Court jurisprudence. His template is the Constitution as the Framers

---

[544]   Ibid, 304.

[545]   Alexander Hamilton, *Federalist Paper* no. 78.

wrote it…"[546] Nevertheless, a Supreme Court justly concerned with precedent would have to find its way gradually. Yet a pattern of decisions in recent years reveals hesitant steps pregnant with possibilities.

Early Steps

Michael Greve outlines these in his book *Real Federalism*.[547] He argues that an enhanced form of federalism requires institutional pathways and political dynamics that can produce federalism despite and against – or at least around – the natural tendencies of democratic government to consolidate central power.[548] For example, decision by decision, the Supreme Court can preserve a proper balance between the federal government and the states as well as enhance competition among the states in terms of regulatory regimes, and packages of government services. This approach "presupposes reliable, judicially enforced constitutional norms that protect competition and thwart monopolistic tendencies – enumerated powers and a corresponding realm of state autonomy."[549]

He suggests that such moves might emphasize the competitive aspects of jurisdictions that are inherent in the federal structure (and are also a centerpiece of the FEO). And, of course, other provisions of the Constitution are designed to protect individual liberty against governmental overreach and could be more effectively deployed to enhance the FEO. Greve writes, "Above all, the Founders endowed us with an awareness of the central political problem – to govern, and yet to control government. They thought of government as a monopoly problem, and they endeavored to solve it by subjecting government itself to competition – the separation of powers and federalism."[550]

An acceptable alternative to limiting the government to the enumerated powers might be disciplining the federal government via antitrust considerations and inter-state competition. Greve's touchstone, which also supports the FEO, is that:

> [T]he free movement of citizens, goods, and capital across jurisdictional boundaries tends to produce smaller government and lower regulatory standards than would a monopolistic, centralized system. … When governments are forced to

---

[546] Myron Magnet, author of *Clarence Thomas and the Lost Constitution*, adapted from a speech at Hillsdale College, September 17, 2019.

[547] Michael S. Greve, *Real Federalism: Why It Matters, How It Could Happen.*

[548] Ibid, 134.

[549] Ibid, 133.

[550] Ibid, 150.

compete for business, investment, and productive citizens, they can ill afford to sustain costly, inefficient schemes. The exit rights are excessively powerful.[551]

Indeed, today, in the United States, the population is decreasing or stagnant in states (2010-2018) that are least hospitable to investment (e.g., Illinois (-0.7%), Connecticut (-0.4%), and New York (0.8%)), in favor of quickly growing states like Texas (14.1%) and Florida (13.3%)[552]. Greve concludes that, to enhance and protect citizens' liberty and welfare, the federal government must not prevent state competition with monopolistic schemes, and nobody but the courts can ensure this restraint.[553] He argues, "[R]estrict the means severely enough, and sooner or later the ends move beyond reach."[554]

In addition, there are many less dramatic ways the Court could facilitate the workings of the FEO. For example, it can decide whether unions continue to enjoy a unique quasi-monopolistic status, determine the extent to which affirmative action is privileged, ascertain whether compulsory health insurance is acceptable, decide whether regulation can proceed absent congressional authorization, determine whether the federal government can compel state action that bears costs without compensation, and identify the extent to which property rights and contracts can be infringed. The list can be as long and varied as is human endeavor.

Despite Greve's measured optimism, thus far, there is little evidence that the Court could operate along these lines without a change in public values and more congressional openness. Still, in recent decades, in response to public concerns about federal overreach, the court has challenged unfunded federal mandates on state and local governments, such as speed limits and welfare programs. Greve also points to a few Supreme Court decisions that move slightly in the direction of Court resistance to federal overreach:

- *United States vs. Lopez* invalidated a federal statute that criminalized the possession of handguns near local schools. For the first time in six decades, the Court found that Congress had exceeded its constitutional authority to regulate interstate commerce. Justice Rehnquist allowed that there must be an "outer limit" on the

---

[551]   Ibid, 4-5.

[552]   *Wikipedia*, List of States and Territories of the United States by Population.

[553]   Michael S. Greve, *Real Federalism: Why It Matters, How It Could Happen*, 14.

[554]   Ibid, 83.

operational extent of the Commerce Clause but didn't suggest what that limit might be.[555]/[556]

- *Printz vs. United States* invalidated key provisions of the Brady Act, which compelled local sheriffs to conduct background checks on would-be gun purchasers, as an unconstitutional intrusion on state sovereignty. The *Printz* decision separates the spheres of federal and state governments precisely because the states and the federal government cannot control one another, and voters cannot choose or control either, when political responsibility disappears into a cesspool of cooperation.[557]
- *City of Boerne vs. Flores* struck down the Religious Freedom Restoration Act, a federal statute that required state and local governments to exempt religious practices from many general laws and regulations.[558]

While these decisions have a narrow scope compared to the larger goal of finding operational principles for constitutional government, Greve believes they have a useful open-ended quality:

> None of the cases forecloses, and some actually invite, a return to more principled federalism. Lopez and Flores at least mention enumerated powers as federalism's lodestar and, as noted, neither decision is easily confined to the bounds of state sovereignty. Both cases are pre-occupied with federal intrusions into "traditional" state concerns ...[559]

In the bigger picture, if a growing body of case law is to strengthen the FEO, it needs to move towards enhancing the inherent discipline of federalism, along with providing for inter-state competition and antitrust protections.

More practically, federalism and competition could be enhanced by pushing for more charter schools; resisting affirmative action; encouraging welfare reform; protecting property rights (see the reaction to the Kelo decision); prohibiting

---

[555] Ibid, 27.

[556] Ibid, 28; Justice Clarence Thomas is more forthright in his concurrence, which called for an originalist, enumerated powers interpretation. He correctly notes that the clause applied to commerce and said nothing about manufacturing, agriculture, and all the other expansions that occurred under the New Deal. None of the other justices joined him in this view. Yet it holds some promise if the Court as a whole should move in a strong conservative direction.

[557] Ibid, 57.

[558] Ibid, 19-20.

[559] Ibid, 83.

"unfunded mandates"; and reinforcing the idea that, despite the Commerce Clause's seeming applicability to everything, "there must be a line" somewhere.

Still, it is clear from recent history, despite the promising decisions cited above, that the Court is a long way from fulfilling such a role. It would require a national zeitgeist and the election of a more conservative Congress. George Will's comments about the Court's decisions regarding the Affordable Care Act (ACA) demonstrate how far we have to go: "Since the New Deal, courts have permitted any legislative infringement of economic liberty that can be said to have a rational basis." Worse, the ACA decision suggests that the Court now believes it also has the power to construe laws to make them perform better than they would as written by Congress.[560] The Court seems to want to become a player rather than merely the umpire.

The days when the citizenry could trust the Supreme Court to interpret the law and police the boundaries of the Constitution are gone; that ship has sailed. The heated confirmation battles of the last decades have occurred because both progressive and conservative forces recognize that the latitude that the Court has taken in interpreting language has vast ideological implications.

*　　*　　*

Given our conservative traditions, there is a lot to be said for the kind of gradual reform outlined above. There are several reasons for this, not least being that revolutionary turns are highly unpredictable. The aftermath of the French Revolution, which began with grand pronouncements and utopian hopes, demonstrates the downsides of precipitate action. Society should not have to uproot itself to deal with governing difficulties like those facing the U.S.

An earlier example, Britain's experience in Adam Smith's time, shows how fundamental change can come about gradually when informed by economic principle. James Buchanan notes:

> The difference [in how reform was accomplished] is methodological, in that the ... emphasis was on structural or institutional change, not on the particulars of programs. Adam Smith sought to free the economy from the fetters of mercantilist controls; he did not propose that the specific goals of policy be laid down in advance. He did not attack the failures of governmental instruments in piecemeal, pragmatic fashion; he attacked in a far more comprehensive and constitutional sense. He tried to demonstrate that, by removing effective governmental restrictions on trade, results would emerge

---

[560]   George Will, *The Washington Post*, June 26, 2015, A21.

> that would be judged better by all concerned. … He and his compatriots proposed genuine "constitutional revolution," and their proposals were in large part, adopted over the course of a half-century.[561]

Unfortunately, given what we know about human nature, it is difficult to be optimistic about the prospects for gradual reform under the existing rules of the road. Individuals and groups can be bloody-minded in their defense of their existing interests in contrast to the public good, even despite compelling evidence. For example, in industry after industry, unions have refused to renegotiate terms of employment, thereby pushing companies into bankruptcy, which (perversely) then causes many union members to lose their jobs.

Many states, such as Illinois, have unsupportable and unfunded pensions for state employees. Their predicament is illustrated by Chicago's circumstances. Chicago's financial situation is dire: "The city, which says it will collect about $8.5 billion in local revenues [in 2018] … is burdened by an astounding $28 billion in unfunded pension liabilities and another $9 billion or so money that it owes to general-obligation bondholders, as well as billions more in other debts." Chicago's pension costs have doubled in the last decade and are projected to double again in the next five years.[562] Even knowing that pension obligations are the greatest threat to Chicago's (and Illinois') fiscal stability, unions resist any retrenchment. Fighting retrenchment, they have argued that pension benefits amount to a contractual agreement that cannot be diminished or impaired. The unions' political power had gotten such language into the State Constitution and the Illinois Supreme Court has ruled in favor of that view against governmental attempts to scale back employee benefits.[563]

At the national level, a similar dynamic holds; virtually every congressman in either party knows how unsustainable the entitlement programs are, yet they refuse to address the problems because of the threat to their own careers due to the "third rail" effect. Their overriding motivation seems to be to kick the can down the road until they have completed their political careers. This alone is an argument for term limits. But such is human nature. It is all too easy to imagine that this downward fiscal spiral will lead to a crisis.

So, the nature of the likely crisis is clear. The solution, however, is uncertain. New Zealand and Sweden were able to move swiftly when the crisis was apparent because of their parliamentary systems, which combine the executive branches

---

[561] James M. Buchanan. *The Limits of Liberty: Between Anarchy and Leviathan* (Chicago: The University of Chicago Press, 1975) 170.

[562] Steven Malanga,"Chicago's Fiscal Storm", *City Journal*, August 9, 2018.

[563] Rick Pearson and Kim Geiger, "Illinois Supreme Court rules landmark pension law unconstitutional", Chicago Tribune, May 8, 2015.

(the prime minister and cabinet ministers) into one institution. The U.S. system, as previously discussed, is far less decisive, suggesting that our response will be much less swift.

Together, a financial crisis and Congress's inability to act could be what opens the door to more dramatic constitutional change. This will be discussed in the final section of this chapter – not a revolution but changes that restore the Constitution's original spirit.

THE PATH OF CONSTITUTIONAL AMENDMENTS

Without a virtuous restoration, and assuming that the potential conservative reforms described above crater on partisanship, what will happen if a financial crisis occurs? For the electorate to support dramatic constitutional change there must be obvious signs that the political establishment is unable to deal with growing threats under the existing rules of the game. The final trigger will likely be a major fiscal crisis, accompanied by widespread despair – something like the crash of 1929. After the 1932 election, Roosevelt enjoyed overwhelming majorities in both houses of Congress along with strong public support. In his first one hundred days, Congress passed sixteen major bills. Unfortunately, those initiatives were largely misconceived, but it does demonstrate the power of a crisis to drive reform.

As seen throughout U.S. history, constitutional change is very difficult. This is by design: Constitutional amendments face a high hurdle; ratification requires agreement from two-thirds of Congress and three-quarters of the states. The founders' rationale seems clear: If power was to be granted to a strong federal government, it should only be able to acquire still greater powers after careful deliberation. After all, once a central government is created, there is probably no going back to what is perceived as safer ground.

The circumstances surrounding the Constitutional Convention of 1787 and its deliberations have a strong parallel with upcoming circumstances that would lead us today to consider a package of Amendments. The Convention had no utopian or revolutionary goals, nor should we. The Convention was addressing a finite number of institutional problems regarding taxation, trade, defense, and negotiating with foreign powers; our modern-day problems are likewise finite in number and well-defined: over-spending, heavy regulation, and out-of-control, poorly designed entitlements. Relatively few changes could address the critical problems.

The central questions going forward are: what specifically needs doing and how can it be done? Regarding the first, changes should: strengthen the conditions favorable to a robust FEO and modify the systemic motivations of representatives and senators so they align better with the needs of the people. The second, of course, is determined by Article V of the Constitution, which lays out two avenues for amending the Constitution.

Strengthen Conditions Favorable to the FEO

The prior section on gradual change has already laid out the prerequisites for reinvigorating the FEO. Constitutional amendments to that end would go further to limit dysfunctional congressional actions through, for example, requirements for a balanced budget, limitations on taxation, and restraints on the regulatory state.

Modify Systemic Incentives Affecting Congressmen

However, something more needs to be said regarding action to address representatives' tendency to buy votes with other people's money. Namely, constitutional change should take into account that a representative's votes have economic value. Perhaps the days of graft and bribery are behind us, but, clearly, consciously or unconsciously, representatives often sell their votes to factions for the monetary or political support they need for re-election. Representatives cast too many votes to support their own interests and those of the most influential factions in their districts rather than the long-term benefit of their entire constituencies.

It is too difficult for the average voter to track these transactions, which are always dressed up in the warmest of sentimentality and good intentions. Average voters cannot conduct the analysis required, and the potential cost to each individual voter is likely not worth the effort. In most instances, the benefits to a special interest are large, while the costs are spread among all the voters and are therefore small to each individual.

Moreover, the balances that Madison intended to control factions have been attenuated by the government's ability to borrow money; the discipline imposed by balanced budget considerations is mostly a memory. If money cannot be borrowed, the budget has to be balanced by less spending or higher taxes. Because the electorate is highly sensitive to tax increases, representatives are compelled to do some serious horse-trading. Currently, tough tradeoffs can be finessed both by borrowing and by the use of last-minute continuing resolutions to keep the government going without passing new budgets. Financial discipline is side-stepped; an obvious prescription for growing deficits.

However, most representatives just do what comes naturally within the rules of the game. It is those rules and the motivations they reward that must be modified – in other words, alter how representatives and senators connect to the electorate. To this end, factional-interests (unavoidable) and the long-term needs of the country must be balanced in a way that can benefit everyone. Different selection processes could make representatives less beholden to the most inflexible, partisan members of their parties and more in tune with the true needs of their broad constituencies. This suggests that, while the original Constitution was ahead of its time in terms of checks and balances, it still failed to provide sufficient protection from the downsides of unfiltered democracy.

Previous sections discussed the easier possibilities for reform, such as redistricting and changing primary rules. Tougher measures requiring constitutional amendments fall in two categories: term limits for representatives and returning the election of senators to state legislatures.

Term limits

In hindsight, establishing term limits for representatives and senators could be considered one of the pieces of unfinished business from the Constitutional Convention. At that time, term limits were common in many state constitutions and in the Continental Congress. For example, the Pennsylvania Constitution required that members of the General Assembly serve no more than four years out of any seven.[564] The objective was to find candidates that wanted to serve their country for brief periods rather than establish long careers benefitting from public monies. At the Constitutional Convention, Benjamin Franklin opposed the idea of paying legislators and executive officers of the federal government. He was concerned about the effect on their motivations because of the unavoidable impact of "ambition and avarice; the love of power and the love of money."[565]

Thomas Jefferson also was a proponent of rotation in office. Of the draft Constitution, he wrote "I dislike … and strongly dislike … the abandonment, in every instance, of the principle of rotation in office…[566]

The Convention debated the point but ultimately moved onto other matters, believing that the relatively short two-year terms of House members made the idea moot. Indeed, for most of the nineteenth century, this was so. On average, during the second half of that century, more than half the House consisted of first-term members.[567]

This pattern, as noted in an earlier chapter, changed noticeably with the rise of Progressivism, the introduction of the income tax, and the dramatic leap in the size of the federal government. Today, there is little evidence of citizen-service being the primary motivation of members of Congress.

---

[564] Mark R. Levin, *The Liberty Amendments – Restoring the American Republic* (New York: Threshold Editions, 2013), 22.

[565] Ibid, 23.

[566] Ibid, 26.

[567] Ibid, 27.

A contrary argument is that government has become so complicated that our representatives must become a "professional class." However, plentiful evidence, as seen in a recent Pew study, suggests just the reverse. States with part-time representatives enjoy superior government and a happier electorate. Today, fourteen states are represented by part-timers; twenty-six have a hybrid model; and ten have converted to a full-time model with professional representatives – and commensurately high salaries. The Pew Study found that, over the last fifteen years, the states with the highest legislative salaries consistently spent more than they took in, relying on debt and gimmicks, while the states with the lowest representative pay consistently balanced their budgets. As for the benefits of experience and professionalism, the most professional legislatures have the worst-managed government pension systems.[568]

One example might show how such a change could help at the national level. As noted earlier, most congressmen recognize the severe defects of the entitlement programs but fear to address them because of the potential impact on their re-election prospects. If a substantial number know that they won't be running for re-election, might they not place their country above their party?

Selection of Senators

The way senators are selected also might offer an opportunity for improvement. The original Constitution established a bicameral legislature in which each house was elected differently; one represented the people directly, and the other the interests of the individual states.

While the potential benefit of returning senatorial selection to state legislatures is speculative, consider the experience of other federal republics such as Switzerland, Germany, and the Netherlands. In those countries, the upper house is obliged to follow the dictates of their cantons, Länder, or provinces. The author believes that it is not a coincidence that those countries have never established grandiose monstrosities such as Social Security, Medicare, Medicaid, or Obamacare.

While the U.S. Constitution did not obligate Senators to follow direction from their states, it did expect them to largely represent their states' interests. In this regard, the Convention clearly opposed the direct election of senators. As Madison argued, the difference between direct election and appointment by the states is the distinction between a unitary national entity and a federal one. More specifically, a member of the Massachusetts ratifying convention feared that direct election

---

[568]   Steven Malanga, "Lawmakers Are Doing a Bad Job – So Give Them a Raise?" *The Wall Street Journal*, January 12, 2019, A11.

by the people would make it easier for the federal government to consolidate state governments under its control.[569]

Nonetheless, this feature of the Constitution was changed with the passage of the Seventeenth Amendment, which provided for the direct election of senators. At the time, it was argued that direct elections were more in keeping with democratic principles. However, the United States is a republic, not a democracy, for good and sufficient reasons. The result was a subtle shift in the political dynamic; senators have become captives of their respective parties and less responsive to state legislatures. Mark Levin argues that "senators now spend more time with, and are more beholden to, Washington lobbyists, campaign funders, national political consultants, and national advocacy organizations."[570]

In short, Levin concludes that repealing the Seventeenth Amendment "returns Congress to a true bicameral institution; provides the states with direct input into federal law-making decisions in real time; [and] decentralizes the influences on a senator from Washington, DC to the states and local communities ..."[571]

One could argue that the two constitutional changes described above would merely complete the work of the Constitutional Convention and restore its spirit.

*   *   *

In short, there are numerous ideas in political circulation that could address the country's threatening circumstances. The ones most likely to help are modest amendments that could be carried out by a Convention of the States. They focus on simple changes without altering the federal-republic form of the Constitution. For the most part, the proposed changes aim at reducing the size of the central government, reducing partisanship, restoring the Supreme Court to its constitutional role, and strengthening checks and balances.

When the time comes, our Constitution provides mechanisms for sober, thoughtful consideration of options for change.

Amendment Mechanisms

According to Article V, amendments to the Constitution can be made in two ways:

> The Congress, whenever, two thirds of both Houses shall deem
> it necessary, shall propose Amendments to the Constitution, or,
> on the application of the Legislatures of two-thirds of the several

---

[569]   Mark Levin, *The Liberty Amendments*, 41.

[570]   Ibid, 46.

[571]   Ibid, 48.

> States, shall call a Convention for proposing Amendments, ...
> which when ratified by the Legislatures of three-fourths of the
> several States, or by Conventions in three-fourths thereof, as
> one or the other Mode of Ratification may be proposed by the
> Congress.

The first of these is the primary route for amending the Constitution; indeed, it is the only one that has been used thus far. In this process, amendments originate in Congress and are ratified by the states. However, George Mason recognized that all institutions attempt to increase their authority, never to reduce it. He astutely predicted that the federal government would someday abuse the enumerated powers described in the document. If and when that happened, Congress might have to be bypassed, because no branch of government should have the power to determine the extent of its own power. Therefore, he proposed a second avenue for constitutional amendments that would curtail federal usurpations and rely only on the states.

His concern has been manifested in later experience; overreaching presidents enabled by an overreaching Congress. Since our difficulties stem from congressional lack of restraint and since congressmen treasure their prerogatives, change will not emanate from that source. They may offer words, but no real change. Thus, the second option of Article V, in which amendments are proposed directly by the states, *skirting* Congress, provides the more likely path forward.

This reality is not that different from the situation in 1787. The founders knew that they had to operate outside the Continental Congress to formulate a different system from that contained in the Articles of Confederation. Moreover, they did not ask Congress to ratify it; they set up a system of unique ratifying conventions in each of the states.

In any event, a narrowly tailored set of amendments under either approach of Article V is unquestionably the appropriate course, rather than an unfettered Constitutional Convention. The changes needed are modest, and any venue that could radically change our federal-republic structure (which has protected individual rights for over two hundred years) would be viewed as too threatening to ever get off the ground. That is why efforts are currently underway to pursue constitutional change in the form of a Convention of the States. The states would authorize a Convention to consider only certain prescribed amendments: those designed to address the commonly perceived inadequacies of the current government.

SPECIFIC POTENTIAL AMENDMENTS

Two sets of proposed changes (of many) are particularly illustrative: Mark Levin's *Liberty Amendments*[572] and amendments suggested by the Cato Institute.

The Liberty Amendments

Levin's proposed amendments are as follows:

1. Set term limits for members of Congress (twelve years for representatives and senators).
2. Restore the selection of senators to the states (repeal the Seventeenth Amendment).
3. Establish term limits for Supreme Court Justices (twelve years) and provide for a supermajority override (three-fifths vote either of Congress or of the states may override a majority opinion of the Court).
4. Limit federal spending (balanced budget plus a 17.5% GDP limit on outlays).
5. Limit taxation (Congress shall not collect more than 15% of a person's income from any source).
6. Limit federal bureaucracy (agencies must be reauthorized every three years, and regulations exceeding an economic burden of more than $100 million must be approved by Congress).
7. Promote free enterprise (the Commerce Clause is stipulated not to mean the power of the federal government to regulate and control economic activity).
8. Protect private property (whenever the government, through either seizure or regulation, reduces the market value of property, the owner must be fully compensated).
9. Grant the states authority to directly amend the Constitution (two-thirds of the states may adopt amendments to the Constitution).
10. Grant the states authority to check Congress (three-fifths of state legislatures may override federal statutes and executive orders).
11. Protect the vote (require voter IDs and limit early and absentee voting).

While Mark Levin addresses the country's obvious problems from his own perspective, virtually all the proposed amendments align with the arguments presented in this book. The first three would change the motivations that drive the behavior of representatives and of Supreme Court Justices so those public

---

[572] Mark Levin, *The Liberty Amendments.*

servants would place the needs of the country over the advancement of their own careers. Amendments four through eight are designed to ensure limited government in terms so binding that even the Supreme Court's ventures into penumbra of meaning would become impossible. Notably, these amendments do not attempt to revive the Enumerated Powers Clause. However, they are consistent with Greve's observation that if you restrict the means tightly enough, undesirable ends move out of reach. Amendments nine and ten strengthen the role of the states and thereby the operation of federalism.

Other possible amendments are suggested by the Cato Institute; these come from a libertarian perspective. They, too, are clearly aligned with the predicates of the FEO.

Cato's Proposed Amendments

The chairmen's message in a *Cato Policy Report* contains several ideas about potential Constitutional amendments.[573] They were written by various staff, including David Boaz, Tim Lynch, John Samples, Roger Pilon, and Ilya Shapiro. Many ideas are similar to Mark Levin's, especially those regarding term limits, procedures to amend the Constitution, empowering the states to amend the Constitution, correcting the misuse of the Commerce Clause, limiting the reach of federal regulation in states and localities, and the principle of legality (requiring all laws be understandable to the average voter). Chairman [at the time] Robert Levy's proposals go further:

1. All major regulations must be approved by Congress and their constitutional authority is explicitly stated.
2. The General Welfare Clause is not a delegation of power.
3. The Necessary and Proper Clause authorizes acts not merely convenient, but integral to executing other authorized powers.
4. Congress may not mandate state or local spending without providing funds.
5. Eminent domain may be exercised only for legitimate public purposes or benefits.
6. Federal, state, or local governments may not alter the terms of lawful private contracts.
7. No occupational licensing or other barrier to entry may be imposed for the primary purpose of limiting competition.
8. No legally owned asset may be forfeited, except for sale or auction to pay a fine properly imposed against the owner.

---

[573]   *Cato Policy Report*, Vol. XXXV No.5, September/October 2013.

9. There shall be no limitation of private contributions or expenditures to fund political speech.

10. The federal government should raise money through a consumption tax, and the Sixteenth Amendment should be repealed.

Most of these simply reinvigorate the spirit of the Constitution regarding the provisions important to the FEO (the Commerce, General Welfare, and Necessary and Proper Clauses). In fact, if the clear meanings intended by these clauses were enforced (see the earlier discussion of the Supreme Court), some of these amendments would be unnecessary. However, these amendments would lend more constitutional muscle to forestall congressional attempts to circumscribe liberty or strive for larger government.

Cato's tenth proposed amendment takes a different approach than Levin's to reducing the fiscal size of the government. Interestingly, rather than putting explicit limits on tax rates, Cato suggests an amendment introducing a consumption tax to replace income taxes. This has the obvious collateral merit of eliminating the egregious tax code, which offers ample opportunities for cronyism, special interests, and attempts to micromanage the economy.

A Convention of the States

Civic-minded institutions have identified an array of constitutional solutions to our fiscal and constitutional woes. As Milton Friedman suggests in the introductory quote, part of their mission is to have solutions ready when the time comes.

When that time comes, it seems more likely that these amendments will originate from the states rather than Congress, for the reasons discussed above.[574] A Convention of the States would not have the authority to rewrite the Constitution or to propose amendments beyond those passed by each state legislature.

While the Constitution has not yet been amended in this way, it has been attempted. Since the Constitution was written, states have applied for amendments some four hundred times, but none of these efforts attained the two-thirds approval required by Article V. At the time of this writing, twenty-eight states have standing calls for a convention to pass a balanced-budget amendment (thirty-four are needed for a convention).[575]

This discussion has dealt almost entirely with amendments congruent with the FEO. This was done for the reasons laid out in Chapter Nine. However, it is

---

[574] Michael Farris and Jenna Ellis, "A Convention of the States to Amend the Constitution," *The National Review*, September 29, 2016.

[575] Steve H. Hanke and Stephen J.K. Walters, "Lying Prices Keep America Hooked on Spending," *The Wall Street Journal*, January 8, 2019, A19.

reassuring that others such as Levin and Cato reach similar conclusions based on other analytical frameworks.

Importantly, this set of changes would restore the spirit of the original Constitution, which in turn built on millennia of value evolution that found ways to reconcile the positive and negative aspects of human nature – that is, to solve Aristotle's conundrum.

Of course, the passage of such amendments would merely be a way-station. Despite the Founding Fathers' clear vision in drafting the Constitution we have seen key provisions of that Constitution unravel. It could easily happen again – ambition and predatory forces never rest. That is why the citizenry need to practice eternal vigilance.

SUMMARY

This chapter is founded on the belief that a crisis is also an opportunity and that coming fiscal crises arising out of a century of failed Progressivism will eventually spur fundamental change. Strengthening the FEO and restoring the spirit of the original Constitution are the obvious solutions to our problems; the empirical evidence is overwhelming.

Nonetheless, the political hurdles are so high that it is not clear how bad things will have to get before change comes. Since none of us can foresee the future, this chapter considered several paths the country might take to reach the more promising land of a fully functional FEO.

The citizenry might collectively learn from our history, our current circumstances, and the examples of other countries to experience a 'Third American Revolution' of values. Politics will inevitably follow. In that event, the country is likely to follow some path akin to the conservative shift discussed above. Should that fail, and should a looming crisis become increasingly difficult to avoid, constitutional change may well be necessary – either in an orderly fashion in a Convention of the States or a more panicky Constitutional Convention. Should none of these things come about, should the fiscal crisis result in virtual insolvency and a hapless Congress, we'll have to deal with hard times. This could take shape in ways similar to Greece's experience, or worse become a leftist autocracy similar to that of Venezuela – in which case we would lose our liberties along with our prosperity.

Still, we, more than any other nation, possess essential values that have evolved over centuries of empirical and political experience, and they would support a positive outcome. Moreover, as Friedman noted, our think-tanks (much more than academia) provide useful roadmaps for forestalling a complete crisis. Fortunately, effective corrective action is truly not complicated.

One is reminded of what Winston Churchill said (admittedly in other circumstances): "You can always count on Americans to do the right thing – after they've tried everything else."

Finally, in the context of the broad sweep of human evolution, our immediate future holds an exciting prospect. We can align humankind's vast and growing creative capability enhanced by the digital revolution with evolved forms of self-governance that corrals his predatory side. If done right, this system will validate the timeless wisdom of:

- Aristotle, who pointed the way, but lacked a final solution,
- Buchanan, who argued that humankind's capacity for successful self-government was attainable, despite predatory inclinations, by limiting the powers granted to government,
- Madison, who identified the predatory challenges of factions and the need to check them, and
- Hayek, who discerned the key underpinnings of the FEO that need to be protected to achieve an optimum system of government.

ETERNAL VIGILANCE
WORKS CITED

Alesina, Alberto, Ph.D., Romina Boccia, Ryan Bourne, Salim Furth, Ph.D., David Howden, Ph.D., *Filip* Jolevski, Miguel Marin, Matthew Melchiorre, Derrick Morgan, Dalibor Rohac, and Veronique de Rugy."Europe's Fiscal Crisis Revealed: An In-Depth Analysis of Spending, Austerity, and Growth," Heritage Foundation Special Report on Europe, June 6, 2014.

Allison, Graham T. and Kalypso Nicobidis, ed., *The Greek Paradox: Promise v. Performance.* Cambridge, Mass.: The MIT Press.

Ayittey, George. *Africa in Chaos.* New York: St. Martin's Press, 1998.

Barnes, Fred. "The Last Redoubt," *The Weekly Standard*, July 13, 2013.

Bartholomew, James. *The Welfare of Nations.* Washington, DC: Cato Institute, 2016.

Bartley III, W.W., ed. and F.A. Hayek. *The Fatal Conceit: The Errors of Socialism.* Chicago: The University of Chicago Press, 1991.

Beito, David. *Critical Review*, Vol. 4, No.4, 1990,

Bethell, Tom. *The Noblest Triumph: Property and Prosperity Through the Ages.* New York: St. Martin's Press, 1998.

"Blue State Budget Breakdowns," *The Wall Street Journal*, July 5, 2017, A16.

Boaz, David, ed. *The Libertarian Reader.* New York: The Free Press, 1997.

Boaz, David. *Libertarianism – A Primer.* New York: The Free Press, 1997.

Boghassian, Paul. *Fear of Knowledge – Against Relativism and Constructivism.* Oxford: Clarendon Press, 2006.

Boston, Jonathan and Martin Holland, ed. *The Fourth Labour Government: Radical Politics in New Zealand.* Auckland: Oxford University Press, 1987.

Bowen, Catherine Drinker. *Miracle at Philadelphia.* Boston: An Atlantic Monthly Press Book, Little, Brown and Company, 1966.

"Brazil Set to Tackle Pensions Overhaul," *The Wall Street Journal*, July 9, 2019, A16.

Brandeis, Louis D. "The Living Law," *Illinois Law Review*,1917, 10.

Breiding, R. James. *Swiss Made: The Untold Story behind Switzerland's Success.* London: Profile Books Ltd., 2013.

Brittan, S. *The Role and Limits of Government: Essays in Political Economy.* Hounslow: Maurice Temple Smith, 1983.

Brooks, Arthur. *The Wall Street Journal,* July 11-12, 2015.

Buchanan, James M. and Gordon Tullock. *The Calculus of Consent – Logical Foundations of Constitutional Democracy.* Ann Arbor: The University of Michigan Press, 1965.

Buchanan, James M. *The Limits of Liberty: Between Anarchy and Leviathan.* Chicago: The University of Chicago Press, 1975.

Buckley, James L. *Saving Congress from Itself: Emancipating the States and Empowering Their People.* New York: Encounter Books, 2014.

Bueno de Mesquita, Bruce, and Alastair Smith. *The Dictator's Handbook – Why Bad Behavior is Almost Always Good Politics.* New York: Public Affairs/The Perseus Books Group, 2011.

Carlyle, A.J. *Political Liberty.* London: Frank Cass & Co. Ltd., 1963.

Carr, William. *A History of Germany 1815–1945.* London: Edward Arnold Ltd., 1969.

Cassidy, Bill and Patrick W. Cobb. "Not Enough Cancer Drugs, Too many Price Controls," *The Wall Street Journal,* November 12, 2012, A17.

Cato Policy Report, Vol. XXXV No.5, September/October 2013.

Churchill, Winston S. *The Birth of Britain.* New York: Dodd, Mead & Company, 1966.

___. *The New World.* New York: Dodd, Mead & Company, 1965.

Conard, Edward. *Unintended Consequences: Why Everything You've Been Told About the Economy Is Wrong.* New York: Portfolio/Penguin, 2012.

Congressional Research Service, "The Legislative Process on the Senate Floor: An Introduction", Valerie Heitshusen, Specialist on Congress and the Legislative Process, Updated July 22, 2019.

Courtois, Stéphane, Nicolas Werth, Jean-Louise Panné, Andrzej Paczkowski, Karel Bartosek, and Jean-Louis Margolin. *The Black Book of Communism: Crimes, Terror, Repression.* Cambridge: Harvard University Press, 1999.

Dawkins, Richard. *The Selfish Gene.* Oxford: Oxford University Press, 1976.

de Rothschild, Lynn Forester, and Adam S. Posen. "How Capitalism Can Repair Its Bruised Image," *The Wall Street Journal,* January 2, 2013, A17.

De Toqueville, Alexis. *Democracy in America.* New York: Mentor Books, 1956.

DeMuth, Christopher. "Capital for the Masses," *The Wall Street Journal,* April 8, 2014, A15.

Department of Justice, Office of Justice Programs, Press Release, April 25, 2019.

Diamond, Jared. *The Third Chimpanzee: The Evolution and Future of the Human Animal.* New York: Harper Collins Publishers, 1992.

Durant, Will. *The Age of Faith*. New York: Simon and Schuster, 1950.

___. *Caesar and Christ*. New York: Simon and Schuster, 1944.

___. *The Life of Greece*. New York: Simon and Schuster, 1939.

___. *Our Oriental Heritage*. New York: Simon and Schuster, 1954.

Durant, Will and Ariel Durant. *The Age of Louis XIV*. New York: Simon and Schuster, 1963.

___. *The Age of Reason Begins*. New York: Simon and Schuster, 1961.

___. *The Age of Voltaire*. New York: Simon and Schuster, 1965.

___. *Rousseau and Revolution,* New York: Simon and Schuster, 1967.

Eastland, Terry. "A New Constitutional Convention?" *The Weekly Standard*, February 8, 2016.

Eis, Rafi. "The Conservative and Progressive Theories of Education", *National Review*, November 25, 2019, 46.

Elkins, Stanley and Eric McKitrick. *The Age of Federalism*. New York: Oxford University Press, 1993.

R.C. Ellickson, R.C. *Order Without Law*. Cambridge, Mass. Harvard University Press, 1991.

Ellis, Joseph J. *The Quartet – Orchestrating the Second American Revolution, 1783–1789*. New York: Vintage Books, a division of Penguin, Random House LLC, 2015.

Epstein, Richard A. *Design for Liberty*. Cambridge: Harvard University Press, 2011.

___. *The Classical Liberal Constitution – The Uncertain Quest for Limited Government*. Cambridge, Massachusetts: Harvard University Press, 2014.

___. *How Progressives Rewrote the Constitution*. Washington, DC: Cato Institute, 2006.

___. *Why Progressive Institutions are Unsustainable*. New York: Encounter Books, 2011.

Evans, Richard J. *The Coming of the Third Reich*. London: Penguin Books, 2004.

Fairfield, Roy P., ed. *The Federalist Papers*. New York: Anchor Books, Doubleday & Company, 1966.

Farris, Michael and Jenna Ellis, Jenna. "A Convention of the States to Amend the Constitution," *The National Review*, September 29, 2016.

Folsom, Burton W. Jr. *The Myth of the Robber Barons – A New Look at the Rise of Big Business in America*, Third Edition. Herndon, Virginia: Young America's Foundation, 1996.

Friedman, Milton and Rose Friedman, *Free to Choose*. Harcourt Brace, 1990.

Gokhale, Jagadeesh. *The Government Debt Iceberg*. London: The Institute of Economic Affairs, 2014.

Gordon, Robert J. "Why Innovation Won't Save Us," *The Wall Street Journal*, December 22-23, 2012, C3.

Grady, Robert E. "Obama's Misguided Obsession with Inequality," *The Wall Street Journal*, December 23, 2013, A15.

Gramm, Phil and John F. Early. "Americans are Richer Than We Think", *The Wall Street Journal*, August 22, 2019.

Gramm, Phil and Michael Solon. "How to Distort Income Inequality," *The Wall Street Journal*, November 12, 2014, A15.

____. "Why This Recovery is So Lousy," *The Wall Street Journal*, August 4, 2016, A11.

Green, David. *The Rediscovery of Welfare Without Politics* London: Civitas, 2000.

Greenspan, Alan and Adrian Wooldridge. *Capitalism in America*. New York: Penguin Press, 2018.

Greve, Michael S. *Real Federalism*: *Why It Matters, How It Could Happen*. Washington, DC: The AEI Press, 1999.

Gwartney, James and Robert Lawson with William Easterly. *Economic Freedom of the World 2006 Annual Report*. Canada: The Fraser Institute, 2006.

Gwartney, James D. et al. *Economics, Private and Public Choice*. Mason, Ohio: South-Western Cengage Learning, 2008.

Hadenius, Stig. *Swedish Politics During the 20th Century: Conflict and Consensus*. Trelleborg: The Swedish Institute, 1997.

Hamilton, Jose Ignacio Garcia, "Historical Reflections on the Splendor and Decline of Argentina," *Cato Journal*, Vol. 25, No. 3, Fall 2005.

Hanke, Steve H. and Stephen J.K. Walters. "Lying Prices Keep America Hooked on Spending," *The Wall Street Journal*, January 8, 2019, A19.

Harrison, Lawrence E. *The Pan-American Dream*. Boulder, Colorado: Westview Press, 1997.

____. *Underdevelopment is a State of Mind*. New York: Madison Books, 1985.

____. *Who Prospers*: *How Cultural Values Shape Economic and Political Success*. New York: Basic Books, 1992.

Harrison, Lawrence E. and Samuel P. Huntington, eds. *Culture Matters: How Values Shape Human Progress*. New York: Basic Books, 2000.

Hayek, Friedrich A. *The Constitution of Liberty*. Chicago: The University of Chicago Press, 1960.

Henderson, David R. *The Wall Street Journal*, March 29, 1996.

Holenstein, Andre, Thomas Maissen, and Maarten Prak, eds. *The Republican Alternative: The Netherlands and Switzerland Compared*. Amsterdam: Amsterdam University Press, 2008.

Horowitz, David. *Barack Obama's Rules for Revolution: The Alinsky Model*. Sherman Oaks, CA: David Horowitz Freedom Center, 2009.

____. *The Black Book of the American Left, Volume II: Progressives*. Los Angeles: Second Thought Books, 2013.

____. *Go for the Heart: How Republicans Can Win*. Bryn Mawr, PA: Go for the Heart, Inc., 2013.

Joffe, Josef. *The Myth of America's Decline: Politics, Economics, and a Half Century of False Prophecies.* New York: Liveright Publishing Corporation, a division of W.W. Norton & Company, 2014.

Johnson, Paul. *A History of the American People.* New York: Harper Collins Publishers, 1997.

Kamaras, Antonis. "The Origins of the Greek Financial Crisis – Letter from Thessaloniki," *Foreign Affairs,* December 13, 2011.

Kirk, Russell. *The Roots of American Order.* Washington, DC: Regnery Gateway, 1991.

Klarman, Michael J. *The Framers' Coup: The Making of the United States Constitution.* New York: Oxford University Press, 2016.

Klein, Aaron and Brenda J. Elliott. *Red Army.* New York: Broadside Books, an imprint of Harper Collins Publishers, 2011.

Kriesi, Hanspeter and Alexander H. Trechsel. *The Politics of Switzerland: Continuity and Change in a Consensus Democracy.* Cambridge: Cambridge University Press, 2008.

Lal, Deepak and H. Myint. *The Political Economy of Poverty, Equity, and Growth.* Oxford: Clarendon Press,1966.

Lal, Deepak. *Unintended Consequences: Their Impact of Factor Endowments, Culture and Politics on Long-Run Economic Performance.* Cambridge: The MIT Press, 1998.

Levin, Mark R. *Ameritopia: The Unmaking of America.* New York: Threshold Editions, 2012.

____. *Liberty and Tyranny: A Conservative Manifesto.* New York: Threshold Editions, 2009.

____. *The Liberty Amendments: Restoring the American Republic.* New York: Threshold Editions, 2013.

Levy, Robert A. "Chairman's Message: Towards a Better Constitution," *Cato Policy Report,* Vol.35, No. 5, September/October 2013.

Lewis, Bernard. *What Went Wrong? The Clash Between Islam and Modernity in the Middle East.* New York: Perennial, an imprint of Harper Collins Publishers, 2003.

Lewis, William W. *The Power of Productivity.* Chicago: The University of Chicago Press, 2004.

Lindsey, Brink. Op-ed, *The Wall Street Journal,* January 9, 2002.

Machiavelli, Niccolò. *The Prince.* Harmondsworth: Penguin Books, 1973.

Magnet, Myron (author of *Clarence Thomas and the Lost Constitution*). Speech given at Hillsdale College, September 17, 2019.

Maier, Pauline. *Ratification: The People Debate the Constitution 1787–1788.* New York: Simon & Schuster, 2011.

Malanga, Steven. "Lawmakers Are Doing a Bad Job – So Give Them a Raise?" *The Wall Street Journal*, January 12, 2019, A11.

Malkiel, Burton G. "The Best Remedy," *The Wall Street Journal*, November 12, 2014, A13.

Malpass, David. "Nothing is Certain Except More Debt and Taxes," *The Wall Street Journal*, January 2, 2013, A17.

McTigue, Maurice. "Making Government Accountable: Reform Lessons from New Zealand", speech to the Mercatus Center, George Mason University

Mecia, Tony. "Plowed Under," *The Weekly Standard*, August 21and 28, 2017, 10.

Mercatus Center, George Mason University. *Research Summary: The Cumulative Cost of Regulations.*

Miles, Marc A., Kim R. Holmes, and Mary Anastasia O'Grady. *2006 Index of Economic Freedom: The Link Between Economic Opportunity and Prosperity.* The Heritage Foundation and *The Wall Street Journal*, 2006.

Miller, Henry I. "Save the Whales, Forget the Children," *The Wall Street Journal*, October 31, 2012, A13.

Miller, John J. "Review of *Constant Battles* by Steven LeBlanc," *The Wall Street Journal*, April 20, 2003.

Miller, Terry and Anthony B. Kim.*2016 Index of Economic Freedom: Promoting Economic Opportunity and Prosperity.* The Heritage Foundation and *The Wall Street Journal*, 2016.

Moore, Stephen."Growth Can Solve the Debt Dilemma," *The Wall Street Journal*, April 26, 2017, A17.

___. "How Did the Great Depression Actually Run Its Course?" *The Washington Times*, B3, October 13, 2014, B3.

Moore, Stephen and Louis Woodhill. "Avoiding Fiscal Armageddon," *The Washington Times*, November 19, 2018, B3

Morano, Marc. *Climate Change.* Washington, DC: Regnery Publishing, 2018.

Morison, Samuel Eliot. *The Oxford History of the American People.* New York: Oxford University Press, 1965.

Morison, Samuel Eliot, Henry Steele Commager, and William E. Leuchtenburg. *A Concise History of the American Republic.* New York: Oxford University Press, 1977.

Morris, Ian. *Why the West Rules – For Now.* New York: Picador, licensed to Farrar, Straus and Giroux, 2010.

Moskowitz, Eva. "Test Scores Don't Lie: Charter Schools are Transformative," *The Wall Street Journal*, August 24, 2017, A15.

O'Grady, Mary Anastasia. "The Americas: Don't Blame the Free Market for Argentina's Woes," *The Wall Street Journal*, New York Edition, May 30, 1997, A19.

___. "The Chile 'Miracle' Goes in Reverse," *The Wall Street Journal*, New York Edition, November 3, 2014.

O'Shaughnnessy, Andrew Jackson. *The Men Who Lost America*. New Haven & London: Yale University Press, 2013.

Ohanian, Lee and Kip Hagopian, "The Mis-measure of Inequality," *Policy Review*, 2011.

Olson, Mancur. *The Rise and Decline of Nations*. New Haven: Yale University Press, 1982.

Ortega y Gasset, Jose (1883-1955). *The Revolt of the Masses*. New York: W.W. Norton & Company, 1932.

Ostrowski, James. Progressivism: *A Primer on the Idea Destroying America*. Buffalo, NY: Cazenovia Books, 2014.

Palmer, Tom G., ed. *After the Welfare State*. Ottawa, Illinois: Jameson Books, Inc., 2012.

___. *The Morality of Capitalism: What Your Professors Won't Tell You*. Ottawa, Illinois: Jameson Books, Inc., 2011.

___. "The Origins of State and Government," *Cato's Letter*, Vol. 10, No. 4, Fall 2012.

___. *Why Liberty: Your Life – Your Choices – Your Future*. Ottawa, Illinois: Jameson Books, Inc., 2013.

Pribram, Karl. *A History of Economic Reasoning*. Baltimore: The Johns Hopkins University Press, 1983.

Przeworski, Adam. *Democracy and the Limits of Self-Government*. Cambridge: Cambridge University Press, 2010.

Rahn, Richard W. "Hong Kong's Miraculous Progress," *The Washington Times*, September 2, 2014, B1.

Rawls, John. *A Theory of Justice*. Cambridge, Massachusetts: Belknap Press of Harvard University Press, 1971.

Ray, Dixy Lee with Lou Guzzo, *Trashing the Planet*. Washington D.C. Regnery Gateway, 1990

Read, Leonard E. *I, Pencil*. Foundation for Economic Education, March 3, 2015.

Ridley, Matt. *The Evolution of Everything: How New Ideas Emerge*. New York: Harper Collins Publishers, 2015.

___. *The Origins of Virtue: Human Instincts and the Evolution of Cooperation*. New York: Penguin Books, 1996.

Riley, Jason L. "An Obama Decree Continues to Make Public Schools Lawless," *The Wall Street Journal*, March 22, 2017.

Rosenberg, Nathan and L.E. Birdzell, Jr. *How the West Grew Rich: The Economic Transformation of the Industrial World*. United States of America: Basic Books, 1986.

Rossiter, Caleb. "How Washington, DC, Schools Cheat Their Students Twice," *The Wall Street Journal*, December 1, 2012, A13.

Rothbard, Murray N. *Conceived in Liberty, Vol. 1*. Auburn, AL: Mises Institute, 1999.

Russell, Bertrand. *A History of Western Philosophy*. New York: Simon and Schuster, 1945.

Scalia, Antonin and Bryan A. Garner. *Reading Law: The Interpretation of Texts*. St. Paul, Minnesota: Thomson/West, 2012.

Schlaes, Amity. *The Forgotten Man: A New History of the Great Depression*. New York: Harper Perennial, 2008.

Schoenfeld, Mathew."The Mythical Link Between Income Inequality and Slow Growth," *The Wall Street Journal*, June 15, 2015, A17.

Schumacher, E.F. *Small Is Beautiful: Economics as if People Mattered*. Canada: Harper Collins Publishers, 1974.

Sharma, Ruchir. "Impeachment Won't Save Brazil," *The Wall Street Journal*, April 19, 2016, A13.

Sirico, Robert. *Defending the Free Market: The Moral Case for a Free Economy*. Washington, DC: Regnery Publishing, Inc., 2012.

Smith, Lamar. "The Climate Change Religion," *The Wall Street Journal*, April 24, 2015, A11.

Smith, Nancy DeWolf. "The Wisdom that Built Hong Kong's Prosperity," *TheWall Street Journal*, July 1, 1997, A14.

Sowell, Thomas. *A Conflict of Visions: Ideological Origins of Political Struggles*. New York: Quill, William Morrow and Company, 1987.

Steele, Shelby. *The Wall Street Journal*, March 11, 2015, A13.

Stephens, Bret. "Doomed to Stagnate?" *The Wall Street Journal*, December 20, 2016, A21.

Stewart, Dugald "Account of the Life and Writings of Adam Smith LL.D.," *Transactions of the Royal Society of Edinburgh*, Jan. 21 and Mar. 18, 1793, section 4, repr. In *Collected Works of Dugald Stewart*, ed. William Hamilton (Edinburgh: Thomas Constable, 1854), vol. 10, 1-98.

Sullivan, Dan. "How to Put Building Permits on a Fast Track," *The Wall Street Journal*, December 5, 2016, A21.

Sykes, Charles J. "Clinton's Bailout for the College-Industrial Complex," *The Wall Street Journal*, August 23, 2016.

Tanner, Michael. *Going for Broke*. Washington, DC: Cato Institute, 2015.

The Wall Street Journal, "Public Pension Funds Miss Their Mark", August 7, 2019, A2.

__ "The Great Student-Loan Scam", August 21, 2019, A14.

__ "U.S. Global Business Ranking Advances," September 27, 2017, B11.

__ "Blue State Redistribution", January 8, 2020, A16.

__ "If You're Riding Through Hell …," *The Wall Street Journal*, July 15-16, 2017, A12.

__ "In Illinois, Long-Term Problems Still Loom," *The Wall Street Journal*, July 6, 2017, A3.

__ "Income Dynamics," editorial, *The Wall Street Journal*, June 16, 1991, A1.

__ "Italy Struggles to Find its Way Back from the Crisis," *The Wall Street Journal*, A12.

__ "Italy's Economic Suicide Movement," *The Wall Street Journal*, October 27, 2014.

The Washington Post, June 19, 2015, A1.

The Washington Times, "No Big Dent Made in Annual Cost of Federal Regulations", May, 8, 2019.

Thomson, David. *England in the Nineteenth Century, 1815–1914*. Great Britain: Penguin Books, 1979.

University of Alabama – Huntsville (UAH) Satellite-Based Temperature of the Global Lower Atmosphere (version 6.0).

Vedder, Richard. "How to Beat the High Cost of Learning," *The Wall Street Journal*, February 16, 2017, A15.

Von Mises, Ludwig. *Human Action: A Treatise on Economics*, Fourth Revised Edition. San Francisco: Fox & Wilkes, 1996.

Wang, Wendy. "The Sequence is the Secret to Success," *The Wall Street Journal*, March 28, 2018, A17.

Weiser, Jay. "Image of a Decade," *The Weekly Standard*, May 29, 2017.

White, Adam J. "Betraying the Constitution," *The Wall Street Journal*, June 30, 2014, A9.

Will, George F. *The Washington Post*, June 17, 2012, A19.

____. "The Closed American Mind," *The Washington Post*, December 2, 2012, A27.

____. *The Washington Post*, June 26, 2015, A21.

____. *The Washington Post*, October 10, 2004, Op-Ed.

Wilson, David Sloan. *Darwin's Cathedral – Evolution, Religion, and the Nature of Society*. Chicago: The University of Chicago Press, 2003.

Wilson, Woodrow. *Constitutional Government in the United States*. New Brunswick: Transaction Publishers, 2004.

Wikipedia: Herbert Croly; the Robber Barons; Alexander Fraser Tyler; Greek Government Debt Crisis; Government of the Netherlands; Singapore; Works Progress Administration (WPA); List of states and territories of the United States by population; Health Care in Germany.

Wood, Gordon S. *Empire of Liberty*. New York: Oxford University Press, 2009.

Wood, John. "New Zealand: A Blueprint for Economic Reform," Heritage Foundation HL 531, June 16, 1995.

Yeatts, Guillermo M. *The Roots of Poverty in Latin America*. Jefferson, North Carolina: McFarland & Company, 2005.

INDEX

legislatures, state, 70, 72–73, 75, 78, 80, 85, 97, 108, 195, 290–92, 294, 296
level, macroeconomic, 187–88
Levin, Mark, 103, 127, 156, 158, 292, 294–97
  Ameritopia, 156
liberty, xi, xv, xviii, 7, 10, 25, 59, 62, 87, 104, 111, 118, 121, 127, 159, 180, 253, 258–62, 282, 284
life, tribal, xiv, 48, 226
Locke, John, 69–70, 74, 259

M

Madison, James, xv, xviii, 39–40, 46, 71–75, 77–80, 82–83, 85, 87, 90, 121, 166, 262, 267, 274, 289, 291, 298
Magna Carta, xvi, 60, 64–65, 68
majoritarianism, 72, 74, 82, 168–69, 201, 222
manufacturing, 91, 93, 104, 285
markets, 2, 7, 9, 18–19, 22, 34, 41, 110–11, 113, 117, 133–34, 159, 170, 180, 187, 192, 207, 215, 226, 228, 249–50, 260–61
Medicaid, 139–40, 163, 253–54
Medicare, 134–36, 138, 163, 254
merchants, 12, 227–28
Middle Ages, 32, 58–60, 62–63, 68, 233
middle classes, 23–24, 37, 54, 63
Model Parliament, 64, 66
monarch, 47, 54, 62, 64, 66, 68, 205
monarchy, 54, 63–64, 79–80, 84, 205
monopolies, government, 86, 114, 142, 165
Moore, Stephen, 167, 221

N

National Industrial Recovery Act (NIRA), 112–13, 119
Netherlands, 67, 193, 201, 204–6, 219, 272, 291
New Deal, xviii–xix, 105, 110–11, 113, 117, 119–20, 122, 124, 128, 198, 247, 280, 285–86
New Zealand, 149–50, 163, 170, 183, 186, 188, 193, 205, 213–18, 223, 251, 272–73
nobility, 33–34, 37, 63–64

O

Old-Age, Survivors, and Disability Insurance (OASDI), 114, 129, 131
oligarchy, xiv, 54–55, 63, 79
Olson, Mancur, 40, 43, 252
order, spontaneous, 7, 9, 14, 21, 98, 141, 147, 228, 236, 242, 260

P

parents, 142–43, 145, 148–50
parliament, xiv, 84, 99, 101, 176, 201, 205, 208, 210, 222
pensions, xviii, 100, 146, 153, 161, 165, 172, 175, 182–83, 198–99, 209, 259, 272
policies, 23, 137, 154, 173, 180, 187, 189, 207, 209–10, 251, 257, 264, 271, 286
  government, 19, 22, 111, 247
politicians, 43–44, 93, 99, 105, 127–28, 130, 146–47, 154, 160, 185, 247, 254–55, 261–62, 269, 272
poverty, xxi, 1, 144, 208, 239–40
predation, xii, xiv–xv, 2, 16, 27–30, 32–33, 36–42, 45–46, 48, 82, 87–88, 96, 253, 256–57

trust, 15, 68, 71, 93–95, 115, 226, 247,
    258, 286
trust funds, 115, 130–31, 136

U

unemployment, 92, 109, 111, 113, 115,
    117, 144, 175, 177, 184, 188,
    203, 205–6, 208–9, 219
unions, 42, 75, 84–86, 100, 106, 112,
    142–49, 161, 177–78, 199, 253–
    54, 284, 287
United States, xvii, xix–xxi, 7, 13, 20,
    22–24, 27, 35, 38, 40, 44, 52,
    62, 74–76, 78, 82, 88, 90–92,
    96–98, 100–103, 106–7, 114–16,
    120, 124–26, 128, 132–34, 136,
    138, 142–44, 146, 150, 152–53,
    163–65, 169, 179, 183, 186, 189,
    192–95, 197–204, 207–11, 214,
    220–21, 223, 237, 239, 241, 247,
    250–51, 253, 255, 262, 265, 267,
    272, 274, 284–85, 292
U.S. Constitution, xii, xv, xxiii, 47–
    48, 57–58, 62, 86, 89, 98, 101,
    106, 123, 155, 169, 192, 195–96,
    231, 259–60, 265, 291

V

values, xiii, xvii, 6–7, 22–25, 37, 47,
    50, 52, 55–64, 71–72, 86, 93,
    96, 171, 173, 186, 216, 223,
    225–28, 233, 235, 244, 246,
    256, 258, 262, 266–67, 269,
    279, 297
  atavistic, 226, 230
  political, xxii, 47, 56, 266, 269
vigilance, eternal, xi, 45, 297
visions, xvi, 95, 128, 151–52, 230–
    32, 282

von Hayek, Friedrich, xi–xiii, 2–3,
    6–11, 44, 48, 89–90, 98, 111,
    224–25, 228–29, 246, 254, 298
  The Constitution of Liberty, 10
votes, xx, 41, 43, 68, 78, 86, 100, 129,
    169–70, 172, 179–80, 184, 190,
    197, 202, 217–18, 275, 277–78,
    289, 294

W

wages, xiii, 19, 22–24, 106, 110–13,
    118–19, 134, 157, 174, 215, 227
Wall Street Journal, 85, 146, 160,
    177–78, 233, 276
war, 30, 33, 56, 71–72, 77, 134, 203–4,
    235, 239, 253
wealth, xiii, xv, xxi, 2, 4, 8, 16–17,
    19–23, 29–30, 32–35, 37, 39,
    41–44, 68, 83, 164, 179, 181,
    183–84, 200, 202, 206, 212–13,
    227, 231–35, 237–40, 248–
    49, 257
  inherited, 237–38
welfare state, Dutch, 205–6
Wilson, David Sloan, 48, 227
Wilson, Woodrow, xviii, 101, 106–7
Wood, John, 188, 214–17
workers, 13, 22–23, 92, 100, 104, 111,
    115, 117, 126, 128–34, 161, 177